The Sun Must Set

The Sun Must Set
Britain's Betrayal of India

Andrew P. Hyde

AMBERLEY

For
Ermias, Wynter, Tayjah, Clöe, Deandre
and Nasya Rae

First published 2022

Amberley Publishing
The Hill, Stroud
Gloucestershire, GL5 4EP

www.amberley-books.com

British Library Cataloguing in Publication Data.
A catalogue record for this book is available from the British Library.

ISBN 978 1 3981 0614 7 (hardback)
ISBN 978 1 3981 0615 4 (ebook)

1 2 3 4 5 6 7 8 9 10

Typeset in 10pt on 12.5pt Sabon.
Typesetting by SJmagic DESIGN SERVICES, India.
Printed in the UK.

Contents

Introduction

The circumstances surrounding African American George Floyd's death in June 2020 provoked a terrific backlash against what was interpreted as further evidence of institutionalised white racism. Under the rallying cry of 'Black Lives Matter' violent demonstrations followed, in which statues of Confederate generals were torn down and reparations called for amid demands that the narrative which has driven much of US history be reappraised. The movement soon travelled across the Atlantic, resonating with those in the UK who drew parallels with Britain's own often contentious past. The so-called *Windrush* scandal had already highlighted for many the existence of pernicious double standards in the treatment of the UK's non-white citizens and these frustrations came to a head in towns and cities all over the country. In Bristol protesters wrenched the statue of slave trader and philanthropist Edward Colston from its plinth and unceremoniously ditched it in the harbour, while monuments to other prominent Britons also came under the spotlight. Vilified for his role in Britain's 350-year domination, appropriation and exploitation of India, demands for Robert Clive's statue to be removed became increasingly uncompromising. Venerated war hero Winston Churchill, too, blamed for blocking nationalist aspirations for decades, has become the target of vehement animus, and his statue in Parliament Square repeatedly vandalised. That of Cecil Rhodes, whose own record as an inveterate imperialist has provoked considerable scorn, is also threatened with removal.

Elsewhere local South Asian communities have sought restitution and a recontextualising of their local heritage. The Sikh community of Southall in London peacefully campaigned to replace a road named after Sir Henry Havelock, a significant figure in the war of 1857, and instead honour Sikhism's founder, Guru Nanak. Even such erstwhile innocuous place names as Canning Town and East India Docks have come in for scrutiny due their connections with the British presence in the subcontinent. Such concessions have been made in the spirit of reconciliation and as part of a general trend within the British establishment to atone for its past. In Edinburgh, a cross honouring what it called 'the Heroes of Lucknow' became the focus of attention, accused of glorifying Britain's subjugation of the Indian Mutiny or War of Independence of 1857. As a result the council have undertaken to recontextualise the monument. Nonetheless, there remain critics who dismiss these gestures as virtue signalling, insisting that it is driven by today's so-called 'woke' agenda instigated by elitist bourgeois liberals.

Defenders of the Raj refer to the benefits of its rule, pointing to the endowments of Western education, law, culture and government that have provided an enduring legacy. In asserting these claims they imply, too, that the earliest Europeans encountered a blank canvas, a vast subcontinent devoid of any political, economic and social structures of its own, and instead one ruled over by ignorant and uncivilised despots. But in fact by the time the shadow of the first European was cast upon the Indian subcontinent, a succession of sophisticated civilisations and empires had already come and gone, their powerful rulers stamping their own long-lasting impressions on their subjects. It was simply an accident of history that the British arrived just as the last of these empires, that of the Mughals, was approaching its nadir, and its last ailing incumbents were ripe for usurpation.

Although the servants of London's Honourable East India Company established themselves in the 1600s ostensibly to engage in trade, the royal charter conferred by Queen Elizabeth I gradually became a licence to insinuate its agents increasingly into other facets of Indian life. Men such as Robert Clive displaced local rulers, supplanted traditional trading patterns and eradicated long-established industries. Monopolies were imposed which systematically strangled native commerce and reduced the country to a producer of raw materials. These were exported to the metropole where British-owned mills and factories transformed them into finished goods, then greedily re-exported at huge profits. At the same time they subjected whatever products survived complete extirpation to unfair commercial competition and manipulation.

Millions were extorted from ordinary Indians through a raft of punitive taxes on a range of necessities, cumulatively burdening them with increasing indebtedness. These billions would be drained away to increase the wealth of the metropole and to support the very administration which oppressed them. They also financed the construction of the canals, railways and other infrastructure projects which later generations of rulers would characterise as acts of altruism rather than profit-driven commercial ventures. In the process, these enterprises inflicted physical, social and environmental suffering on a shocking scale, changing landscapes and physical environments beyond recognition. Their construction furthermore came at the cost of thousands of lives, all the while supplanting traditional sources of employment and destroying livelihoods. Despite opposition from sympathetic British critics and an increasingly educated Indian middle class, the impoverishment continued, starvation and penury becoming a feature of everyday life, exacerbated by frequent famines and food shortages.

Zealous self-appointed philanthropists also sought to replace long-established beliefs, religions and traditions with their own. Widow burning, child marriage and other practices of which Christian missionaries disapproved were among those banned and suppressed, further provoking the resentment of Muslim and Hindu alike. Others sought to transform the people into subservient and pliable mirror images of themselves, imposing English education, legal processes and other forms of westernisation. To suppress dissent, laws were incrementally enacted curtailing free speech and denying Indians the rights taken for granted by Europeans. Moreover, by pursuing a policy of divide and rule, distrust and enmity between Hindus and Muslims were deliberately fostered in the hopes that this would stymie any concerted efforts to create a common front against the ruling British.

A great civil service and army were created, their ranks strictly controlled in order to ensure that they posed no challenge to the status quo. The army exploited the subcontinent's vast human resources in particular, first to establish control of the country itself and then to further British interests beyond its shores in numerous wars and campaigns of conquest. When discontent within its ranks erupted into open rebellion in 1857, the British responded without mercy, ruthlessly suppressing the uprising and quashing any opportunity for further armed resistance. Nonetheless, increasing numbers of progressive Indians emerged from the ranks of the sullen majority to demand a greater share in the management of the country. Eventually, political movements such as the Congress Party and later the Muslim League sought to influence liberal opinion at home and abroad, and to expose the reality of the Raj as an instrument for repression and extortion. They also enjoyed the moral and practical support of farsighted British benefactors, and together these trailblazers laid the foundations for the struggle upon which later freedom fighters were able to build.

Meanwhile, marginalised and impoverished in their own country, tens of thousands despaired of their lives as subjects of the Raj and sought a better future in the far-flung outposts of the British Empire. They travelled to British Guiana, the West Indies, Fiji, East and South Africa, Mauritius, Malaya and Burma, only to experience the same exploitation they had sought to escape. These were primarily indentured labourers, their lives blighted by treatment little better than that of the slaves they replaced, contracted to work long hours for little pay, mistreated, abused and subjected to discrimination and humiliation. Traders and entrepreneurs arriving in their wake sought to establish themselves in the nascent colonies, but despite the huge contribution they made to the commercial and economic prosperity of territories such as South and East Africa, Burma and Malaya, they too experienced rejection and systematic discrimination. They were also faced with concerted efforts to refuse them their rights to live as equal subjects of the Crown anywhere in the British Empire, as European colonists in what were increasingly referred to as the 'White Dominions' used every means at their disposal to exclude people of the subcontinent from their colonies. In these endeavours they were aided and abetted by the British government, which connived to draft immigration laws that admitted Europeans but excluded anyone darker.

Back home, minor reforms to the civil service, the army and the administration of the country, especially after the First World War, were accompanied in equal measure by greater oppression, brute force and even massacre. But while they had to fight tooth and nail over decades for every small advance, nationalists watched as the white-governed Dominions were granted incremental concessions which by 1931 would render them virtually independent. Even the landmark Government of India Act of 1935 failed to square the circle, leaving them as second-class citizens of the Empire whose fortunes remained almost entirely within the gift of their rulers. Offers of further concessions were then stalled by the Second World War, with the country threatened by invasion and conquest. Nonetheless, in spite of the die-hard opposition of men such as Winston Churchill, the writing was now on the wall. Having signed up to such high-minded documents as the Atlantic Charter in 1941, pressure mounted for Britain to apply it to its own empire. Furthermore, having helped to deliver hard-won victory in 1945, any justification for delaying further had been removed. Faced with growing nationalist agitation and domestic and foreign pressure, the British were forced to relent. Too exhausted and war-weary to continue to resist, in August 1947 they finally departed.

But they left behind a divided land. Rule that had fostered longstanding intercommunal hatred resulted in a partition which left outstanding territorial disputes for the successor states of India and Pakistan to resolve, and they also faced considerable domestic challenges. Religious and ethnic, economic and social legacies remained as a consequence of 350 years of British rule while the legatees themselves appeared ill equipped or unwilling to undo all of the injustices of the past. Pakistan repeated the 'Drain' experienced under the British and exploited its Bengali population to the point where they revolted in 1971 to secure their own independence as Bangladesh. The country also experienced decades of political instability, lurching from one dictatorship to another, fostering fears it would become a failed state. Once freed of Punjabi rule, Bangladesh itself experienced years of turmoil and economic and political upheaval which dogged its development. Seventy years from partition, all three nations continue to spend billions on arms and Pakistan and India compete both in space exploration and in the acquisition of nuclear weapons. This has largely been at the cost of widening social problems, and none of the successor states have succeeded in bridging the gulf between the haves and the have-nots.

Under the leadership of India's Jawaharlal Nehru, successive Congress Party governments made strident efforts to coalesce its people around a united secular, democratic republic. Nonetheless, alienated groups such as the Sikhs, unable to reconcile themselves to life as minorities in the new state, renewed demands for their own homeland. By engaging in acts of terror in pursuit of their aims, however, they were met with ruthless repression, which in turn provoked more violence and even mutiny in the ranks of the army. Furthermore, confronted by successive wars against Pakistan and China over border disputes left over from the Raj, the country moved away from Nehru's vision of non-alignment, frequently becoming involved in peripheral regional disputes to protect its interests and maintain political stability within its sphere of influence.

Although India has largely been spared the dictatorships that have dogged progress in Pakistan and Bangladesh, decades of government by the Congress Party, headed by a succession of educated elites, was seen as little more than an extension of the Raj. Only in 2014 was its grip finally loosened when Narendra Modi and his Bharatiya Janata Party (BJP) came to power, bringing with them a more assertive foreign policy and Hindu-centric domestic agenda. Against a backdrop of criticism for violations of civil and human rights, ethnic and religious tensions have resurfaced, resulting in deteriorating relations with Pakistan and with India's significant Muslim and Christian minorities, and even a resurgence of caste discrimination. Nonetheless an unapologetic BJP has foresworn calls for rapprochement and instead ploughed ahead with its strategy of creating a Hindu state, responding to criticism by curtailing freedom of speech and suppressing expressions of dissent. Partly in response to this increasingly hostile atmosphere, many among its huge middle class have abandoned the country and joined the expat community that had first emerged under the Raj, seeking better lives outside of India. Many have been welcomed by those countries which once went to such lengths to exclude them, such as Canada, Australia, New Zealand and particularly the United Kingdom, where they now play significant roles in political, social, cultural and economic life.

This work seeks therefore to gainsay those commentators who seek to justify the Raj, using balanced, impartial and empirical evidence to demonstrate how India was largely the object of extortion and exploitation over many years. This will be seen to have come in many guises, and through accounts from which Britain rarely emerged with very much credit. This I have sought to do by drawing upon an eclectic range of sources from an array of contemporary printed material, documents, official records and other published papers. Wherever possible, accounts have been those written not by European commentators, no matter how sympathetic, but natives of the subcontinent who witnessed the events at first hand and whose experiences are of greater value than the interpretations of well-meaning outsiders. This approach will, I trust, provide context and depth, and afford a thorough and balanced appreciation of this unique and remarkable 350-year relationship. I should therefore like to record my gratitude for the endless possibilities for study and research that are now offered through the medium of the internet, saving long and costly journeys to libraries, museums and other repositories. There are now countless facilities that provide facsimile copies of original books, papers and other documents, revolutionising the way in which primary information is gleaned and drawn upon. There is also a wealth of quality websites covering nearly every topic imaginable, containing well-referenced sources which in turn permit cross-checking to ensure all material used is verified and authenticated. Undertaking such a task during the Covid lockdown would furthermore otherwise have been nearly impossible, so I am immensely thankful for the resources available now in this digital world.

Finally, while I was working on this book a good friend of mine, John Ablett, had been struggling with ill health. His underlying condition made him, like many thousands of others, susceptible to Covid. It finally contrived to intervene in his fight and took him from us early in 2021. I should like, therefore, to humbly dedicate this work to the memory of a kind and gentle man who gave me every encouragement in my literary endeavours.

Andrew Hyde

1

'There shall be perpetual friendship'

With Britain's presence in India approaching its three-hundredth anniversary, commentators of various stripes were taking stock of its impact on the subcontinent. Imperialists extolled the virtues of their civilising mission, having guided and educated native peoples across the world, and of which the shining example was India. There stood a textbook example of how they had enlightened and educated millions who otherwise would have languished in darkness and ignorance. There were nonetheless others, including men such as conservative turned Marxist Henry Mayers Hyndman, who vigorously disputed such assertions. He postulated rather that 'three thousand years ago, the nations of India were a collection of wealthy, and in a sense, highly civilised peoples, with at least one great language, and an elaborate code of laws and social regulations,'[1] a fact which was both ruefully overlooked by his counterparts and resented by an educated and increasingly assertive Indian middle class.

In thus reproving his contemporaries, he was referring to civilisations such as the Bronze-Age peoples of the Indus Valley in the north-east. Dating from around 3300 BC, it was one of the world's earliest urban cultures, rivalling Egypt and Mesopotamia. Before it succumbed to invasion around 1,500 BC it had developed sophisticated architecture, including dockyards, granaries and warehouses. Its homes enjoyed complex sanitation and drainage, with drinking water provided through sophisticated irrigation systems and wells. The Indus people also pioneered metallurgy, handicrafts, ceramics and jewellery, and utilised a form of writing. There were also uniform weights and measures, and a religion believed to have been related to Hinduism and Buddhism. Its decline began as the climate changed and the monsoon patterns started to render the region less fertile, and there is evidence that clashes with Aryan migrants led to regular conflicts which caused further disruption to its way of life. Among such interlopers may have been the Vedas, semi-nomadic pastoralists who emerged from central Asia at around the same time as the Indus civilisation was coming to an end. Their many tribes in turn fought and warred among themselves, and they were already in decline by the time that the Mauryan Empire was founded by Chandragupta Maurya. This survived from 325 to 185 BC, and was arguably the first all-India empire, covering nearly 2 million square miles at its greatest extent with only the southern tip remaining outside its influence.

After its decline internecine struggles between local warlords became endemic, followed in turn by the first conquests of the Arab Empire between AD 664 and 750. As waves of Muslim invaders from central Asia gradually came to control the north and east, the beginnings of India's largest religious minority were becoming established. In the first half of the tenth century a Muslim ruler of Afghanistan, Sultan Mahmud of Ghazni, invaded the Punjab. At Peshawar he met and defeated a force commanded by Rajah Jaipal of Lahore. He then embarked upon the first of seventeen campaigns of rape and pillage, which between 997 and 1030 expanded the Afghan kingdom from the Tigris to the Ganges and northward to the Amu Darya (Oxus). In 1173, Mohammed, the Persian Sultan of Ghor, seized power in Ghazni and launched further invasions of India. Four years later he was turned back by a Hindu army on the Saraswati (Sarsuti) River, but in 1192 he returned and crushed the Hindus at Taraori. His conquests took him as far as Delhi.

From 1221 until around 1327 the Mongols staged frequent invasions of India, and one of Genghis Khan's successors, Tamerlane, mounted an invasion in 1398 to plunder and exploit its riches. His empire would ultimately disintegrate and become a number of smaller factions, intermarrying and warring intermittently. One of the products of these intermarriages was Babur, founder of the empire which is most associated with modern-day India and Pakistan, the Mughal. Having emerged from the ashes of the Mongols of fifteenth-century Turkestan, they converted to Islam and simultaneously assimilated the culture of both the Middle and Far East. They also retained their warlike predilections and were among the earliest adopters of gunpowder and guns. Babur began raiding northern India in 1510, and nine years later he crossed the Indus with an army 2,000 strong, determined to establish a permanent presence. At Panipat, 53 miles north of Delhi, Babur met a much larger Afghan army under Ibrahim Lodi. On 20 April 1526, the Afghans were routed and Ibrahim killed. Babur then occupied Delhi and Agra, founding the great Mughal dynasty of northern India that would not be finally expunged from the history books until 1858.

In 1538 Sher Shah assumed the mantle of emperor. Before his reign ended in 1545 he had completed a comprehensive program of administrative and fiscal reforms, establishing the rupee and, of most significance for generations of peasants, founding the basic framework for the collection of land taxes – the *Diwani*. In 1556 Abu Akbar became emperor, leading a coalition of Muslim sultans from the Deccan Plateau to defeat the Hindu empire of Vijayanagari at Talikota, and by the time of his death in 1605 Abu Akbar ruled over most of north, central and western India. He had endeavoured to bring all of his subjects under one religion, marrying a Hindu princess and placing Hindus in positions of authority. He also abolished the *Jizya*, a tax previously imposed upon non-Muslims, and exempted them from the obligation to obey Muslim laws – a philosophy which served to hold the empire's various peoples together. He also merged the teachings of Islam, Buddhism, Hinduism and Christianity into a short-lived new religion called Godism, but it faded away with him having never spread beyond his court.

Abu Akbar's son Jahangir embarked upon ambitious building projects and adopted Urdu as the official language of the empire. He in turn was succeeded by Jahan, who built the Taj Mahal and moved the empire's capital to the Red Fort at Delhi. He was followed by Aurangzeb, who ruled for fifty years, expanding the empire to its furthest extent but reversing the policy of religious toleration. He imposed Sharia law and had thousands of Hindu temples and shrines demolished. He also reimposed the *Jizya* and generally destabilised the empire and made it increasingly difficult to govern. The Muslim Governor of Hyderabad in southern India finally revolted and established a separate Shia state, restoring the policy of religious toleration. Other areas, particularly Hindu, also started to show dissent and rebellions began to increase in intensity.

The subcontinent had not been developing in isolation, however. Alexander the Great invaded the Punjab between 327 and 325 BC, inspiring his historian Megasthenes to write how astonished he had been to find people who were the equal of the Greeks in civilisation and art.[2] Romans then penetrated the border between 27 and 14 BC, but it was not until the sixteenth century that the next substantial incursion by Europeans occurred. Portuguese activity, led by adventurer explorers like Vasco da Gama, gradually established links which expanded as the Europeans increased their presence. In February 1509, a fleet commanded by Francisco de Almeida seized the Muslim-held island and town of Diu on the southern end of the Kathiawar peninsula of western India. This victory secured a firm presence for the Portuguese and Almeida became the first Viceroy of Portuguese India. In 1510 a Portuguese expedition under Alphonse de Albuquerque attacked Goa, which then became the capital. But as Portuguese power declined during the latter part of the century, the Dutch and English became increasingly active. The English came under the auspices of the Honourable East India Company, which operated under royal charter, and of which we will learn more later. The Dutch were the first to appreciate the enormous profits to be made from the trade in spices, but the English were not far behind. However, although the Dutch had long-standing interests on the subcontinent, including Malabar and Bengal, they proved less profitable than their East Indian islands. Consequently, by 1741 their presence in India was all but eclipsed.

The British were nonetheless kept on their toes by other European rivals, such as the Danish East India Company, which engaged in trade from 1616, acquiring Serampore in Bengal as late in the game as 1755. There was also the Ostend Company, which attempted to compete from 1723 until giving up in 1731, and even the Swedes and Prussians tried their hands. The main source of competition came from the French, who set up five trading posts between 1668 and 1674. Pondicherry in particular would serve as the launching pad for a series of ambitious forays against the British, while the emerging Maratha Confederacy of the Western Deccan also developed as a threat. The most important of these were the Bhonsles, who consolidated their power during the 1630s and 1640s and expanded to the south and south-west. Shahji Bhonsle was the first prominent member of the clan, and between 1670 and his death in 1680 his son Shivaji engaged in wide-ranging expeditions extending from Thanjavur in the south-east to Khandesh and Berar further north. By the mid-1740s, Maratha influence expanded far beyond the Deccan, consisting of a loose confederation of ninety branches. As this alliance began to falter the East India Company sought to exploit the situation, and by 1800 it would find itself increasingly subordinated to the British. In 1803 Sir Arthur Wellesley, later the Duke of Wellington. defeated them at Assaye and Argaon, and by 1818 they were a broken reed. This really left only the French as a serious contender for control of the subcontinent.

By the time the War of the Austrian Succession spread to India in 1746 the Mughal Empire was in a state of disintegration, and both Britain and France were keen to fill the growing vacuum. In what would be known as the First Carnatic War, Pondicherry's governor Marquis Joseph Dupleix persuaded the Nawab of the Carnatic to stand aside while he attacked the British settlement at Madras. A siege was mounted on 5 September 1746, which forced it to surrender, and an obscure twenty-one-year-old clerk by the name of Robert Clive was among those who managed to escape to nearby Fort Saint George.

As was the fashion during the wars of this period, the French held on to Madras until the Treaty of Aix-la-Chapelle in 1748, when it was exchanged for the city of Louisberg in Nova Scotia. Also typical for the age, peace did not endure for very long. In September 1751, the Second Carnatic War broke out in which Dupleix hoped to influence the outcome of a civil war between claimants to suzerainty in southern India and install a ruler friendly to France. He laid siege to the town of Trichinopoly 200 miles south-west of Madras where Mahomet Ali, the British candidate, was trapped. Clive had by now enjoyed a meteoric rise from clerk to general, and took command of 200 Europeans and 600 Indians, marching on Arcot, capital of the French-aligned potentate 65 miles west of Madras. This manoeuvre obliged the French and their Indian allies to transfer their forces from Trichinopoly to relieve Arcot, and they assaulted the town until Clive was relieved by a friendly Maratha chieftain. The inconclusive fighting dragged on until Dupleix's failure to force a decision led to his ignominious recall to France. Mahomet Ali was appointed Nizam of Hyderabad, and another peace was signed between France and Britain in 1755 that recognised him as ruler and brought the fighting to a close.

War broke out again just a year later, centred around Britain's Fort Saint David, just north of Cudalore on the east coast. In the spring of 1758 the new French commander in the East, the Comte de Lally, laid siege to the fort on 2 June and the garrison was forced to surrender. The French then moved against Madras from Pondicherry and besieged the port, but the arrival of a British relief force compelled them to abandon their efforts. This proved to be the turning point in the war with the French in India. Under Eyre Coote, the British led several thousand troops out from Madras early in 1760. At Wandiwash they met a combined French-Indian force under the Comte de Lally, aided by a strong force of mounted Marathas. In the event the Marathas stood aside, allowing the British to force the French all the way back to Pondicherry. By August Eyre Coote had the town under siege, assisted by a Royal Navy blockade, and on 15 January 1761 the city surrendered. As was the pattern of give and take in those days, however, it was later returned to France under the terms of the Treaty of Paris of 1763, which concluded the war. In the meantime, in 1757, the Nawab of Bengal Siraj-ud-Daula and his army of 50,000 allied with the French, hoping to turn the war with the British to Bengal's advantage. Clive allied himself with Mir Jafar, who opposed the nawab, and marched on Plassey, 80 miles north of Calcutta, with 3,000 troops. Although outnumbered seventeen to one, Clive inflicted a seven-hour artillery bombardment on the enemy which broke their ranks and they fled the field in disorder. Clive became master of all Bengal and a few days later Siraj-ud-Daulah was assassinated and Mir Jafar installed in his place.

These stunning victories placed Britain's position on the subcontinent almost beyond question, but the Company's exploits in India were also attracting the attention of their masters in London. Clive had been appointed Governor of Bengal, where he served until 1767, during which time he reformed its administration and put more money into the coffers, but he was also implicated in the Company's growing reputation for graft and corruption. He became part of an investigation into Company practices, and although officially exonerated, he died, allegedly having committed suicide, in 1774. His death did not diminish government scrutiny, however, especially as the charter was coming up for renewal. Under its terms the Company had to pay the British government £400,000 a year in tribute, equivalent to £46 million today, but it was sinking into debt and there was a realistic prospect that it might default. Of course, the infamous corruption endemic to the organisation was a major factor, but it was one of those cases where, like the massive banking concerns of today, it was considered too big to fail.

Therefore, threatened with possible bankruptcy the Company approached the government of Lord North for a loan of £1,500,000. Accepting that British prosperity depended on the proceeds of the Company, he agreed but demanded root-and-branch reform in return. First, the dividends paid by the Company had to be limited to 6 per cent until the loan was paid off in full, and he also insisted on a raft of measures which would impose stricter supervision and oversight of its operations. These were enshrined in the Regulating Act of 1773, which restricted its Court of Directors to four-year incumbencies and increased government control over its activities. The post of Governor of Bengal was upgraded to Governor-General, and his responsibilities would include management of the Madras and Bombay Presidencies, hopefully creating a more unified and efficient administration. To further ensure greater oversight, supreme courts were established at Fort William and Calcutta, to which British judges would be appointed in order to administer the law in a more impartial and efficient manner.

The first man to oversee the new structure was Warren Hastings. He had served in various capacities in India since 1750 and although he helped to expose corruption and fraud, he was not entirely immune from its pernicious effects himself. Nonetheless, he proved his abilities sufficiently to be appointed Governor of Bengal in 1772 and then first Governor-General in 1774. In the meantime, with America's Thirteen Colonies lost India had become an even more important asset, and the Company's activities again came under scrutiny. Hastings found himself increasingly at odds with the government in London, particularly prime minister William Pitt, and when further reforms were being discussed he concluded that enough was enough and resigned in 1784. The subsequent Pitt Act of that year was intended to give the British government an even greater role in the Company's operations. This provided for joint management by the government and the Company, but with the former having the final word. A Board of Control, headed by a president and consisting of six privy counsellors, including the secretary of state or the Chancellor of the Exchequer would serve as 'Commissioners for the Affairs of India' to oversee political matters. A second body, the Court of Directors, was now responsible for financial matters and day-to-day operations. The governors of Bombay and Madras were to be less independent of the Governor-General in Bengal, but he in turn would have greater prerogatives to act in matters of war, revenue and diplomacy, albeit under greater scrutiny from the government.

A supplementary Act of 1786 appointed Lord Charles Cornwallis Bengal's second Governor-General. He had served as aide-de-camp to the King, Lord of the Bedchamber and Constable of the Tower of London, although he also enjoyed the less enviable position of having surrendered to the Americans and French in Yorktown, effectively losing the Thirteen Colonies. Being more of a soldier than a politician, he also had Sir John Shore, his principal adviser and eventual successor, to help with the administrative side. Shore would in turn be replaced in 1798 by Lord Richard Wellesley, elder brother of Arthur, later Duke of Wellington. Wellesley began his tenure with the routing of Tipu Sultan at Seringapatam in 1799, ending French influence outside of its enclaves and bringing more princes under the tutelage of the Company. These princes agreed to adopt a benign attitude towards Company rule and recognise it as the 'Paramount Power', in return receiving British 'protection' and the right to domestic sovereignty, an arrangement which would survive for another 150 years. Some might have other conditions placed upon them, such as an obligation to maintain sufficient forces to be at the disposal of the Company if need be, or to accept agents, political officers or Residents. These men would act as representatives of the government and keep a wary eye on their charges. Depending upon their territories, the rulers would be entitled to handsome pensions and gun salutes to underline their status, and their dubious internal machinations might be tolerated to a greater or lesser degree. To this end the treaties they signed would be couched in fine words and admirable intentions, each tailored to the nuances of the prince. In nearly every case the preamble would be the same:

> There shall be perpetual friendship, alliance and unity of interests between the Honourable East India Company and the Maharajah, his heirs and successors; and the friends and enemies of one party shall be the friends and enemies of both.[3]

Governor-General Francis Rawdon-Hastings, who served from 1813 to 1823, accelerated the program of negotiating treaties with the princes so that by 1818 only the Sikh and Punjabi kingdoms remained truly autonomous. In the meantime, the Company itself was being monitored, and when Lord Minto took over the role in 1807 he laid the foundations for the Charter Act of 1813, which further entrenched the hegemony of the British government but also heralded another massive change. While the Company's servants anchored British political and military dominance over the subcontinent, close on their heels would come those with an entirely different agenda. Missionaries and other reformers arrived with far-reaching ambitions that would profoundly challenge the very foundations of the country's religious and cultural framework.

Baptist missionary William Carey had already established himself in 1793, intending to translate the Bible into Indian languages to facilitate the spread of Christianity, endeavours which soon enjoyed the support of reformers such as Hindu Ram Mohan Roy. Born in the Bengal Presidency in 1772, Roy became a staunch advocate for change, at one stage enjoying the ear of Mughal Emperor Akbar Shah II. When Carey and Roy met they agreed to collaborate with Tantric Salhardana Vidyavagish in producing the 'Book of the Great Liberation' or *Maha Nirvana Tantra*. This was produced between 1796 and 1797, but despite the ambitions of men such as Carey, any notion of entirely supplanting Hinduism with Christianity faced an uphill struggle, especially as Mohan Roy was no abolitionist. His stance clashed with one of the most vocal and uncompromising proponents of reform, Evangelical Christian William Wilberforce, who believed Hinduism in particular to be incompatible with Britain's civilising mission. The renowned anti-slavery campaigner insisted that India should 'exchange its dark and bloody superstitions for the genial influence of Christian light and truth' and furthermore that 'those absolute monsters of wickedness and cruelty', the Hindu deities, should be completely expunged.[4]

What Wilberforce and other abolitionists were advocating was the elimination of a religion which dated back as far as 3000 BC. One of its fundamental tenets was the caste system, comprising four primary castes and thousands of sub-sets originally denoting a person's trade or profession. When they became hereditary they instead predestined social status, and the most significant were the Brahmins, or priests; Khastrya, warriors or nobility; Vaisya, farmers and traders and artisans; and the Shudra, tenant farmers and servants. Those with little or no hope of a better life were condemned to Untouchability, performing the most menial and unpleasant of tasks such as leatherworking, killing rats and other vermin, and collecting and disposing of human waste. Because it was believed they also polluted everything they touched or upon which their shadow fell, they were completely ostracised by the rest of society. They could not draw water from the same wells as those of higher caste, nor could they eat among them or be cremated when they died lest their ashes pollute and corrupt others.

But what most appalled the Christian zealots was the fact that Hinduism seemed to validate the killing of daughters to avoid paying dowries, and the practice of widow sacrifice, either by fire or by drowning. Vigorous efforts to stamp out the former began in the 1790s, but it was still not unheard of as late as the 1870s. The equally appalling practice of burning to death a widow on her husband's funeral pyre derived from the goddess Sati, which translates as 'pure and virtuous woman',[5] and was seen as the ultimate expression of wifely devotion. It was first recorded around AD 510 in what is now Madhya Pradesh and the custom grew, spreading further north to Rajasthan and Bengal. It was already on the wane by the time that the British took a serious interest, and it was in any case far from universally popular among the Indians themselves. As one commentator, Henry Jeffreys Bushby, explained in 1855, it had been proved by scholars 'to be an innovation and a heresy; but it was an innovation of two thousand years standing, and a heresy abetted by the priesthood since the days of Alexander'.[6] Nor were the British to be the first to try to eradicate it. As long ago as 1510 the Portuguese explorer Albuquerque had prohibited its practice within the confines of Goa, Guru Amar Das had condemned it, and Mughal Emperor Jahangir had outlawed it entirely in 1620.[7] It was theoretically not even obligatory for widows to undertake the rite, but it was common enough to attract the disapproving attention of missionaries, soldiers, officials and other Europeans who chanced upon the ceremony. A witness in 1611 wrote of one husband having 'four hundred wives [who] burned themselves along with him'.[8]

Although *sati* was therefore claimed to be an act of free will, many practitioners harboured less virtuous motives. Priests encouraged it because the widow's family might grant them first refusal of any property left behind. It was also made very clear that unless they sacrificed themselves they would be a burden on a family ill equipped to provide food and shelter. Those who still resisted their fate could be drugged and tied to the husband's corpse, and if they succeeded in fleeing the flames would be thrown back on the pyre. W. Ewer, superintendent of police in the Lower Provinces of the Bengal Presidency remained convinced that 'few widows would think of sacrificing themselves unless overpowered by force or persuasion,'[9] and C. M. Lushington, magistrate at Trichinopoly, recorded in 1830 that 'the act I apprehend is always voluntary, providing being in a state of stupefaction and delusion can be said to possess the power of volition.'[10] Some widows were spared the horror of the funeral pyre but instead faced being buried alive or drowned,[11] but it was the grotesque sight of a human being burned alive which mostly concentrated the minds of the missionaries and officials.

Gradually, therefore, the authorities sought to ameliorate the worst excesses of the practice. In 1812 the government issued a compromise edict stating that officials would tolerate it where 'it is countenanced by their religion, and prevent it where it is, by the same authority, prohibited',[12] while the use of drugs was banned, and girls under sixteen years of age or pregnant were prohibited from being involved altogether.[13] Further instructions were issued in 1817, exempting 'women in a state of menstruation ... nor such as had infants at the breast or under four years old, nor such as had children under seven, unless responsible persons would engage to maintain the orphans'.[14] These measures still did not go far enough for committed abolitionists, and in some areas magistrates took it upon themselves to ban the practice entirely, while the Residents of Princely States also used their influence to persuade the nawab or maharajah to do likewise.

Debate as to the extent of the ritual was hotly debated, and whereas a Company administrator in Central India in 1823 claimed 'there had been no more than three or four instances in twenty years,'[15] officials in the Bengal Presidency reported 707 cases in 1817, 839 in 1818 and 463 in 1828,[16] representing nearly two burnings a week. Responding to pressure for more resolute action, Governor-General Lord Amherst doubted in March 1827 that it 'would long survive' in any case.[17] Nonetheless, the issue continued to vex those in authority, and in November 1829 his successor, Lord William Bentinck, pondered 'whether the question is to continue or discontinue the practice of *sati*, the question is equally surrounded by an awful responsibility. To consent to the consignment year after year of hundreds of innocent victims to a cruel and untimely end, when the power exists of preventing it, is a predicament which no conscience can contemplate without horror.'[18]

Nonetheless, the practice stubbornly refused to die a natural death so it was finally decided that prohibition was the only course of action. Regulation XVII of 1829 finally proscribed the burning or burying alive of widows and stated that anyone participating in the rite would be guilty of culpable homicide, punishable by a fine and/or imprisonment. If drugs had been used then it would be treated as murder. The Act came into immediate effect in Bengal and in Madras and Bombay six months later,[19] the latter further amending its provisions to make the killing of a widow under eighteen by any means an act of murder.[20] As anticipated, the law provoked outrage among traditional Hindus, and an 800-name petition was drawn up and taken to London to be presented to Parliament. Mohan Roy was in London when it arrived and, despite preferring persuasion, concluded that enough was enough. He decided to put his weight behind the measures and the law was upheld.[21] Despite the final abolition of the practice, the semi-autonomous rulers of the Princely States also had to be persuaded to act, and it would be many more years before the practice died out. There were instances in 1895 in the State of Datia, and in Bihar between 1901 and 1906, and in Cawnpore, Calcutta and Allahabad as late as 1913.[22]

Another practice confronting successive Governor-Generals was slaver...y. This institution was of course Wilberforce's bête noire, but the government could hardly be justified in sweeping it away in India when it remained legal in the British Empire. Furthermore, it was another practice firmly enshrined in both Hindu and Muslim law, and as with *sati* the British were initially wary of interfering. Under Hindu law, 'infidels captured in war were the religious prize of what was looked upon as a sacred duty,'[23] and once enslaved a captive saw little hope of salvation. Moreover, 'the Hindoo [*sic*] Law ... makes no provision for the protection of the slave from cruelty and ill-treatment ... and the Mohammedan ... is restrained by no provisions of the law adapted to protect the slave from ill treatment.'[24] Slavery was therefore a bleak and sorry prospect, and one accompanied by few if any of the protections afforded even to the slaves of the Americas.

Nonetheless, it was accepted that some form of regulation was required to address the buying and selling of humans, and in 1774 measures were taken to prohibit 'all persons ... from selling or buying a slave who had not already been proven such by legal purchase',[25] while in 1793 Lord Cornwallis expressed his intention to go further and suppress the practice if it could be done 'without doing much injury to the private interests or offering great violence to the feelings of the natives'.[26] This approach was felt to be too half-hearted by abolitionists such as John Shore, who argued that legislators were still 'more interested in personal profit to their Company than in the welfare of the people'.[27] But of course the fact remained that slavery was not illegal anywhere else in the British Empire, and that efforts to suppress it within the subcontinent were therefore technically unlawful.

It was only when Parliament banned the slave trade entirely in 1807 that the authorities in India could act, and in 1811 the importation of slaves from outside India was outlawed.[28] It remained stubbornly resistant to the law nonetheless, and in 1823 the *Calcutta Journal* drew its readers' attention to the fact that Arab traders were still importing African slaves into the country,[29] and realistically the total extinction of the practice could only be pursued once London took the initiative. But even then, when it was finally outlawed everywhere else in 1833, India was exempted. Instead, the renewal of the Company Charter in 1833 stipulated only that slavery had to be eradicated as 'soon as such extinction shall be practicable and safe',[30] which many interpreted as tacit approval for it to continue for the foreseeable future.

Slavery certainly remained a highly popular and profitable undertaking, whatever the abolitionists might think. In 1840 a Mughal merchant was reported as having sold three Abyssinian women, seven Abyssinian men and two native girls to the King of Oudh for 20,000 rupees,[31] and in 1841 it was estimated that there were anywhere between 300,000 and 800,000 slaves in British India alone.[32] Consequently, on 15 January 1841 the impatient Anti-Slavery Society demanded 'at the opening of the next session of Parliament ... its immediate and entire abolition',[33] and finally, fully ten years after the curse of slavery was banned throughout the rest of the empire, Act V of the Law of 1843 put an end to the practice by 'declaring and amending the law regarding the condition of slavery within the territories of the East India Company'.[34] Nevertheless, for all the moral rectitude of the measure, it left yet another section of Indian society affronted by intrusions into their way of life.

A further bane of the British administration was dacoitry – effectively hereditary banditry – whose practitioners operated in the countryside raiding and ambushing at will. Such was the extent of the danger they were believed to present to law and order that in 1772 Warren Hastings advocated applying collective penalties on their home villages, so that as punishment 'the family of the criminal shall become the slaves of the state'[35] and could also be jointly subjected to capital punishment. Even more pernicious was the sinister cult of Thuggee (from the Sanskrit word meaning 'concealment'), followed by groups of professional robbers and, unlike dacoitry, using religion as a motive. This was essentially ritualistic murder and robbery carried out in the name of Kali, the Hindu goddess of destruction and renewal. Its other distinction from plain dacoitry was the fact that it was evidently governed by strict guidelines. High-caste Brahmins, the sick and women were meant to be protected as they were considered to be reincarnations of Kali, while children were usually spared and instead trained up as apprentices to carry on the work. Ostensibly, a range of other trades were also considered sacrosanct, including potters, carpenters, blacksmiths, goldsmiths, even elephant drivers and musicians,[36] but in the heat of the moment these distinctions were often overlooked.

Although driven by religious devotion, greed clearly played a predominant role in Thuggee. The Thugs would infiltrate groups of travellers during the daylight hours and by the evening, when the group had settled down for the night around the fire, talking, smoking, singing or perhaps playing the sitar, they were ready to strike. Upon a prearranged signal, one Thug would seize the victim's hands, the second his legs and the third would apply the *roomal*, a handkerchief, which was used to strangle him or her.[37] Although one Thug conceded that as little as eight annas or a shilling was enough motivation to murder, in 1826 one ambush returned £2,500, and in 1827 a haul of

£2,200 was achieved. In 1829 £8,200 was stolen in a single crime in which six people were murdered.[38] It was clearly a potentially highly lucrative undertaking, and in Oudh alone some 1,400 miles of road was infested by Thugs, who had 274 murder sites set aside in which they would commit their crimes.[39] It would therefore prove no easy task to stamp out this widespread and pernicious practice.

The British first became aware of Thuggee around 1799, but probably because it was confused with the outright banditry of the dacoits it was some time before active steps were taken. In 1829 Governor-General Bentinck asked Colonel William Sleeman to plan a campaign of suppression in north-east India, and by employing his skills as civil administrator Sleeman set about gathering intelligence prior to embarking on his crusade. Villagers, officials and captured Thugs taught him how they worked, under what circumstances and in many cases when they were most likely to strike. He then started to track them down, staging ambushes and pre-empting their attacks. Slowly his efforts bore fruit, with some Thugs convinced that Kali had sent Sleeman to punish them and surrendering themselves to the authorities of their own volition. Others betrayed fellow gang members in exchange for leniency, and travellers were educated in the hopes they could avoid being infiltrated in the first place.

The success of Sleeman's campaign led to him being charged with destroying Thuggee throughout India, and in 1835 he was appointed 'General Superintendent of the Operations for the Suppression of Thuggee'.[40] He was also supported by a series of Thuggee and Dacoitry Suppression Acts, the first of which, Act XXX of 1836, ordained that any person known 'to have belonged ... to any gang of Thugs' could be sentenced to life imprisonment with hard labour.[41] By 1848, by a combination of intelligence and ruthlessness, Seeman had captured over 4,000 Thugs and the menace had been largely but not entirely wiped out. Well into the 1890s travellers venturing into isolated and lonely areas of the country would have been well advised to take measures that would not leave them exposed to attack. Again, the British may well have eradicated a historic and cruel crime, but in doing so they added to the stock of ill feeling that was aggregating against them. Still, they had not come to the end of their list yet.

In the earliest days language was of little concern to the Company servants as long it did not affect the bottom line. Indeed, among many early Europeans there existed a healthy respect for such ancient languages as Sanskrit and Arabic. It had cultivated such a reputation that a college was established by Jonathan Duncan, Governor of Bombay, in 1791 in Varanasi to study the subject, but eventually it, too, came within the orbit of missionaries and reformers. A furious debate began to develop between so-called 'Orientalists' who advocated teaching in India's own languages, and 'Westerners' who opposed them and fought for learning to be undertaken in English. This argument had been partly stimulated by the influx of Christian missionaries like Carey, who understandably believed that the gospel would be easier to spread if their potential converts were conversant in English. Indeed, after Carey came to India he established Baptist missions and primary schools in Serampore in Bengal for this purpose.

The government in London soon became involved, and included the subject in their current review of the operations of the Company. But although the Charter Act of 1813 appropriated £10,000 for the purpose of educating Indians it did not stipulate how it ought to be spent. With the argument between the Orientalists and the Westerners ongoing, it was not until 1823 that a General Committee on Education came to its decision, allocating the funds to Orientalist education. But the Westerners were undeterred and continued to fight their corner. With the issue becoming increasingly weaponised they eventually gained the support of men such as Thomas Macaulay, who had served as Secretary of State for War and Paymaster General, and was now to play a major role in reforming Indian education. A firm advocate of extending British influence and power, in 1834 he was appointed Law Member of the Governor-General's Council, and upon his arrival made no bones about his position on the matter. In his famous minute of 2 February he declared that education would henceforth serve to produce graduates 'Indian in blood and colour, but English in taste, in opinion, in morals and in intellect'.[42]

The English Education Act of 1835 followed, with Governor-General Bentinck confirming in the State Resolution of 7 March that 'the great object of the British government ought to be the promotion of European literature and science among the natives of India ... and the funds appropriated for the purpose of education would be best employed on English education alone.'[43] He began to put this mantra into practice when he founded the Calcutta Medical College, a medical school and hospital in which tuition was to be in the English language only. Medicine was not unique in becoming the first beneficiary of Anglicisation, and as we shall see later, the same code would be applied to the civil service and the military. Nonetheless, these far-reaching measures would be slow to blossom, and even by 1845 there were still only 17,360 Indians in Government funded education.[44]

It was to be nearly a decade more before further meaningful measures were proposed, when in 1854 Sir Charles Wood, President of the Board of Control, issued his Educational Despatch or 'Intellectual Charter for India'.[45] This proposed further sweeping reforms, such as the creation of a Department for Public Instruction and the foundation of universities in Madras, Calcutta and Bombay, alongside grant-in-aid to assist poorer students.[46] Most controversially of all, he advocated educating girls on an equal basis with boys, incurring in the process the ire of orthodox Hindus who viewed such developments as completely at odds with traditional values and mores. Moreover, the decades that followed saw higher education favoured increasingly over elementary education, and although various efforts were undertaken to redress the balance, education policy tended to stagnate.

After he became Viceroy, Lord Curzon organised a conference in Simla in September 1901. Educationalists and other stakeholders were invited, but there were no Indian representatives. The conference lasted for two weeks, during which time 150 resolutions were passed, proposing massive changes from primary to university education. It was agreed that the government should be more pro-active, provide better funding, abolish payment by results and better train and pay teachers. There was one other, highly problematical proposal, concerning the reform of the curriculum. This involved replacing some of the more esoteric traditional subjects with practical ones such as agriculture and physical education. These, however, were interpreted by traditionalists not as expanding and modernising education but, as in the case of Sir Charles Wood's earlier plans, as further undermining the influence of Indian educators and religious organisations.[47] Faced with challenging budgets and a population constantly outstripping resources, as well as the resistance of vested interests, education would in any event prove excruciatingly slow to reach the wider population. Large-scale illiteracy among the overwhelming majority would, perhaps *could*, not be resolved. Fifty years after Wood's Despatch, 94 per cent of Indians would remain unable to read or write.

Justice and law and order were other areas upon which the British looked with increasing disdain. Hindu law was mainly concerned with family matters such as marriage, divorce and inheritance, interpreted according to centuries-old Hindu and Buddhist texts contained in the 2,685-verse Code of Manu. Muslim personal law was based on the Quran, but there was also a criminal code created by the Mughals. Some Islamic and Hindu legal systems operated only in village councils, or *panchayat*, but they had no authority to impose their judgments. Inevitably the British sought to rationalise and unravel this conundrum, Warren Hastings creating district courts in which the Indian systems could be interpreted by British judge-magistrates with the assistance of Indian law officers. These courts were subject to the Supreme Court set up in 1773, which it was hoped would facilitate the administration of a dual system of British law for the British and customary law for the Indians. Warren Hastings also established a madrassa in Calcutta in 1781 for the teaching of Muslim law, and during his tenure Cornwallis had attempted modifications of the Muslim Criminal Code.

Nonetheless, India remained a melting pot, and when Thomas Macaulay was sent out in 1834 to deal with education he was also charged with a root-and-branch reform of what he referred to as 'this strange tribunal'.[48] Appointed chairman of the committee to draw up the new penal code and code of criminal procedure, he applied himself to the issue with the same vigour as he had for education. Consequently, the draft he left behind when he returned home in 1838 provided a document which, according to one Justice Stephen, was 'to the English Criminal Law what a manufactured article ready for use is to the materials out of which it is made'.[49] In doing so he had attempted to remove as many of the privileges as possible previously accorded to Europeans in legal proceedings, as well as to eliminate the common law and rationalise English criminal legislation,[50] proposals which unsurprisingly met with strong opposition, and his much-vaunted code would not see the full light of day until 1862.[51] Nonetheless, he is credited with having introduced a template not just for India but for the entire British Empire,[52] and when it was finally brought into effect there arrived a major milestone as the Calcutta High Court was established.[53]

Although these reforms may have been interpreted by their exponents as motivated by a simple desire to improve the lot of the people, others, among them the Indians themselves, saw a far more sinister incentive. A nation heretofore governed by its own rules and guidelines might be harder to penetrate and influence than one slowly divided by new and, to some, refreshing ideas. We have already seen how traditionalists resented changes instituted by Macaulay and Curzon, but those enforced against the Thugs, widow burners and slavers might in fact have had ulterior motives. Indeed, in 1821 a British officer, signing himself 'Caraticus', insisted in the *Asiatic Journal* that '*Divide et Imperia* should be the motto of our administration, whether political, civil or military.'[54]

Certainly Lord Dalhousie, who served as Governor-General from 1848 to1852, made no effort to conceal his intentions. He cynically implemented the hated 'Doctrine of Lapse', which denied dynasties the traditional right to adopt a successor if there was no natural heir. This highly unpopular policy not only ran a coach and horses through longstanding convention but gave him spurious grounds to acquire more territory. Oudh, which controlled the Upper Ganges Valley and Samalpar, came under the doctrine, as did Kolaba, Jalaun, Satara, Jhansi and Nagpur, along with another 20,000 small estates in the Deccan. All this was achieved through the simple device of refusing to recognise the heirs who had been adopted by their rulers.[55] He also stirred the cultural pot further when he permitted the remarriage of Hindu widows and entitled sons to inherit their father's possessions even if he had changed his religion.

Dalhousie's intrusions served to further exacerbate the growing and compelling fears that traditional Indian life faced an existential threat. His abject indifference to the anger he was provoking also resulted in his later being condemned by one of his harshest critics, Henry Hyndman, as an 'arbitrary bigot'[56] who had embarked upon 'a course of unscrupulous annexations and wholesale Europeanisation from which our Empire is now suffering'.[57] Another sympathetic ear was proffered by Anglo-Irish author and civil servant Montgomery Martin. He accused Dalhousie of being indifferent to the feelings of the Indians because 'he governed India for the Company, and looked at every question from the Leadenhall point of view ... and entirely overlooked the accumulation of grievances pent up in the native mind.'[58] Henry Hyndman naturally saw in such bull-headed arrogance the storing up of considerable problems, warning how 'one civilisation, trying to act upon and improve another, ought to be exceedingly cautious in what it either removes or introduces.'[59]

But such warnings fell on deaf ears, as Dalhousie and his ilk could respond to any criticism by simply invoking one of a number of repressive statutes dating back to the earliest days of Company rule. Irish-American journalist William Duane had travelled to Calcutta in 1788 to open the *Bengal Journal*. But when his paper incurred the displeasure of the Governor-General by printing scurrilous criticisms of the Company it was arbitrarily shut down. When he persisted with his negative comments he was deported in 1794 and returned to America.[60] Freedom of speech was further compromised in 1799 when Lord Wellesley introduced the Censorship of the Press Act, which prevented any paper being published until it had previously been inspected by a government official and received a clean bill of health.[61] This was strengthened by the Bengal Regulation Act of 1818, which authorised preventive arrest and incarceration without trial for those guilty of publishing 'animadversions' or articles likely to cause alarm or incite dissent. This stifling of press freedom led to many editors suffering the lighter indignity of being censured and forced to publish apologies and imposing self-censorship to avoid the harsher penalties.[62] An 1823 law also required all newspapers to be licensed, so that if they published anything likely to be considered seditious the licence could be revoked and the publication shut down. These measures muzzled European editors, which was outrageous enough to liberal thinkers, but they also served to completely gag any Indian voices. In spite of the disgust they engendered there was little or no sympathy forthcoming from the Government of India. It argued that a free press only applied in a representative democracy, and as India was not one, 'the people had no voice in its establishment, nor have they any control over its acts.'[63]

The organs of freedom may have been effectively stifled in India, but back in Britain they were active in censuring the Company and its activities. Despite the vigour of successive Governors-General, distrust of the Company in London had never abated and demands for its charter to be revoked entirely were growing. During 1852 and 1853, with the charter due for review, a select committee took evidence and received numerous petitions calling for reform, the system of 'double government' that had existed since the Pitt Act of 1784 coming in for particular censure.[64] It was also subject to excoriating condemnation beyond the confines of Parliament. At a public meeting in Manchester one speaker after another called for its abolition and for the administration of India to be exercised solely by the Crown.[65] As a consequence of such appeals and the accumulated evidence of decades, the charter was renewed in 1853 with one significant caveat: the status quo was only to be tolerated until the government had framed the country's long-term future. In the meantime, the number of company directors was reduced and the membership of the Governor-General's Executive Council increased. Moreover, the Governor-General's duties were split between executive and legislative functions. To this end the Indian (Central) Legislative Council was created, four of its six members to be appointed by each of the governments of Madras, Bombay, Bengal and Agra. Pointedly, though, there was no significant role for Indians. Then, out of the blue, in 1857 came the catastrophe that turned everything on its head.

Just four years after the charter was grudgingly renewed, Indian discontent exploded into open rebellion. The details of the Indian Mutiny, or First War of Independence, will be covered in greater detail later, but as an immediate response to the disaster, Prime Minister Lord Palmerston announced that he intended to introduced a bill bringing forward plans to transfer responsibility for India to the Crown. Despite their incompetence being exposed for all to see, the directors of the Company continued to insist that the status quo was 'an indisputable necessity for good government in India'.[66] The slaughter witnessed across the country gave the lie to this preposterous claim, however. Against their vehement protests, the Government of India Act of 1858 saw the East India Company dissolved after 258 years. Governor-General Lord Canning duly convened a durbar (a court gathering) at Allahabad on 1 November 1858 at which he read out a royal proclamation in the name of Queen Victoria announcing this monumental milestone in the country's history. Her Majesty promised a new dawn, respecting freedom of religion and undertaking to 'stimulate the peaceful industry of India, promote work of public utility and improvement and administer the government for the benefit of all our subjects'.[67] The Charter Act, just five years old, had become a dead letter and was to be superseded by a document of far more ambitious proportions.

The new Legislative Councils Act followed, legislating for all the necessary changes to the structure of government and administration of the country. The Governor-General assumed the additional title of Viceroy, overseeing an Executive Council of four, while the Board of Control and the Court of Directors was abolished. Sir Charles Wood ceased to be its president and became the first Secretary of State for India, assisted and advised by a fifteen-member Council. As the overriding motive for abolishing the Company was to provide for the better governance of the country, an Imperial Legislative Council was established in 1861, replacing the Indian (Central) Legislative Council. This would operate as a cabinet, with its members being assigned specific portfolios. Three of its members were to be appointed by the Secretary of State for India and two by the sovereign, although by 1869 all would be appointed by the Crown. In addition, the Viceroy could designate an additional six to twelve members. The five appointed by the secretary of state and then the Crown headed the executive, and those appointed by the Viceroy were empowered to debate and vote upon subsequent legislation.

In addition, the legislative powers of Bombay and Madras were restored, and although they could only pass laws for their own Presidencies, Bengal's laws would apply throughout the country. The Governor-General was also empowered to create new provinces and appoint their Lieutenant-Governors. The Presidencies of Bengal, Madras and Bombay, however, would continue to have direct access to the Secretary of State and be appointees of the

Crown. The status of the Princely States was unaffected, but to emphasise that the British Parliament was the final arbiter of Indian affairs, the Colonial Laws Validity Act was also passed in 1865. Although it also applied to the increasing number of representative legislatures being granted to the 'white' colonies, its intentions were clear:

> Any Colonial Law which is or shall be by any respect repugnant to the Provisions of any Act of Parliament extending to the Colony to which such Law may relate, or repugnant to any Order or Regulation made under Authority of Such Act of Parliament or having in the Colony the Force and Effect of such Act, shall be read subject to Act, Order or Regulation, and shall to the Extent of such Repugnancy, but not otherwise, be and remain absolutely void and inoperative...[68]

Wood hailed the reforms as 'a great experiment. That everything is changing in India is obvious enough, and that the old autocratic government cannot stand unmodified is indisputable.'[69] Yet there was still little for native Indians to savour, an opportunity Montgomery Martin felt the British had missed. He insisted that they were now duty bound to go much further and use their authority to 'prepare the people of India for independence',[70] but that possibility was still a long way from the minds of the Act's architects. Rather than loosen the relationship with London and the Crown, British Prime Minister Benjamin Disraeli sought to tighten it further. In 1876, he sponsored the Royal Styles and Titles Act, which recognised Queen Victoria as Empress of India. The idea worried William Gladstone, who feared that the country was now moving far beyond the role envisaged by the Act. He wondered whether 'we are now going by Act of Parliament to assume that dominion the possible consequences of which no man can foresee,'[71] fearing in particular that the measure inferred a radical change in the Crown's relatively loose relationship with the princes. Liberals also disliked the term 'Empress', associating it with those despotic and autocratic rulers who presided over countries such as Russia and Turkey. Disraeli denied both charges, especially that the step carried with it any changes 'to the dignity and honour of the Native Princes',[72] and ploughed ahead with his plans. Thus, with much fanfare, the Queen's new title, *Kaiser-e-Hind*, was duly announced at the Delhi Durbar of 1877, officiated by Viceroy Lord Lytton.

But if it were hoped a new title alone would improve relations between rulers and ruled, Disraeli would be left disappointed. Ever since the earliest days of the Company, British power was based on an acceptance that they were different to and apart from those over whom they exercised their suzerainty, and that was the way it had to be. Some limited intimacy had existed in the early days, but the devastating consequences of the Mutiny swept aside any pretensions that the two cultures should mix. Henry

Hyndman noted as late as 1886 that 'it is in general sadly true that Englishmen in India today live totally estranged from the people among whom they are sojourning,'[73] while another commentator, Theodore Monson, observed that 'the English newspapers ... often betray the insolent contempt of conquerors without being aware of it.'[74] Indeed the British seemed more preoccupied with increasing their hold over their Indian charges than reaching out to them, a frame of mind no better illustrated than by the raft of laws the Government contrived to pass. One source of paranoia was the ongoing determination to quash dissent at its slightest manifestation. The Vernacular Press Act of 1878 was one which added to existing statutes by attempting to restrict the dissemination of those Indian-language newspapers perceived to be challenging British policies, while an Arms Act of the same year sought to pre-empt open rebellion by forbidding Indians from manufacturing, trading in, owning or possessing any firearms whatsoever.

Yet one of the basic tenets which held British rule to be superior was that all were equal before the law. Despite Macaulay's best efforts this chimera was exposed in 1873 when a further statute was enacted which spared Europeans the indignity of a trial in any court presided over by Indian magistrates. Whites were particularly mortified at the prospect of an Indian judge having jurisdiction in a case in which it was their word against that of another Indian. Therefore, under such circumstances, the accused could instead demand to be heard in the High Court. As Monson freely admitted, 'very few Europeans in India believe that an English jury ... would even on the clearest evidence convict one of their countrymen for the murder of a native.'[75] Such egregious expressions of contempt for the people in whose country they were living inevitably produced concern among the more liberal minded, as well as being a pointed snub to Indian sentiment. Nonetheless, it remained stubbornly on the statute books until Viceroy Lord Ripon sought to reverse its worst aspects. Hoping to mollify growing nationalist sentiment without alienating the European population, he introduced the highly contentious Ilbert Bill in 1883.

Named after Sir Courtney Ilbert, a well-meaning law member of the Viceroy's Council, the controversy stirred up by this bill instead simply served to highlight the huge gulf between the two communities. A campaign was financed by British businessmen and furious letters were sent to Europeans of influence demanding something be done. The Lieutenant-Governor of Bengal, the Chief Justice and ten British judges of the Calcutta Court also made their opposition known. The Hon. Mr Justice Stephen KCSI wrote to *The Times* on 1 March 1883 pompously calling the bill 'utterly needless [and] of a determination to try to govern India upon principles inconsistent with the foundations on which British power rests'.[76] On 24 June, Sir Arthur Arbuthnot KCSI CIE, a former member of the Supreme Council in India, demanded 'the withdrawal of a measure which nearly all Englishmen who knew India believed to be highly prejudicial to the best interests of the country'.[77] There were nonetheless somewhat more level heads advocating more rational contemplation. In its leading article on 26 June *The Times* reasoned:

> ... there will not be a general exodus if the Ilbert Bill passes, any more than there will be a collapse of Indian society if it is withdrawn. But the change of the law would unquestionably add to the risks of capital and unpleasantness of life in India ... it would consequently be a mistake to encourage the present dangerous temper of the natives by ostentatiously defying the universal and strongly expressed opinion of the English community.[78]

But such measured tones were in the minority. Lord Ripon was booed in the streets, and there were rumours of a plot to kidnap and throw him out of the country and unleash anarchy if the bill went through. Under such sustained pressure he was inevitably forced to backtrack, and a form was passed that was so watered down it left the Europeans in more or less the same privileged position as before. Educated middle-class Indians were also appalled by the controversy, reminded once again of their second-class status. The relative ease with which the Government of India caved in to the pressure of European vested interests led men such as Dadabhai Naoroji, later known as 'the Grand Old Man of India' and one of few Indians to serve in the House of Commons, to warn that 'the Secretary of State ... has to make Parliament lay down by clear legislation, how India is to be governed for India's good ... Hindus, Mohammedans and Parsees are alike asking whether the English rule is to be a blessing or a curse. Politics now engross their attention more and more.'[79] His views also chimed with sympathetic British critics, who saw that demands for radical change could not be avoided for much longer.

British civil servant Allan Octavian Hume put the lack of an Indian voice down to the fact that 'there existed no recognised channel of communication between the rulers and the ruled,'[80] and urged that some action be taken to amplify the voices of the Indian people. This position was shared by Annie Besant, a strongly pro-Indian socialist who was determined to change the European mindset. The idea also gained traction among Anglicised Indian elites who were influenced by the Brahmo Samaj movement and agitation for home rule in Ireland. Much of this new radicalism came from the pen of Bengali writer Bankim Chandra Chatterjee, whose writing extolled the virtues of Hinduism, and especially its past glories. One poem, *Vande Mataram* ('We pay homage to our mother'), would become the anthem of the Indian nationalist movement. Those proponents of an organisation to articulate Indian concerns were eventually heeded, and within a couple of years of the Ilbert controversy an embryonic Indian National Congress was founded in 1885.

The first three-day meeting of the Indian National Congress was convened in Bombay in December 1885 to form, in the words of one speaker, 'the germ of a Native Parliament ... an unanswerable reply to the assertion that

India is still wholly unfit for any form of representative institutions'.[81] A branch office was also set up in London in 1888 under the management of William Digby to spread the word of Indian nationalism through lectures and the distribution of leaflets. This was followed by a permanent British Committee of the Indian National Congress in 1889, with William Wedderburn as its chairman and Digby as secretary. Within a couple of years it had so transformed the political landscape that in 1890 Viceroy Lord Lansdowne was moved to concede that 'the Congress Movement is regarded as representing in India what in Europe would be called the more advanced Liberal Party.'[82] Nevertheless, it was still too small and moderate to have any chance of winning over imperialists. They were still convinced of their divine mission, and now turned their attention to another long-running bone of contention between traditionalist Hindus and reformist Europeans.

The arranged marriage of girls as young as ten to much older men appalled British sensibilities and had been the subject of debate for decades. The main issue was that marriageable age and the age of consent were essentially one and the same. Some progress had been made in 1860 when the Indian penal code defined rape as intercourse with any child under the age of ten, but marriage was still legal from as young as eight; the law simply compelled the parties to abstain from sexual activities until the bride was twelve.[83] Indian poet and social reformer Behramji Malabari shared the concerns of Europeans and had campaigned against the practice for many years. He published pamphlets entitled *Infant Marriage* and *Enforced Widowhood* in 1887, hoping, like Moham Roy in his day, to persuade rather than compel. In 1888, the case of a young bride of eleven dying as the consequence of attempted congress by her husband of thirty-five outraged most informed people, but still the Hindu elders stood firm against change. Professor D. R. Bhandarkar reminded zealous reformers that the practice had been permitted within the Code of Manu for generations. He even quoted the appropriate passage, which stated that 'a man thirty years old should marry a girl pleasing to him of the age of twelve years' but that the marriage should not be consummated until the bride was fifteen.[84]

One problem was that Britain had itself been slow in reforming laws regarding the age of consent. It had been twelve from 1275 until 1875, but in 1885 it was raised again to sixteen. This provided the fillip the reformers in India needed, and finally in 1891 the Age of Consent Bill was drafted and submitted for approval. This proposed to raise the age for girls from ten to twelve years and make sexual intercourse with a girl below that age punishable by ten years' imprisonment or transportation for life.[85] It inevitably met with a storm of protest from traditional Hindus who accused its authors of trying to further imperil their religion. Meetings and demonstrations were organised, petitions drawn up and appeals launched to stop it passing into law.

One meeting on 18 January 1891 passed a resolution condemning the measure as 'direct interference with the Hindu religion and usage',[86] and on 5 March, Sir Ramesh Chunder Mitter, the first Indian Chief Justice to be appointed to the Calcutta High Court, insisted it 'met with the strongest opposition from the people'.[87] Counterintuitively, it also met with resistance from the other side of the divide, with most of them advocating stricter laws. Among them was Bal Gangadhar Tilak, a rising star in the nationalist movement. He and his supporters looked to the glory days of the Marathas before the arrival of the British interlopers, using his newspaper *Kesan* to spread his views and promote festivals honouring Maratha hero Shivaji Bhonsle and the Hindu god Ganapati. Tilak was an ardent reformer who advocated marriage for girls at age sixteen and boys at twenty years. He also wanted an end to the dowry system, but he did not want these changes to come as a consequence of laws passed by Englishmen. He insisted that 'we should not like that the government should have anything to do with regulating our social customs or ways of living, even supposing that the act of government will be a very beneficial and suitable measure.'[88] Henry Hyndman sympathised with such sentiments, and although he too abhorred child marriage he was firmly against the idea that 'a handful of foreigners, who do not even live in the country, can safely introduce their ideas and methods, irrespective of the opinions of their subjects.'[89] Nevertheless, Viceroy Lord Lansdowne signed the legislation into law on 9 March 1891, leaving Tilak and his followers incensed and more than ever convinced that the solution was not simply a greater say in the government of their country but the expulsion of the Europeans altogether. The watchword was henceforth to be *swaraj*, self-rule, and as one of its most vocal exponents Tilak would prove to be the bane of the British establishment until his death in 1920.

Amid this ill feeling and animosity it was grudgingly recognised that some concessions ought to be made to placate moderate Indian sentiment, and so came the Legislative Councils Act of 1892. This modest measure increased the number of seats on the councils to sixteen, and permitted a limited number of elected Indians to be inducted through local governments, universities, chambers of commerce and cultural associations. The Act also permitted councils to discuss each year's financial statement, and as a result 'each important class should have the opportunity of making its views known in Council by the mouth of some Member specially acquainted with them.'[90] Furthermore, the number of additional members on the Governor-General's Executive Council was raised to sixteen, two-fifths of whom would be non-official and allowed to ask questions of public interest. It was naturally hoped that these limited reforms would appease nationalist opinion and kick demands for further concessions into the long grass. Instead they opened a different can of worms. Theodore Monson observed at the time that instead of assuaging native calls for a bigger say, 'the Muhamadans [*sic*] oppose the introduction of the principle of representation because they are in the minority and are well aware that the elections would always be contested on racial and religious lines, and that therefore Muhamadans would always be defeated at the poll.'[91] Muslims were therefore aware that the biggest gainers from any reforms would be the Hindus, arousing latent feelings of hostility which having the British as a common enemy had so far held in check. The Muslim *Rohilkand Gazette* of 8 March 1898 reported a Hindu paper warning darkly of the troubles to follow, advising its readers to guard against 'cultivating friendship and affection towards the Mussalmans, who are their enemy, oppressors and murderers'.[92]

Others saw the British as the real problem, particularly when its servants demonstrated their own fallibility and incompetence. This was graphically demonstrated when famine and bubonic plague broke out in the Bombay Presidency in 1897 and the response of Poona's Chief Plague Officer Walter Rand proved clumsy and inept. This was highlighted by the blind insensitivity with which he attempted to contain the problem, opening plague hospitals and segregation camps in which he forcibly confined anyone suspected of carrying the bacteria. Entire districts were cordoned off and the soldiers who entered homes to take the victims were accused of wanton damage to personal property, harassment, disrespect towards religious shrines and even looting. The effects of the famine and plague were bad enough but Rand was held personally responsible for the unnecessary suffering and the inept manner in which the crisis was handled. His actions were even condemned by fellow Europeans, but for one nascent nationalist group, the 'Society for Removing Obstacles to the Hindu Religion', there could be only one answer to the manner in which their compatriots had been tyrannized and humiliated. Two of its members lay in wait while Rand attended a dinner party celebrating Queen Victoria's Jubilee in Government House, Poona, on 22 June 1897. As he left he and a colleague were gunned down, provoking a manhunt in which suspects were rounded up and arbitrarily arrested. Among them was Tilak, but although no evidence of complicity in the murder could be found he was still charged with sedition, put on trial and sentenced to eighteen months' imprisonment.

It was indeed ironic that this tragic chain of events should occur in the midst of celebrations for Queen Victoria's sixty years on the British throne and twenty as *Kaiser-e-Hind*. As the seat of a vast empire encompassing 11 million square miles and 372 million people, London, not Poona, was the centre of attention. Over £30 million in today's money had been lavished on an exposition of British might and power while the Bombay Presidency suffered. A voluptuous procession through London was organised in which India held centre stage, pride of place given to representatives of famous regiments such as the 2nd Lancers (Gardiner's Horse), the 10th Bengal Lancers (Hodson's Horse), the 6th Bombay Lancers (Jacob's Horse) and a contingent from Hyderabad. *Daily Mail* reporter George Warrington Steevens, described 'Indian Princes in their magnificent native costumes and riding the most splendid horses'[93] processing through the city and wowing the crowds. Later, the Queen reviewed them at Horse Guards Parade and on her return to Windsor met four sons of native princes who were studying at Eton

College. Simultaneously, communities across India held festivities to express their fealty and loyalty. Speeches in her honour were hosted at sumptuous banquets such at that at which Rand met his fate, by the Governors of British India and at the Viceroy's summer residence at Simla. Ostentatious durbars were organised at which prayers were held for her health and longevity, while princes competed to show their love and affection, founding schools and hospitals, erecting statues and memorials and feeding the starving masses in her name. No expense was spared in expressing the extent of India's love and devotion; an outward show of unity which belied its widening schisms.

Yet with Tilak and other nationalists languishing in prison and Congress agitating for a greater share in government, the bitter irony of such spectacles was not lost on more astute observers. Henry Hyndman was among the more thoughtful students of the Raj who ran scathingly counter to the popular mood. Instead of lauding her rule, he accused Queen Victoria of being 'the Empress of famine and the Queen of Black Death',[94] and of presiding over a despotic and illegitimate regime. Yet he remained in the minority. To the less perceptive among his peers, British rule was an unmitigated success.

2

'Settle a new branch of the nation in the strong places of India'

While the country wrestled with its social and political metamorphosis, changes of a more structural nature had been transforming the subcontinent. These had been formulated in statute but crafted in stone and steel, making possible a network of canals and railways so extensive and all-pervading that they would dominate the landscape as well as much of the economy by the time of the Jubilee. Hailed by enthusiastic imperialists as tangible proof of the Raj's commitment to progress and advancement, they nonetheless visited debt, social upheaval and ecological disaster upon the very people they were supposedly built to benefit.

Canals had, of course, been a feature of the landscape for centuries, axiomatic totems of the achievements of old India. The Greek Megasthenes, ambassador of Seleukos Nikator at the Court of Sandrakothos near Patna, wrote as early as 3000 BC that thanks to them 'the whole country was under irrigation',[1] but by the middle of the eighteenth century warfare and neglect had left many canals in a state of disrepair, broken, silted up or drained away. Eventually it was decided that something ought be done, and during his tenure as Governor-General Lord Hastings toured Upper India and subsequently proposed a scheme of large-scale restoration of the canals built in the reign of Firoz Shah Tughlaq east and west of the Jumna River, a tributary of the Ganges. Hastings wrote to the Board of Directors confidently that 'my own inspection has fully convinced me of the facility and the policy of immediately restoring this noble work ... inspired by the knowledge that ... the land revenue of the Honourable Company [and] the dues to be collected for the distribution of the water from it would make a most lucrative return.'[2] When their potential was finally grasped, a Committee of Enquiry was appointed in 1810 under Lord Minto to make recommendations upon how they might be resurrected.

Following its findings the Board of Directors appointed one Lieutenant Blaine in 1817 to commence the restoration of the West Jumna, and in 1823 Colonel John Colvin was appointed Superintendent of Irrigation at Delhi; under his supervision the project was completed by 1833.[3] Once the potential for profit was grasped, their prospects did not escape the nation's entrepreneurs for long. But there were obstacles to be overcome before they could begin in earnest, particularly in obtaining the necessary finance. Before 1854 public works were the domain of the somewhat cash-strapped Engineers Department of the Army under the supervision of a military board,[4] which was not an arrangement designed to foster speedy and energetic enterprise. Lord Dalhousie had made some strides in streamlining its functions, however, and created a Central Public Works Secretariat in Calcutta under the oversight of a chief engineer. This removed some of the bureaucratic tumbleweed, but public works could only do so much as the cost of any major project would be astronomical and so required contributions from Company revenues.[5] Dalhousie had suggested that loans instead be raised in London, but for some time the parsimonious Court of Directors opted for a more cautious approach and preferred to use private companies.

Nonetheless, it was evident that serious investment was needed if major works were to be undertaken, and this could only be secured from financial institutions in the UK. Fortunately, this came at a time when India's investment potential was being widely promoted in the metropole. The decision was therefore taken to enlist the services of joint-stock companies in London to provide the necessary capital, but this meant borrowing on an unprecedented scale. Alfred Deakin, an Australian politician who visited in the 1890s, later observed that 'the great irrigation works of India are constructed with borrowed money raised in London and charged to the works at from three and half to four per cent,'[6] sums which brought a wince from the cost-conscious Board of Directors. Serious expenditure only truly began in earnest, then, after the Crown took over, with a planned investment of £1,600,000 in 1869–70, £2,500,000 in 1870–71, £3,000,000 in 1871–72, and further spending each year thereafter of £4,000,000.[7] But raising money and spending it wisely were not always compatible, and early endeavours proved disappointing.

In 1858, hitherto highly respected British Army general and irrigation engineer Arthur Cotton proposed constructing a network of canals from Madras to Mangalore. This, he assured his potential backers, would exploit the waters of the Krishna River, which almost bisects the subcontinent and bring life to thousands of acres of potential farmland. Furthermore, it was claimed, the scheme would increase trade to the tune of some £5,000,000 a year.[8] Cotton already had a reputation for competence and efficiency, having worked on irrigation projects as a servant of the Company, so he seemed like a safe pair of hands. His Madras Irrigation Company therefore had little trouble securing an initial government guarantee of 5 per cent on a loan of £1,000,000 towards the total outlay of £2,000,000, and work proceeded.[9]

The project succumbed to crippling cost overruns almost from its inception. It exceeded its initial budget long before it had even covered a fraction of the proposed route, resulting in a series of blunders that would bring to mind modern-day overspends. A sluice and lock that was meant to cost £11,000 was installed incorrectly and had to be replaced at the cost of another £12,900, and an entire aqueduct cost £45,000 instead of the intended £14,500 because it had been so poorly constructed it had to be completely rebuilt.[10] The grandiose project was going nowhere fast, and as one critic pithily observed, 'the canal runs from nowhere, to nowhere in particular, and consequently there is nothing and nobody to carry.'[11] By 1866 the project threatened to become one huge white elephant, leading an exasperated Secretary of State for India to offer to buy the company out to prevent any further pointless leeching of money. However, the shareholders knew they were on to a good thing with a guaranteed return of 5 per cent on their investment, and they cynically declined the offer.[12] As Viceroy Lord Lawrence admitted to a parliamentary select committee, 'with a guarantee of five per cent, capitalists will agree to anything; they do not care very much whether it succeeds or fails.'[13]

Projects that were actually finished on time proved equally disappointing. A scheme that was supposed to have cost £550,000 eventually consumed £1,240,000 and instead of yielding the promised 20 per cent return ran at a loss.[14] The Sone in Bengal returned only 0.1 per cent for many years, while the Chenab Canal in Punjab paid back just 0.08 per cent,[15] prompting Robert Burton Buckley in 1905 to observe candidly, if with sublime understatement, that 'the modern works, which have been entirely constructed by the British government in the last thirty years, were for a time a drain upon the finances.'[16]

Some projects went ahead despite not really being necessary. John Dacosta wrote in 1873 how their builders frequently demonstrated 'no practical knowledge of Indian agriculture ... and no intercourse with cultivators, only an imperfect acquaintance with the actual wants which they were called upon to supply'.[17] As a result, schemes were laid across lands already well provided for by monsoons, rivers and wells, and in one case of 2,500,000 acres of land introduced to a canal system, 1,900,000 were already under crops and 900,000 of these already sufficiently irrigated.[18] As a result, wrote Deakin, 'in all Presidencies, crops can be seen which have been impaired or destroyed by untimely and excessive soaking.'[19] Lack of understanding of the landscape and topography wrought further problems, construction drawing saline or salt-laden moisture up from the subsoil, rendering existing wells unusable and creating conditions in which malaria-bearing mosquitos flourished.[20]

As we have seen, whatever the merit of the schemes, they had to be built on borrowed money, and revenue had to be secured to repay the investors.

This was achieved in part by charging for transit and by selling irrigation services to the end user. Such charges varied according to region and type of crop; it was one rupee per acre for rice crops in some parts of Bengal and Sind, for example, and up to twenty rupees an acre in Bombay for sugar crops.[21] Yet the huge shortfall between income and expenditure often meant that when there were too few consumers of the water it was decided that irrigation cesses, or charges, should be imposed on farmers whether they used the service or not.[22] This often left cultivators with little choice but to pay for water instead of relying upon their own resources, and forcing them to cultivate cash crops rather than foodstuffs to fund this extra burden on their already tight budgets.[23] John Dacosta was among those who realised the consequences of such tactics, and warned that '[such] additional taxation would consequently further impoverish the people,'[24] a matter of little concern to shareholders comfortably accruing their 5 per cent per annum.

Yet despite the cost, the burden on the taxpayer and the environmental damage, these public works remained an article of faith to their champions. In the 1860s Superintendent General of Irrigation Colonel Turnbull remarked how the east of India had been transformed into 'one huge garden due to canals and irrigation ... [producing] ... wheat, lentil, mustard ... cotton, indigo [and] barley',[25] and by the end of 1903, £24,000,000 had been lavished on forty-two major works consisting of 7,500 miles of canals and 27,000 miles of distributaries designed to irrigate between 13,000,000 and 15,000,000 acres.[26] Furthermore, it was alleged that they brought other, political benefits. In 1905 Buckley asserted that not only had the Chehab Canal produced a 'new and prosperous home for more than a million inhabitants ... [it had also] done more to convince those colonists of the beneficial intentions of British rule than the Queen's Proclamation of 1858 and all the resolutions of the Indian Government since Queen Victoria assumed the sovereignty of the country'.[27] With men such as Sir Bamfylde Fuller adding in 1910 that the lowest estimate of the financial benefits obtained through irrigation works was £30,000,000 a year,[28] the British remained doggedly faithful to this awesome phenomenon. But canals were only one side of the coin. There was another wonder, more ambitious in concept and monumental in scale, to be introduced to the national landscape.

By the middle of the nineteenth century the East India Company claimed ownership of much of the vast subcontinent. But its various territories and responsibilities remained isolated and far from the key coastal factories of Calcutta, Madras and Bombay. However, recent innovations in Britain were pointing to a possible solution. In 1831–32 the parliamentary select committee of the East India Company looked into the advantages to be gleaned from the construction of railways, and concluded that they would serve to bring the various corners of the vast landmass together. An early exponent of the idea was Arthur Cotton, the civil engineer who would play such a disappointing role in the canal building debacle. In 1836 he presented an ambitious plan to lay 862 miles of track between Madras and Bombay, and further such proposals quickly followed in his wake. In 1842, fellow soldier and railway engineer Charles Blacker Vignoles submitted plans, and in July 1844 Sir Rowland Macdonald Stephenson proposed building a line from Calcutta to the North-West Frontier. In November 1844, the Great Indian Railway Company submitted plans to the Court of Directors to build a line across the Deccan with branches extending to the north and south. Such enthusiasm was shared by influential figures within the Indian community, and in 1845 Sir Jamsetjee Jejeebhoy and the Honourable Jagannath Shankarseth formed the Indian Railway Association, determined to pursue their dream of establishing a comprehensive network across the subcontinent. In 1846, the revenue commissioner of Bombay, Thomas Williamson, wrote to the chairman of the Great Indian Peninsular Railway in London:

> The great trunk line, running by the Malseje Ghaut in the direction of Nagpur, would be most direct which could possibly be selected to connect Bombay to Calcutta, commercially it would be best for the cotton of Berar, whilst for the first 120 miles from Bombay we would proceed in the immediate direction of the military stations of Ahmednuggar, Jaulna and Aurangabad.[29]

The arguments were almost irrefutable. Trade largely relied upon the fickle and unreliable river systems, themselves subject to monsoons, currents and the shifting of channels. The River Ganges from Calcutta, for example, was only safe for navigation during the dry, cool months of November and January following the monsoon, and even in good conditions it still took a steamer twenty-four days to travel to Allahabad.[30] Such modes of transport also exposed travellers to the perils of dacoits and Thugs, a situation which critics such as engineer, philologist and author Hyde Clarke considered intolerable. He was one of a growing band of men who advocated the wholesale development of railways, free from the caprice of both nature and banditry. He described how a 'locomotive which takes down a train with 100 tons of goods from Allahabad [to Calcutta], would be back in another day, so as on the third morning to be ready to start again from Allahabad with another train ... it would make ten trips backwards and forwards while the steam boat made one.'[31] He insisted moreover, that the transport of 'fruits, vegetables and vegetable juices ... [would benefit from the] ... savings effected by superior speed and less time in the conveyance of produce to market.'[32]

The *Calcutta Review* also took up the cause in March 1846, explaining how 'where it takes three months now, it will take only as many days, to bring distant consignments to market, and the same capital, consequently, which at present can be returned only three or four times a year, may be returned, probably, twenty.'[33] An East India Company agent believed railways could improve traffic in both directions, explaining that 'if we can cheapen carriage, we may greatly increase the imports of foreign articles into the interior; and in a corresponding degree, export cotton and other agricultural produce.'[34] Karl Marx, writing in 1853, also recognised the enormous commercial advantages, writing that 'the English millocracy intend to endow India with railways with the exclusive view of extracting at diminished expense the cotton and other raw materials for their manufactures.'[35] Moreover, Hyde Clark believed that railways 'will [also] have a direct tendency to promote the formation of roads in connection with the railway stations; and in many cases they will most efficiently assist them by bringing stone and other suitable materials at a cheap rate into districts where the construction of roads is now so expensive as to be economically impossible.'[36]

Lord Dalhousie was convinced enough to minute on 20 April 1853 how 'it cannot be necessary for me to insist upon the importance of a speedy and wide introduction of railway communication throughout the length and breadth of India ... great tracts [of India] are teeming with produce they [the growers] cannot dispose of, others are scantily bearing what they would carry in abundance if only it could be carried whither it was needed.'[37] Furthermore, the savings to the average traveller were clearly laid out by Hyde Clarke:

The expense of travelling ... from Calcutta to Darjeeling, with eight bearers, two *mussalchees* [torch bearers], and two *bangby-burdars* – say 372 miles, for twelve men at an average of fifteen annas and two pie per mile, is 259 rupees nine annas ... [or] £25.00, and the time employed about seven days. By the East Indian Railway, and Northern Bengal Railway, the cost of a first-class express passenger will not exceed £5.00 nor the time ten hours.[38]

Hyde Clarke also had a darker, ulterior motive. He saw railways attracting to India 'an effective English population',[39] and believed 'an immigration of 50,000 men, women and children per year ... would constitute an effective and powerful colonisation.'[40] These numbers, he calculated, would be further increased 'by births, so as to settle a new branch of the nation in the strong places of India',[41] giving 'us a hold which can never be shaken off ... An English population of one million will render revolt or revolution in India impossible, and secure peaceable settlement and our perpetual domination.'[42] Montgomery Martin was probably among a minority in thinking primarily of the benefits they might bring ordinary Indians. 'The excessive poverty of the labouring classes everywhere,' he reasoned, 'and the terrible famines which periodically occurred, were the direct consequences of the want of proper means of transit.'[43]

Yet again, if India was to fully embrace these possibilities, finance was critical. The railway boom in Britain had been accompanied by a frenzied period of speculation, with mad and impractical schemes attracting investors only to prove impossible to fulfil. In 1846 alone the government authorised the establishment of 246 companies, attracting more money and creating bubbles which would burst with alarming frequency. This cycle of madness only came to an end at the close of the 1840s, when the Bank of England increased interest rates and people started to come to their senses. Thus, with opportunities in the UK becoming relatively moribund, financial institutions started to look to India, just as its government was looking for investors. Nonetheless, just as with the canals, India was to prove only slightly more circumspect than Britain, offering guaranteed returns of 5 per cent as well as undertaking to purchase the land, pay for surveys and meet the costs of supervision.[44]

There was much to learn, too, from the challenges encountered in pioneering railway building in the UK. George Stephenson had been responsible for the Stockton and Darlington Railway in 1825, and Isambard Kingdom Brunel delivered the Great Western Railway, running from London to the West Country and opening its first section in 1841. So, for all the home-grown enthusiasm of the army engineers, it was agreed that railway experts from Britain should also consult the government on the best way forward. Consequently Frederick Walter Simms was among those invited by the East India Company to accept the post of consulting engineer and under the supervision of such men the various parties involved knuckled down to the nitty gritty of planning and preparation. It was no easy prospect. Those advocating a line between Calcutta and Delhi were talking about a route of 811 miles, almost the distance between London and John O'Groats, a scale of construction equating to the UK's HS2 programme today. Such an endeavour required careful consideration and the assessment of numerous variables.

One of the earliest subjects for debate was the gauge to be adopted, as the wider the track the greater the construction costs. George Stephenson had adopted the same gauge as the tracks used in coalmines – 4 feet 8½ inches – but Isambard Kingdom Brunel advocated the much wider 7-foot gauge, clearly more expensive but offering greater speed, stability and travelling comfort. Such debates had not accompanied the experimental work undertaken by men such as Arthur Cotton, whose lines were short and designed primarily for the transportation of material for road and dam construction, but now that both freight and people were to be conveyed over considerable distances the question commanded greater attention. In consideration of India's unique terrain and geographic and climactic conditions it was agreed that a gauge capable of safeguarding against the effects of high winds on bridges, curves and exposed stretches of track would be best. Stephenson's gauge was therefore rejected as too narrow, but Brunel's probably too wide and unnecessary. Lord Dalhousie ordained, therefore, that India should settle for something midway between the two. The compromise reached was 5 feet 6 inches.[45]

Tentative steps were already underway and in July 1850, Dalhousie had approved the building in Bengal of two experimental lines of 25 and

15 miles in length respectively,[46] but these were early, modest and relatively cheap practice lines. Once serious finance was secured the first service to be completed was the 21 miles of line opened between Bombay and Thane on 16 April 1853. In May 1854 the line was extended to Kalya, while the first in eastern India was constructed over 24 miles from Calcutta to Hoogley and opened on 13 August 1854. These were not cheap undertakings by any means. The Calcutta to Hoogley stretch – the work of the East Indian Railway – cost £15,000 per mile, although other companies managed lower costs, the Madras Railway coming in under budget at £12,000 a mile and the Great Southern somewhat less again at £8,000 a mile.[47] These disparities were partly due to the inevitable optimistic estimates given, with quotes of £15,000 a mile soon proving to be much nearer to £21,000.[48] Nonetheless, they were still much lower than in the UK, where by the late 1840s each mile of line cost upwards of £35,000.[49]

Such costs often reflected unexpected physical and environmental challenges, and nowhere were they greater than in India. They included the need to cross vast plateaus, deep ravines and broad, furious rivers, penetrate mountains and mitigate against hostile weather. As Montgomery Martin admitted, 'the formation of railways in India is tedious and costly, owing to the numerous bridges and viaducts required ... the Jumna Bridge has fifteen spans of two hundred feet each ... on eight other rivers the spans vary from fifty to one hundred and fifty each,'[50] and that meant more expense. Palta Ghat near Barrackpore, for example, had been considered as the crossing for the East Indian Railway, until it was surveyed and engineers realised they would have to span a river 710 yards wide and 45 feet deep, the bed of which consisted of bottomless, soft alluvial soil. When it was estimated that such an undertaking might incur an outlay of up to £459,000, they decided to look elsewhere.[51] Sometimes a planned route proved completely impractical, and further time and effort had to be spent on rerouting. Then floods and cyclones would wash away lengths of track and they would have to be reinforced and relaid,[52] all adding extra expense.

Arguably the greatest stumbling block to the programme of construction came in 1857 when the Mutiny broke out, and sabotage, attacks on workers and the general disruption caused by the conflict exacerbated the practical and logistical issues. On one occasion, when the sepoys at Danapur mutinied on 25 July, they marched on the East India Railway's partially built bridge over the Soane River in Bengal, forcing the European engineers and their families to flee for their lives,[53] and then proceeded to try to knock the bridge down.[54] The conflict did, however, serve to highlight the vital role railways were destined to play in India's future, as in this piece from *The Times* of 7 July 1857:

The late disastrous events in India have produced a very powerful effect on the Indian Railway Department, and the authorities are pledged to the development of the railway system. Had the East Indian Railway been complete from Calcutta to Delhi, as it ought to have been, instead of halting half way, the late disastrous events at Meerut and Delhi would never have occurred …[55]'

As Montgomery Martin explained, 'it is not easy to exaggerate the national importance of being able to despatch troops from England, via the Euphrates and the Persian Gulf, to Karrachee [sic] in one month, and thence by rail to most parts of India in twenty-four hours.'[56] Nonetheless, it was commercial considerations which commanded the shareholder's attention, and on the face of it once building began again in earnest the railways boomed. Between 1864 and 1869 passenger journeys increased from nearly 12,000,000 to 14,000,000 a year, growing by an average of 234 per cent between 1882 and 1902,[57] or 196,500,000 passenger journeys a year.[58] Freight traffic too, just 23 tons in 1854, had grown to 200,000 tons by 1859 and would be 12,000,000 tons ten years later. In percentage terms, the income from freight traffic increased from just 4 per cent in 1853–54 to nearly 66 per cent in 1869,[59] and would grow by 207 per cent by 1902.[60] By the turn of the century more than 14,000 miles of broad gauge and 11,000 miles of narrow gauge had been built over ninety-six different lines administered by thirty-three railway companies.[61] Nonetheless, such statistics proved deceptive and did not necessarily translate into profits.

Returns on investment proved painfully slow in coming. Most of the companies levied passenger fares ranging from just over two pennies a mile to about three-eighths of a penny, and freight from four pennies per ton per mile,[62] but even with the growth in human and cargo traffic these prices were nowhere near enough to defray the construction and running costs. The total loss for 1868–69 alone was £3,600,000,[63] producing a massive shortfall which the Government of India would have to make up for and remit to investors in the UK. In fact, there was only one brief half year, that of 1865–66, in which income outstripped interest paid on the debt, and this was only by a fraction.[64] In an attempt to cut costs the Government of India offered subsidised contracts in 1862 instead of the fixed guarantee, but by 1869 it was apparent that only guarantees would attract the necessary investment,[65] and so the expense and indebtedness carried on. From 1858 to 1900, the Government of India would pay a total of £51,527,307 out of general revenues,[66] and in Henry Hyndman's calculation 'up to the present time [1886] the public works, especially the railways, have represented a dead pecuniary loss to the country … [because the expenditure on them] did not show a return of even one per cent upon the capital.'[67]

This was a situation which in the words of William Digby had made payment of interest on the railways little more than 'a tax imposed on the Indian public for the benefit of the British shareholder'.[68] Henry Hyndman agreed, explaining scathingly how the greatest burden of building the railways inevitably fell upon the ordinary Indian ryot (peasant cultivator), 'who had to borrow an additional five, ten or twenty rupees off the native moneylender, at twenty-four, forty, or sixty percent in order to pay extra taxation ... every poor famine stricken creature whom that small sum might have tided over to a better day, has better reason to ask whether this is what Europeans mean by development ... railways will not put back that money into the pockets of the cultivators which has been drained away from them, or for which they have been forced to run into debt'.[69]

Buying the companies out and cutting their losses did not always solve the problem either. The contract for the East Indian Railway ran for thirty years, and when it was bought up in 1879 it still cost £32,750,000, which had to be repaid in annual instalments until 1953.[70] In his report for 1900, the Director-General of Railways admitted that 'the expenditure side of the account is further heavily weighted by the terms of the contracts of the guaranteed railways. Under these contracts payment of interest has to be made at a higher rate than is now necessary, and the calculation of the surplus profits has to be made at twenty-two pence to the rupee, while the current rate of exchange is nearer sixteen pence. Until these contracts terminate, the State is unable to obtain any advantage from cheaper money, or from the improved credit of the country, or from a favourable exchange.'[71] A further example of the extent to which the entire enterprise had bypassed Indians was the fact that out of a total of 17,000 share owners, only 679 were registered in India, and of these only 336 were native Indians.[72]

Another problem lay in the fact that practically every element required to build the railways originated in and profited Britain, which meant that 80 per cent of the capital was spent in the UK, on British-made goods and services.[73] Montgomery Martin described how 'during the year 1860–61, the raw materials despatched from England for the nine Indian lines amounted to 235,000 tons, valued at considerably more than £2,000,000 sterling,'[74] including the rails, locomotives, girders and rolling stock. Ironworks for bridges were prefabricated in Britain and reassembled in India. Nearly 30 per cent of all the locomotives manufactured in the UK were destined for the Indian market,[75] built by companies including Kitson, Thompson and Hewitson of Leeds and Stothert and Slaughter of Bristol. Furthermore, the railways often colluded in this one-way traffic. Considering India was covered in forests, even sleepers were imported at first because they were cheaper to bring from the UK than to source, extract and transport internally. At one point, home produced sleepers commanded the princely sum of 8-12-0 rupees each, whereas creosoted sleepers were available in the UK for just 3/6d each, roughly equivalent to 1-10-0 rupees, and therefore far cheaper even with freight costs added.[76] The East Indian Railway also enjoyed a monopoly over access to Indian coalfields, making it more expensive to transport local coal than import it from the UK. This not only suppressed India's coal industry, but stifled domestic iron and steel production, which could have benefited from local coal.[77]

Fortunately, the situation did slowly change for the better towards the end of the century as Indian railways matured and companies became more savvy. The East Indian Railway, for example, began to appreciate the earning potential from hauling Indian coal rather than suppressing it in favour of imports. Consequently, whereas during the first half of 1885 over 45,000 tons of Welsh coal had been imported, this number fell to just 1,000 tons for the corresponding period in 1889. Instead the company earned income by carrying Bengal coal for export, rising from some 250,000 tons a year in 1893 to 2,767,000 tons in 1905.[78] The Indian railway industry also became less dependent upon Britain for its rolling stock. In Jamalpur in Bihar, the East Indian Railway established its own workshops which by the early 1900s had become known as 'the Crewe of India',[79] with its 100-acre site employing 9,428 men capable of building and maintaining its own rolling stock and with the facilities to build almost every part in-house at a much lower cost than importing them.[80] It opened its own steel and iron foundries and a rolling mill in 1879, and in 1894 the construction of crossings and signals commenced.[81] Jamalpur remains a major workshop and manufacturer of key aspects of the Indian railways to this day.

Naturally the first builders, engineers, supervisors, traffic managers and locomotive superintendents were recruited in the UK, but as Dadabhai Naoroji explained, this had a further knock-on effect for India's finances. He explained that when 'you build a railway in England ... all the employees ... are Englishmen. Every farthing that is spent from the gross income is so much returned to Englishmen ... and ... England at large, as a part of the general wealth ... [but] in India the case is quite different. First, for the directors, home establishments, Government superintendence, and what not in England, a portion of the income must go from India; then a large European staff of employees ... must eat up and take away another large portion of the income.'[82]

These men also had to be highly paid if they were to be asked to risk the perils of mosquitos, cholera, prickly heat, sunstroke and other unpleasant climactic conditions. Subsequently the maintenance of European staff included additional allowances, passage money between India and home and often three times the pay that could be earned in the UK.[83] A resident engineer received pay and allowances of more than 700 rupees a month,[84] and a stationmaster £7/10 to £15.00,[85] whereas skilled native labourers, carpenters, masons and blacksmiths were paid nearer ten pence to a shilling, and ordinary labourers two pence-halfpenny to four pence a day.[86] The maximum pay for a European engine driver in India was £480 a year[87] – two-thirds more than an Indian could expect[88] – although when the penny finally dropped, £150,000 was saved during the five years ending 1880–81 simply by employing cheaper Indian drivers and shunters.[89] The ratio of maximum to minimum salaries on Indian railways compared to European lines was nonetheless glaring well into the 1920s. In India it was 500 to one, yet in Denmark it was twelve to one, in Norway eight to one, in Germany eleven to one, and in France twenty-one to one.[90] Nevertheless, despite the Government of India issuing instructions in 1879 for superior grades to be opened to Indians, by 1912 the Traffic Department still employed only twelve out of the ninety-nine posts and there was not one Indian earning more than 2,000 rupees a month.[91]

Being in their infancy, the railways also posed dangers to their employees with some 109 being killed in the course of their work in 1869 alone. But as the network grew the authorities began to take health and safety concerns more seriously. In 1870 and 1871 Acts provided for better fencing of track to stop cattle and people from straying onto lines,[92] and in 1880 rules were framed for the guidance of railway officers, police, civil officers and the government inspector for procedures to be followed in the event of a serious incident.[93] Nonetheless, by far the greater risk of death and injury was faced by those who worked on the tracks. The spread of diseases such as malaria was exacerbated by excavations for embankments, which filled huge pits with water and created vast breeding grounds for mosquitos.[94] Moreover, a cholera epidemic in 1859 killed thousands of labourers, while smallpox, typhoid, pneumonia, dysentery and diarrhoea could cut through a workforce rarely provided with adequate medical care.[95] To disease had to be added the perils of drilling and blasting rock to build tunnels and viaducts, explosions sending lethal shards in all directions. The construction of the Bengal–Nagpur Line in 1888 caused the deaths of between 2,000 and 3,000 workers, their bodies left where they died to rot or be eaten by carrion.[96]

However, such perils did not deter poor and desperate Indians attracted by a regular if miserly wage, and between 1859 and 1900 there were on average 180,601 to 221,253 men in employment on the lines each year, around 126 to 155 for each mile of track.[97] By 1881–82, 162,000 out of 200,000 railway employees were Indians,[98] and by 1902 there were 378,373 employed in various capacities.[99] In 1920 the railways would employ 6,941 Europeans, 10,865 East or Anglo-Indians and 694,884 Indians.[100] Such large numbers of men in employment seemed positive at first sight, but Dadabhai Naoroji explained that in fact the 'building of railways took men from working in agriculture'[101] and consequently there could be shortages of much-needed labour to grow food. Furthermore, higher-paid labourers with greater buying power could push up prices, creating local inflation which could badly affect non-railwaymen on lower incomes.[102]

The railways also affected traditional life in other ways, confronting Indians with a technology to which they were ill-equipped to adapt. In 1884 Sir Henry Waterfield, Financial Secretary at the India Office, told a parliamentary select committee, 'I think it more important that the people should become gradually familiarised with the extension of railways, than that they should be put down in every district before people have learnt to take advantage [of them].'[103] He could have had in mind the peasant who in 1880 told of the living he once made carrying goods on his bullock cart from Cawnpore to Aligarh and back, a distance of 220 miles, before the railways came and took away his livelihood. He went on to lament how thousands of his colleagues, too, had lost similar means of earning a living as a result of being overwhelmed by this innovation.[104] One of the arguments submitted in favour of the railways was, of course, that they would make the transport of produce cheaper and more economical. Instead, whereas exports were improved, the ordinary ryot often through ignorance continued to sell to his buyers at the old price, losing out on the extra money to be made.[105]

In Britain, this new and innovative form of transport was seen as a great social leveller, but in India served to emphasise the country's endemic racism. Should a European step into a carriage, its Indian occupant was expected to vacate it regardless of how crowded the rest of the train was,[106] and despite providing the overwhelming majority of their customers, third-class passengers were also packed into the starkest and most spartan accommodation imaginable. They were packed, in the words of one commentator, 'like animals bound for the slaughter, twenty or more in one compartment',[107] and in 1903 Mr Thomas Roberton admitted that the 'average number (154 to 267) of passengers in a train is greater than in any other country in the world'.[108]

In 1884, Sir Alexander Rendell, Consulting Engineer for Indian Railways, told a select committee that lack of competition was largely to blame for these conditions. In the UK, companies provided double or quadruple the seating space required because if one line was overcrowded they could easily change to other lines, an option not available in India's captive market.[109] Another cause of overcrowding was frequency. While in England scores of trains ran daily up and down the line, Indian passengers were lucky of there were more than four trains a day,[110] and it was not until 1905 that express trains first started to be provided for lower-class passengers.[111] The absence of competition led to Indian third-class customers being taken advantage in other ways, with an absence of toilet facilities or buffet cars. Stations also lacked adequate catering, waiting rooms were left open to the elements, and general overcrowding meant a mad rush for a seat when the train pulled in.

Despite the appalling service, Indians paid up to 40 per cent more for their fares than for a comparable journey in the UK, where the third-class accommodation was frequently better than the first-class offered on Indian lines.[112] Moreover, for all the bravado of their supporters, there would only be one mile of railway for every 82.36 square miles of territory, and for every 12,231 people even by the end of the century.[113] But, as had been admitted in a despatch to the Court of Directors as early as 1845, 'remuneration for railroads in India must, for the present, be drawn from the conveyance of merchandise and not from passengers.'[114]

This great technological and engineering marvel also proved to be an environmental disaster for large swathes of the country. The construction of the lines required supplies of wood for sleepers and fuel for brick kilns of herculean proportions once Indian wood became accessible. The 17 miles of one line on the East Indian Railway built in the second half of 1858 required 4,500,000 bricks to be in kilns preparatory to burning, and a further 7,000,000 moulded and ready to be baked. To meet such voracious demand there were fifty brick kilns and sixteen lime kilns consuming wood from such places as the Deodar forests of the Punjab Hills in Kashmir.[115] Each mile of track also needed 1,700 sleepers and 1.5 tons of wooded keys for securing the track,[116] although the railway from Delhi into Jaipur alone consumed timber for 80,000 sleepers.[117]

The Indian climate also meant that they needed to be replaced more frequently, putting an even greater strain on the country's forests. Consequently, those in Tenasserim and Lower Burma were exhausted by the middle of the nineteenth century,[118] and in the western United Provinces during the 1870s loggers removed up to 1,046,000 trees, a number which doubled again in the 1880s.[119] Nonetheless, experts considered the supply to be almost inexhaustible even at these rates of loss. German botanist and forestry specialist Dietrich Brandis, who was appointed inspector-general of Indian forests in 1864, surveyed the Himalayas in 1878 and calculated that they should comfortably be able to yield around half a million trees a year.[120] In spite of such bounty, the resulting deforestation left entire hillsides exposed to the elements, causing soil erosion and the loss of natural habitat. The roots which once gave the earth stability had gone, and when the monsoons arrived there was little to stop the soil washing away. As Henry Hyndman put it, 'only now are we beginning to understand that forests [and] groves ... do more to enrich a poor tropical country than vast systems of railroads.'[121]

Their supporters, however, remained bullish. In 1876 Viceroy Lord Northbrook bragged that he 'did not think anyone who had any knowledge of the subject could doubt that the expenditure on the Indian railways was one of the most profitable investments that ever was made by a great nation',[122] and in 1884 a parliamentary select committee claimed that railways had benefitted the Indian people to the tune of some £30,000,000 to £40,000,000.[123] In any case, as one Major Pears of the Madras Engineers remarked at the height of the building boom, 'we are in danger of doing great injustice to the people of this country by looking upon these great works as mere commercial speculation ... [they are] essentially peaceful. They have arisen out of and naturally belong to an era of peace, civilisation and commerce.'[124] This was a specious claim, considering the railways had been achieved largely at the expense of the Indian people.

3

'Great traffike for all sorts of spices and drugges'

Even before the advent of canals and railways, the rich cultural heritage that early European visitors encountered had been enriched by the existence of an equally sophisticated and flourishing economy. As Annie Besant explained, India 'was trading with ancient Babylon, and three thousand years before Christ ... to 1613 ... there was no break in the commercial and the industrial property of India'.[1] As well as Babylon, early contact with Rome fostered a thriving trade which greatly advantaged canny Indian merchants. Sales of popular luxuries such as muslin peaked under the reign of Emperor Nero and prompted historian Pliny to write tetchily in AD 79 that 'in no one year does India drain our Empire of less than 550,000,000 of Sesterces, giving back her own wares in exchange which are sold among us at fully one hundred times their cost price.'[2] Commerce also blossomed closer to home. In 1406 a Chinese envoy to Bengal mentioned trading in five to six varieties of cotton fabrics besides silk handkerchiefs and caps embroidered with gold, painted wares, steel, guns and scissors.[3] By the end of the sixteenth century such enterprises realised a market share of approximately 23 per cent of the known world's economy. But by the end of British rule in 1947 this would plummet to just 4 per cent. This staggering decline was due almost entirely to the commercial policies of British traders, aided and abetted by their politicians back home.

This transformation in fortunes had as its genesis the activities of adventurers such as the English merchant Ralph Fitch. Around the beginning of 1583, he and other likeminded men looked to exploit the prospects for lucrative trade with the east. He would later describe how he 'did ship [himself] in a ship of London called the *Tyger* ... [*sic*]',[4] and set off through the Mediterranean, the Levant and Mesopotamia in search of fame and fortune. He surveyed several likely trading opportunities, including in Burma, the Malay Peninsula and Malacca, but it was India that captured his imagination. When he finally returned to London in April 1591, he enthused about the

... great traffike for all sorts of spices and drugges, silk, and cloth of silke, sandales [sandalwood], elephants teeth, and much china worke, and much sugar, which is made of the nut called Gagara. The tree is called the Palmer [Portuguese Palmeiro], which is the profitablest tree in the world. It doth always bear fruit, and doth yield wine, oyle, sugar, vinegar cordes, coles; of the leaves are made thatch for the houses, sayles for shippes, mats to sit or lie on; of the branches they make their houses and broomes to sweep; of the tree wood for shippes ... [sic] [5]

Fitch's flamboyant claims may have sounded like exotic tales, but when they were substantiated by the discovery of a cornucopia of goods aboard a Portuguese galleon captured in 1592,[6] they further whet the appetites of astute and profit-minded London merchants. Keen to cash in on the bounty offered by the mysterious East, a number of them pooled their resources and secured initial capital of £30,133,6-8,[7] over £9,000,000 today. With this considerable sum they formed the Honourable East India Company, and were granted their royal charter from Queen Elizabeth I on 31 December 1600 under the name of 'Governor and Company of Merchants of London Trading into the East Indies'.[8] The monarch presided over the General Court and the Court of Directors, with management consisting of a direction board of seventeen members, later increased to twenty-four, who were termed 'committees'. From among these worthy notaries a chairman or governor was elected who would serve for one year, the first being Alderman Thomas Smythe, an experienced financier of explorations of discovery to the New World. The business of the committees was initially the purchase and exporting of goods for sale in India, as well as the provision of agents with bullion to purchase Indian spices, goods and manufactures.

The Company's first five ships set off under the command of one Captain Lancaster in 1601, laden with iron, tin, cloth, cutlery, glassware and hides worth 68,000 rupees, along with hard cash. Eight more voyages followed, together yielding average profits of 200 per cent,[9] one particular consignment purchased for £386,000 realising £1,915,000 back in England.[10] Inevitably, as Montgomery Martin later recorded, these first ventures were destined to be followed 'by a rapid increase of commerce, the products and manufactures of India being exchanged for the coined gold and silver of Europe'.[11] Gradually the Company extended its footprint, and with the cooperation and consent of the Mughal emperors and local potentates they established their first 'manufactories' or trading posts, starting with Surat in 1612. Bombay Island, part of the dowry of Catherine of Braganza upon her betrothal to Charles II, was also gifted to the Company in 1668, and in 1684 the seat of government was transferred there from Surat.[12]

By 1690 the Company had firmly established Presidencies in Madras and Bombay, so named because the chief officer or president was appointed by the Company. Eight years later permission was obtained from Prince Azim, one of the grandsons of Aurangzeb, to purchase Calcutta (Kolkata) in Bengal, while Azim also permitted the Company to exercise judicial authority over both its English and native inhabitants.[13] As the Company extended its interests and its power and influence grew, it became only a matter of time before its ambitions evolved likewise. In 1686 it declared its intention to 'establish such a polity of civil and military power and create and secure such large revenue ... as may be the foundation of a large, well-founded, sure English dominion in India for all time to come'.[14] It was to prove true to its word as, slowly but surely, the Company tightened its hold on the lives of those Indians with whom it came into contact.

An early coup was to be granted royal *firmans* by the nawabs of Bengal, exempting the Company from the transit duties which applied to native merchants. These had been given on the understanding that the Company acted as an import/export agent and confined itself to inland trade. When it began to trade in its own right the concessions took on an entirely new dynamic. Natives, subjected to unfair and unscrupulous competition, found themselves increasingly marginalised by the Company's ability to undercut them.[15] This situation accelerated when England's Industrial Revolution took off in the eighteenth century. Inventions such as the flying shuttle in 1760, Watt's steam engine in 1768 and Hargreaves's spinning jenny in 1776 transformed the British economy, while in India products of the highest quality were still being cheaply produced in humble dwellings using a few crude tools and requiring no elaborate machinery. Scottish economist and political theorist James Mill explained that as a domestic industry weaving had always been 'a sedentary occupation ... it requires patience ... little bodily exertion ... and the finer the production the more slender the force which he is called upon to apply'.[16] This undemanding approach to manufacturing clearly conflicted with the productivity required by the Directors in London, and would have to change.

So, in 1769 the Directors issued instructions that although the manufacture of raw silk was to be permitted, the production of finished goods must be actively discouraged. Furthermore, silk winders should no longer work for themselves at home but exclusively for the Company, 'under severe penalties by the authority of the Government'.[17] Cotton producers faced a similar fate. Consequently, as historian Romesh Chunder Dutt later expressed it, 'men who worked on their own capital, produced commodities in their own homes and villages and made their own profits, were made dependents of the Company.'[18] There were nonetheless principled Westerners who sympathised with the conditions being imposed on native manufacturers and the effect they were having on their traditional way of life. In 1772, merchant William Bolts, a former servant of the Company turned whistle blower, wrote a lengthy exposé:

> ... the whole inland trade of the country, as at present conducted ... has been one continued scene of oppression: the baneful effects of which

are severely felt by every weaver and manufacturer in the country, every article produced being made by a monopoly ... in which the English ... arbitrarily decide what quantities of goods each manufacturer will deliver, and the price he will receive for them ... [manufacturers] are in general now monopolised by the English Company and their servants, as so many slaves ...[19]

In the course of the next forty years the situation would deteriorate even further. 'It was the British intruder who broke up the Indian hand-loom and destroyed the spinning wheel,' wrote Karl Marx. 'England began with driving the Indian cottons from the European market; it then introduced twist into Hindustan ... From 1818 to 1836, the export of twist from Great Britain to India rose in the proportion of 1 to 5,200. In 1824 the export market of British muslins to India hardly amounted to one million yards, while in 1837 it surpassed sixty-four million of yards.'[20] In monetary terms the effects were even worse. In 1815 Indian cotton goods exported from India to the UK were worth £1,300,000, but by 1832 they had plunged in value to just £100,000, while British exports to India had increased in value from £26,300 to £400,000 in the same period.[21] The social consequences were, as William Bolts foretold, devastating. Karl Marx described how as a result of British actions, 'the population of Dacca decreased from 150,000 inhabitants to 20,000';[22] as Henry Hyndman succinctly put it, 'the unfortunate Indian weavers ... perished silently on the battlefield of commercial war.'[23]

Even while this transformation was taking place, a heated debate was raging as to the capacity of ordinary Indians to absorb British exports. Warren Hastings had admitted that 'the poor in India may be said to have no wants ... their wants are confined to their dwellings, to their food, and to a scanty portion of clothing,'[24] while Company servant John Malcolm conceded that Indians 'are not likely to become consumers of European articles because they do not possess the means to purchase them'.[25] Instead, admitted Robert Rickards, Lord President of the select committee of the House of Lords on East India Affairs in 1830, 'India requires capital to bring forth its resources, but the fittest capital for this purpose would be one of native growth, and ... would be created if our institutions did not obstruct it.'[26]

In 1866, Scottish physician and writer on India Dr Forbes Watson wrote that 'the British manufacturer must not look for his customers to the upper ten millions of India, but to the hundreds of millions in the lower grades. The plainer and cheaper stuffs of cotton, or of cotton and wool together, are those which he would be able to sell.'[27] Yet even by this stage in the nineteenth century Montgomery Martin was still having to argue that if Britain wanted a worthwhile trade with the country then it needed a healthy Indian consumer base. He explained how 'estimating the population of all India at 200,000,000, it seems reasonable to suppose that the import of British manufactures might be raised to twenty shillings' per head[28] if only the Indian consumer could afford to purchase more. But even after twenty years Indians were spending an average only two shillings and sixpence a head on British goods.[29]

But instead of trying to improve Indian buying power the decision had been taken to undercut Indian goods by dumping those of Britain on its markets as cheaply as possible. To this end, as British humanitarian William Digby elucidated, India was obliged 'to take our goods either with no import, or with a merely nominal import duty' of only 2.5 per cent.[30] But no reciprocity was to be given to Indian manufactures into Britain. Instead, as Company Director Henry St George Tucker explained in 1823, 'silk manufactures and ... goods made of silk and cotton intermixed have long been excluded altogether from our markets ... partly in consequence of the operation of a duty of sixty seven per cent.'[31] It was not just wool and silk goods which faced such impenetrable barriers; by 1831 duties ranged from 105 per cent to 378 per cent for coffee, 400 per cent for pepper, 393 per cent for sugar, and 100 per cent for tea.[32] By comparison, duties on goods imported into India from the UK were still as low as 3.5 per cent by 1852, and rarely higher than 10 per cent.[33]

This one-sided commerce continued to weigh down upon India, until by 1914 tariffs had been applied to around 400 items, one-third of the revenue from which was cotton goods, 10 per cent silver and sugar, 14 per cent alcohol, and 7 per cent petroleum and metals.[34] But Indian exporters were not only faced with prohibitive tariffs. Freight costs, too, favoured the British because raw produce is much bulkier than finished goods and Indian exports to the UK attracted much higher charges than those from Britain into India.[35] Because India was almost literally a captive market there was nothing that could be done to redress this exploitation. If instead, as British Orientalist Horace Hayman Wilson asserted, India had been a sovereign and independent state, she could have retaliated and imposed her own tariffs on British goods.[36] No such recourse was open to a people ruled by the very nation which was holding all of the cards, and this litany of inequality inspired men such as Montgomery Martin to accuse Britain of having done 'everything possible to impoverish ... the miserable beings [Indians] subject to the cruel selfishness of English commerce ... Under the pretence of free trade, England has compelled the Hindus to receive the products of the steam-looms of Lancashire, Yorkshire, Glasgow.'[37]

Even the financial basis of the two countries' transactions were weighted in favour of the British by fixing the exchange rate between their currencies. As late as 1873 there were two shillings to the rupee,[38] but then it gradually lost ground until Jamsetjee Ardaseer Wadia of Bombay explained the implications in a furious letter to the Times of India in May 1901:

for the year 1899-1900 the import trade is given at ... £47,000,000, exclusive of treasure and government stores. Our export trade is given at ... £72,000,000 for the same year on the basis of the artificial rupee, viz one shilling and four pence. The same figure on the basis of the true value of the coin, viz eleven pence [and] one half penny, would ... amount to about £65,000,000 for imports and about ... £100,000,000 for exports ... We would have paid ... £16,000,000 more for our imports, and it would have come out of the pockets of the well-to-do Europeans and natives, as they are the chief consumers of imports, whilst the producers would have got ... £26,000,000 more for their exports, which would have remained in their pockets.[39]

Certainly, India's importing of shoes and boots, which more than quadrupled from 1900 to 1914, and that of tobacco, mainly cigarettes, which increased from 3,750,000 to 7,300,000 tons between 1900 and 1909,[40] were among the luxury items which the poor and impoverished masses would not have been able to afford. The problem was that the rupee had been the currency of India from the Mughals through to the East India Company and was firmly entrenched in India's internal market. Efforts had been made to try to address the effect this had on the relationship with sterling, but in 1913 a royal commission on Indian finance concluded that the rupee was still the most suitable currency 'for the internal needs of India'[41] and ought to be encouraged because 'the vast mass of people make transactions for very small sums and cannot possibly use gold coins.'[42] This was cold comfort to long-suffering exporters.

As Horace Wilson had pointed out, if India had been an independent trading partner she would have been much better placed to make the arrangement more equitable. After all, Henry Hyndman contended, 'our trade with India does not depend upon the continuance of our domination ... commerce would not cease and the demand for British goods would continue.'[43] Other liberal-minded intellectuals and statesmen were similarly vexed by the exploitative nature of the relationship. John Bright insisted that this did not need be Britain's legacy on the subcontinent. As early as 1858 he reasoned that 'there are but two modes of gaining anything by our connection with India. The one is by plundering the people of India, and the other by trading with them. I prefer to do it by trading with them. But in order that England may become rich by trading with India, India herself must become rich.'[44] This was a philosophy not lost on men such as Jamsetjee Ardaseer Wadia, and slowly the mood was changing. Ordinary Indians were among those who decided that a more proactive approach was needed. This new mindset inspired the formation of the so-called Swadeshi movement on 7 August 1905. It was, it announced,

... [a response to] the subordination of India to Europe, the life-death struggle of the cotton industry of Bombay against the powerful and long established mills of Lancashire, and the economic neutrality of a government that refused to initiate, pioneer or (directly) assist home industries ... the ethical value of Swadeshi is even greater [than the economic] … each of us, however poor his means, can make a small silent sacrifice for his country every time he goes to market…[45]

Such an initiative could not come too soon, for the British had not sought to suppress just the country's silk, cotton, tea, coffee and sugar industries. Others experienced a similar fate and eventually required the same spirit of defiance to reverse its decline. Indian ships had carried trade goods to Phoenicians, Assyrians, Greeks, Romans, Turks, Venetians and later the Portuguese, Dutch and the English for 3,000 years. This achievement had marked it, in the words of one admirer, as the 'Queen of the Eastern Seas',[46] and India's reputation for shipbuilding had spread far and wide. Those of Sylhet in Bengal had earned such renown that the Turkish sultan found it cheaper to have his ships built there rather than at Alexandria,[47] and later still British visitors appreciated the advantages offered by Indian teak. William Taylor Money marvelled in 1811 at its 'abundance for all the purposes of naval architecture, for which it is known to be eminently adapted',[48] and there was little doubt that Royal Navy ships constructed in Madras did not compromise on quality. The captain of one Bombay-built frigate, HMS *Salsette*, wrote confidently that his vessel 'sails as well as any of ours',[49] prompting Money to declare that the docks at Bombay 'promise to be lasting monuments of the British power in India'.[50]

Yet in the eyes of too many industrialists at home, this prowess simply threatened their own businesses with unwanted competition. Consequently the industry gradually and steadily declined until, in the words of William Digby, 'the Mistress of the Seas in the Western World has stricken to death the Mistress of the Seas in the East.'[51] The change did not come overnight, however, and it was only after the 1840s that larger ships stopped being built, and not until around 1863 that their construction ended altogether.[52] Nonetheless, by the end of the century the situation was such that of the 9,115,646 tons of shipping employed in 1898–99 just 122,033 was of Indian origin, whereas forty years before it had been a third.[53] As Radha Kumud Mukherjee succinctly summarised the situation, 'there can hardly be conceived a more serious obstacle in the path of her industrial development than this almost complete extinction of her shipping and shipbuilding.'[54]

While supplanting India's own maritime commerce, the British proceeded to create cartels and monopolies which ensured that competition from Indians was shamelessly strangled.[55] A particularly bold but inevitably doomed attempt to compete was that of V. O. Chidambaram Pillai's aptly named Swadeshi Steam Navigation Company. From humble beginnings it had proven so successful that by 1907 it threatened to challenge the British Steam Navigation Company where both competed in the southern Bay of Bengal between Tuticorin and Colombo in Ceylon. A ruthless price war ensued, which drove down fares and led to ludicrous perks being offered to passengers such as free food and other refreshments. The British became increasingly frustrated, and in the end turned to sympathetic European port authorities to hamper their rivals. They obligingly denied the Swadeshi Company berthing facilities and refused to give medical and customs clearance to passengers, slowly driving them away.[56] Still the Indians held out. So because Pillai was also a well-known nationalist, the Assistant Collector of Tuticorn, Robert Ashe, schemed to have him arrested under trumped-up charges of sedition. While he languished in prison, further pressure was piled on the shipping line until its investors finally sold up and in 1911 it folded entirely.[57]

Shipping was just one sector of the country's heavy industry to suffer such a fate, William Digby writing how 'Indian manufacturing generally, on the theories prevalent early in the nineteenth century ... [was] deliberately throttled.'[58] Among them was Indian steel, which had made the chisels that drilled the granite of the great Egyptian pyramids[59] and was employed in the famous Damascus blades said to have come from the kingdom of Golkonda in Central India in the sixteenth century.[60] The Iron Pillar at Delhi was also used as an exemplar of Indian skill, made of wrought iron dating from the fourth century in the reign of Samudragupta.[61] Sixteenth-century Mughal vizier Abdul Fazl had written glowingly of prosperous iron industries in the provinces of Bengal, Allahabad, Agra, Berar, Gujarat, Delhi and Kashmir,[62] and as late as 1800 one Dr Francis Buchanan-Hamilton recorded the smelting and forging of iron into agricultural implements and weapons, and wrote of artisans skilled in making the most delicate wire required for musical instruments.[63] It was also claimed by contemporary historians that 'the iron [of Hyderabad] has the remarkable property of being obtained at once in a perfectly tough and malleable state, and is considered better than English iron, and even superior to the Swedish varieties.'[64] But under the British all these skills and the natural resources which supplied them were allowed to fall into disuse and decay. The reason was clear. Annie Besant wrote that even though 'traces of iron were found in the Central Provinces ... nothing was done to extract the metal [because] England [was] then ... the world's shop for iron to her own huge profit ... not desiring a rival'.[65]

Some industries, however, were spared the more ruthless application of British commercial hubris. The earliest exploitation of coal began around 1774 in the Raniganj field in Bengal, and although it was considered inferior to British coal and later abandoned, prospecting was resumed in 1814, and in 1843 the Bengal Coal Company was founded. Progress was slow due to inadequate transport, but as we have seen, the construction of railways not only provided the means to move the coal but also stimulated demand. The mines established in the Burdwan District of Bengal would eventually yield up to 15,000 tons a year,[66] and as further collieries were opened between 1880 and 1919, production doubled every ten years.[67] As a result, coal mining employed 95,000 workers by 1901 and 151,000 by 1915, production rising from 6,600,000 tons in 1901 to 17,000,000 tons in 1915.[68] However, the industry was seriously underfunded and this was reflected in poor productivity, Indian colliers only extracting 163 tons of coal a year compared to an average of 362 tons extracted by a British miner.[69] As we saw in the previous chapter, it nonetheless increasingly made commercial sense to use home-hewn rather than imported British coal, even on negligible tariffs. As a result this industry was one of a handful that escaped being strangled entirely.

Nonetheless, through its application of stiff tariffs, exchange rate manipulation and the suppression of India's ability to compete, Britain enjoyed 53 per cent of India's foreign trade by 1866.[70] Although this fell to 37 per cent by 1900. Britain would have a trade surplus of £60,000,000 by 1910.[71] Out of a total of £1,756,448 worth of raw wool exported in 1912–1913 the UK took £1,704,785 worth. In 1909–1910 the UK took £7,000,000 out of £8,500,000 worth of wheat; in 1911–1912 the UK imported £6,741,190 out of £8,989,972, rising by 1912–1913 to £8,830,422 out of £11,795,816 exported.[72] Nonetheless, the approach of the twentieth century witnessed a gradual re-evaluation of India's industrial potential, so long as there was no threat to the metropole. It was particularly under the viceroyalties of Lord Lansdowne and later Lord Curzon that serious efforts to stimulate an Indian industrial renaissance emerged.

Various products and manufactures were promoted in foreign exhibitions in Chicago and Antwerp but were largely restricted to niche items such as artwork, tea, coffee, tobacco and high-end timber.[73] More promising were the explorations being undertaken for commercially viable sources of raw materials for export, and many of those long suppressed were now being offered a new lease of life. Alongside surveys for oil in Baluchistan, iron ore in Madras was prospected, gold in Anantapur, Bellary and Chuddapah, copper in Sikkim and tin in Tenasserim. New companies were also emerging, keen to exploit the opportunities and profits on offer. These included the Bengal Iron and Steel Company, the Godavery Coal Company, the Burma Oil Syndicate, the Burma Oil Company, the Assam Oil Syndicate and the Burma Ruby Mines Company.[74] Some were to prove more durable than others, as speculation and the search for a quick profit saw as many fall by the wayside as succeeded. But one name in particular would emerge from the scrum and go on to become a world-renowned, multinational business empire.

Pioneer industrialist Jamshedji Tata sought to succeed where others had failed in creating the country's own sustainable iron and steel industry. A long-time believer in Indian self-sufficiency, he also benefited from the sponsorship of Viceroy Lord Curzon,[75] who like his predecessor favoured India achieving its industrial potential. At the time, the country was still importing an average of 415,000 tons of steel a year, and it was proposed that a well-sited and constructed domestic plant could comfortably match this.[76] Tata's ideas also chimed with the aspirations of the Swadeshi Movement, which eagerly embraced this potentially spectacular symbol of Indian regeneration. The main problem was the raising of capital, so in keeping with the philosophy of self-sufficiency a public appeal was launched in 1907 which secured the £1,630,000 required to start the mammoth project. In fact it would later be claimed that just 8,000 investors, described by Tata's colleague Axel Sahlin as the 'old and young, rich and poor',[77] stumped up the money, and the Tata Iron and Steel Company was born.

In the meantime, exhaustive prospecting and surveying had been undertaken to locate the right site. Not only did the site require sufficient deposits of iron ore, access to water and coal and close proximity to rail communications, but it had to be flat and large enough to house the complex of furnaces, workshops and other buildings that would be necessary. Sakchi, in present-day Singhbaum in the state of Jharkhand, was finally identified as ticking all these boxes, and with the capital secured, foundations were laid in May 1909 and the first iron smelted in December 1911. Tata's vision and energy had realised a major milestone in the country's progress from an impotent consumer of foreign produce to one with the increasing potential to compete with the rest of the world. It is not surprising, therefore, that Tata came to be lauded as the J. P. Morgan of East Asia.[78]

This growing confidence in India's economic prospects meant that it was attracting more capital, and investment in coal companies alone quadrupled between 1901 and 1910.[79] In 1913 there were 2,588 joint stock companies with two-fifths of the share capital invested in cotton, jute and other mills and presses and 8 per cent in private railways and tramways.[80] While only £10 million of nearly £36 million invested in joint stock companies in 1881 was held by Indians, this situation was changing as domestic investors started to appreciate the profits to be made.[81] But although the number of jute mills in British India had grown from thirty-six in 1901 to seventy in 1915 and wool mills from four to six in the same period,[82] three-quarters of them were still in the hands of Europeans and the profits were inevitably going to Britain.[83] But it was a start, and coincided with a world event that would transform the industrial landscape almost overnight.

India's gradual conversion had begun just as the outbreak of war in August 1914 brought huge demands on the country. The disappearance of the German merchant navy and the reallocation of 70 per cent of British and neutral shipping for the war effort had cut trade with countries which had accounted for 14.2 per cent of Indian exports,[84] and in the eight months following the start of the war to March 1915 total imports decreased by 43 per cent and exports by 34 per cent,[85] compounded by the flight of European capital. This prompted a search for new partners, the most promising of which was Japan. In 1913, for example, it exported only 44 per cent of India's matches but this grew to 83.4 per cent by 1915,[86] but there was still scope for a more proactive approach. In a speech to the Council Session of 1914–15, Viceroy Lord Hardinge assured the assembly that 'my Government have been giving such assistance as they can to Indian industries, in its endeavours to take advantage of the opportunities for expansion afforded by the cessation of imports from Germany and Austria,'[87] and to this end openings left by the Germans and Austrians led to more energetic promotion of Indian goods and manufactures across the country.[88]

Initially, the stoppage of chemicals and dyes such as synthetic indigo, which used to be supplied from Germany, was a problem for Indian cotton mills,[89] but with the development of vegetable indigo it proved possible to overcome this hurdle. Subsequent demand from the French, British and Russians for sandbags, grain bags and ginny cloth created a surge in demand,[90] while Tata supplied 291,562 tons of steel for the construction of rail lines throughout the war theatres of the Middle East.[91] Such measures coincided with a more robust application of the war effort in general. The Defence of India Ordinance of 10 November 1915 empowered the government to 'take possession of, regulate, control ... any factory, workshop, mine or other industrial concern for the manufacture of any article which can be utilised in the prosecution of the war'.[92] An early start was made when fifteen German merchant vessels in port at the start of the war were seized and turned over for the use of Indian trade,[93] and businesses previously owned by enemy aliens were also taken over. Of these 114 were closed down, fifty were allowed to continue as they benefitted Indian interests and seventy-nine were permitted to continue with restrictions.[94] In 1916 the general import duty was raised from 5 per cent to 7.5 per cent; duty on sugar was increased to 10 per cent, on iron and steel imports to 2.5 per cent and on other imported metals to 7.5 per cent. Articles previously imported free of duty were now to be subject to tariffs of between 2.5 per cent and 7.5 per cent and in 1917 the import duty on cotton goods was raised to 7.5 per cent.[95]

Together, these developments opened the door for greater Indian post-war economic prosperity, galvanising its industrialists, merchants and entrepreneurs who, Annie Besant was convinced, 'now realise that in the trade war after the end of the present war, they will go down unless they have power in their own country'.[96] This power was partly delivered through the constitutional reforms being enacted, and would give far greater scope for the government to make decisions on its own. These included the right to impose even higher import tariffs to protect domestic producers. In 1921 a 15 per cent import tax was applied to sugar, and the *ad valoreum* duties, based upon the value of the item involved, increased from 7.5 per cent to 20 per cent. In 1922 a 15 per cent import duty was applied to cotton goods and machinery, and iron and steel were subject to a 10 per cent tariff. In 1924 the Steel Industry Protection Act was passed raising import duties on steel and wrought iron based on a sliding scale, and bounties were granted on the manufacture of rails and steel plates.[97] In order to protect workers from the side effects of the small post-war boom, the Indian Factories Act of 1922 was also passed. This limited the working hours for adults in factories to sixty a week or eleven per day, and children below twelve could no longer be employed at all. Furthermore, the hourly limit for mine workers was set at fifty-four underground, and sixty above.[98] The following year, the employment of children, who had up until that time been working in mines from as young as ten or twelve, was finally forbidden.

The opportunities unleased by the war were not lost on titans such as Tata and led to the company expanding and consolidating in the years following the return of peace. Even the British stranglehold on shipping was being slowly and grudgingly loosened. In 1919 Walchand Hirachand formed the Scindia Steam Navigation Company to compete on the lucrative India to UK route, carrying freight and passengers. It was the first such venture to see the light of day since the sabotaging of the Swadeshi Steam Shipping Line, and consequently the first such Indian-owned venture. Encountering the predictable resistance from vested British interests, he nevertheless persevered and went on to create a fleet of ships that made him the great name in Indian industrialism that has lasted to this day. Nonetheless, these developments came only after the British had enjoyed a veritable three-hundred-year free-for-all at India's expense. It would remain a long uphill struggle to regain the industrial and trading position enjoyed before Ralph Fitch and his colleagues had come to visit.

As well as having exercised free rein over India's manufacturing, industrial and trading activities, the British, first under the Company and later under the auspices of Crown protection, granted themselves the right to exercise complete control of its revenue and expenditure. They had learnt a bitter lesson about taxing colonies when the Americans rose up in revolt and gave them a bloody nose in 1776, and this led to the Taxation of Colonies Act of 1778. Although it proved too late to prevent them from breaking away it established a convention that no duties, taxes or assessments should be imposed in future upon any of its colonies or dependencies – all, that is, except India. Its card had effectively been marked a decade earlier when the Company began passing its debts onto the profit-and-loss sheet of the three Presidencies. Also, perhaps because of its unique status under the management of a commercial enterprise, the Directors and the government in London were able to impose upon it any costs they chose, with the result that it was in the red to the tune of £7,000,000 by 1792, £21,000,000 by 1805 and £30,000,000 by 1829.[99] When the Company lost its monopoly of the opium trade under the Charter Act of 1833, it had to be compensated with a 10.5 per cent dividend on its capital of £6,000,000. But the British government in London did not bear this financial commitment; instead it was to be paid out of Indian revenues over a period of forty years. Furthermore, a fund of £1,200,000 was established to meet this obligation in the event that it defaulted, and this too was to be reimbursed out of Indian revenues.[100] By 1858 the national debt stood at £69,000,000,[101] of which some £40,000,000 was due to the huge cost of the Mutiny. Nonetheless, Indian national debt would continue to rise inexorably, totalling £173,000,000 by 1885,[102] and climbing further to £307,000,000 in 1914.[103]

The problem of the national debt was not helped by what were euphemistically referred to as the 'Home Charges', which India paid to the UK every year. These consisted not only of the annual interest on the Indian debt but also dividends to Company and railway shareholders, plus the eyewatering cost of maintaining an army and civil administration. These stood at £2,399,000 in 1815, paid out of revenues of £21,000,000,[104] and rising to £3,500,000 by 1850. By 1914 they were running at £20,000,000 a year,[105] although revenues were only double those of 1815 at £55,000,000.[106] The costs of running the country therefore were by no means modest. The India Office List for 1905 gives the salary for the viceroy as £16,720 per year, or adjusted for inflation over £2,000,000 in 2020; his private secretary was paid £1,700, or more than £208,000 today; chief justices earnt £4,111 and lieutenant-governors of provinces £6,666, or £503,000 and £815,000 respectively in today's values, and their private secretaries the equivalent of £156,000 in 2020. This was only the tip of the iceberg; the salaries of commissioners of police, their deputies, and many more of the Empire's functionaries could be added to the list.[107] There was also the Secretary of State for India in London costing another £5,000 a year,[108] his salary alone equal to the annual incomes of 90,000 Indians.[109] His London headquarters, completed in the 1860s, cost £215,000[110] and this expense too had to be met by Indian taxpayers. Lord Curzon's departmental and police reforms alone added nearly £9,500,000 to the bill by 1908.[111]

As one Major Wingate explained as far back as 1859, 'taxes spent in the country from which they are raised are totally different in their effects from taxes raised in one country and spent in another.'[112] This was because, as Henry Hyndman explained, 'an English official in India receives say £3,000 a year and saves one-third of his salary. In ten years, he will have remitted to England the sum of £10,000 in addition to any pension ... A native filling the same post at the same salary would undoubtedly save at least twice as much; but assuming that he saves only £1,000 a year, at the end of ten years he would have £10,000 in his hands for remunerable employment in India, his pension would also be spent in India ... the capital of India would be £10,000 larger in the one case than in the other, and the pension would be used to feed Indian mouths instead of foreign ones.'[113] Romesh Chunder Dutt, an Indian civil servant and economic historian, published the first detailed and most thorough study of the economic exploitation of India and calculated that Home Charges in the financial year 1900–01 alone were equal to an entire year's land revenue.[114] Nonetheless, despite the glaring injustices these and other critics exposed, little would improve. By 1921 the Indian taxpayer was having to find between £3,500,000 and £4,000,000 alone in pension payments for retired claimants in England,[115] and together these expropriations came to be known collectively as the 'Drain'. These exactions were also shrouded in almost mystical bookkeeping, as one critic attempted to explain:

Every year the Secretary of State for India has to spend twenty million pounds sterling in England on our behalf, which must be paid to him out of the revenue of India. At the same time merchants in England have to send money to India to buy our produce for export. To avoid this double transport of money, the Secretary of State in Council sells in London documents called 'council bills' (or telegraphic transfers) for which the merchants pay to him in gold, whilst the agents of these merchants cash the bills for rupees at the Government treasuries in India, and buy our raw materials, grain etc. with the money. When, owing to famine or war, the Indian treasuries are short of money and can pay only a portion of the Home Charges in cash, the secretary of State sells bills to that amount only and raises the balance needed for his expenses by contracting a debt in England. Sometimes certain sums due to India are reduced to that extent. Very often trade requires more council bills than are necessary for the Secretary's expenses in England. In that case he draws bills for the surplus amount, but they are paid in India out of the paper currency or Gold Standard Reserve, while their price, paid in London, is afterwards transmitted to India in silver bullion to fill up the gap in the reserve. Thus, the Secretary of State is the greatest banker working between England and India...[116]

Of course, civil servant salaries and pensions, the railways and canals were not the only expenses charged to Indian taxpayers. When the Company was finally dissolved in 1858 all of its debts, along with the accrued interest on them, were added.[117] In the 1860s, largely due to the increased number of European troops posted there as a result of the Mutiny, the cost of the army mushroomed. This too, it was assumed, would be borne not by the British but by the Indian taxpayer. Despite John Bright calling it 'a grievous burden' at the time,[118] it was nonetheless added to the subcontinent's growing list of financial impositions. It was estimated that if every regiment of infantry cost £85,000 a year to maintain, and a cavalry regiment £102,400 a year, the total would amount to £8,000,000 a year, nearly £1,000,000,000 in today's prices.[119] India also had to pay their transport expenses, plus the recruiting and depot charges in England for the annual reliefs of British units sent to India.[120]

This was an increasing burden which after 1885 was among the first things the nascent Congress had tried to address. As Annie Besant explained, 'in the First Congress, Mr. P. Rangiah Naidu pointed out that military expenditure had been £11,463,000 in 1857 and had risen to £16,975,750 in 1884. Mr D.E. Wacha ascribed the growth to the amalgamation scheme of 1859 and remarked that the Company in 1856 had an army of 254,000 at a cost of £11,500,000, while in 1884, the Crown had an army of only 181,000 at a cost of £17,000,000 ... year after year Congress continued to remonstrate against the cost of the army, until in 1902, after all the futile protests of the intervening years, it condemned an increase of pay to British soldiers in India which placed an additional burden on the Indian revenues of £786,000 a year.'[121] As a result, prior to 1914, while the UK defence budget was £28,000,000, and Canada and Australia were spending only £1,500,000 and £1,250,000 respectively, India was estimated to be spending

£21,000,000.[122] In 1904 and 1905, long before the fresh demands of a world war added to the pressure, Congress declared that the military expenditure was beyond India's power to bear, and 'prayed' that the additional £10,000,000 sanctioned for Lord Kitchener's reorganisation scheme might instead be allocated to education and reducing the burden on the silver rupee.[123] Inevitably, such pleas continued to be dismissed, whilst the simple injustice of paying such a disproportionately high cost for being ruled from London provoked increasingly shrill protests.

Indian civil servant Sir William Hunter was among those who admitted long before that enough was enough, and in 1880 conceded that Indians were so heavily burdened by the costs of government that 'any [further] increase in the revenue involves serious difficulties.'[124] Henry Hyndman agreed. He asserted that 'Indian society, as a whole, has been frightfully impoverished under our rule, and that process is going on now at an increasingly rapid rate.'[125] Income tax was added in 1858 to an already lengthy list of duties, and in just twelve years of Crown rule, the government effectively doubled salt, spirit and sugar taxes, as well as increasing stamp and customs duties, court fees, succession taxes and local and municipal taxes in an effort to make ends meet.[126] When Viceroy Sir John Lawrence admitted candidly in 1869 that 'the non-official European community ... desire that all taxation should fall on the natives,'[127] Lord Mayo obligingly increased income tax in 1870 from 1 per cent to 2.5 per cent and then to 3.5 per cent, and local provincial taxation was also introduced.[128] With gross national income in 1900 only £2.00 compared with £42.00 in the UK,[129] Indians were on average faced with a taxation regime 40 per cent higher.[130] Yet there would be a long way to go before India could hope to spread the burden and for the wealth to be distributed sufficiently to show results. By 1923, out of a population of 240,000,000, still only 238,242 would be eligible to pay income tax, even though the minimum threshold was just 2,000 rupees a year.[131]

But while this regime was bleeding the country, critics other than Congress had not been idle in seeking redress. On 12 February 1885, Dadabhai Naoroji had moved an amendment to the royal address in the Legislative Council of Bombay in the hope of reducing at least some of the burden of taxation weighing his countrymen down, proposing

> to adjust the financial relations between the United Kingdom and British India ... that some fair and adequate portion of [expenditure on the Indian Civil Service] ... be borne by the British Exchequer in proportion to the pecuniary and political benefits accruing to the United Kingdom from Your Gracious Majesties sway over India ... [132]

Nonetheless, there was no material change until, under pressure from nationalists such as G. K. Gokhale and Naoroji, the government finally relented. Having taken his lead from some Irish nationalists who sat in the House of Commons, Naoroji decided that the best way to oppose

British policy was from within. Consequently he stood twice for the British parliament, and in 1892 was successful, taking the seat of Central Finsbury. Having won by a slim margin of just five votes, he inevitably earned the soubriquet Dadabhai Narrow-Majority. Nonetheless, having secured this unique position of influence, he used it to press his demands for an enquiry. Finally, a commission under the chairmanship of Lord Reginald Welby, Permanent Secretary to the Treasury, was formed in 1895 to 'enquire into the administration and management of the Military and Civil Expenditure incurred under the Secretary of State for India in Council, or of the Government of India, and the apportionment of Charges between the Governments of the United Kingdom and of India for purposes of which both are interested'.[133] On 21 March 1896, Naoroji, having by now lost his seat in Finsbury, sat on the commission, urging Lord Welby to 'stop the material and moral bleeding, and leave British India a freedom of development and progress in prosperity which her extraordinary natural resources are capable of ... treat her justly in her financial relations with Britain by apportioning fairly the charge on purposes in which both are interested'.[134] He was to be bitterly disappointed. Furthermore, having lost Naoroji as a voice of dissent in the House of Commons, it had instead gained the more accommodating Parsi Conservative MP for North-East Bethnal Green, Mancherjee Merwanjee Bhownaggree, who had been elected to the seat the same year his compatriot had lost his.

The commission took evidence over several years, but when it published its findings in 1900, they did little to assuage the nationalists or their supporters. Despite copious proof to the contrary, the report maintained that 'the financial machinery of the Indian Empire is well organised, and ... its action is effectively controlled.'[135] While it called on the House of Commons to have impartial oversight of India's finances, to see that British costs were not passed on to Indian taxpayers and to ensure that India's payments should not be tied to a fixed exchange rate, it concluded that as a member of the British Empire the country had an obligation to support its upkeep.[136] The report justified this by insisting that 'the Indian taxpayer of the present obtain ... the benefit of a vast railway system at a comparatively light cost,'[137] and that the defence burden in particular was justified because 'India has a direct and substantial interest in keeping open the Suez Canal ... [and to protect its borders with] ... Persia ... Afghanistan ... [and] Siam.'[138] There were nonetheless some modest concessions with regards to defence expenditure, and the commission recommended that the UK should make a £50,000 contribution towards the upkeep of the India Office, pay half the cost of maintaining the base at Aden – at that time an Indian dependency – and £5,000 towards ongoing commitments in Persia. Britain should also pay half of the costs of transporting troops to and from India, a total rebate of about £293,000.[139] It also recommended that 'in every case where the two Governments are not agreed, no contribution should be made by India until the sanction of Parliament has been obtained.'[140]

Clearly, this would not go nearly far enough for the system's harshest critics. Annie Besant complained how 'the Government ... will not allow the people's money to be spent on the systems they prefer,'[141] noting bitterly that 'a budget framed by an Indian Finance Minister would aim at a much increased expenditure on education and irrigation ... Railways would be constructed out of loans raised for the particular project, not out of revenue. Administration charges would be reduced by the reduction of salaries and greater economy ... the taxation on land would be lightened.'[142] Despite her pleas, however, the British would be holding the purse strings for many years to come and its wealth would continue to feather the beds of its rulers. With Britain able to tap into so many profitable revenue streams and enrich itself at the country's expense, it would use every tool at its disposal to maintain the status quo.

4

'The pivot of our empire'

What irked many Indians was the fact that much of the wealth being drained away was spent maintaining an image of the Raj the British rulers wanted to project, and which was completely at odds with reality. As William Digby explained in 1901, 'ninety-nine visitors to India out of one hundred, if not indeed nine hundred and ninety nine out of one thousand, leave that country with an impression that they have been visiting a land of great prosperity and a people fairly well-to-do and generally content ... [because] the route taken by the ordinary traveller ... can leave but one impression on the mind.'[1] This chimera was perhaps most conspicuously displayed during the incumbency of Lord Curzon, a staunch advocate of the Raj who maintained that it was 'the pivot of our Empire ... If this Empire lost any other part of its dominion we could survive, but if we lost India the sun of our Empire would be set.'[2] He was also a firm advocate of the need for ostentatious displays of power and majesty, by which British prestige could be maintained. When he arrived in 1899 he wasted little time in putting this philosophy into practice.

Beguiled by the romance and opulence of the country's history, Curzon enthusiastically sponsored the arts and the preservation of India's ancient monuments and buildings. He lavished a fortune on schemes to conserve its heritage and increased the £7,000 a year budget to £40,000. He is credited with singlehandedly saving the Taj Mahal in Agra, and authorised the expenditure of £50,000 on that one famous monument alone. Even parsimonious nationalists would have approved of such expressions of philanthropy, but far less well received were his eye-wateringly expensive plans for the Durbar of 1903. It was held in late December 1902 and early January 1903 to celebrate the accession to the throne of King Edward VII. Although the princes and loyal Indians participated willingly enough, others condemned it as a great show of flummery and bluster which many boycotted in disgust. The final cost was approximately £213,000[3] (close to £26,000,000 in 2020 figures), an astronomical sum Congress condemned for 'its extravagance ... the humiliating treatment accorded to the Indian princes ... and [for] forcing vastly expensive celebrations upon a starving country'.[4] But if sheer financial profligacy was enough to galvanise popular opposition, there might have been at least one repetition of the Mutiny in the past forty years. Instead, the subcontinent had become inured to the apparent inertia of its people and their sullen resignation to alien rule. Theodore Monson was among those sympathetic to India's suffering but equally despairing of their being aroused sufficiently to take action. He believed that this could happen only if the people were 'provided with a central idea which will unite them all ... to which they can all be equally loyal and round which the feeble beginnings of nationality can cluster'.[5] Gangadhar Tilak had demonstrated that this was possible when the reforms to child marriage were resisted and the mishandling of the famine and plague in 1897 were exposed. But these were short lived and soon fizzled out in the face of concerted official action.

Ironically, it was Curzon who reinvigorated nationalist sentiment when in 1905 he controversially approved the partitioning of the Bengal Presidency. At 189,000 square miles and with a population of 78,000,000 it had come under frequent scrutiny for its administrative unwieldiness, combined with the fact that the Muslim east had been largely neglected by the Hindu-dominated west. Curzon was therefore sympathetic to the idea of two smaller provinces, holding the present arrangement to be 'antiquated, illogical and productive of inefficiency'.[6] Assam was consequently united with fifteen districts of the eastern portion of Bengal to create an entirely new province of East Bengal, with its own lieutenant-governor presiding over 18,000,000 Muslims and 12,000,000 Hindus from its capital at Dacca. The rest of the old province became West Bengal, with 42,000,000 Hindus and 12,000,000 Muslims. To Curzon it was a perfectly rational solution to a longstanding problem, but as news of the plan became public disquiet soon turned into howls of protest.

The Hindus of East Bengal, who dominated commerce and the professions, balked at the prospect of becoming a minority and immediately protested. Maharaja Mahindra Chandra Nandi claimed the plans meant that 'Bengal Hindoos [sic] will ... be strangers in our own land,'[7] while the Moslem Chronicle of 9 January 1904 warned, 'We cannot recollect that there has been ... ever before so much unanimity of voice as that which is raising its shouts of protest against the proposed partition of Bengal.'[8] Congress leader Gopal Gokhale insisted that a 'cruel wrong has been inflicted on our Bengalee brethren, and the whole country has been stirred to its deepest depths with sorrow and resentment'.[9] There were some among the British too who doubted the wisdom of the proposals. The Englishman of 9 August 1905 asked dryly whether 'the Government of India, in its wisdom, realised the gravity of the precedents of the partition business'.[10] There was nonetheless some support for the plan, at least among the Muslims of Bengal. The educated and ambitious among its community saw the possibilities for a new province in which they would be the majority, and they resented Hindu protests as hypocritical and churlish. Partition therefore proceeded as planned on 16 October 1905, but it did nothing to quieten the mounting anger and increasing protests.

It was in the midst of this uproar that Curzon executed his timely departure, leaving the ramifications of his decision to be dealt with by his successor, Lord Minto. Formerly Governor-General of Canada, and great-grandson of an earlier Governor-General, he was as fervent an imperialist as his predecessor. He was convinced by Britain's moral claim on the subcontinent, and felt that the nationalist agitation emerging from partition was little more than a flash in the pan. As he informed the Prince of Wales, later George V:

> At present, if things were left alone here I do not think that the Congress movement is much to be feared: the danger exists at home, where a few Members of Parliament, with a very doubtful Indian connection, manage to keep the pot of disaffection boiling, and to disseminate entirely fake views upon the position of affairs in India ...[11]

Congress nonetheless had the bit between its teeth, and seized upon the issue of partition to amplify its voice further. It had tried but failed to influence government decisions almost from its inception, achieving very little by attempting to cooperate with and cajole the administration, so when in 1905 Gokhale became president he was instrumental in drafting a constitution which left no one in any doubt as to its future direction:

> ... the objects of the Indian National Congress are the attainment by the people of India of a system of government similar to that enjoyed by the self-governing members of the British Empire and a participation by them in the rights and responsibilities of the Empire on equal terms with those members ...[12]

This radical change of tack rattled leading Muslims. An organised and well-led Congress could side-line Muslim opinion and leave them without a voice. On 1 October 1906, the Aga Khan reminded the Viceroy that while Congress was articulating its demands, there also existed 'grievances and aspirations'[13] among his community which needed to be addressed. Hoping to allay the Aga Khan's fears, Lord Minto gave an undertaking which would have far-reaching consequences. He assured him that 'the Mohammedan community may rest assured that their political rights as a community will be safeguarded by any administrative reorganisation with which I am concerned.'[14] But prominent Muslims remained convinced that they needed more than assurances and concluded that only an organised body like Congress could defend their interests. Consequently, during an educational conference in Dacca in December 1906, Syed Hussain Bilgrami, Khwaja

Salimullah Bahadur, Viqar-ul-Mulk and Aga Khan III Sultan Sir Mahomed Shah founded the All India Muslim League.

It was a timely move, because since January 1906 preparations for the planned reforms hinted at by Lord Minto had been in train. The UK Liberal Party had won a landslide victory under Henry Campbell-Bannerman and enjoyed a mandate to implement sweeping social reforms. These included old-age pensions and national insurance, as well as changes to employment law and education. The new administration also planned constitutional change in India, and this was to be enacted under the incumbency of the new Secretary of State for India, John Morley. He hailed this opportunity as 'the greatest appointment I have ever hoped for,'[15] but he was no maverick; rather he thought in terms of 'slow and steady' reform'.[16] Nonetheless, although he had supported the partition of Bengal, stating it to be 'a settled fact',[17] he did reluctantly recognise the need for engagement with the nationalists and urged the Viceroy to 'deal with the Congress Party and Congress principles – whatever you may think of them'.[18]

But the obstacles to any meeting of minds were considerable, as Morley revealed in a despatch to Minto on 2 August 1906: 'Gokhale ... made no secret of his ultimate hope and design: India to be on the footing of a self-governing colony. I equally made no secret of my conviction that for many a long day to come ... this was a mere dream.'[19] He further insisted that anything so ambitious would be 'startling ... fantastic and ludicrous'.[20] Instead he appointed Muslim League co-founder Syed Hussain Bilgrami and Hindu Krishna G. Gupta, a member of the Indian Civil Service, to his council in London, and Minto was asked to make a similar gesture with regards to the Viceroy's Executive Council. The Viceroy demurred, warning that 'such a colleague would necessarily become acquainted with all our state secrets.'[21]

Such modest tweaks to the status quo did little to temper the growing violence in Bengal. There were two assassination attempts on Lieutenant-Governor of West Bengal Sir Andrew Fraser, a Dacca lawyer was murdered, and the Nawab of Dacca's private secretary was viciously assaulted.[22] In April 1908 two European women were killed in the town of Muzaffarpur in Bihar by a bomb intended for the local magistrate – the first reported use of such a tactic[23] – while Swadeshi activists assaulted shopkeepers and traders who stocked British-made cloth and attacked anyone they encountered wearing Western clothes.[24] Such escalations prompted Minto to warn Morley that 'there is a great deal of nervousness everywhere; even ladies are buying revolvers.'[25] Moderate Indians were also concerned by the anarchy spreading throughout the province. Nationalist Mahatma Munshi Ram Vij went so far as to admit that 'our nation has reached depths of moral degradation which it is difficult to fathom. How utterly unfit are we for *swarajiya* [self-rule] just at present ... I believe, now, that for another three hundred years, British supremacy alone can ensure peace and order in this land.'[26]

Much of the blame for the increasing tempo of disorder was laid at the door of the Indian-language press, which was blamed for stirring up anger and inciting its readers to commit violence. This prompted Minto to write to Morley on 5 March 1907 insisting that 'we must consider seriously how to deal with the native press, for in many cases the utterances of newspapers are outrageous.'[27] Consequently the Indian Newspapers (Incitement to Offences) Act was passed in June 1908, empowering magistrates to confiscate any publications judged to be sponsoring the violence. This was accompanied by steps to limit access to bomb-making equipment, with the Indian Explosives Substances Act making the possession, manufacture, storage or use of explosives punishable by a lengthy prison sentence. The Bengal Regulation Act of 1818 was also invoked, allowing for the arbitrary round-up and arrest of suspects without trial.[28] Minto was also keen to impress upon the British government that the trouble was not widespread or even enjoyed popular support. He reminded Morley that 'it is the voice of Bengal which is so largely heard at home; the silent loyal strength of India on which we must rely is hardly heard at all.'[29] To this end he also assured the Muslim League that 'you will never again have the combination of a Secretary of State and a Viceroy who are more thoroughly in earnest in their desire to improve Indian Government, and to do full justice to every element of the Indian population.'[30] Yet for all his bold words, he delivered a damp squib.

All that the royal commission had been asked to examine was the 'great mischief for over-centralisation ... [and] ... how this great mischief might be alleviated',[31] and 'to enquire into the relations now existing for financial and administrative purposes between the Supreme Government and the various Provincial Governments'.[32] It was hardly surprising, therefore, that for all the expectations Morley and Minto had raised, the final report constituted little more than extensions to the 1892 Act, seen by many as mere window dressing. There were now to be 135 elected Indians in the legislative councils of British India, and a maximum of sixty in the Imperial Legislative Council. Membership of the provincial councils of Bombay, Madras and those of a number of other councils was to be increased to fifty, and elected members would be entitled to informally question the annual budget and to propose their own legislation.

Perhaps Muslim hopes were most satisfied with the introduction of separate electorates, while Minto finally relented and allowed an Indian to sit in the Viceroy's Executive Council. This honour went to a Hindu, eminent lawyer Satyendra P. Sinha, who became the Legal Member. Minto hailed this development as 'acceptance of entirely new principles in respect to the government of India'.[33] Yet this thin veneer of reform barely concealed the fact that the overall power structure of the country remained intact. The British Secretary of State and the Viceroy remained firmly in charge, answerable only to Parliament in London, as enshrined in the India Councils Act, which received royal assent on 12 March 1909.

Clearly these measures were as far removed from Gokhale's dream of self-government as could have been imagined, but he chose to be magnanimous and play a waiting game. He welcomed Sinha's appointment as 'a red letter day in the history of British rule in India',[34] and although disappointed, conceded that 'first we must prove that we can bear these responsibilities before we ask for any more.'[35] The reforms also served to highlight the vying for advantage which would dog future efforts to introduce change. The League, irked at the appointment of a Hindu to the Executive Council, insisted that a Muslim be afforded similar status by a system of alternating nominations,[36] while Congress balked at the creation of separate electorates, and immediately proposed a motion in the imperial legislature to abolish them.[37]

Those nationalists who had rejected reform and instead embraced violence had in any case decided that freedom could only come at the point of a gun or from the fragments of a bomb. They adhered to the teachings of men like Gangadhar Tilak and having turned Bengal into a battleground, they now looked to extend their campaign to the Imperial capital itself. Taking a leaf out of the Irish nationalists' book, Vinayak Damodar Savarkar, Shyamji Krishna Varma, and Madan Lal Dhingra plotted to overthrow the Raj from within. Following their arrival in London, Savarkar and Varma acted as magnets for the large number of idealistic dissidents studying in the capital and began planning a spectacular coup which would stun the complacent British establishment. They decided upon the murder of Indian government official and *aide-de-camp* to the Secretary of State William Curzon Wyllie, a longstanding administrator and a figure well known for his opposition to self-government. On 1 July 1909, he and his wife were attending an event at the Imperial Institute organised by the Indian National Organisation when Dhingra opened fire and killed Wylie instantly. He was arrested at the scene, tried and hanged, while Savarkar went on the run. He was eventually arrested and sent to India to face trial, where he received two life sentences, remaining incarcerated until 1937. Varma was more fortunate and escaped the clutches of the authorities entirely.

With little evidence that the situation in Bengal was improving, additional measures were implemented, including further inroads towards press freedom. The Act of 1910 sought to 'provide for the better control of the Press' due to the 'recurrence of murderous outrages [which] has shown that the measures which have hitherto been taken to deal with anarchy and sedition require strengthening'.[38] Suspect newspapers and other publications now had to deposit financial securities of anything between 500 and 5,000 rupees with the government. These would be held by the authorities and forfeited if the newspaper published anything which breached the provisions of the Act. But for moderates such as Annie Besant such measures went too far, transgressing 'the fundamental principles of the unwritten law of England on which the allegiance of the subject depends',[39] and Ramsay MacDonald, later Britain's first Labour prime minister, condemned them as 'contrary to [the] freedom of peoples and responsibility of governments, [and] ... ought to appear on the Statute books of no free country'.[40] But Minto insisted they were working. With scurrilous press statements suppressed and terrorists being rounded up, he boasted that the 'political movement of which they were leaders has degenerated into an anarchical plot.'[41]

On 6 May 1910, while Bengal was in turmoil, George V had ascended to the throne, and felt that perhaps he might play a role in drawing the various parties together. He wrote optimistically to Lord Morley on 8 September 1910 with a suggestion:

> [If] it were possible for me, accompanied by the Queen, to go to India and hold a coronation Durbar in Delhi, where we should meet all the princes, officials and vast numbers of the people, the greatest benefits would accrue to the country at large ...'[42]

Such a display could hardly be expected to bring round the bombers and rioters, who continued to plough their own bloody furrow. In the course of 1911 three policemen were killed in Calcutta, a bomb was thrown in the city at the motorcar of an official of the Public Works Department and Robert Ashe was murdered, purportedly in retaliation for his role in scuppering the Swadeshi Steam Navigation Company. Officers executing a search warrant were attacked in July, and in September another police officer was gunned down in Dacca.[43] On the other hand, as Minto had been keen to point out, loyal Indians – particularly men such as Mahatma Munshi Ram Vij, the princes and those still trusting in British rule – deserved some reassurance that their world was not about to crash about their heads in a tsunami of violence. On Tuesday 12 December 1911, Their Majesties, resplendent in their jewels, crowns and robes, rode in grand procession to the Delhi Durbar, accompanied by a 101-gun salute and cheered by crowds of thousands. The princes and potentates over whom they reigned then strode towards their dais one by one to offer their obeisance.

It was a grand spectacle, representing continuity and permanence and, as was traditional, the opportunity was taken by the King-Emperor to announce reforms and demonstrate to the assembled Indians the beneficence of his rule. He announced that there was to be more money available for education, that soldiers and civil servants were to receive a pay rise, and that his humanity and sense of justice was to be expressed by the release from prison of some criminals and debtors. Then he pulled a massive rabbit out of his crown when he declared that the controversial partitioning of Bengal was to be reversed. The government had relented. The announcement at once elated and stunned the assembled crowd. Those who had agitated, rioted and killed for this outcome took to the streets crying jubilantly, 'No bombs no boons.'[44] Others, however, felt betrayed and abandoned. Nawab Salimullah condemned the climbdown as 'a ready concession to the clamours of utterly seditious agitation',[45] and a vindication of deep-seated Muslim suspicions that when push came to shove the British would always accede in matters of policy to Hindus, irrespective of their feelings.

An announcement that the capital would be transferred from Calcutta to purpose-built accommodation in New Delhi was equally galling, as losing the capital would also cost them prestige and deprive Calcutta of one of its key functions. The reasons for the decision were manifold, but significant among them was the desire to weaken nationalist activity in Bengal by shifting the seat of power to the more pacified west. Secondly, with the centre of gravity of British interests moving to the areas threatened by Russian encroachment in the north-west, it made sense to underline the fact by having the capital of the empire there. Finally, it would allow magnificent new administrative buildings to be constructed, designed by renowned architects Sir Edwin Lutyens and Herbert Baker. Obviously, none of these gestures would cut any ice with the extremists; indeed, they were ploughing ahead with their terror campaign. When the newly installed Viceroy Lord Hardinge arrived they decided to strike while the iron was hot.

On 23 December 1912, Lord and Lady Hardinge were in state procession in the new capital where, despite the violence and attacks on Europeans, few extra security precautions had been taken. Their only protection was the ceremonial arrangement of troops lining the route, stiff to attention and eyes straight ahead, not surveying the route or looking out for bombers. As they processed atop an elephant in their elaborately decorated howdah, a device was lobbed from a rooftop, bouncing off but exploding and killing a servant seated behind. Another died along with a bystander, and many others were injured by shrapnel. Both Lord and Lady Hardinge suffered only minor injuries, Lady Hardinge escaping almost unscathed. Reports of the attack immediately swept round the world, and as the *Waikato Times* of New Zealand later reported, 'two operations under chloroform were subsequently performed on Lord Hardinge, with the result that several small nails and some particles of iron were removed from his right shoulder and back.'[46]

Subsequent frenetic police investigations revealed that the assassination attempt had been part of a wider plot, traced to revolutionary Bengali and Punjabi terrorists masterminded by Rash Behari Bose. Although he managed to elude the authorities, his co-conspirators felt the full weight of the law, being arrested, tried and punished. Inevitably the episode perpetuated the cycle of violence, and the period between 23 December 1912 and 4 August 1914 was 'troubled and anxious' according to official reports. Although there were successes for the authorities, with arms, explosive caches and bomb-making literature seized in Calcutta, Lahore and Delhi, the perpetrators changed tactics and started sending letter-bombs to their intended victims.[47] The worsening atmosphere was also reflected in escalating inter-communal violence. One of the most serious incidents occurred on 3 August 1913 when it was claimed that a road-widening scheme in Cawnpore threatened a mosque, provoking an angry confrontation which soon descended into a riot. When the situation got out of control the police opened fire, killing eighteen demonstrators and wounding twenty-seven. One policeman was also killed and forty-one injured before order was restored, but the subsequent trial of 104 rioters exposed the entire episode for the avoidable tragedy it was. Hoping to ease tensions, Lord Hardinge intervened, overruled the decision to take the mosque's land and even pardoned the rioters,[48] but there seemed to be no hope of an end to the violence.

It was against this backdrop that hostilities erupted with Germany and Austria in August 1914, and later with Turkey. As was the convention, the declaration of war was made on behalf of the entire British Empire, and naturally India was thus automatically drawn into the conflict. Although Lord Hardinge insisted that 'the war was none of our seeking, but it has been thrust upon us,'[49] there was no guarantee that in such a highly charged atmosphere Indians would support their involvement. Ironically, though, more than any Durbar or political concession, King George's cousin Kaiser Wilhem II managed to coalesce loyalty around the Crown.

Of least surprise, among the first to offer their support were the rulers of the Princely States. Hardinge wired the Secretary of State, now the Marquess of Crewe, on 7 September that they had 'with one accord rallied to the defence of the Empire and offered their personal services and the resources of their States for the war'.[50] The Nizam of Hyderabad spent 1,530,000,000 rupees equipping and supplying a regiment of the Hyderabad Imperial Service,[51] as well as subscribing 1,640,000 rupees to War Loans and 639,000 rupees to various relief funds.[52] The Maharajah of Kashmir also volunteered the services of the Kashmir Rifles, the Kashmir Imperial Lancers and the Kashmir Mountain Battery; Sir Ganga Singh, Maharaja of Bikaner, promised 25,000 men and offered his own services into the bargain,[53] as did the Aga Khan, Sir Pratap Singh of Idar and His Highness Lt Sumer Singh, the Maharaja of Marwar.[54] In all, eleven regiments of volunteer horse and forty-two volunteer infantry regiments – a total of 40,000 men in all – would be put at the disposal of the British,[55] in the process freeing up regular troops so that the 34,000 men of the frontier militias and military police could be sent overseas.[56] Many other princes also contributed horses, non-combatants and auxiliaries, hospital ships and ambulances.

British India and particularly Congress was where the potential for serious opposition lay. Instead, many saw the war as an ideal opportunity to earn their political spurs, and amid an air of surprising magnanimity, the twenty-ninth session of the National Congress was held in Madras, shortly after the declaration of war. In his opening address President Bhupendra Nath Bose announced, 'India has recognised that, at this supreme crisis in the life of the Empire, she should take a part worthy of herself and the Empire in which she has no mean place.'[57] On 8 September the Imperial Legislative Council followed suit, offering its 'unswerving loyalty and enthusiastic devotion to their King-Emperor'.[58] Founder of the Indian National Association Surendranath Banerjee even toured his home province encouraging fellow Bengalis to join the army, confident that 'if we sought the privileges of Imperial citizenship, we must share its burdens.'[59] Mahatma Gandhi too, soon to become one of the bêtes noires of the British, expressed support for the cause. Despite his avowed pacifism he expressed his conviction that 'the gateway to our freedom is situated on French soil ... if we could but crowd the battlefields of France with an indomitable army of Home Rulers fighting for victory for the cause of our allies, it would also be a fight for our own cause.'[60]

Annie Besant was optimistic that 'we cannot doubt that the King-Emperor will, as reward for her glorious defence of the Empire, pin upon her breast the jewelled medal of self-government within the Empire.'[61] Former Conservative MP for Bethnal Green Sir Mancherjee Bhownaggree agreed, believing that participation would herald 'nothing short of the privileges and rights enjoyed by other parts of the British Empire ... with every distinction of race and colour at present in vogue eliminated'.[62] Even the Indian community in the UK, many of whom were students and usually the more radical elements of Indian opinion, not to mention would-be assassins, offered their services and rallied to the cause.[63] Such high expectations appeared to have been vindicated when in November 1914, the Under Secretary of State for India announced in the House of Commons that as a result of her almost unanimous expressions of loyalty, 'it is clear that India claims not to be a mere dependent but a partner in the Empire, and her partnership with us in spirit and on battlefields cannot but alter the angle from which we shall look at the problems of the government of India.'[64]

Nonetheless, staunch nationalists such as Lala Har Dayal Mathur remained unmoved. An expat living in the United States, he had founded the Pacific Coast Hindustani Movement in 1913, later the Hindi Association of the Pacific Coast, and started the newspaper *Ghadr* or 'Mutiny', which also became the name of his movement. To spread the word of Indian nationalism he embarked on tours, speaking to fellow Indians and trying to stimulate a movement among the largely Punjabi community. The British Embassy, having become aware of his activities, tried to have him arrested and deported. Instead, he managed to stay one step ahead and in March 1914 left for Switzerland, ultimately fleeing to Berlin.[65] But his philosophy continued to thrive among his adherents, and early in 1915 a group of conspirators inspired by Ghadr concocted a plot to sail to India to foment a rebellion, aided by German agents in the US who promised to supply guns and cash. A vessel loaded with arms and ammunition landed in Java in March from where smaller fishing boats would ferry the cargo to Bengal.

The plot soon started to unravel with many conspirators betrayed to the police, so Rash Behari Bose, having eluded the authorities following the attempt on the life of Lord Hardinge, attempted to inject some vim into the conspiracy. Nonetheless the plot enjoyed mixed fortunes, and although in the Punjab there were twenty-four bombings and eleven sabotage attempts,[66] many more plotters were rounded up and taken into custody. In what became known as the Lahore Conspiracy Trial, which followed in April 1915, twenty-four were sentenced to death, twenty-seven to transportation for life, and many more to varying degrees of lesser punishment. Bose again left his colleagues to face the music and fled to Japan to establish the Indian Independence League, while in response to the attempted revolution the government passed the Defence of India Act. This gave the authorities even more far-ranging powers to suppress dissent, silence criticism and intern suspects without trial, with no right of appeal.

Constitutionalist nationalists, meanwhile, had decided to take the British at their word. In October 1916 they called upon the British to institute 'not merely good government or efficient administration, but government that is acceptable to the people',[67] presenting the Viceroy with a memorandum of thirteen demands for post-war reform. They were drafted by nineteen non-official members of the Imperial Legislative Council, and constituted an agenda for immediate self-government, including creating a majority of elected representatives to all legislative councils, the conferring on the Imperial Legislative Council the power to legislate on all matters, and the abolition of the Council of the Secretary of State.[68] Clearly, these were ambitious proposals and went far beyond the remit of the 1909 Act, and the reaction was understandably mixed. Mr A. P. Smith, editor of the *Anglo-Indian* newspaper, was highly supportive, stating that 'no country can be really happy unless she is self-governed. India under self-government may make mistakes ... but she will emerge purified, stronger and more able to stand on her own feet.'[69] Founding member of Congress and former president Sir William Wedderburn lauded the proposal as 'a remarkable document, breathing a spirit of reasoned loyalty to the British Empire'.[70]

But such sentiments were far from unanimous. Businessman and entrepreneur Sir Jamsetjee Jejeebhoy Bt was more guarded, viewing self-government as a laudable aspiration and then only 'within certain limits'.[71] The new Viceroy, Lord Chelmsford, who replaced Lord Hardinge in 1916, was even less enthusiastic and condemned the proposals as potentially 'catastrophic',[72] a point of view shared by former Governor of Bombay Lord Sydenham. He called them 'revolutionary changes',[73] so egregious that their impertinent authors should be punished 'with a strong hand'.[74] In a lightly veiled threat of the possible use of force, Governor of Madras Lord Pentland also warned 'educated Indians' to abandon any hope of early self-government or face the consequences.[75] Instead, in January 1917, the Maharaja of Bikaner was invited to attend the Imperial War Cabinet as an assistant to the Secretary of State for India and representative of the Princely States. Prime Minister Lloyd George couched this small step in his usual flowery oratory, claiming it to be 'not the whim of any individual ... but attributable largely to the welcome accorded by the heads of the Dominions to the representatives of India as equals in the Council Chamber of the Empire in its greatest emergency'.[76] But it added little or no voice to British India, and Gokhale's Congress was determined to press ahead with what became known as the Thirteen Demands.

Gokhale appreciated that more could be achieved by Congress and the League working together, and endeavoured to foster closer cooperation between the two parties. These efforts culminated in a joint session in Lucknow between 29 and 31 December 1916 which produced the Lucknow Pact. Although it was basically a reaffirmation of the Thirteen Demands, it now had the combined weight of Congress and the League behind it. Their perseverance seemed to have paid off when on 20 August 1917, recently appointed Secretary of State Lord Edwin Montagu appeared to recognise the validity of their demands. He proclaimed that forthwith 'the policy of His Majesty's Government, with which the Government of India are in complete accord, is that of the increasing association of Indians in every branch of the administration and the gradual development of self-governing institutions with a view to the progressive realisation of responsible government in India as an integral part of the British Empire,'[77] but 'by successive stages'.[78] He added that to this end he would embark on a fact-finding trip and take soundings on how best to deliver such reform. But he was also going to have to tread warily. Lord Sydenham, now co-founder of the Indo-British Association which he formed in October 1917, balked at such a prospect and insisted that he would 'oppose all measures tending to destroy or weaken the paramount authority of British rule in India or to transfer power to a small oligarchy unrepresentative of the masses of the Indian people and having interests opposed to those of the masses'.[79]

Lord Montagu nonetheless embarked on his mission, and alongside Lord Chelmsford spent several months in the country, assessing the situation and speaking to prominent Indians of all hues evaluating their opinions. Their deliberations produced a report on 8 July 1918 which, to Sydenham's great satisfaction, made no mention of either the Thirteen Points of October 1916, or indeed the terms of the Lucknow Pact. These he had dismissed as 'unworkable [and] bound to fail'.[80] Instead, the 'self-governing institutions' to which he referred would be subject to a convoluted hybrid arrangement called 'dyarchy'. This provided for parallel or double rule, in which the central government would share 'transferred' and 'reserved' subjects with the provinces, which would in turn practise a form of dyarchy within their own governments. In the latter case certain responsibilities would be within the gift of the governor, his ministers and the legislature, and in other cases the governor and his ministers only. There would be bicameral legislatures, the majority of both being elected on a franchise based on property ownership, tax liability or educational qualifications. Separate electorates would continue to protect Muslim, Sikh, Christian, Anglo-Indian and European minorities, and the number of Indians on the Viceroy's Executive Council would be raised to six. This system, the authors insisted, would allow sufficient time for 'smooth and harmonious progress'[81] towards the next unspecified phase, which would not be considered for a further ten years.

Clearly, this did not constitute self-government. Responsibility for foreign affairs, defence and relations with the princes would remain vested in the Viceroy, and he and his provincial governors retained crucial vetoes. Annie Besant was among those who upbraided its authors for producing a plan 'penetrated with distrust of Indians, and the desire to keep all real power in the hands of Englishmen ... It is petty where it should have been large, banal where it should have been striking. There is about it no vision for India or even future evolution into freedom.'[82]

Nonetheless the Secretary of State and the Viceroy pressed ahead and the reforms produced the Government of India Act, scheduled to come into operation on 1 January 1920, leaving nationalists deflated and angry. But this was not the only bone of contention concentrating the minds of nationalists and rulers. Discussions were underway over peace terms with Turkey, and throughout India concerns were growing for the fate of the Sultan who, as Caliph, was still the spiritual head of the world's Muslims. There was a concerted effort by both Muslims and Hindus to use the issue to extract more concessions and box the government into a corner. Instructions were issued for more boycotts, demonstrations and protests to be staged, most of which were likely to degenerate into further violence. The prospect of more assassinations, bombings and perhaps a repeat of the Lahore Conspiracy frightened the authorities into considering what they could do to suppress further unrest. Consequently, with the Defence of India Act of 1915 due to expire, a sedition committee chaired by Justice Rowlatt was established 'to investigate and report on the nature and extent of the criminal conspiracies connected with the revolutionary movement in India'.[83] This produced the Rowlatt Acts, passed in February 1919, and destined to inflame passions rather than temper them.

Their passage initially appeared to be justified when, in Amritsar in the Punjab on 10 April, several Europeans were killed and property set alight by marauding gangs. In response the army shot and killed several rioters, putting more Europeans at risk as the cycle of violence escalated. When Church of England missionary Marcella Sherwood cycled down a narrow alley she suddenly encountered a furious mob, and despite the intervention of several passers-by she barely escaped with her life. As described by an increasingly enraged Gandhi, in order to make an example of those thought responsible, the authorities compelled randomly selected 'innocent men and women ... to crawl like worms on their bellies'[84] down the same alley. Many soldiers, unsympathetic to the locals at the best of times, used the situation to harangue, bully, degrade and generally abuse any civilian who came within sight. It was almost inevitable that matters would reach a tragic denouement.

On 13 April 1919, General Reginald Dyer responded to reports of an unlawful assembly in the Jallianwala Bagh and led a unit of soldiers into the crowded square. Under the provisions of the Rowlatt Acts he was within his rights to disperse the crowd, but having decided to teach them a salutary lesson he ordered his men to open fire, allegedly without warning, killing somewhere between 400 and 1,000 people and wounding as many again, including forty-one children. Furthermore, because he refused to lift the curfew, the bodies of the dead had to be left out in the open until the next morning. The slaughter inevitably became known as the 'Amritsar Massacre', polarising opinion and intensifying already heightened emotions.

Dyer was hailed as a hero by many Europeans and almost universally vilified by nationalists. The subsequent Hunter Commission was highly critical of his failure to even count the casualties, and although the British House of Lords was ambivalent about his actions the Commons was outraged. The *Daily Telegraph* of 27 May covered the fallout in some detail, echoing the dismay expressed at his actions, which were called 'inhuman and un British' by Indian members of the enquiry, and which the Government of India called with some considerable understatement 'beyond the necessity of the case'. Those expressing sympathy for Dyer interpreted his actions as those of a man upholding law and order in the face of anarchy and terrorism. A fund raised £30,000 of which £28,000 alone was donated by one sympathetic old lady, and this popular sentiment also exposed the vein of racism which lay behind support for his actions. Someone was alleged to have said, 'This'll be a slap in the face for that ... Jew secretary of state for India! We'll show him what we think of his so-called reforms!'[85] Dyer, too, appeared unrepentant, a witness claiming to have overhead him on a train calling the episode 'a jolly good thing'.[86]

Such experiences served as an epiphany for many. Moderate voices such as Dadabhai Naoroji, Gopal Gokhale and Sir William Wedderburn, who had now passed away, and others such as Annie Besant who were getting old, yielded to a new generation of uncompromising nationalists. Renewed battle lines were being drawn as the disciples of men such as Gangadhar Tilak, Vinayak Damodar Savarkar and Rash Behari Bose began vying for control of the levers of power with the pacifist Mahatma Gandhi, the mercurial Ali Jinnah and the socialist republican Jawaharlal Nehru. Between the two remained the British, steadfastly resolved to hold fast against both camps.

5

'That remarkable man, Sir Salar Jung I'

Among those levers crucial to maintaining control of the subcontinent was the civil service, staffed by men of the highest calibre, well educated and dedicated to an organisation renowned for integrity and probity. But unfortunately for aspiring Indians nearly every senior position remained the jealously guarded preserve of Englishmen. From its inception, it had been regarded as only fit and proper for Europeans to hold the reins of an agency responsible for the good governance of hundreds of millions of people. To admit that they could indeed perform this role themselves would be tantamount to admitting that the British were not needed at all.

In fact, the earliest of the Company's administrators were men not well versed in the art of administration at all, described as civil servants only to distinguish them from those in the naval and military arms of the Company. They were expected to gain experience as they went, picking up pointers and learning from older hands. But in 1675 this rather rudimentary approach changed when the lowest rung on the ladder became the apprentice, serving an indenture of seven years, upon the completion of which he might achieve the post of 'writer'. At this point he was covenanted, or contracted, to perform his duties 'faithfully and efficiently' for a minimum of five years.[1] He could then earn promotion to Factor, and then perhaps the lofty heights of Senior Merchant. Even so, the only qualifications required of the early writers were youth, stamina, loyalty and a working knowledge of bookkeeping, Persian and Arabic. Duties initially included all the administrative functions associated with running any commercial enterprise, such as recording and logging the Company accounts and transactions in ledgers. Only gradually, as the Presidencies expanded and the Company accumulated more power, was further experience gained through working in municipal government and judicial administration.

One of the earliest of the Company employees to move into a role whose functions would be recognisable in 1919 was Ralph Sheldon. In 1700 he was appointed to the post of Zamindar, or collector, to administer estates in the three villages of Calcutta. His brief was 'to collect the rents and to keep the three Black Towns in order',[2] with his own court to try civil and criminal cases and to adjudicate on matters relating to revenues. A similar position, that of land customer, was established in Bombay, where a Company official was charged with collecting rent, customs dues and taxes from the villages and lands round the fort.[3] Such demanding roles involved working long hours in unhealthy, inhospitable and alien environments for very little remuneration. But as responsibilities increased, pay and promotion remained stubbornly stagnant. In 1744 the annual salary of a chief merchant was only £40, that of a junior £30, while a factor received just £15 and our humble writer a mere £5.[4]

Inevitably, the pecuniary advantages offered through extramural activities became irresistible. Penurious employees increasingly exploited opportunities for private trade and became embroiled in corruption and graft, prompting Lord Clive to confess to the Council of Directors in 1765 that 'the evil was contagious and spread among the civil and military down to the writer, the ensign and the free merchant.'[5] As a consequence, wrote Henry Hyndman, 'the earliest members of the Indian service, civil and military, must be pronounced to have been the most corrupt body of officials that ever brought disgrace upon a civilised government.'[6] As we have seen, it was such notoriety which brought the Company increasingly under the scrutiny of both the Directors and the British government. This led to the trials of men such as Clive and Warren Hastings, accompanied by increasingly robust measures to draw in its horns and curtail its activities.

The Company also became synonymous with white privilege, employing native Indians in none but the lowest positions. As if to enshrine in statute this culture of exclusion a standing order was issued in April 1791 confirming that 'no person, the son of a Native Indian, shall henceforward be appointed ... to employment in the Civil, Military or Marine Service of the Company.'[7] Thus, the door was to be firmly closed to all but well-connected Englishmen, anointed by God but appointed by the Directors to rule over and govern lesser mortals. Furthermore, as the huge profits to be made by securing a position in the Company became more widely appreciated, the demographics of its servants also changed. Families and individuals were prepared to offer considerable sums to buy a post, knowing they would be able to recoup their investment many times over. This made the civil service even more exclusive, and rendered admission to anyone without the financial wherewithal all but impossible.

This philosophy was further entrenched when in 1800 Lord Wellesley established a college in Calcutta where all new arrivals would spend three years of education in subjects deemed appropriate to their new duties. The Directors, however, then decided that instead such training should be undertaken in England, further precluding native Indians. Nonetheless in 1805 they duly sanctioned the purchase of the estate of Haileybury in Hertfordshire as a purpose-built college to 'provide a supply of persons duly qualified to discharge the various and important duties required from the civil servants of the Company in administering the Government in India'.[8] Selection was of necessity kept within strict limits, and when the college opened in 1809 it permitted only nominees of the Directors and those who could meet the fee of 50 guineas a term. Subjects included Oriental literature, Arabic, Persian, mathematics, natural philosophy, classical and general literature, law, history and political economy. It soon became clear, however, that the curriculum was too narrow and parochial, failing to equip its students with the essential knowledge they needed to administer a subcontinent. Both Persian and Arabic, for example, were spoken in India by only a handful of people, although the former remained the official language of government until 1837. As a consequence their studies culminated in examinations which Ramsay MacDonald later condemned as 'too often mere book papers, and too rarely searching tests of original ability and intellectual common sense'.[9] This inevitably meant that, as civil servant Sir Bampfylde Fuller admitted, 'young British officials go out to India most imperfectly equipped for their responsibilities. They know no law worth the name, little Indian history, no political economy, and gain a smattering of Indian vernacular.'[10] Modest attempts would be made to reform the institution, but for too many years the very location and curriculum of the college left it beyond the reach of any but the most fortunate.

There was also a wide gulf between the education provided by the Company and that available in India to any would-be applicants. Higher education for Hindus particularly was almost exclusively for Brahmins in the dead Sanskrit language. Muslim education in theory was open to all classes but conducted in Arabic, equally obscure to the majority of people. As we have seen, the education of Indians was largely neglected until the Charter Act of 1813 and even then the government was tardy in applying the sums allocated for the purpose. It was hardly surprising therefore that even by the 1830s there were just 1,197 Indians in the entire civil administration, all in lower, poorly paid positions.[11] Impatience was growing nonetheless, and in 1833 the Bombay Association passed a resolution insisting that 'the time has arrived when the natives of India are entitled to a much larger share than they have hitherto had in the administration of the affairs of their country.'[12] A parliamentary committee agreed, concluding that 'natives are only employed in subordinate positions ... such exclusion is not warranted on the score of incapacity for business or want of application or trustworthiness; while it is contended that their admission ... would strengthen their attachment to British dominion.'[13] Consequently, when the charter was renewed in 1833 clause eighty-seven overturned the standing order of 1791 and stipulated that henceforth 'no native of India shall by reason only of his religion, place of birth, descent, colour or any of them, be disabled from holding any place, office or employment.'[14]

The government could not have been clearer, but, as Montgomery Martin maintained, the Company consistently 'refused to appoint natives to offices of trust or emolument. No public employment was given to the higher class of natives in any degree proportionate to their social position.'[15] Moreover, there could be little improvement so long as patronage played a significant part in appointments, a situation which would stubbornly hinder progress for another twenty years. When finally the Government of India Act of 1853 abolished nominations and threw the service open to 'all natural born subjects of the Queen',[16] it might have been hoped that things would soon improve.

Moreover, with the role of the civil service evolving quickly, there were other reasons why change was becoming essential. The limited skillsets with which its Haileybury men departed for India were disadvantages that became more glaring as the service assumed greater responsibilities. On average, the area of an Indian district would grow to some 3,875 square miles containing around 880,000 people. At the very core was the District Officer, working virtually alone on his own initiative, arbitrating on subjects as diverse as land rights and inheritance, tax, boundary disputes and a range of other matters. These men, as Henry Hyndman put it bluntly, would 'soon find that they form part of an inexorable machine which grinds minutes, reports and judgments out of them to such an extent that they have no time for friendly intercourse with the natives'.[17] The organisation would therefore have profited early on from having men with local knowledge and a deeper understanding of customs, traditions and languages. Home-grown officials would also be able to use their interpersonal skills to develop a closer affinity with the population they served and present the Raj in the best possible light. Instead, by persisting in its unofficial 'whites-only' policy and 'by separating itself from the organic life of India', Ramsay MacDonald warned 'it has over-emphasised the fact that India is ruled by foreigners.'[18]

Even after the civil service was opened to natives in 1853, only a handful could apply for posts because they had to steam all the way to London at their own expense to take the examinations and do so before they reached the age limit of twenty-one. For many orthodox Indians, the prospect of travelling overseas in itself served as a bar, compounded by the fact that only the wealthiest could afford the associated costs.[19] This restriction also flew in the face of Queen Victoria's proclamation of 1 November 1858, issued upon the transfer of control to the Crown, which assured Indians that 'Our subjects, of whatever Race or Creed, be freely and impartially admitted to Office in Our Service, the Duties of which they may be qualified, by their education, ability, and integrity, duly to discharge'.[20] The only wise and fair solution would have been to hold simultaneous examinations in India, but this idea was repeatedly rejected.[21] Instead, in 1861 the shape of the new Indian Civil Service was formalised, in which there would be a distinction between those servants Covenanted under the Company, and those Uncovenanted after the Crown took over. The Covenanted posts would be reserved almost exclusively to Europeans, while the Uncovenanted Service would be made available to some Indians. It was however, immediately seen for what it was: a two-tier civil service, with most Indians inevitably consigned to the second.

Nonetheless, applicants battled against all the odds to secure a position. In 1863 Satyendranath Tagore made the six-month journey to the UK and passed the examination, returning home to serve in the Bombay Presidency until retiring in 1897. His achievement was all the greater when one considers the hoops through which he had to jump, and by 1870 he was still the only Indian civil servant out of a total complement of 916 in a higher post.[22] Not everyone in the British establishment was entirely comfortable with the status quo nonetheless, and some counselled caution. Lord Salisbury warned on 22 January 1867 that 'it would be a great evil if the result of our dominion was that the natives of India who were capable of government should be absolutely and hopelessly excluded from such a career.'[23] Unfortunately, such fine words were not backed by action. When the Government of India established nine £299 scholarships to enable Indian students to travel to the UK to study law or prepare for the public services, the scheme was later scrapped.[24] Instead, Parliament passed another half-hearted Act in 1870 purporting to provide 'additional facilities for the employment of Indians of proved merit and ability in the Civil Service of Her Majesty in India, notwithstanding that he had not competed in the Civil Service examination held in England'.[25] In theory it was supposed to open up any office to native Indians, including the Covenanted Service, but in practice that would prove harder to realise. In the meantime, aspiring Indians continued to avail themselves of the limited opportunities thrown open to them.

In 1868 Surendranath Banerjee, Behari Lal Gupta, Romesh Chunder Dutt and Sripad Babaji Thakur all followed in the footsteps of Satyendranath Tagore, just meeting the age deadline for the examination. All passed, practically quadrupling the Indian contingent of the ICS in one fell swoop, but it was Banerjee's experience after he was appointed Assistant Magistrate which would shine a light on the racism and bigotry endemic within the service. Despite his perfectly legitimate right to serve, he was virtually ostracised by his white colleagues who resented having to work alongside a native on an equal basis. Passing a promotion exam in 1873 over the head of a white superior was like a red rag to a bull, and it was only a matter of time before some excuse was found to get rid of him altogether. When he later committed a minor clerical error the book was thrown at him. Censured and forced to go before a commission, he was found guilty of neglect and summarily dismissed. He then had to make the long journey all the way back to Britain early in 1874 to appeal the decision and exonerate himself. But, finding the officials at the India Office 'distinctly cold and unsympathetic',[26] he knew he was unlikely to receive a fair hearing, and was told that his dismissal had been upheld. Although perhaps not unexpected, the news nonetheless came as a 'crushing, staggering blow'.[27] It also had serious consequences for his future. Although a qualified barrister, his dismissal meant that he could not now be called to the Bar: 'From the Civil Service

I had been dismissed. From the Bar I was shut out.'[28] Years later he candidly recounted his experience and the anger he felt:

If I were not an Indian, I would not have been put to all this trouble ... the head and front of my offence was that I had entered the sacred preserves of the Indian Civil Service, which so far had been jealously guarded against invasion by the children of the soil ...[29]

His treatment prompted the Lieutenant-Governor of Bengal to condemn the entire episode as a 'wicked proceeding',[30] and the Duke of Devonshire to warn that 'it is not wise to ... tell them they shall never have any chance of taking any part or share in the administration of the affairs of their country except by their getting rid in the first instance of their European rulers.'[31] It was a wise prophecy, but it went unheeded in the white heat of Britain's conviction of the superiority of European rule. Bitter and angry, and considering himself 'a ruined man',[32] Banerjee joined those of his contemporaries who were beginning to feel British rule to be the root cause of their misfortune. He also blamed the lack of any real political voice on his failure to gain redress, and so in July 1876, some years before the Indian National Congress came into being, he established the Indian Association,[33] to 'represent the views of the educated middle class community'.[34] It very soon found a cause célèbre worthy of its aims.

Despite outward signs of engagement with Indian concerns, the mood music continued to be that of obfuscation and delay, and the same year that Banerjee founded his nascent organisation the country was embroiled in controversy. The newly installed Viceroy Lord Lytton persuaded the Secretary of State to agree to reduce the maximum age limit for the ICS examination from twenty-one to nineteen years. This was in direct contravention of the longstanding convention that the upper limit of twenty-one allowed Indian candidates time to meet the criteria and to make the lengthy sea voyage to the UK. Although the Suez Canal had opened in 1869 and cut the sailing time considerably, Indians having to make the journey were still at a disadvantage. Lytton, however, had another motive, a desire to ingratiate himself with the Princes, many of whose sons wanted to join the civil service but lacked the acumen to do so. So he came up with the Statutory Civil Service, by which candidates could circumvent the need to pass an examination entirely. Instead, the Governor-General could simply facilitate their 'right to command'[35] by nominating them, with the new age limit freeing up the necessary vacancies.

The whole scheme backfired, however, because class-conscious princes considered an appointment to a post junior to the Covenanted Service beneath them, while Indians in the Uncovenanted Service resented being passed over by unqualified aristocrats. This situation wrote, Banerjee, 'created a painful impression throughout India ... [and] was regarded as a deliberate attempt to blast the prospects of Indian candidates for the Indian Civil Service'.[36]

On 24 March 1877, the first of a series of public meetings was organised to demand that the decision be reversed. The Association also sought to inspire widespread protests across the subcontinent and in Banerjee's own words create 'a spirit of unity and solidarity among the Indian people'.[37] An attempt to assuage their anger was made through a proposal that candidates who showed sufficient aptitude could be 'listed', thereby gaining access to higher posts, although they would only occupy them at two-thirds of the salary paid to European contemporaries.[38] This simply added fuel to the mounting anger and frustration, while once the Indian National Congress came into being it renewed agitation for simultaneous examinations in India.[39] Under this mounting pressure, the British government was forced to finally get to grips with the issue and undertake a thorough review of the entire system.

In 1886, new Viceroy Lord Dufferin appointed highly respected Lieutenant-Governor of the Punjab Sir Charles Umpherston Aitchison to chair a public services commission. Its goal was simple enough: to put the matter to bed by devising 'a scheme which might reasonably be hoped to possess the necessary elements of finality and to do full justice to the claims of natives of India to higher employment in the public service.'[40] Publishing its recommendations in 1887, it certainly fulfilled its brief. It proposed replacing the Covenanted and Uncovenanted Services with three distinct bodies: the Imperial, Provincial and Civil Services. Indians would have 108 posts reserved in the Provincial Service and could then be promoted to vacancies reserved to them in the Imperial Civil Service. The unpopular Statutory Civil Service would also be abolished, and the upper limit for recruitment raised to twenty-three.

This solution would, it was hoped, bring the finality that its authors had been asked to achieve. Its efficacy would soon be put to the test, as when the new system came into effect in 1892, just twenty-one out of its 939 members were Indian.[41] Meanwhile, there was no resolution to Congress's increasingly shrill demands for simultaneous examinations. Although in 1893 the House of Commons finally passed a resolution in favour of the move, it was immediately vetoed by the government, which insisted that an 'adequate' number of Europeans in the service had to be maintained.[42] The examination also needed to remain in the UK, supposedly to maintain its 'English character',[43] but one loose-lipped official let the cat out of the bag when he confessed that 'the appointment of a native of India to a very prominent position hitherto held by an Englishman, would undoubtedly create a very serious social difficulty'.[44]

Regardless of any such potential social improprieties, Indians were growing increasingly impatient for change and it was evident that if they looked to the British they were destined for a long wait. Instead, in 1892 Jamsetji Tata created higher education scholarships for gifted Indian students to study in prestigious universities around the world. One condition was that they agree to apply to sit the ICS examination,[45] and it was so successful that by 1924 a third of all Indian ICS officers would be Tata scholars.[46] Yet even his considerable influence could do little in the immediate term, and despite the overwhelming evidence to the contrary, Lord Curzon, in his inimitable way, still felt justified in complaining in 1900 that 'an increasing number of the 900 and odd higher posts that were meant and ought to have been exclusively and specifically reserved for Europeans ... [are] being filched ... by the superior wits of the native.' How he could have come to make such an astonishing assertion is all the more difficult to fathom when they still constituted just 4.24 per cent of the total.[47] In fact of the entire wage bill of £10,488,147 for 1898–99, £5,333,334 alone was allocated to just 8,000 Europeans, one-eighth of whom were the sacred '900-odd' posts that so troubled Curzon; the balance, of course, went to the remaining 136,000 Indian staff.[48] Moreover, a decade after his ill-considered outburst little had changed. In 1912 only three of the 208 posts in the Indian Education Service were held by Indians,[49] while in eight districts in Bengal there were only thirty-nine Indian civil servants, and nine of these lacked full magisterial and executive powers. This left only thirty fully qualified officers for an area of 28,000 square miles and 15,500,000 people.[50]

There were nonetheless suggestions that change was in the air, but no thanks to the success of the Aitchison Commission. A career in the ICS was losing its attraction to Englishmen, with candidate numbers falling from 226 in 1899 to 166 in 1906 despite the number of vacancies increasing from fifty-six to sixty-one.[51] These bright young graduates were instead being increasingly drawn to London, the throbbing engine of Empire, rather than to Calcutta. Here careers in the law, commerce, maritime insurance and banking offered highly lucrative alternatives to a life of drudgery in a fetid jungle or under the merciless heat of an arid desert. In essence the ICS could not compete with the salaries which lured talented men from the top schools and universities. Perhaps socio-economics was finally achieving what reformers were as yet still unable to resolve. Then came the tragedy of the First World War, where young men who might have studied for their examinations instead volunteered to fight, and where others who might have returned home to take up public service remained. The war would consume approximately 35,000 possible applicants, boys from public schools and colleges, or 18 per cent of all those who marched off to war. Harrow School alone lost 27 per cent, most other boarding schools 20 per cent and many public day schools up to 17 per cent of those callow youths who enthusiastically answered Lord Kitchener's call.[52] They left a worsening staffing dilemma which needed to be solved if the ICS were to continue to function, and one which had to be addressed before the war came to an end.

The government subsequently established the Islington Commission, which recommended in 1915 that a minimum of 25 per cent of posts should be reserved for Indians, a figure which the Montagu-Chelmsford reforms four years later increased substantially to 48 per cent.[53] Although the headline figure appeared ambitious, it was to be achieved by gradual, incremental increases of 1.5 per cent a year, meaning that the end objective might take twenty years to reach. In the meantime, European recruitment would be encouraged by inviting ex-servicemen to apply for posts by selection and a simpler test, rather than the full civil service examination.[54] But it was still too slow if the ICS were not to implode. By 1922, despite these initiatives, the flow of British candidates had reduced almost to a trickle,[55] prompting the Lee Commission of 1924 to urge that even more affirmative action be taken. It recommended that in future 40 per cent of successful applicants should be British and the same percentage Indian, with the remaining 20 per cent being made up of Indians through promotion from the Provincial Service.

Nonetheless, in spite of declining European recruitment and the adoption of the positive discrimination of Indians, ratios remained stubbornly one-sided. In 1928, while in-post Europeans occupied only 12,000 out of a grand total 1,500,000 jobs,[56] 8,000 of these were still in the most senior positions.[57] Whatever one commission or other might propose or recommend, and however generous the ratios, they were not shifting quickly enough. In the opinion of Ramsay MacDonald this lack of progress could be laid at the door of the civil service itself because while 'the politicians at home have regarded India as a political problem, the Governors in India have regarded it as an administrative one. They have been unwilling to surrender or share authority, and so when acts and resolutions have been passed by Parliament liberalising the administration of India, their application has been delayed and their intention twisted.'[58] Nor was it a mindset limited to bureaucrats. In 1922, Lloyd George told the House of Commons that Indians could never entirely dispense with a substantial nucleus of British civil servants because they were the 'steel frame of the whole structure', without which the country could not function.[59] Even by 1939, despite all of the initiatives and programmes, growing nationalist agitation and threats of civil disobedience, half of all senior positions were held by Europeans.[60] Yet when Liberal Member of Parliament Dr Vickerman Rutherford maintained that 'for every post held in India by Englishmen ... [there are] five or ten Indians well qualified to discharge its duties,'[61] he was not just cocking a snook at his contemporaries but perhaps referring to those parts of the subcontinent where Indians had been running their own affairs for decades.

The situation in British India stood in stark contrast to the conditions prevailing in the Princely States. Britain's snail-pace reforms in both the political and administrative spheres were predicated on the argument that Indians 'were not ready' for more responsibility. This intransigence overlooked the fact that apart from ceding powers including defence and foreign affairs, their neighbours were self-governing with functioning civil administrations of varying kinds. Overseen by the guiding hand of a British Resident, they managed their own affairs with various degrees of competence, some evolving to become at least as efficient as those run by Europeans in British India, such as Hyderabad, 82,000 square miles in the south-east. As we have seen, it featured heavily in the final stages of the battle for the subcontinent between Britain and France until falling under the former's orbit at the end of the eighteenth century. After becoming the first Treaty State in 1800, its autocratic Nizams governed at their own pleasure through a Diwan or prime minister, the earliest of them under the often despairing eyes of British Residents. For many years, its mismanagement resulted in debt and instability, actually prompting the Company to consider invoking its treaty rights and intervening. A major cause of its increasingly lamentable condition was the chaotic manner in which revenue collection was practised, leaving massive shortfalls in the Nizam's budget. As in eighteenth-century France, this duty was 'farmed out' to bidders in exchange for advances to the government. They in turn recouped their investment from the taxes they raised, but there were no proper records or accounting and little consistency in the valuations levied for example on farm tenants, resulting in an ad hoc, burdensome and corrupt system.

Matters were further complicated by the fact that there was no uniform currency.[62] Company representative Captain Meadows Taylor wrote of its 'wretched system of coinage',[63] consisting of twenty-six separate mints producing three distinct types of rupees, all with different weights and values. There was also widespread debasing of the coins, making transactions highly problematical, particularly with the Company. In addition there were fifty different varieties of silver and numerous copper coins in circulation at any one time. Successive Residents had urged the Nizams to close the private mints and adopt the Company rupee as the sole currency instead, but each stubbornly resisted all entreaties to do so.[64] It was also alleged that millions more were lost meeting the 25 per cent interest rate charged for loans advanced by English banker William Palmer and his Gujarati partner Benkati Das. These were often needed to offset the shortfall between income and expenditure, and during the 1820s had reached a staggering £300,000 a year.[65]

The state was not only a victim of its own shortcomings, as it was further burdened by an obligation written into the treaty of 1800 to raise and maintain 5,000 infantry, 2,000 cavalry and four field batteries of artillery to be placed at the disposal of the Company.[66] The salary of its commander alone was £5,000 a year, with running costs around 1,500,000 rupees a month.[67] Finding this money was another crippling drain on resources. It was therefore no surprise when one candid member of the British Residency, Colonel Stewart, conceded in a letter to the Government of India in 1834 that 'many of the evils that exist in the State ... are unquestionably the most avoidable result of our connection with it.'[68] Nonetheless, to most men on the spot the major culprit was the governing class of Hyderabad itself. Another observer lamented how the decline of the state had been 'marked by a series of administrative and financial adversities ... The government was overwhelmed with debt, the State Treasury was empty, and the whole of the Nizam's private funds were expended in endeavouring to partially satisfy the claims of the State's creditors; even some of His Highnesses jewels were mortgaged for the same purpose.'[69] As a result, wrote Sir John Kaye, the state was 'rotten to the core ... Nothing seemed to flourish there except corruption. Every man was bent on enriching himself at the expense of his neighbour.'[70]

When serving as British Resident, Sir Charles Metcalfe, believing matters had come to a head, sought the Directors' permission to oversee a complete overhaul of the state's administration. He hoped to staunch its expenditure and return the economy to the black,[71] but was again thwarted by the Nizam, his current Diwan, Raja Chandu Lal, and a reluctance on the part of the Company to interfere. Later, however, when he became Governor-General, he turned his gaze once again upon the ailing state and determined that only affirmative action could save it. In 1835 he wrote to the Nizam, warning that unless meaningful reform was implemented 'it would be the duty of the British government to urge upon His Highness the necessity of changing his Minister, as well as of adopting such other arrangements as might appear to be advisable for the purposes of securing good government.'[72]

Nonetheless there was little sign of improvement, and by the middle of the 1850s the Nizam had reduced his dominion, in the words of one commentator, '[to] a deplorable condition',[73] prompting renewed debate on the part of the Company as to whether to take control. In May 1853, with the Nizam's debts to the Company now standing at 4,500,000 rupees and the wages of the Contingent seven months in arrears,[74] it assumed the administration of Berar, Shorapur and the Raichur Doab in lieu of payment, but without meaningful change the decline continued. That same year saw the resignation of another major hurdle to reform, Diwan Siraj ul-Mulk, heralding a sea change in the fortunes of the state. In his place the Nizam appointed his twenty-four-year-old nephew Salar Jung. Jung was the same age as William Pitt the Younger when he had assumed the premiership of Great Britain in 1783 and there were doubts as to whether he would prove equal to the task. As his biographer Syed Hussain Bilgrami admitted, 'It was not unnatural that many people would prophesy his failure.'[75] He too found himself understandably daunted by his responsibilities. Unsure of himself, he confided to the British Resident, 'I shall nevertheless, do my best, with God's help, to restore order in the affairs of this country and endeavour to extricate the government from its embarrassments.'[76]

In fact, Jung's appointment proved to be a game changer. He immediately threw himself into the role, adopting a strict daily regime which demonstrated a work ethic that would put many British administrators to shame. Once he got into his stride, his average day would begin at 6.00 a.m., when he rose, washed and dressed and took a cup of tea. Then he held his first durbar, at which some of the poorest had the opportunity to air their grievances and seek redress. The Nizam's officers then made their reports and afterwards he returned to his private rooms to deal with state papers. He then had his own audience with the Nizam, after which he breakfasted, dealt with more business until about 12.30 p.m., and held a second durbar. After lunch and a short siesta, he spent some time in quiet contemplation and prayers, following which he received various officials to discuss any further matters which required his attention. At around 5.30 p.m. he took a stroll or went for a ride. After dinner and evening prayers he attended to more correspondence before retiring to bed at 10.00 p.m.[77] Despite the burden of his responsibilities he nevertheless developed a reputation for being personable and for having a good sense of humour. One of those with whom he came into contact referred to his 'charm of manners ... Nothing ever seemed to disturb his equanimity, though he was always on the alert to defeat intrigues in a capital which has been termed the Constantinople of the East.'[78] He would certainly need those qualities to survive as he embarked upon his campaign of reform.

The obvious immediate challenge Jung faced was the rescue of the state from its dire financial situation. With the creditworthiness of the government at rock bottom moneylenders were refusing to advance it any more funds,[79] but with one of the state's main sources of wealth – land revenue – mortgaged to the hilt his options were limited. It was therefore critical to return its management to professional and salaried civil servants, appointed by the government and to which they would be directly responsible.[80] But in adopting this strategy he was clearly playing a dangerous game, as opposition from vested interests, particularly those who profited from the old system, immediately made itself felt. There were soon rumours of a palace coup, which would oust him and keep the state in the same anarchic condition. Fearing the worst, Jung wrote to the British Resident in September 1853, asking the Government of India to underwrite his efforts. He advised him starkly that 'unless I have the avowed support of the British Government I shall find it difficult to carry out any measure whatever. I am anxious that in any communication made by the Governor-General to this Court a hint should be given of the corruption and malpractices prevalent amongst the principle revenue offices. An intimation of this kind would instil some dread into the minds of these people and strengthen my hands.'[81] The British, understandably keen to give their backing to anyone who was finally getting to grips with the state's crumbling economy, obliged him. As one historian later confirmed, 'in matters in which the Paramount Power was interested, the whisper of the Residency was the thunder of the State.'[82]

With the relevant parties duly chastened, Jung was able to proceed with his reforms. By the beginning of 1854, his strategy had led to the recovery of districts from one of the leading Arab chiefs yielding 850,000 rupees in revenue, and by the middle of the year nearly 4,000,000 rupees more of mortgaged land was restored to the state.[83] State revenues increased by another 800,000 rupees in 1855, and when transit duties were abolished an additional 200,000 rupees were realised.[84] The state's finances were further stabilised when in 1855 he established a central treasury which finally minted a uniform currency, the *Halli Sicca* rupee,[85] with a fixed exchange rate against the British Indian rupee.[86] The farming out of taxes levied on exports and imports would also be brought to an end, and in 1861 a professional customs department was established. Jung's willingness to cooperate with British India extended to the decision to ban exports of salt, sacrificing the revenue from this product so that the British could instead consolidate their own monopoly.[87] It would however prove a small price to pay for the continued approval and benevolence of the Paramount Power, and he followed this move with an agreement in 1881 banning the cultivation of poppies, which would instead be imported.[88]

Jung was not entirely preoccupied with the country's financial wellbeing. State education commenced in 1854 when Dar-ul-ulom was founded in Hyderabad City and further expanded in 1859, 1868 and 1871. By 1872 there would be sixteen schools in the city and its suburbs and 125 in the districts,[89] but although continued efforts would be made into the twentieth century, even by 1901 only 6 per cent of all children of school age would be in education.[90] Such statistics, however, did not reflect so badly on his own record, considering the equally poor achievements in British India. More effective was a royal proclamation in 1856 which banned the trafficking of both Muslim and Hindu children. Then, just as he was fully committed to his reforms, his greatest diplomatic and military challenge came in 1857 when his loyalties to the Nizam and the British were put to the test. But he was well aware of the extent to which he owed his survival to his British allies, so instead of throwing in his lot with the rebels he suppressed all signs of unrest and detained any mutineers who sought sanctuary inside the state. When the British Residency came under attack he provided help for its defence until it was finally relieved, his management of the situation winning him laurels from the British and the gratitude of the Nizam. Furthermore, for their part the British were sufficiently grateful to restore Shorapur and the Raichur Doab, ceded to the East India Company seven years before, which returned another 2,100,000 rupees to the state coffers.[91]

Moving ahead with his reforms, in 1859 Hyderabad was divided into four distinct divisions,[92] later increased to five. In each of these he replaced the assessment of land tax obligations at harvest time with one annual valuation based upon a regular system of measurements for fields,[93] while freeing fallow land from assessment altogether. He also exempted the land attached to a peasant's home from taxation and conferred proprietary rights upon tenants.[94] In 1864 a five-member board was formed to improve the revenue department, prompting British Resident Richard Meade to report that the manner in which it was now managed was 'admirable', not least because this liberalisation of the system saw revenues grow by another 1,300,000 rupees.[95] Goods ranging from food grains, fruits, oil seeds and oils, silk and cotton and cotton seeds, indigo, scents, drugs, timber, hardware cutlery, sugar, livestock, minerals and silk began flowing from the state.[96]

Nonetheless, in growing income Jung failed to achieve a concomitant reduction in poverty. Famine persisted and there were shortages in 1854, 1862, 1866, 1871, 1876–77 and 1896–97.[97] Even by 1901, 49 per cent of the state's population, scattered among more than 21,000 villages, remained tied to the land.[98] As late as 1935 a survey revealed that at any one time, out of an average village of thirty-five families, twenty-seven might be in debt to a moneylender to the tune of 173 rupees.[99] There were also 130,000 beggars, and up to 10,000 women reportedly driven by poverty to prostitution.[100] His Nizam, however, as befitted his exalted position, fared much better than his subjects, supplementing his income from the state's growing prosperity and burgeoning diamond industry with an income of some 36,000,000 rupees between 1853 and 1900.[101] Consequently, its last Nizam, the truculent Mir Osman Ali Khan, who ruled from 1886 to 1948, would be renowned as the world's richest man.

In the meantime, more prosaic changes were undertaken. Energetic efforts were made to suppress the bandits who had for so long harassed and robbed villages throughout the state, and in 1866 Jung reformed the police and abolished the practice by which criminals could effectively buy their way out of jail. Instead they faced the prospect of a long sentence in British India's penal colony on the Andaman Islands. The administration was further enhanced in 1868 with the appointment of *sadr-ul-mahams* or assistant ministers to the judicial, revenue, police and miscellaneous departments,[102] and in 1869 the first municipal administration was introduced in Hyderabad City. It was divided into four divisions, and its suburbs into five.[103] Then in 1870 he appointed a commission of Muslim lawyers to frame laws for the state on the model of British India,[104] and five years later completely reorganised the administration, laying the ground for the Hyderabad Civil Service.

In other areas, however, Salar Jung's judgement proved to be more questionable. Hyderabad's slow decline into near-bankruptcy had seen vital infrastructure badly neglected and left in dire need of investment. But in addressing this Jung fell under the spell of railway speculators who had convinced him that salvation lay in the construction of a railway linking Hyderabad with the Great Indian Peninsula Railway. He was beguiled by assurances that the line would encourage rail connectivity with British India and open up new markets to the state's coal and diamond reserves while attracting inward investment and facilitating the export of the country's produce. There was some opposition within the state, but the death in 1869 of Nizam Asaf Jah V gave Jung his opportunity when the throne passed to the two-year-old Mir Mahmud Ali Khan. With British support, Jung had himself appointed regent, which conferred upon him considerable powers, and these he used to forge ahead with his plans. It nearly proved the state's undoing.

Although the railway line was primarily the brainchild of the British, who wanted the extension through the state territory because of their own strategic interests,[105] it was Hyderabad that ultimately footed the huge bill. What would be christened the Nizam's State Railway would be built on the same basis as those in British India, and Jung used intermediaries to secure finance from London of 5,500,000 rupees, the state guaranteeing a return of the usual 5 per cent. The first track, from Hyderabad City to Wadi Junction, was laid in 1870 and finished four years later. But the expense soon proved to be crippling, and it was evident that it would take years to return a profit; as it was, it consistently failed to yield returns higher than 1.5 per cent.[106] The British then submitted a plan to extend the railway north to Chanda and the Godivari coalfields and thence to Nagpur in British India. In 1881 the Nizam's State Railway became the Nizam's Guaranteed State Railway, but the expense proved equally prohibitive at some 3,000,000 rupees,[107] and ultimately the entire scheme was as great a charge on Hyderabadi taxpayers as British India's. The episode brought Jung's government in for considerable opprobrium, which many attributed to the state's close relationship to the Paramount Power. The British now effectively controlled concessions over salt, opium, tariffs and excise, the currency exchange rate and the railways,[108] with some detractors attributing this close collaboration to Jung being appointed a Knight Commander of the Star of India in 1870. Certainly, his popularity with the British was not to be underestimated.

In 1876 Jung visited the metropole, meeting the pope along the way and hoping to use his charm to secure some concessions. Among these was the restoration of Berar, the annulment of debts owed to the East India Company and financial backing for the railways. Although he secured a private audience with Queen Victoria, the meeting consisted largely of small-talk and the topics he wished to raise did not materialise. His subsequent meetings with Disraeli, Salisbury and Lord Derby proved equally fruitless, but he was invited to be guest of honour at a banquet hosted by the Prince of Wales. His popularity among the wider public had also preceded him, and he received a number of municipal awards, not least of which was an honorary degree conferred upon him by Oxford University. Later he would also be remembered in the Memorial Hall named in his honour at the Shah Jahan Mosque in Woking.

When Salar Jung died of cholera in 1883, aged just fifty-four, he undoubtedly left behind a mixed legacy which may have been contentious in many areas but saw Hyderabad among the wealthiest of the Princely States, with trade growing in value to £10,000,000 a year – double that of any other state and equivalent to about 165,000,000 rupees of British Indian currency.[109] Furthermore, his reforms did not end with his untimely death. In 1884, Act I of 1304 recognised the right of the people to share in the work of framing laws and representation,[110] while a legislative council consisting of a president, vice president, eight government officials and six non-official members followed in 1893.[111] A cabinet council consisting of a minister serving as president, and assistant ministers acting as advisers was also established; its main remit was consideration of the annual state budget and the discussion of questions arising out of the proceedings of the legislative council.[112] Changes to the judiciary also continued, and by 1909 there were 123 civil and 271 criminal courts including a high court.[113]

Among the plaudits Jung received was one from William Digby, who said that he had proven himself to be 'head and shoulders above his contemporaries – Anglo-Indian and Indian'.[114] John F. Law wrote in 1914 that 'no one can form an opinion on modern Hyderabad and appreciate its present condition without studying the life of that remarkable man, Sir Salar Jung I.'[115] Others were convinced that he was far from unique, however. In March of that year Sir Walter Lawrence, an Indian civil servant who had travelled widely across the subcontinent, addressed the Royal Institution in London. His speech contained a ringing endorsement of Indian administrators as a whole:

I am of the opinion that the people in the Indian States are happier and are more contented than are their brethren over the border in British territory. They have Government that is more congenial, more in accordance with their own ideas, in short a Government that is Indian. If I were an Indian, I should most certainly elect to live in an Indian State ...[116]

6

'Striving to bring about a revolution'

Irrespective of role models such as Sir Salar Jung, the implementation of the Morley-Minto reforms or the India Act of 1919, the prospects for constitutional parity with the so-called 'White Dominions' remained remote. Although token representation of nominated princes at imperial meetings and separate membership of the League of Nations had been approved, these were superficial, perhaps even artificial concessions. At the Imperial Conference of 20 June to 5 August 1921, Canada, Australia, New Zealand, South Africa and of course the UK were all represented by their prime ministers. India, however, having no such political representation, had the Secretary of State Lord Montagu as its official delegate. Membership of the League meant nothing so long as its delegation was ultimately answerable to the Secretary of State rather than the Imperial Legislative Council. The heady promises and undertakings made at the outset of war and reiterated during its prosecution had therefore produced a settlement which fell far short of the constitutional concessions enjoyed elsewhere in the Empire.

Canada had secured self-government as a dominion as long before as 1867, when the British North America Act effectively federated the separate colonies of Nova Scotia, New Brunswick, Quebec and Ontario into provinces, with their national capital in Ottawa. Its system of self-government would form the template for the subsequent evolution of Australia, New Zealand, South Africa and the Irish Free State, based as closely as possible on the Westminster model, with a Senate instead of a House of Lords and a House of Commons. There was a strong federal government, with reserved rights over the provinces, and responsibility for relations with the UK and the passing of federal laws; the provinces would have legislative powers, and the country would be subject to the Colonial Laws Validity Act of 1865. Canadians also had the right to appeal to the Privy Council in London, which could override or veto any laws or decisions about which an appeal was made. Ultimate power resided in the Governor-General, who was both the personal representative of the sovereign and the British government and was appointed not by the dominion but by the monarch, whose constitutional functions he exercised on behalf of the monarch.

Canada had therefore been created under an Act of the British Parliament which could only be amended or abolished by Westminster. Nevertheless, the Governor-General had less power than the Viceroy, and Canadians were not left with the same sense of being governed by an alien and distant power. Many Canadians, along with Australians, New Zealanders and to a lesser extent South Africans, were transplanted Englishmen and women and did not feel the same sense of distance from London as the average Indian. The governors in each of its provinces likewise exercised executive authority and could veto legislation which was considered contrary to the interests of the Raj. Clearly, under such an arrangement Indians had a long way to go to emulate their white counterparts. At the Colonial Conference of 1907, the status of Dominion had already been conferred upon the self-governing countries to distinguish them further from Britain's other dependencies and protectorates, and of course India. The move was given legal effect by UK statute in 1911,[1] creating a two-tier empire and laying the groundwork for the establishment of a separate British Commonwealth. This would emerge as the model for moderate Indian aspirations, as had been articulated during the war – an equal partnership devoid of the restrictions from which the other dominions had divested themselves.

As part of the second-tier, India held its first direct elections in 1920 for seats on the Imperial Legislative Council and the provincial councils. These, too, only served to underline the differences in rights enjoyed by the so-called White Dominions and the people of the subcontinent. The new Central Legislative Assembly – the lower chamber of the Imperial Legislative Council – was based in Delhi and had 104 seats, of which sixty-six were contested and eight reserved for Europeans who would be elected by their local chambers of commerce. The upper chamber, the Council of State, had thirty-four seats, of which twenty-four were contested, five reserved for Muslims, three for Europeans, one for Sikhs and one for the United Provinces. Elections for the 637 seats in the provincial assemblies were also held, of which 440 were contested, and 188 had single candidates elected unopposed. Thirty-six seats were reserved for white voters. But the number of electors was lamentably small. The census of 1921 revealed that only one in fifty women in British India could read or write, and one-tenth of the adult male population. Consequently, only 909,603 out of a total population of 247,000,000 in the British provinces were as yet eligible to share in even this limited concession towards democracy.[2]

The usual qualification was one of residency along with the payment of a small amount of land revenue or local rates in rural areas and of municipal rates in urban areas. As few women owned property on which to pay taxes, they found themselves further disadvantaged.[3] The process for voting was also lacking in sophistication, and special devices had to be used to assist voters who could not read, such as pictorial symbols – another barrier to the franchise.[4] By contrast, the Dominions at this time had almost unanimously instituted universal male and female suffrage, eschewing property, income and educational qualifications. Some had achieved these reforms during the course of the war as a recognition of both sexes' contribution to achieving victory, although in New Zealand all men could vote from 1879, and women from 1893. The Union of South Africa was the least progressive of the Dominions, and would not introduce universal male and female voting rights until 1930. Their Black population, moreover, would be incrementally disenfranchised as successive segregationist Afrikaner governments imposed increasingly oppressive laws. Even in the UK it took until 1928 before both men and women of all classes could exercise their right to vote on an equal basis. Nonetheless, Indians were far behind, and the exercise of democracy in any true sense was further hampered by additional safeguards which had to be put in place to protect various vested interests.

Arguably the most powerful of these were the princes, who wore their treaty rights like a security blanket, determined to outfox any measures which impinged upon their privileged lifestyles. For their benefit alone, a grandly named Chamber of Princes was established by the Act of 1919 to serve their interests. The Viceroy was president and its 120 members consisted of 108 princes entitled to eleven-gun salutes or over, and twelve others elected by the rulers of non-salute states. The members also elected a chancellor annually who would serve as a kind of speaker. They would meet once or twice a year to provide a forum for discussion and resolution for matters of common interest and a platform to air grievances and recommendations to be put forward to the government for consideration. However, for the rulers of Hyderabad and Mysore, two of the largest and most important states, even these safeguards were not enough and they declined to take part. The Nizam of Hyderabad considered that his particular status as 'Faithful Ally', granted by King George V in recognition of his help in the First World War, entitled him to direct access to the King-Emperor through the Political Department. For his part, the Maharaja of Mysore did not believe that any decisions arrived at by the Chamber could be of any relevance to his state. Involvement did however afford other opportunities for those princes who participated. The Maharaja of Bikaner and the Jam Sahib of Nawanagar became involved with Indian affairs at the League of Nations and represented their country at various imperial conferences.

British interests were also well-served by keeping the princes on-side, as they recognised that the Paramount Power was still their best insurance policy against internal dissent or external threats. This was a fact Dadabhai Naoroji had clearly long appreciated:

> ... the present form of relations between the Paramount Power and the Princes of India is un-English and iniquitous ... I have not the least hesitation in saying that, as much from self-interest alone as from

any other motive, the Princes will prove the greatest bulwark and help to perpetuate British supremacy in India ... I say from personal conversation with some of the princes, that they thoroughly understand their interest under the protection of the present paramount power ... [5]

All three centres of power were opened on 9 February 1921 by the Duke of Connaught, and three days later he laid the foundation stone for the new Parliament Building. First envisaged when the capital was moved from Calcutta years before, it would be an impressive structure 560 feet in diameter and covering 6 acres, and its construction would take six years. He also dedicated India Gate, a national memorial to the 70,000 men who died in the war. But if the British believed they had put further reform on hold and secured a few more decades of unchallenged rule, they were in for a rude awakening. Mahatma Gandhi was by now a dominant voice in the nationalist movement and had secured the rejection of the India Act and the adoption of a novel and tacitly non-violent form of resistance. The Rowlatt Acts, the humiliation of the Crawling Lane and the massacre in the Jallianwala Bagh had turned the diminutive and once loyal if restless subject of the King-Emperor into a man determined to rid his country of the foreign oppressor. On 1 August 1920, he wrote to the Viceroy declaring that 'half of India is too weak to offer resistance, and the other half is unwilling to do so. I have, therefore, ventured to suggest the remedy of non-cooperation.'[6]

However, the other leading light emerging from within the Muslim ranks of Congress, Muhammed Ali Jinnah, did not believe that such a response was the correct line to take. Jinnah had begun his working life as a barrister, first in London and then in Bombay, joining Congress in 1906 and then simultaneously becoming a member of the League in 1913, of which he became president in 1916. He then helped to draft the Lucknow Pact, instrumental in bringing about the Congress–League rapprochement. He had been uneasy about Congress policy for some time, but when it opted for non-cooperation he decided it was time for a parting of the ways and resigned. Annie Besant too had strong reservations about such an escalation. She believed that boycotts would harm ordinary Indians far more than the government and mean 'the destruction of clothing, so terribly needed by the people, with the consequent rise in prices ... to meet the sudden demand ... Only the really poor suffer by the bonfires.'[7] She therefore believed that 'Mr Gandhi's proposal ... is wrong in principle and will be disastrous to the country in proportion as it is carried out.' She accused him of 'striving to bring about a revolution', and warned that 'non-cooperation stirs up hatred between Government and people' and furthermore 'stirs up race hatred'.[8] This, she added, 'will inevitably lead to violence and bloodshed, which can only have one result – repression and the putting off of all improvement in our civil conditions'.[9] Nonetheless, non-cooperation was adopted as policy, while the movement also found growing support in Britain as attitudes towards the very idea of imperialism experienced a sea-change.

Longstanding British sympathisers such as Annie Besant, Henry Hyndman and others going back to Montgomery Martin found their ranks swelled by men such as socialist and author H. G. Wells and Arthur Conan Doyle. The latter felt that few of his compatriots in Britain cared very much about the India Act or indeed the non-cooperation movement that it helped to inspire. He believed that nineteen out of twenty British people had as little interest in or knowledge of India as 'they had about the Italian Renaissance',[10] and therefore would care little if it should become independent. He was joined by Leonard Woolf, husband of Virginia, who had served as a civil servant in Ceylon and returned chastened by what he experienced there. He turned into an avid anti-imperialist and in 1919 published *Empire and Commerce – a Study in Economic Imperialism*, which laid bare the injustice and exploitation that it wrought. These and other influential writings spread the word and led others to acknowledge the evils of one race governing another against their will. These elder statesmen of anti-imperialism were later to be joined by someone who had also witnessed the dark side of imperialism: Eric Blair, later to find fame as the prolific author George Orwell. He joined the Burmese police in 1922 but left after five years, later writing of the iniquities he encountered in his novel *Burmese Days*. The British Labour Party and Trades Union movement – bodies which associated the wrongs of imperialism with their own class struggle – also joined the chorus of disapproval, their views articulated by men such as Ramsay MacDonald and another future leader of the party, Clement Attlee.

Nonetheless, there remained a strong body of opinion which saw the Empire as a positive influence and essential for British prosperity. Growing hostility prompted imperialists to search for some fillip which might reinvigorate patriotic fervour and restore national pride. One proposal was the holding of an annual Empire Day, an event observed on an ad hoc basis around the Empire since the death of Queen Victoria, on her birthday, 24 May. During the war, Lord Reginald Brabazon, the Earl of Meath, sought to revitalise the idea and in 1916 moved that it be formalised as a national holiday, telling the House of Lords that 'I found to my astonishment that Empire Day had been observed in many parts of India ... in Mahomedan mosques and Hindu and Sikh temples'[11] but not more widely. He observed wryly that although it had become a statutory holiday in most of the self-governing colonies by that time, it was not in South Africa, adding, 'I need not go into that question.'[12]

Concurrent with this train of thought was the decision to revive an idea which had also lain dormant since it was first mooted by Lord Strathcona in 1912: a great exhibition to showcase the Empire,[13] like one mounted in 1886, but on a far grander scale. This idea too was adopted and Wembley was chosen for the site, with India taking centre stage. As the exhibition commissioner for India, civil servant and administrator Diwan Bahadur T. Vijayaraghavacharya explained to the *Asiatic Review*, he believed his country's participation was recognition of India's role in the war, and 'the change in India's political status as a member of the Empire'.[14] The extent of its exhibition space certainly seemed to reflect its new-found status, consisting of a huge Mughal-style pavilion of 402 by 450 feet, 'similar to those on the Victory Gate at Fatehpur-Sikri',[15] in fact a stylised pastiche of everything the casual observer might expect to represent the vast country. The entire site covered 216 acres, with a 50-acre amusement park, a play area for children and even a dance hall which, many sceptics claimed, proved to be the most popular attraction of all. Officially opened by King George V on 23 April 1924, it was to receive some 17,000,000 visitors and when reopened a year later with additional attractions, another 10,000,000 went to take a look. In the opinion of socialists, Indian nationalists and cynics the whole show was a sham, attempting to prop up a philosophy of rule which was looking increasingly anachronistic.

Stalwart supporters of imperialism like Winston Churchill, a member of Stanley Baldwin's shadow government and vehement opponent of any constitutional concessions, believed there was more to Empire than pride and patriotism. He viewed with horror the 'frightful prospect' conducted 'recklessly [and] wantonly' of policies which would lead to Britain losing India altogether. He added that to do so would simply lead to its people being left to suffer 'measureless disasters'.[16] William Joynson-Hicks' views if anything were even more full of invective than Churchill's. He insisted that 'we conquered India by the sword and by the sword we should hold it,'[17] sentiments not designed to ease the passage of further reform. The violence in the country may or may not have vindicated their points of view, but Baldwin nonetheless was among those who saw the tide was turning against Britain: 'There is a wind of nationalism and freedom blowing around the world and blowing as strongly in Asia as anywhere.'[18] He would soon be given the opportunity to put his words into practice.

Early in 1924, having concluded that dyarchy was a non-starter, Bahadur Rangachari moved a resolution in the Imperial Legislative Council, once again calling for immediate self-governing Dominion status on the same basis as the other members of the British Commonwealth. His motion received the firm support of fellow Congress Members, not least of whom was Pandit Motilal Nehru, Jawaharlal Nehru's father. He also proposed a round-table conference to discuss drafting a new constitution. Both proposals were adopted by the Council on 18 February 1924 and put to the British. Having hoped to have put off further changes for at least a decade, they instead grudgingly agreed to look into the workings of the Act, and appointed a commission under civil servant Sir Alexander Muddiman 'to enquire into the difficulties arising from, or defects inherent in the working of the Government of India Act ... [and] to investigate the feasibility and desirability of securing remedies for such difficulties or defects, consistent with the structure, policy and purpose of the Act'.[19] But behind this grand-sounding brief there was no concession of a wholesale revision and certainly no intention of ditching the Act. After all, as the report stated in its preamble, 'it may be argued that the period for which it has actually been in force is too short to afford sufficient experience for a well-rounded analysis.'[20]

The British having therefore already pre-empted any findings, eminent official and non-official members Sir Tej Bahadur Sapru, Ali Jinnah, Sir P.S. Sivaswami Iyer and R. P. Paranjpe set about their pointless task. They interviewed or received written evidence from 130 witnesses, bodies, organisations and individuals, but the conclusions arrived at only succeeded in producing two quite distinct camps. There were those who believed the British government was right and the Act ought to be given more time, and those who were convinced it was a failure and could not be made to work. While Fazlul Huq, a member of the Bengal Legislative Council, told the committee that he did not believe dyarchy had 'had a fair trial', believing the 1919 Act to be 'an essential and indispensable first step towards ... full responsible government',[21] Sir Surendranath Banerjee believed 'it should go as quickly as possible' simply because it had been 'condemned by educated public opinion'.[22] Others believed Banerjee simply represented the opinions of those who had been determined all along that it should fail. Representatives of the Government of Bombay felt that because 'the successful working of the Act depend [s] to a large degree upon the spirit in which it is worked by all parties,'[23] such spirit was singularly lacking.

Nonetheless, those who offered constructive criticism exposed serious and deep-seated flaws which had only been revealed through its application. Sir Kurma Reddy, a minister in the Government of Madras, described the inconsistencies of the partial devolution represented by dyarchy. He gave as examples how 'I am Minister for Development minus forests, and you all know that development depends a good deal on forests. I am Minister of Industries without factories, which are a reserved subject, and industries without factories are unimaginable ... I am Minister of Agriculture without irrigation. You can understand what that means.'[24] Moreover, under dyarchy transferred departments were very often managed not by the Indian ministers but by their permanent secretaries who were British civil servants, and they had the ear of the governor. If the minister issued a directive of which his permanent secretary disapproved, he often went over the head of his superior, straight to the governor who could be persuaded to simply overrule the minister.[25]

Nonetheless, the British remained unmoved, and inevitably an impasse was reached. The committees' inability to agree produced, appropriately, two reports. The 'Minority' report authors claimed that the Act was working 'creakily' and whilst 'minor remedies may cure a creak or two'[26] they could not address the fundamental flaws described by Sir Kurma. Instead, Jinnah, Bahadur Sapru and others returned to their original demand for a 'Constitution ... with provisions for automatic progress ... so as to secure stability in the Government and [the] willing cooperation of the people'.[27]

The 'Majority' report predictably echoed the gentlemen from Bombay and blamed the 'evil influence'[28] of the non-cooperation movement for much of the problems the reforms had encountered. Adamant that it was far too soon for the giant leap demanded in the Minority report, Muddiman advocated instead the very tweaking vilified by his fellow committee members. He proposed that the power of the Secretary of State be relaxed, for some reserved powers to be delegated to the provinces, greater joint working between the parties, plus greater representation for the depressed and labouring classes and greater enfranchisement of women.[29] The status quo would therefore be maintained, producing a chimera which, in the opinion of commentators at the time, 'looks like *Swaraj* to India and like British Raj to England'.[30] But of course few nationalists saw this as anything like *Swaraj*.

Nationalist anger was further fuelled by the swift advances still being made by the Dominions. This perhaps explained British reticence to accede to their demands, with authority already ebbing away from Westminster at an unexpected rate. By the time of the Imperial Conference of 1926, South Africa's new prime minister, James Hertzog, who had won the South African general election of 1924, arrived in London determined to establish his nation's credentials as a fully sovereign state. His ultimate objective was a South African republic, but he had to mark time. Nevertheless, further reform was demanded and although Canada's Mackenzie King was no republican, he too sought clarifications on such issues as the role and powers of the Governor-General. The Irish Free State, with South Africa the most unwilling member of the Commonwealth, was also seeking to exploit any loopholes which could hasten its severing of political ties with Britain. Unable to staunch such aspirations, the British government had to try to concede the sovereignty demanded without losing allegiance entirely. After much discussion and debate, a form of words was agreed upon which now recognised members of the British Commonwealth as:

> ... autonomous communities within the British Empire, equal in status, in no way subordinate to one another in any aspect of their domestic or external affairs, though united by a common allegiance to the Crown, and freely associated as members of the British Commonwealth of Nations ...[31]

This was not a legally binding undertaking, merely a statement of intent. London was giving assurances that it would never seek to invoke the residual powers enshrined in their respective constitutions. They were technically free to pass whatever laws or amendments to their constitutions they wished so long as they did not include removing the British monarch as head of state. This half-way house naturally left die-hard nationalists dissatisfied. For the Irish and South Africans cutting ties with the British ruler was the ultimate goal, and this statement did nothing to address such demands. Inevitably another committee was established to decide what further measures would need to be taken and it arrived at further recommendations. One was to assign to the Governor-General of each Dominion the same functions as the King, without recourse to the UK parliament or the monarch. Furthermore, London would accredit to each Dominion a separate High Commissioner, to serve as the political representative of the British government, quite distinct from the constitutional role played by the Governor-General. Still they fell far short of what the South African and Irish governments wanted, but they stood in stark contrast to what was on offer to India. It still had a Secretary of State and a Viceroy answerable directly to the British government, while the India Act, notwithstanding the Muddiman tweaks, left it subject to a system of government which vested ultimate authority in a foreign power.

Therefore, many nationalists who sought more than the crumbs on offer continued to feel they had no alternative but to seek their ends by other means. Non-cooperation, instigated in 1920, continued to dog the government and cause disruption, but it also became increasingly violent, culminating in February 1922 with a bloody incident in Chauri-Chauri in the United Provinces that compelled Gandhi to call off the campaign. This did not sit well with Motilal Nehru and others who felt that an isolated incident should not be allowed to bring a successful campaign to an end, and a rift opened up which resulted in the forming of a breakaway Swaraj Party.

The split among the leading nationalists did nothing to de-escalate the violence, even with Gandhi's growing influence over events. In fact the violence was intensifying, from eleven riots in 1923 to eighteen in 1924, then sixteen in 1926 and thirty-five in 1927. These often became conflated with inter-communal tensions, and a serious riot in Lahore was followed by another in Nagpur in the Bombay Presidency which resulted in twenty-two deaths and in excess of a hundred injuries. Non-cooperation and the subsequent disorder also saw movements aimed at overthrowing dyarchy growing in Britain. The foundation of organisations such as the India League by Krishna Menon would attempt to bring home to the British public the extent of the discontent in India, and underscore the growing disenchantment with British policy. As the situation deteriorated and the negative publicity it engendered around the world threw a spotlight on British intransigence, Stanley Baldwin parked the findings of the Muddiman Commission and brought forward slightly the ten-year review provided for in Section 84A of the Government of India Act, which had promised:

> within ten years ... [there] shall be a commission for the purpose of inquiring into the working of the system of government, the growth of education, and the development of representative institutions, in British India, and matters connected therewith, and the commission shall report as to whether and to what extent it is desirable to establish the

principle of responsible government, or to extend, modify or restrict the degree of responsible government then existing therein …[32]

This would, therefore, be far more thorough and have a wider gift than the Muddiman Committee, which most had dismissed as a whitewash anyway. In November 1927 Baldwin asked lawyer Sir John Simon to head the statutory commission, which would travel to India and hear evidence in two tranches, from 3 February to 31 March 1928 and from 11 October 1928 to 13 April 1929. He would be accompanied by four Conservative MP, plus two from Labour and one Liberal, among whom was the young socialist and ardent anti-imperialist Clement Attlee. Predictably, the all-white composition of the commission immediately set hackles rising, and the nationalists saw it as yet another attempt by the British to weigh the findings in their favour and so maintain the status quo. As soon as it was discovered that no Indians were included in the commission, it met with a hostile reception and cries of 'Simon Go Back!'[33] Jawaharlal Nehru told a meeting on 11 April 1928 that 'none of you here want any argument from me to boycott it. That boycott is going to continue.'[34]

With Congress having turned their backs on Simon, he and his colleagues sought to do the best they could. Travelling 7,000 miles on the first trip and 14,000 on the second, they took evidence over a total of seventy-five days, and found vital factors which they would claim as critical impediments to further progress. These included the limited franchise, the canker of corruption in the election process and ultimately the incessant intercommunal violence which undermined any efforts to make progress. Despite some changes since 1920, the proportion of enfranchised women remained pitifully small, there being only 116,000 in the Madras Presidency, 39,000 in Bombay, 37,000 in Bengal and 21,000 in the Punjab, the latter representing just 1 per cent of the province's entire female population.[35] This was bad enough but even male enfranchisement was restricted to property owners, title holders and members of the University Senate, which meant that only 10 per cent of the entire male population of voting age could yet do so.

Inevitably, illiterate farmers or disenfranchised women would not stand as candidates either, but as Simon recognised, 'landowners, moneylenders, medical practitioners … retired Government servants … [and] businessmen'[36] would seize the opportunity to extend their power and influence. Plus the reforms so far had seen a rise in a new class of persons, those who could afford the financial costs of pursuing office and subsequently 'make politics their main profession'.[37] With few scruples but deep pockets, such individuals, the report alleged, exploited the 'ignorance and superstition [of] some classes of the electorate' and put them 'at the mercy of ingenious and unscrupulous canvassers' so that 'undesirable forms of pressure are probably fairly common'.[38] This could mean anything from threats by landowners on their tenants to bribery and the buying of votes. The commission, seeing the venality to which this could lead, urged that 'any step that can be taken to reduce the extent of corruption in elections ... should be adopted.'[39] These deductions were damning enough, but Simon considered something else more serious still:

> ... in spite of much neighbourly kindliness in ordinary affairs, and notwithstanding all the efforts made by men of goodwill in both communities to promote Hindu-Muslim accord, the rivalry and dissention between these two forces are one of the chief stumbling blocks in the way of smoother and more rapid progress ...[40]

Certainly, even within the close-knit villages there were always underlying tensions, allowing situations to escalate if not handled delicately and nipped in the bud. The commission recognised how something as innocuous as when an 'anniversary of Moslem mourning synchronises with a day of Hindu rejoicing' or 'when communal feeling is roused on some matter of secular interest, religious zeal is always present to stimulate conflict.'[41] This mutual hatred was writ large in the increasing riots being experienced across the country, the commission concluding that 'the true cause [of communal tension], as it seems to us, is the struggle for political power and for the opportunities which political power confers.'[42] In other words, the British risked leaving power vacuums that both sides were eager to fill to their own advantage, which no responsible British government could allow to happen.

Finally, Simon touched on two other fundamentals. The first was that unlike the British Cabinet, or those of any of the Dominions, which could survive only for as long as they enjoyed the confidence of the House of Commons, the Governor-General in Council faced no such censure, being 'entirely independent of and indeed, can seldom count with confidence on, a majority of the Indian Legislature'.[43] But under the terms of the India Act he could in any case continue to function, as there was no mechanism for forcing him out. The second was that 'there is nothing in the Indian Legislature which corresponds to the working of a party system, as that expression is understood in Britain,'[44] a function which neither Congress or the Muslim League was fulfilling, or seemed prepared to. This absence of pluralism, and any apparent desire to nurture it, was further entrenched through the application of the system of separate electorates, which 'appeal to communal sentiment, instead of developing political associations along the lines of broader citizenship'. Nonetheless, as 'the true cause lies deeper and arises from conditions which are far more difficult to change than the mechanics of representation,'[45] abandoning the practice would do little to mend fences.

The main points of the report, published in May 1930, made for sober reading for nationalists. From the British point of view there were many hurdles to surmount before India could expect to function as a democratic Dominion on the same basis as Australia or Canada. The inference to be taken from this could only be that the British believed they would have to remain at the helm for some considerable time to come. Perhaps because it essentially meant maintaining the status quo, the King's private secretary, Lord Stamfordham, was among many in Britain who considered the report to be 'a very remarkable achievement'.[46]

The commission's findings naturally cut little ice with the nationalists, who instead responded with their own proposals. These were yet another iteration of the demands made on numerous occasions, and inevitably ran counter to the assessment of the situation at which Simon had arrived. Motilal Nehru published his own report on 10 August 1928 calling for Dominion status, a Bill of Rights, freedom of religion, equal rights for men and women, the creation of a Supreme Court, and the realignment of provinces based on language. Jawaharlal, although endorsing his father's report, was now among a growing faction who now openly questioned the value of Dominion status. As a socialist and a republican, he told the All Parties Conference at Lucknow on 29 August 1928:

What does the British Commonwealth of Nations, as it is now called, stand for? It stands for one part domineering and exploiting the other. There are England and the self-governing dominions, exploiting India, parts of Africa, Malaya and other parts of the world. When we obtain Dominion Status, are we going to get promotion from the exploited part to that of the exploiting?[47]

Instead, at the Bombay Presidency Youth Conference in Poona on 12 December 1928, he described an India that did not share in a 'world imperialism [which] is the direct outcome of a system of society which prevails in the greater part of the world today and is called capitalism'.[48] He believed that instead 'we must aim ... at the destruction of all imperialism and the reconstruction of society on another basis. That basis must be one of cooperation, and that is another name for socialism. Our national ideal must, therefore, be the establishment of a cooperative socialist commonwealth and our international ideal a world federation of socialist states.'[49] Furthermore, in Kerala on 28 May 1928 Nehru had made reference to the future status of the princes in the Dominion which his party was demanding. The British saw the Princely States as a separate issue from British India, but in an ill-disguised threat they and British India would 'stand together and nothing must be allowed to separate us'.[50] He was even more explicit when in October he put them on notice that 'the days of kings and princes are numbered'.[51]

The Muslim League, in the meantime, had been considering its own political strategy. Jinnah rejected the Nehru report,[52] responding with his own so-called Fourteen Points which were published on 9 March 1929. He repeated the demand for separate electoral rolls, for a federal system of government, a constitution guaranteeing equal rights for all regardless of race, religion or gender, and provincial autonomy as the means by which Muslim rights could be protected.[53] The British response to both sets of demands was decidedly cool, if not off-hand, so with their patience finally at an end Congress decided the time had come to act. Nehru and others were inspired by the events in Ireland following the British general election of 1918, when the Irish nationalists simply refused to take their seats in Westminster. They stayed in Dublin and proceeded to operate their own parliament, ignoring the authority of the British government and announcing that they were going it alone. On 26 January 1930, Indian nationalists sought to emulate this gesture by holding meetings throughout the country where the Congress flag was raised accompanied by the announcement of '*Purna Swaraj*', unilateral declarations of independence as a republic. Thus, to non-cooperation was to be added non-violent civil disobedience until the British acceded to their demands.

In a world now shrunken by the speed of news and the media, Gandhi decided to give the government no choice but to take notice. He opted to gain publicity by defying one of the most iconic totems of British rule, its monopoly over the production and distribution of salt. The plan was to walk the 241 miles to the Arabian Sea coast and ostentatiously gather salt from the shore. Accompanied by a somewhat sceptical Jawaharlal Nehru, the Bengali radical Chandra Bose and Chakravarti Rajagopalachari – two personalities who would later become prominent figures in the struggle in their own right – he set off on 12 March 1930 from Ahmedabad with seventy-nine devotees. On 6 April 1930, at the end of a march during which he had collected thousands more followers and priceless publicity, he symbolically picked up a lump of salt from the beach. Within days Indians all over the country were emulating this brazen act of defiance.

Gandhi naturally wanted the protest to be peaceful, but inevitably matters took on a different hue when a group of marchers reached Dharasana Salt Works 150 miles north of Bombay. They were met by policemen with drawn truncheons and staves, who ordered them to disperse, and when they declined to do so the officers proceeded to beat them mercilessly. A stunned Webb Miller, European News manager of the *United Press*, reported, 'I have never witnessed such harrowing scenes as at Dharasana ... sometimes ... so painful I had to turn away.'[54] Another eyewitness, Miss Madeleine Slade, confessed that the scenes made 'my skin creep and my hair stand on end as I saw those brave men ... lying before me battered and broken from head to foot.'[55] The brutality of the authority's response was interpreted worldwide, and particularly in the United States, as symptomatic of British cruelty and oppression. The appalling public relations disaster this incident produced was compounded by the government's decision to arrest anyone they suspected of being complicit in the protests, and Gandhi was promptly taken into custody. This in turn produced more violence, with extreme radical nationalists more than ever convinced that only a revolution like that seen in Ireland could hope to achieve their objectives.

Among these was Surya Sen, who was inspired by the Easter Rising of 1916 and determined to achieve freedom by the same ends. On Easter Friday 18 April 1930, three groups of sixty men undertook an audacious raid on the armouries at Chittagong in the eastern Bengal Presidency. They hoped thereby to seize the weapons with which they could arm a force which would foment rebellion in the name of the Indian Republican Army and force out the British. They succeeded in raiding the armoury and setting fire to the buildings, and also managed to cut communications and wreck the railway line, but after that it all went wrong. The police were quick to respond and in a bloody gunfight nineteen rebels were killed and the rest took to the nearby hills. They were pursued by the authorities and a series of skirmishes flushed them out one by one over the succeeding months. Surya Sen was among those who managed to hold out, only finally apprehended three years later. The main result of the uprising was further severe clampdowns, and following the passage of the Bengal Criminal Law Amendment Act thousands more suspects were rounded up and interned without trial. Nevertheless, the violence continued, with the intelligence branch of the Bengal Police recording another 250 terrorist incidents between 1930 and 1932, mostly murder, attempted murder and bombings.[56]

While Sen and his comrades were hiding from the British, his Irish role models were proceeding with their own plans to detach themselves further from the British Empire. The King-Emperor's title of 'Brit Omni' or King of all the Britons was now about to be challenged. When the next Imperial Conference was convened on 1 October 1930, the Irish delegates arrived armed with quite startling proposals. One of these was to 'eliminate the description British subject and obtain for Irish, Canadian, Australian etc ... the [same] recognition, rights and privileges at present attaching to British subjects'.[57] This measure would transform the British Commonwealth into a completely new body consisting not of British subjects sharing a single nationality under the Crown but entirely separate and distinct nations in their own right. To further distance themselves from British institutions, the Irish announced that they wanted the jurisdiction of the Privy Council in London removed as well. To them, it was 'obnoxious because it is an extra state institution exercising a judicial control over the internal affairs of the State without any form of democratic sanction ... The Privy Council must disappear and is already decaying because of its inherent incompatibility with [the] constitutional evolution of the Commonwealth.'[58] Furthermore, the South Africans wanted an official end to the right of the Westminster Parliament to 'disallow' legislation passed by a Dominion government, dismantling one more pillar of British authority.

To keep the British Commonwealth intact, Westminster had little choice than to accede to Irish and South African demands. To refuse simply risked their walking out of the club altogether. So the government relented, conceding that it would no longer advise the King in respect of any reserved bill if this advice was contrary to the view of the Dominion concerned,[59] and furthermore that 'the power of disallowance can no longer be exercised in relation to Dominion legislation.'[60] It also relented to Ireland's demands over nationality, agreeing that:

> ... it is for each member of the Commonwealth to define for itself its own nationals, but that, so far as possible, these nationals should be persons possessing a common status, though it is recognised that local conditions or other special circumstances may from time to time necessitate divergencies from this general principle ...[61]

This was a set of massive constitutional concessions which changed overnight the definition of the British Commonwealth. Clearly, should India now achieve Dominion status, the implications were far graver from Britain's point of view than had existed even a couple of years before. Like South Africa and the Irish Free State, it could seize the compromises which had been made to become almost completely sovereign and independent overnight. The Viceroy would go, along with his responsibilities to London, replaced by a Governor-General obliged by constitution to effectively rubber-stamp any legislation passed by the Indian government. Under the influence of men such as Nehru it would only be a matter of time before all links with Britain were severed entirely. But still the British prevaricated, while the court of public opinion was not in Britain's favour. Its refusal to allow India what was now being assented to elsewhere was becoming an impossible position to maintain.

These stark realities served to inform the decision of an increasingly beleaguered Ramsay MacDonald, who succeeded Baldwin as Prime Minister, to hold the round-table conference demanded by Motilal Nehru. Labour politician Joseph Kenworthy felt that the conference would inevitably coalesce into two camps consisting of 'those who mean to struggle for complete independence, and those who still desire their country to remain within the Empire as a self-governing Dominion',[62] while others suspected the British of using the conference to kick the can back down the road. One critic saw it as a cynical ploy to 'show the world, particularly America that Indians were hopelessly divided among themselves and were not fit for self-government'.[63] Certainly few of the issues identified by the recent commission had come close to being addressed, let alone solved. Therefore it was questionable whether anyone could hope to achieve any sort of meaningful consensus.

Nonetheless, the first conference was opened on 30 November 1930 by King George V, attended by fifty-eight delegates from British India and sixteen from the Princely States, the Muslim League (which sent the Aga Khan and Ali Jinnah), and an assortment of other largely sympathetic Hindus and Muslims. The British government also fielded sixteen attendees, including Ramsay MacDonald and representatives of the Conservative and Liberal parties, but it was boycotted by the Congress whose leaders, including Gandhi and Nehru, were in prison. Furthermore, the Princes took with them their built-in veto because although Viceroy Lord Irwin expressed his conviction that the ultimate objective of British policy was to be the creation of a self-governing federation, the Princes would only agree if India remained within the British Empire.[64] Furthermore, Jinnah appeared ambivalent about the route map to be taken, with the result that the other delegates all seemed to interpret his motives in different ways. The *Manchester Guardian* claimed that 'the Hindus [think him] a Muslim communalist, the Muslims [take] him to be pro-Hindu, [and] the Princes [consider] him a rabid extremist, with the result that he was everywhere but nowhere.'[65] Certainly, he still appeared to share at this time the Princes' belief that only membership of the British Commonwealth offered protection from Hindu domination,[66] presenting a stumbling block which prompted another commentator, A. A. Ravoof, to conclude that 'there was no hope of unity' among the nationalists.[67] So, although those parties who participated agreed in principle on a federal form of government as the ultimate aim, with all but defence and finance devolved to Indians, the conference ended inconclusively. The absence of Congress meant that whatever decisions were reached meant little, while a dejected Jinnah decided to stay in the UK, and would not return home until 1934.

The machinations in London did not mean that fellow Muslims closer to home were waiting on events. Indeed on 29 December 1930, during the annual meeting of the Muslim League, eminent Islamic philosopher Allama Mohammed Iqbal gave further thought to their prospects should India quit the Empire altogether. He offered the prospect of 'the Punjab, North-West Frontier Province, Sind and Baluchistan amalgamated into a single state. Self-government within the British Empire, the formation of a consolidated North-West Indian Muslim state appears to me to be the final destiny of the Muslims at least of north-west India.'[68] But to Congress an independent India was one and indivisible, and such Balkanisation unacceptable. In any event, this was simple speculation so long as its leaders languished in prison. It was evident to many, including Kenworthy, that 'without the consent and agreement of Mahatma Gandhi, no proposals for an Indian Constitution will have much chance of acceptance.'[69] It was therefore reluctantly conceded that he would have to be released, and the current Viceroy Lord Irwin agreed to the so-called Gandhi–Irwin Pact of 5 March 1931. It meant that Congress rights would be restored, all prisoners released, and a moratorium placed on the application of arbitrary arrest, and in exchange Congress would enter into dialogue. Gandhi agreed and travelled to London for the second conference which started on 7 September 1931.

British policy was now in something of a state of flux because not only was there yet another Viceroy, Lord Willingdon, but since the end of October Ramsay MacDonald headed a national government. It included representatives from other parties, and especially the Conservatives who held starkly divergent ideas on the future direction of Indian policy from Labour's. Furthermore, suspicions had not been allayed that most of the pro-British delegates were essentially stooges and were being referred to as Khandar Ghulams or 'traditional slaves' in the pocket of the British.[70] Sceptics also knew that many imperialists looked forward to another debacle because it would prove that '[she] could not loosen her grip on India because India was a house divided in itself ... there would be bloodshed and civil war ... and by giving freedom to India, Britain would not be discharging its moral obligations towards the minority [Muslims].'[71]

In a way the British position was vindicated because Gandhi arrived armed with just two substantive aims: immediate self-rule and recognition of Congress as the sole representative of all Indians. He also reflected Nehru's position on Dominion status, announcing that 'Congress contemplates a connection with the British people – but that connection to be such as can exist between two absolute equals ... I have aspired – I still aspire – to be a citizen not in an Empire, but in a Commonwealth,'[72] but not in a British Commonwealth, entitled to only the status of a Dominion, but one in which 'either party should have the right to sever the connection.'[73] Such assertions naturally panicked the princes and alarmed the Muslims, and proved that there were indeed too many conflicting interests and contradictory demands for anything constructive to be achieved. Sardul Singh Kavishar, editor of the *Sikh Review*, was scathing in his assessment, describing 'wheels within wheels; wire pullers set to administer jerks to different parties from different positions. The result of such machination was that the conference ended without coming to any definite conclusion.'[74]

A third round-table conference followed from November 17 to 24 December 1932, but this too left all parties as divided as ever. Boycotted by Congress and the British Labour Party, only the princes and the Aga Khan plus a motley collection of forty-six other individuals participated, none with any real power to negotiate or speak with any authority. Resigned to the impossibility of reaching any consensus through negotiation, the British government decided instead to proceed on their own initiative, and produced a White Paper in March 1933. To rub salt into the wounds of nationalists the new arrangements agreed with the Dominions had also been codified and given formal expression through the Statute of Westminster Bill. It was hailed as 'an Act to give effect to certain resolutions passed by Imperial Conferences held in the years 1926 and 1930' and received royal assent on 11 December 1931. It released the Dominions, and any potential Dominions, from being bound by any legislation passed in London, unless 'the Dominion requested, and consented to the enactment thereof'.[75]

By contrast the White Paper offered India comparatively thin gruel. It ditched dyarchy and proposed a federal constitution devolving more power to the provinces with some financial independence through the creation of a reserve bank, and judicial freedom via a federal court. There was to be a central legislature consisting of two houses; a Lower House or Federal

Assembly, and the Upper House or Council of State, in which Muslims were guaranteed a third of the seats. The princes would also have the right to nominate one-third of the members of the Lower House, and two-fifths of the Upper House, but accession was voluntary, and federation could not become a reality unless they agreed to it. This was music to the ears of those blocking progress, like the Nizam of Hyderabad, but the patience of ordinary people was wearing thin. He was now being challenged by the Mulki League, which argued that 'federation is the right solution to the Indian problem ... Hyderabad must join to share the responsibility for the good government of a United Indian Empire.'[76] Nonetheless the Nizam held firm, his obduracy enraging even King George V, who admitted that he felt 'disgusted' by such 'vacillation'.[77] Another stumbling block was Congress, to whom the proposals were equally unacceptable. They saw in them a wasted decade of constitutional stagnation which had advanced Indian interests hardly at all, Nehru calling the White Paper little more than a 'charter of slavery'.[78] Jinnah too claimed that they were being imposed 'in the teeth of opposition in India and contrary to the solemn declaration of His Majesty's Government before the first Round Table Conference, that only those proposals which received the greatest common measure of agreement of the people of India would be placed before Parliament'.[79]

Inevitably temperatures boiled over again. Violence broke out, allegedly fomented by Indian newspapers, and in response the British rushed through yet more repressive legislation. A Criminal Law Amendment Act was passed on 19 December 1932 decreeing that, 'whoever publishes, circulates or repeats in public any passage from a newspaper, book or other document copies whereof have been declared to be forfeited to Government ... shall be punished with imprisonment for a term which may extend to six months, or with fine, or with both ... '[80] Such heavy-handedness was a red rag to the Congress bull, prompting Nehru to condemn it in the harshest terms. He argued that the need to pass such legislation was an admission that the Government was losing control, and one that:

> ... has to rely on the Criminal Law Amendment Act and similar laws, suppresses the press and literature, that bans hundreds of organisations, that keeps people in prison without trial and that does so many other things that are happening in India today, is a government that has ceased to have even a shadow of a justification for its existence.[81]

Despite such emotive oratory, there was no unanimity of purpose. Gandhi declined to join in the chorus of indignation, and declared he was going to dedicate more time and energy to the cause of the so-called 'Depressed Classes' and leave the struggle for self-government to others. He also called for an end to civil disobedience, leaving his erstwhile disciples crestfallen and feeling abandoned by their messiah. Subhas Chandra Bose, who had been his adoring protégé only three years before, scathingly referred to him now as 'an old, useless piece of furniture',[82] and set off to chart his own course. Congress naturally rejected the White Paper and repeated its demands for a new draft constitution and constituent assembly elected on the principle of universal adult suffrage. There was stalemate once again, while the British used the political vacuum to push through their latest initiative.

Yet while the key warring parties reached yet another impasse, there were many who felt their views and opinions had been side-lined and ignored in the haste to placate Congress. Although it continued to claim to represent all Indians irrespective of religion or race, Kenworthy reminded his readers that in fact, out of a total population of 350,000,000, Congress could at most command the allegiance of half a million members at any one time,[83] a statistic even prominent nationalists were hard-pressed to refute. Nehru himself was forced to admit that 'we represent largely the intelligentsia of this country only ... directly at any rate, the 2 or 3 or 5 per cent,'[84] leaving 95 per cent of Indians effectively with no voice. For them all the conversations about constitutions and assemblies, the franchise and self-government were mere abstract semantics with no relevance to their day to day lives. Indians content with moderate reform were also being marginalised. In addition to the princes there were moderate Muslims, Hindus and Sikhs, plus numerous other minorities drowned out by the better organisation of the Muslim League and Congress. Kenworthy went so far as to claim that 'there will be irreconcilables whatever settlement is reached ... I, for one, would feel easier about the future if we showed half the anxiety to satisfy the legitimate concerns of our friends that we have to placate the implacable ... [demands] of our avowed enemies.'[85]

But while Congress was charged with being unrepresentative, the League was accused of being virtually impotent. In the opinion of many of its erstwhile supporters it had become practically a 'dead organisation' staffed by 'a cockpit of retrograde title holders and communal wranglers'[86] which needed to be rescued from its inertia. Others accused it of existing 'only in name'.[87] Combined, these factors did not augur well for the future, further underlined by the outcome of the 1934 elections to the Central Legislative Assembly. Congress, fighting the election on a platform of opposing the White Paper, emerged as the largest party with forty-two seats. The recently formed Congress Nationalist party, a breakaway group which opposed Congress over communal electorates, won another twelve and Jinnah, having been persuaded to return from London to lead the party, was also elected. He was, however, joined by only forty other Muslim independents. Congress then proceeded to exploit its victory not only to move a resolution opposing the British government's proposals, but to reject a trade agreement which was being negotiated between the two countries.

As the acrimony and instability continued, Westminster was progressing the White Paper to its next stages through Parliament. Here Churchill, one of its most vocal opponents and for all the wrong reasons at one with the Congress, condemned it as a document 'built by pygmies'[88] which was attempting to introduce a form of 'democracy [that] is totally unsuited to India'.[89] It would, he added, simply lead to 'liberty for one set of Indians to exploit another',[90] echoing Muslim fears as well as those of other minorities. Nonetheless, the government had the votes and despite such resistance, in 1935 the bill had passed successfully through its various stages to become the Government of India Act. The government wanted it to be seen not just as a landmark in constitutional reform but more representative of the previously disenfranchised millions. To this end the vote was extended to 30,000,000 Indians, of whom many more were women. Although the usual property qualifications remained, and voters were still primarily landowners and better-off farmers, at least some progress had been made. It was intended that this great stride in the country's road to independence should be put to the test in the provincial elections of 1937.

Inevitably, the Act was the topic of heated debate at the 1936 Session of Congress. Some, among them Nehru, proposed boycotting the elections in protest, but it was finally agreed to fight the Raj from within. A resolution was passed condemning the Act but accepting participation in the elections on a manifesto which would include the demand for a Constituent Assembly to define the country's future status and constitution. Electors, including the new raft of recently enfranchised voters, went to the polls as planned in all eleven British provinces over the winter of 1936–37. The results were declared in February 1937, Congress winning 758 of 1,500 seats and forming governments in the United Provinces, Bihar, the Central Provinces, Bombay and Madras. The Muslim League only won a quarter of the seats reserved for Muslims, the remainder being taken by regional Muslim parties, a further body blow for its prestige and undermining its claim to represent all Muslims. It was the largest party in only three provinces and in these Congress jealously guarded its successes and refused to form any coalitions. Furthermore, although Congress only fought fifty-eight of the 482 Muslim seats, their candidates won twenty-six of them. Nehru then seized upon the results to announce confidently that they 'proved that the Congress was the real representative of the people, Hindu and Muslim; and it nailed to the counter the claim of the Muslim League to be the sole representative of Muslims in India'.[91]

The elections may therefore have been the best reflection of democratic opinion the country had achieved so far, but they also served to further expose the deep divides running through its various communities. Nor did they advance the aim of real self-government as long as the legislation that enabled it to be realised remained in British hands. Nehru explained the new reality in February 1938 during a visit to London:

If the British Government itself changes the India Act [improvements could be made] but as it is, even if ninety-nine or a hundred per cent of the people of India want to change it they cannot do so. It has no seeds of change in it; it is a permanent fixing of chairs ... The only choice that is offered to the Indian people is to submit to it, or if they want to change it, to revolt against it in some form or other. The League of Nations might perhaps help India, [however] the so-called Indian representatives ... are nominated by the Government of India in consultation with the British Government so that they really represent in the League the viewpoint of the British Government, they do not represent in the slightest Indian public opinion ...[92]

The prospects therefore appeared bleak as the country approached the close of the 1930s. Indians could only believe that the promises being made by politicians, British and nationalist, might bear fruit sometime in the future. But for many thousands of the desperate and disenfranchised, a different route out of poverty and despair had been attempted. Having forsaken hope of any improvement in their lot at home, they decided instead on a huge leap of faith, seeking a better life elsewhere, far beyond India's shores.

7

'A new slave trade'

The prospects for a new life arose for many from the abolition of slavery. The Emancipation Act of 1833 released from bondage millions who for centuries had toiled throughout the Empire without reward, often brutally treated and exchanged like cattle. But having been made aware of their newly conferred rights, they refused to work instead for paltry wages under conditions little better than those from which they had been liberated. Consequently, as one European observed, 'now that the slaves were free ... [the Africans] refused to engage themselves as labourers, and the planters' position became serious.'[1] Suddenly confronted with a dire manpower problem, unless the planters secured alternative sources of labour quickly they would soon go out of business. India, it was concluded, offered the most suitable substitutes, containing an endless supply of labourers who could be exploited well beyond the reach of the Indian government.

Clearly the plantation owners did not want to pay decent wages, so the system of recruitment called 'indenture' was adopted instead. In theory, under a scheme formalised by the Government of India in 1837, a worker was supposed to sign up for a set number of years to work for an employer who would then discharge him and fund his passage home. During his indenture, he would be entitled to decent working and living conditions and enjoy the protection of the terms of his contract. But instead, swiftly opened to criminal abuse and corruption, it degenerated into a system which was damned as having created 'a new slave trade'.[2] Scheming, unscrupulous and corrupt Indenture Agents deliberately misled unwary recruits, in the words of one critic 'by the most fraudulent contracts, to labour for years for scanty wages and scanty fare, separated from their families and from their homes; compelled to perform the hardest agricultural labour known, at the discretion of their masters and without the protection of an upright, impartial, and efficient magistracy'.[3] In the light of such exposés, reformers began campaigning for 'all the fraudulent contracts into which the coolies have been induced to enter ... [to] be immediately cancelled and the unfortunate victims of cupidity be permitted to return home'.[4] But with huge profits to be made, the lure of hard cash far outweighed any humanitarian considerations and the system would endure for nearly a century.

The first ordeal to which they were subjected was the long and sometimes fatal sea journeys in cramped, insanitary conditions little better than those of eighteenth-century slavers. One account describes migrants being unceremoniously 'hurried on board, put under hatches ... and shipped in large numbers on board vessels without the requisite accommodation, food or medical assistance',[5] and if this was not bad enough, many 'were made to pay for the privilege of coming on deck ... for a few gasps of precious fresh air'.[6] This horrendous experience was invariably the consequence of one of the first lies: few of the labourers signing up for work had any idea whether British Guiana was in southern India or South America, or Fiji in the South Pacific or southern Africa. When, in 1884, labourers in British Guiana absconded from their plantation and were eventually caught, the deceit used by agents was laid bare. Asked why they had fled into the jungle they replied that they had been reliably informed that if they kept going they would eventually reach a mountain, on the other side of which was a road that would take them back to Calcutta.[7]

One of the first consignments to endure this experience was that of the so-called 'Gladstone Coolies', who landed in British Guiana on 22 May 1838 after a nightmare passage from Calcutta.[8] Out of 104 that started out, fourteen died en route,[9] a mortality rate that would plateau during this early period to around twenty-six per thousand. Among the approximately 100,000 Indians who travelled to British Guiana in the twenty-five years after 1875, the average death rate did improve to 6.4 per thousand per month, although it increased again to 7.3 between 1901 and 1917.[10] Nonetheless, these numbers were still not much better than the death rate for slaves transported from Africa to the West Indies and South America, which was approximately 10 per cent.

The treatment meted out when they arrived was little better. With no time to recover from the hideous journey or acclimatise to their new home, they were promptly allotted to their master in a manner, wrote one observer, 'suggestive of the transfer of a flock of sheep'.[11] One group who landed at Demerara encountered further indignities because 'there was no building prepared for their reception ... [instead] the sick house was emptied of its patients to make room for them; and ... in dour rooms in that sick house, the whole eighty-two coolies were thrust ... men, women and children, without regard to delicacy or decency ... and kept in that loathsome den for three months before a shed could be erected for their shelter.'[12]

These sheds were generally constructed in areas segregated from Europeans in so-called 'lines'. They were invariably little more than mean rows of substandard hovels affording little shelter, poor sanitation and precious little if any privacy, no better than the shacks allocated to the ex-slaves. Living in such conditions inevitably affected their health, inflicting ailments such as hook worm, nausea and diarrhoea, sores, yaws, tuberculosis and other debilitating and often fatal ailments.[13] Such were the conditions in which they were expected to exist that out of ninety who survived the journey to British Guiana in 1838, nineteen did not survive longer than two years on the plantation.[14] Nor were these outcomes unique to British Guiana. Labourers on the distant island of Mauritius in the Indian Ocean regularly faced mortality rates of 8 to 9 per cent a year.[15] Workers' health was not only affected by their dire living conditions; they were also regularly subjected to unremitting and brutal ill treatment. Of 335 labourers admitted to the colonial hospital of Port of Spain, Trinidad, in 1863, eighty-two died[16] as a result not just of illness but also 'the whip, the bamboo and the dungeon [which] were constantly resorted to to compel labour or gratify revenge'.[17]

Owners sought to justify such abuse by claiming that unless labourers were beaten, often they would get no work out of them. This was because, as one employer admitted, 'their simple wants are confined to a few yards of cotton ... a small quantity of coconut oil, a few pounds of rice, and a few peppers ... [and] one or two days' work is enough to provide them with a week's subsistence.'[18] Thus, having fulfilled their contracted number of hours or tasks for the week, they assumed the rest of their time was their own. But when beatings failed trickery and sharp practices were employed instead. What constituted a day's work, or a required number of tasks, was decided by the employer, and therefore how much or whether they had earned their wages. Deductions were made for lateness, illness – interpreted as malingering – and most especially alleged poor and substandard work. As one Edward Jenkins noted, although their needs were modest they were also 'living hand to mouth [so] the stoppage of their wages ... is a very serious matter for them'.[19]

But the chicanery of the employers did not end with these cunning ruses. Throughout the system, planters were also magistrates who found other ways of extending not just their working hours but, where possible, their months or years of contract. This was often achieved through the imposition of punitive punishments for petty infractions or minor crimes. On Trinidad there were 686 convictions in 1863 for offences ranging from arson, assault, breach of the peace, fraud, theft, larceny, riotous and disorderly conduct and trespass.[20] In British Guiana, a total of 32,876 charges were brought by Europeans, most of these being against indentured labourers.[21] In many cases, the prison sentences which they had to serve were added to the time outstanding on their contract,[22] holding them in servitude for additional months or years. In Trinidad, another ingenious trick was played on labourers who had worked their contract. Their employers could insist that they had to work for a further five years in order to earn an 'industrial residence' certificate to qualify for their free passage home.[23]

Locked into this feudal and arcane system, the labourers were almost defenceless. Many employers simply avoided any sort of censure by abusing their power and intimidating their labourers to dissuade them from complaining in the first place.[24] Those who did try to get justice faced an uphill struggle and insurmountable barriers. Edward Jenkins recorded how 'the indentured labourer finds himself convicted often upon the sole evidence of his employer or a subordinate; he is not allowed to give evidence on his own behalf,'[25] and few even had any understanding of the legal processes to which they were being subjected. Even if they were to have any knowledge of the law, they could not afford to pay for legal representation or to challenge the word of a white man, the consequences of which could be further beatings or punishment on another trumped-up charge. Often, only the support of sympathetic Europeans gave them any chance of redress. In 1871 a German resident on Mauritius, Mr Alphonse de Plevitz, came to their aid when he published a pamphlet exposing the planters' 'shameful injustice towards the Indian labourers',[26] and who had sufficient clout to prompt the despatch of a royal commission from India to look into the accusations. Its members remained on the island from April to October 1873 taking evidence and investigating the claims, but the outcome showed the extent to which the planters held all the cards. Although in their subsequent report they recommended a 'series of stringent measures for the welfare of Indians',[27] they amounted to little more than a slap on the wrist, and after a brief respite the abuses continued much as before.

As well as abuse and mistreatment, life in this twilight world involved trying to adjust to a strange society and an alien culture where plantations became melting pots and microcosms of society back home. However, whereas there the various religions and distinct communities largely kept themselves to themselves, once allocated to a plantation they were all thrown together. Of the 143,939 Indians who migrated to Trinidad between 1845 and 1917, for example, most were from north India but there were also Bengalis and south Indians, of whom 85 per cent were Hindus and 14 per cent Muslims between the ages of twenty and thirty.[28] Of the 45,833 labourers who made the trip to Fiji from Calcutta between 1879 and 1916, 16 per cent were high caste, 31 per cent middle agricultural castes, 6.7 per cent artisan castes and 31 per cent so-called Untouchables. The remainder were Tamil and Telegu speakers from Madras and the Malabar Coasts, also mostly middle agricultural castes.[29] It was therefore inevitable that frictions would emerge and confrontations result. Such tensions could perhaps be taken for granted in male-dominated environments, but they were also exacerbated by an acute shortage of the opposite sex.

The reason was that contracts were limited to 'labour units' rather than family groups. Only those capable of the hard work expected of them were wanted, and consequently women were rarely recruited. It was not unusual to find a ratio of just forty females to every hundred men, and of 19,050 labourers who went to work in Mauritius in 1840, only 205 were female. Numerous lonely and frustrated men fighting over or having to share the same woman was a recipe for trouble, and invariably, 'one woman in the lines was expected to satisfy three or four unofficial husbands besides many other outsiders.'[30] In some cases, the situation was made worse by overseers or managers also deciding to 'form temporary connections with coolie women',[31] resulting in 'the worst possible consequences for the good order and harmony of the estate'.[32] Consequently, the most 'horrible and revolting depravity and demoralisation'[33] was encountered in the lines, which frequently took on the appearance of glorified bordellos. Florence Garnham, one of many campaigners fighting for better conditions, visited Fiji as late as 1918 where even after eighty years little had improved. She uncovered a still 'unspeakably corrupt' society, where it 'was quite impossible … for a woman to preserve her chastity'.[34]

It was therefore perhaps hardly surprising that the employers and white society in general looked down upon their Indian workers. Many dreaded the consequences should their influence reach the black populations of their colonies. A Jamaican missionary wrote, 'I need not say how extremely dangerous it is to our poor negroes, who are just emerging from darkness … to be called upon constantly to mingle with a people so debased in all their habits as the coolies.'[35] Distressed white Mauritians shared his feeling of foreboding, scared that their 'pagan superstitions … and the vices inseparable from them'[36] might spread from the confines of their own communities. On Fiji, Methodist missionary Cyril Bavin reflected, 'It is a matter of surprise and thankfulness that the life of the "lines" is not worse, considering the undue proportion of India's criminal classes who emigrate to Fiji.'[37]

By no means did all Europeans despise the Indian labourers, however. Some indeed found them for the most part industrious and hardworking. In Mauritius one noted how 'if the emancipated blacks had the good conduct of the Indian labourers … not only on the score of labour, cleanliness etc. but general good behaviour, it would add to the general welfare and prosperity of the colony.'[38] The chances of this were for the most part remote, because the black population, irked by being undercut by these interlopers, 'looks down on the coolie as an inferior'.[39] Such attitudes served to foster instead a mutual hostility which could have tragic consequences. In June 1890 Herbert Thomas, a white Jamaican policeman, arrived at the scene of the drowning of an Indian woman in a river. He discovered that the Africans were refusing to retrieve the body unless they were first paid five or ten pounds, which the Indians would not hand over. After he waded into the river and dragged her body out himself, 'the coolies went wild with delight ... cursing the negroes in English until their stock of invectives in that tongue was exhausted.'[40]

Sometimes the bad blood fostered by such sectarianism could lead to greater tragedies, pitting Europeans against both the other communities. In October 1884 on the island of Trinidad the atmosphere was already sour when the annual Hasay Festival approached. Scheduled for the 30th was a celebration of the martyrdom of Mohammad's nephews Hosein and Hassan, which Indians had introduced to the island and which had been adopted by many Africans. Crowds of 8,000 or 10,000 revellers were quite usual, but the authorities and white planters were nervous and feared trouble. When the crowds approached San Fernando, where the festival was to conclude, the local police had been instructed to prevent them entering the town. When this failed, and orders to disperse were refused, the police panicked and opened fire. Several volleys were poured into the unarmed and helpless festivalgoers, killing as many as twenty-two marchers and wounding more than a hundred.

One might have assumed therefore that they could not wait to see the back of such regimes, but many did choose to remain, most likely because they felt the poverty they would return to held little better prospects for them. Consequently, out of 40,220 labourers who went to British Guiana from 1871, between 17,000 and 18,000 opted to re-indenture; just 3,063 returned out of the 26,231 who had originally migrated to Trinidad between 1851 and 1865.[41] Furthermore, it was not considered unusual for some workers to renew their contracts several times and clock up a total of thirty years' service.[42] A minority of those who did finally make the voyage back home did so as self-made men. An envious European recorded how the 'amount of savings of the coolies taken away by them on the *British Trident*, which left Trinidad on the 14 December 1865 was £12,408 4s 2d'.[43] Another man who left the island in 1869 after ten years of indenture had allegedly amassed the princely sum of $10,000,[44] while 2,828 labourers who returned to India between 1834 and 1869 took with them a total of £95,000.[45] Of course these sums were hardly likely to have been accrued by ordinary labouring, but far more likely from various commercial enterprises entered into after their contract expired. After all, as Edward Jenkins conceded, 'no attempt has hitherto been made to discover whether the method by which the well-to-do among them have made their money was one equally open to the majority of their compatriots.'[46] In fact, a report of 1924 concluded that the average labourer in British Guiana was unlikely to save more than $162 after even ten years' hard work.[47]

Those who did stay on also transformed the demographic profiles of their adopted homes. One Trinidadian observed how 'the coolies may be regarded ... as a rapidly growing portion of the population ... and if the increase should go on in the same ratio ... then in 1871, their numbers are likely to be about 40,000 or more,'[48] an assessment echoed elsewhere. Between 1845 and 1921 36,000 Indians, mainly Hindus, travelled to Jamaica and two-thirds of them also remained, having been offered incentives such as land grants to stay and continue to develop the island's economy.[49] It was a strategy that seemed to work. In 1906 it was noted that 'in Jamaica are to be found today many East Indians who thrive in the island and do much useful labour in a characteristically unostentatious manner.'[50]

A total of 450,000 Indian labourers also made the trip to Mauritius[51] and their impact on the island's demographics was also considerable. A census in 1846 indicated that there were already 48,935 male and 7,310 female Indians living on the island,[52] but by 1934, out of a total population of 393,733, 265,429 were former labourers or the descendants of Indian workers.[53] Here too, observers were impressed by their diligence and industry. An official report explained how 'one of the most striking features of the progress Mauritius has made has been the social and economic development of the Indians who today own and cultivate more than two-fifths of the whole area under sugar cane,'[54] living in arguably one of the most ethnically diverse of all Britain's colonies. Author and traveller Lanka Sundaram wrote at the time that 'Indians enjoy the same civic and civil rights as any other citizen without distinction of caste or creed,'[55] concluding optimistically that the island 'could well be a standing example to other units of the British Commonwealth of Nations wherever Indians find themselves entrenched today',[56] although unlikely to sway the views of men such as Nehru. One of its biggest success stories was that of Doohkee Gungah who, born to Indian migrants, began his working life on Mauritius cutting cane sugar in the 1870s. He died in 1944 one of its richest men.[57]

Not all Britain's colonies were quite so effusive. Between 1879 and 1916 60,000 Indians made the journey to Fiji, and by 1906 a *Times* correspondent predicted that 'it seems as if they … are about to replace the natives and become the permanent population.'[58] This was precisely what concerned many ethnic Fijians, reservations not assuaged by the fact that despite many returning home or moving to New Zealand, there were 77,000 on the island by the end of 1930, and by 1935 constituted 85,892 out of a total population of 202,052.[59]

Despite the many abuses and shortcomings of the discredited indenture system, it persisted well into the twentieth century. But by 1916 a combination of factors pushed the Government of India to announce its intention to phase out the practice. This was largely due to the growing influence and authority being exercised by Indians under the new reforms but, as Mahatma Gandhi recalled, 'the Viceroy had made no secret of the meaning of "eventual abolition", which, as he said, was abolition "within such reasonable time as will allow of alternative arrangements to be introduced."'[60] The canny employers had secured a 'slight' five-year transition so that, with the need for existing contracts to expire, it did not entirely come to an end until 1921,[61] by which time they hoped to have devised an equally exploitative scheme.

However, the indenture system was not the only by-product of the demand for Indian brawn. Unlike the islands of the West Indies and the Indian and Pacific Oceans, nearer neighbours such as Burma had acted as pull factors for much longer. Before indenture became a byword for migration, the highly lucrative spice trade of the sixteenth and seventeenth centuries attracted Indian entrepreneurs, traders and merchants, a movement accelerated with Britain's expansionist policies in the nineteenth century. The incremental annexations of Burma from 1824 also brought its immense potential as a major rice producer to the fore, and farmers were offered grants as incentives to develop the land.[62] Such enterprises would eventually expand the area under cultivation from 700,000 to 6,000,000 acres and the amount of rice and paddy exported from Lower Burma would increase from 162,000 tons in 1855 to 2,000,000 tons by 1905-1906.[63] But like plantations elsewhere around the Empire, this massive industry needed labourers. People were required to clear swamps and jungle for the paddy fields and maintain the banks which protected the crops from saltwater inundation. Then labourers were needed to work the fields and sow and harvest the rice, but the native Burmese proved unwilling to undertake such work. Thus employers and estate owners again had to look for alternative sources of labour.[64]

At first Indians were engaged for the season and then returned home, but as the industry developed many entered into three-year contracts,[65] which exposed them to the same sharp practices as their countrymen elsewhere. Agents, in collaboration with mill owners and plantation managers, circumvented the Government of India regulations, making all sorts of promises to secure the workers as bonded rather than bona fide contract labourers. This became known as the so-called Kangani system, the main result of which was an unsupervised free flow of workers into the country where they could be mistreated, exploited and overworked. They also fell prey to moneylenders of the Chettiar caste, mainly from the Madras Presidency, who followed them. By 1901 there were 3,200 of them in the Delta, contributing to the plight of labourers already caught in the trap of indebtedness and poverty by the Kangani System.[66]

Despite such abuses, conditions at home provided a continuous source of volunteers, so that by the 1930s 53 per cent of all labourers on the rice fields were from the subcontinent.[67] In their wake also came entrepreneurs and small businessmen to service their needs and add to the growing Indian presence, and as a consequence the Indian population continued to rise exponentially. Whereas in 1872 they were just under 5 per cent or 136,504 out of a total of 2,747,148, by 1931 they constituted 1,017,825 out of 14,667,146 or just below 7 per cent.[68] By 1901 Bengali had become the third most widely spoken language in the country,[69] and in 1931 Rangoon's total population of 400,415 included 212,929 Indians, with Hindustani the city's virtual lingua franca.[70] Their contribution to the economy also reflected their growing importance to the country. Out of 198,760 main earners in the city

145,715 were Indian businessmen, as were 27 per cent of all male earners in Burma as a whole, together contributing half of the government's tax take.[71] The prosperous port of Sittwe, which had become one of the busiest rice-exporting cities in the world by 1931, had an Indian community comprising 97 per cent of its 210,000 people, half of whom had been born there.[72] Yangon, Bassein, Moulmein and the rice-processing mills were almost exclusively operated by Indians,[73] with Indian labour also constituting 26 per cent of the food industry, nearly 29 per cent of the metal industry, over 37 per cent of the workforce in bridge and road construction, and nearly 60 per cent of those employed in posts and telegraphs. Furthermore, half of those in water transport and 53 per cent of those employed in the chemical industry were Indian.[74]

By the time Burma was detached from the rest of the Indian Empire and became a separate colony in 1937, Indians had also come to dominate many other walks of life, especially in the administration and civil service, their posts effectively protected from Burmese competition by the British establishment. As Burmese nationalism took on a new dynamic, however, they now faced growing calls from native graduates for a greater share in government.[75] This resentment had long led to Indians bearing the epithet *kala lumyo*, or 'dirty aliens', but now it was boiling to the surface throughout the country and anti-Indian activity became more common.[76] The animosity was such that when the Japanese invaded many Burmese initially welcomed them as saviours, and when the Indians fled the country vengeful locals sacked their shops and warehouses and burnt down their homes.

Ironically it was only the arrival of Japanese troops that halted the carnage,[77] but the invaders had something far worse in store for those who had failed to escape. Apart from using them for bayonet and target practice, thousands were impressed to work on the infamous Burma–Thailand Railway, many of them among the 154,000 Commonwealth prisoners of war and other forced labourers who are believed to have perished in its construction.[78] On 1 August 1943, the Japanese cynically granted the country its independence, imperilling the now helpless Indian population even more, and although the British succeeded in reoccupying the country, it was only a few years before genuine independence from Britain was achieved in 1948. Without the restraining hand of the former colonial power to protect them, many more Indians lost their livelihoods and their homes in a country that became increasingly insular, isolated and hostile to foreigners.[79]

Farther south, the entire Malay Peninsula had been a magnet for Indian pirates from as early as the eleventh century,[80] sacking and raiding coastal communities and hauling away any booty that could be seized. They were followed by Muslim missionaries seeking to convert the local populations to Islam,[81] and when the British established themselves here they soon realised its potential. The Government of India began transporting convicts from the Presidencies to Penang in 1788, and then from 1825 to Malacca and the island of Singapore. Singapore had only been settled in 1819, and received its first inmates on 18 April 1825, seventy-nine men and one woman followed by another shipload of 122 a week later.[82] The island soon became the preeminent prison of the expanding Straits Settlements, and in 1857 it had 2,139 convicts, mostly the Thugees and dacoits the British had been flushing out. Many were put to work establishing the new colony's infrastructure, building St Andrew's Cathedral, Government House and other public buildings.[83] Others were used to build its roads, lighthouses, prisons and some even served as firefighters and auxiliary riot police.[84] Trusted convicts were often paroled and granted tickets of leave, and subsequently remained on the island or went on to work elsewhere along the peninsula.

After the penal settlement closed down in 1867, most inmates were transferred to the Andamans, but many of those who had been released married female convicts and set up small businesses or settled down as smallholders.[85] By 1871, when the agricultural potential of the peninsula had been recognised and its plantations were well established, the original community in 1786 of 2,000 had expanded to over 33,000.[86] The demand for Indian labour was also stimulated by the fact that, as in Burma, the native Malays spurned the kind of work which was being offered[87] because, as one commentator rather drily put it, 'the indigenous population ... has been content to secure with a minimum of human effort the means of maintaining a stagnant and non-exigent standard of life.'[88] So the ambitious and profit-hungry planters who needed a ready supply of reliable, hardworking and above all cheap labour obtained the required manpower from nearby India. Many served as indentured labourers or under the Kangani system, but their exploitation began even before they commenced their new jobs. Before being paid they were required to pay off any transport or other costs incurred getting to Malaya, which meant that many started off indebted to employers who immediately had a hold over them,[89] and like their compatriots in Burma made them prey to moneylenders. Moreover, despite the high demand, every effort was taken to drive down costs further and further and this could mean that because, as one observer admitted, 'naked methods of slavery could not be employed ... [other] methods were adopted which undoubtedly involved some form of serfdom.'[90]

Sometimes the desperation of Indians with few options was nakedly exploited, as in the case of those weavers who had lost their livelihoods to the British and instead were given free passage to work on the sugar and coffee plantations and tin mines.[91] As well as being cheap, plentiful and sometimes desperate, they had to be able to endure the climate of the region. Recruitment was therefore mainly restricted to South Indians because they were already acclimatised to the harsh conditions they were to encounter.[92] Consequently, up to 80 per cent of the migrants were Tamil speakers and the remainder Telugus, Malayalis, Canaris and Oriyas,[93] many of whom were in such poor physical condition that they had to be screened before they left India. Upon arrival they were quarantined for a week and given smallpox inoculations to make sure they did not spread sickness and disease throughout the colony. Following these indignities, the familiar pattern of abuse and exploitation became a feature of their lives, although being closer to home they could at least have their complaints addressed more easily.

In response to reports of maltreatment, some effort was made in 1884 to regulate the system when the Straits Ordinance was passed. This statute attempted to improve the wages for indentured workers by setting them at twelve cents a day for the first year, rising to fourteen cents a day for each subsequent year.[94] But the bosses still held the whip hand, and they knew that there was no shortage of desperate Indians willing to undercut existing wages; supply always outstripped demand. This also had drastic consequences for the Malays. By 1891 the Indian population had grown to 76,000 and in 1901 stood at approximately 119,000,[95] with 90,000 new arrivals annually.[96] By 1911 the figure stood at 268,269, by 1921 470,180, by 1931 621,847,[97] and in 1941 640,000,[98] constituting over 80 per cent of the labour force.[99] These numbers inevitably had a profound effect on the population. For example, by 1911 Indians were a quarter of Selangor's population, rising to a third in 1921, and by 1941 they were in the majority,[100] with similar consequences for other parts of the peninsula.

Until 1887 the majority had come to work in the sugar, coffee and rice industries, but after 1900 these were gradually displaced by global demand for rubber and palm oil.[101] Rubber in particular proved to be a boon for the planters, and it was arguably the industry in which Indians were most exploited. Whenever the price of the commodity fell the planters simply used the threat of supplanting Indian labour with Chinese coolies to drive their wages down further.[102] As one contemporary observer noted, 'it is unnecessary to emphasise the value of cheap Indian labour'[103] as inevitably 'modern big business will pay lip sympathy to humanitarianism and benevolence in the interests of its business.'[104] It was therefore thanks largely to white business acumen and Indian sweated labour that the colony grew, expanded and boomed. Tin production rose from 4,200 tons in 1874 to 51,335 tons in 1913, rubber exports from 104 tons in 1905 to 56,782 tons in 1915, with total trade increasing in value from £3,000,000 in 1885 to £15,000,000 in 1905.[105]

Nonetheless, pressure for reform and improvements was growing. In 1904 an Immigrant Protection Act required planters to meet minimum standards of medical care and access to hospitals,[106] and slowly, male workers' wives were allowed to accompany them.[107] But this was no panacea; the death rate among workers in 1911 was still 62.9 per thousand, many succumbing to their appalling treatment and conditions which allowed tuberculosis and malaria to flourish.[108] Finally, in an attempt to stem these losses an ordinance was passed in 1912 requiring planters to notify the authorities of all malaria deaths,[109] a measure intended to both assist in monitoring working conditions and make the planters more accountable. But even into the 1920s the 'lines' remained dangerous placed to live, with infant mortality still as high as one in five.[110] Matters took a new turn when their plight reached the ears of the International Labour Office in Geneva, which had been founded as an arm of the League of Nations in 1919. Its findings resulted in demands for better sanitation, medical services and even maternity benefits and education,[111] and was followed by a commission appointed in 1921 to investigate conditions and suggest improvements. These recommendations formed the basis of the Health Board Enactment of 1926,[112] but only when pressure from the Government of India joined forces with Malayan Indian welfare bodies would higher standards of housing begin to appear prior to the Second World War.[113]

Nonetheless, their position remained precarious, and as many as 53,367 labourers were repatriated to India in 1932 when a slump in world trade rendered them surplus to requirements.[114] Between 1930 and 1933, a total of 250,000 were repatriated, among whom were those who, because there was no social security or old-age benefits, were callously returned purely because they could no longer work.[115] This policy was in part, too, the consequence of the authorities' determination to discourage permanent residency, which would have given them greater security and more rights. In the words of one critic, the 'Indian labourer is welcome not as a prospective or potential settler, but as a wage-earning worker only'.[116] A greater voice in Malayan affairs was finally secured with the establishment of the Central Indian Association of Malaya in 1937, which alongside stronger labour unions improved wages and conditions, and there was further reinforcement of workers' rights through improving representation on the legislative councils.[117] Jawaharlal Nehru also showed sympathy for their plight by paying two visits in 1937 and 1938, but despite all these efforts, as one critic observed, 'the vast majority of them [Indians] have risen no higher than their miserable starting point and have lived out their brief Malayan lives within a radius of a few miles from the dingy coolie lines in which they slept.'[118]

The higher-caste Brahmins and Christians arguably had a more positive experience, often performing white-collar work for the government or in the plantations offices,[119] and Sikhs and Muslim Jats were recruited as policemen and as watchmen in the tin mines and estates. Thus, by 1939 the Indian colony in Malaya as in Burma was well established in all the higher echelons of public life from commerce and trade to politics and civil rights, creating a petite bourgeoise or middle-class clique all of its own.[120] They also dominated the civil administration, with the seven key government departments employing 3,181 Indians against only 1,742 Malays.[121] They therefore attracted the enmity of ethnic Malayans, who wanted a greater share of the wealth being created in their country. Having eschewed an active role in the building of the peninsula's prosperity, they now felt overlooked and marginalised.

Inevitably, intercommunal tensions increased throughout the 1930s and when strikes broke out in Selangor in 1941 they soon turned violent. The demands were reasonable enough: pay equal to that offered to the Chinese, a shorter working day, the right to free speech and assembly and to form a trade union. They even felt the need to include a demand that European men desist from molesting their wives.[122] But the plantation owners, abetted by the authorities, were in no mood to negotiate. As the atmosphere deteriorated the government declared a state of emergency, provoking more violence and the arrest of over 300 strikers. Five were killed and many more arrested, prosecuted and subsequently deported back to India.[123] When the Japanese conquest of the peninsula materialised, the pre-war tensions exploded into an orgy of brutality as thousands shared the fate of their compatriots in Burma. Those who failed to escape found themselves burnt out of their homes and businesses by Malays or sent to work and die on the railway. Only liberation in 1945 returned the few survivors to any kind of normality, but their lives would never be the same again.

8

'Provide against the influx of Asiatics'

After Britain annexed Natal in southern Africa in 1845, colonists soon appreciated the suitability of the climate and the soil for large-scale agriculture, particularly the cultivation of sugar. Experiments began in 1848 exploiting the experience of Mauritian indentured labourers who prepared the land and built the necessary infrastructure. When these proved successful the first mill was opened in 1850. It did not take long for the businessmen, landowners and politicians to grasp the vast profits to be made by massively expanding the industry but once again the indigenous population was noticeable for its reticence to undertake the work involved. There followed considerable debate as to the best means to acquire the right labour, until at a meeting held on 10 October 1851 it was finally agreed that 'the introduction of the coolies [from India] would be the salvation of the colony.'[1] In anticipation, 15,000 cane tops were imported from Mauritius in 1852 and more mills were opened. But it would be some time before the necessary legislation could be enacted due to protracted negotiations with the Indian government. Eventually in 1859 Coolie Law 14 was enacted, paving the way for the importation of the required manpower,[2] and the wherewithal for the colony to proceed with large-scale cultivation of the crop.

A year later, on 17 November 1860, the first shipload of 341 labourers arrived aboard the SS *Truro*, the vanguard of 152,184 Indians who would make the trip between 1860 and 1911 under the well-tried indenture system.[3] Their three-week journey was slightly less arduous than the one month it took to sail to Fiji or nearer five weeks to Trinidad, but as usual they encountered working and living conditions far from those they were led to expect when they signed their contracts. In addition to poor food (especially a shortage of rice), inadequate medical treatment and accommodation was the state of near-permanent penury through the usual arbitrary deductions imposed for the slightest of excuses. They were also overworked and forced to undertake more than their contracted hours. For those suspected of malingering or feigning illness and exhaustion, there was always recourse to the lash.[4]

However, being closer to India than most of the other plantations around the world, more of those with the right to return home at the end of their indenture did so. They then used the opportunity to expose the extent of their ill treatment to the authorities and as the evidence mounted up, the Indian government was compelled to take notice. In 1871 it suspended further transports and put the Government of Natal on notice that no more would be permitted until the claims of maltreatment were investigated. In response, the Natal Government reluctantly instituted a so-called 'Coolie Commission',[5] which was established in 1872 to look into the claims and produce recommendations. Superficially, they represented a sea change in attitudes towards the workers. They included the maintenance of proper records of wages, as well as of births, deaths and marriages, improved medical care and the appointment of a so-called 'Protector' who would adjudicate in disputes between the labourer and the employer. It was also proposed that a grant of between 8 and 10 acres be made at the end of their indentures in lieu of passage home. The Indian government expressed itself satisfied with the investigation, and sailings were resumed.

But it was not long before the bad old ways started to creep back in, and thirteen years later the same litany of complaints became impossible to ignore. In 1885 the Governor of Natal, Sir Henry Bulwer, appointed Justice Walter Wragg to chair another commission of investigation which confirmed his worst fears. Living and working conditions were still appalling, with no sanitation or clean drinking water. A hospital existed in all but name, which was understaffed and with insufficient medicines, although it was the only real 'improvement' from the previous investigation.[6] Its findings had not only exposed the inaction that followed the previous commission but its recommendations simply reiterated what had been called for previously. However, Wragg also recommended that more regular inspections of accommodation be undertaken, sanitary arrangements improved, and wells driven to provide fresh water. As usual, though, the life of poverty that had been left behind was little inducement to rock the boat or seek serious reform, and the labourers continued to grin and bear their appalling treatment.

In spite of this, many opted to stay at the end of their indenture and soon demonstrated their value to the growing colony. Some made successes of their land grants, and Natal politician Harry Escombe was the first to appreciate their apparent horticultural acumen. He cited one example where Indian farmers had 'turned a sandy delta into a useful, profitable piece of land',[7] and Member of the Legislative Council of Durban Mr Maurice S. Evans conceded that he was proving himself as good as, if not 'a better cultivator'[8] than many of his white counterparts. These sentiments appeared to vindicate the arrival of a fresh tranche of so-called free or 'passenger'

Indians. They were settling in the colony to engage in trade, commerce and the professions, represented by early pioneers such as Sheth Abubakar Amod, who had opened an establishment in Natal as early as 1880. His was followed by another six such enterprises, which expanded to a total of 132 by 1891,[9] until by 1904 there were 1,260 Indian merchants competing with 658 Europeans.[10]

Watching as they grew and became more prosperous, envious white colonists attributed each success not to hard work but rather to their wily character and a skilful propensity to engage in devious business practices. One observed that they were prepared to 'keep open perhaps nineteen hours out of twenty four [and] systematically infringe the Sunday Closing Act and the Half Holiday Act'.[11] Writer Violet Markham attributed their prosperity to a 'lower standard of life and … greater standard of thrift [which had] crushed out the English trader in many localities'.[12] Secretary of State for India Lord Crewe also believed he knew the secret of their success, specifically that the Indian merchant was 'content on rice and water, and does not require pork, beef and rum, he naturally is able to support his family on a very much lower scale'.[13] Whatever their successful business model was, it worked, and the opportunities on offer in the young colony attracted increasing numbers of like-minded entrepreneurs.

The census of 1891 revealed that while there were now 46,788 Europeans in Natal, 41,142 Indians, indentured and 'free', had also made it their home.[14] By 1904 these figures reached 94,226 and 100,749 respectively,[15] numbers which were interpreted as a growing challenge to white economic and political domination of the colony. As the Wragg Commission had already deduced, 'the majority of the white colonists were strongly opposed to the Indian as a rival and competitor, both in agriculture and in commerce,'[16] and were naturally anxious to solve the problem by whatever steps were necessary. Some argued for their freedom of movement to be restricted and for Indians to be compelled to carry identity cards. Others rued the day that Indian migration had ever started and felt the indenture experiment had been a mistake. They wanted the entire system scrapped and Africans forced to do the work whether they wanted to or not.[17]

The obvious solution would have been to arbitrarily refuse further entry and to repatriate those who were in the territory, but it was still a young colony, with considerable oversight by the metropole, and its legislators were mindful of the possible ramifications if the Colonial Office thought they were taking too much upon themselves. This position was primarily predicated upon the premise that any British subject in one part of the Empire was automatically free to travel to and reside in another. Any attempt to threaten this principle would be contrary to British law as it stood and Parliament could invoke the Colonial Laws Validity Act to have such a measure annulled. Patience was therefore needed, so instead of overt policies that might incur the wrath of London, petty ordinances were passed in various towns and cities designed to keep them in their place. These included curfews, colour bars in hotels, restaurants and other public places, and vindictive rules obliging Indians to ride on the outside of public tramcars,[18] on the roofs of coaches, and to vacate train carriages if requested to do so by a white passenger.

Meanwhile, the colonists waited for Responsible Government to be granted, hoping it would give them greater scope to enact more egregious legislation. When it came in 1893, however, it proved not to be the panacea they had been hoping for. In 1894 a bill was drafted which would deprive Indians of the right to vote, but by now they had an idealistic young Indian lawyer by the name of Mohandas Gandhi to contend with. He had arrived in the colony to represent a Natal merchant, but almost immediately experienced for himself the extent of the discrimination meted out in what was British territory and in which ostensibly he had every right to be. Despite holding a first-class rail ticket he was ejected from the compartment of the train he had boarded at Pietermaritzburg Station after a white passenger objected to his presence in the carriage. Having refused to leave he found himself and his luggage dumped unceremoniously on to the platform, and because there were no more trains until the next morning, he had to spend a long, freezing night in the waiting room.[19] He had also purchased a first-class stagecoach ticket for the remainder of his journey, but again found himself humiliated when he was told to sit on the roof with the driver.[20]

Dumbfounded by such treatment, he made the first tentative steps in his long fight for equality, and once established in his legal practice began to campaign against all forms of discrimination. He led a huge campaign against the bill, collecting hundreds of signatures and securing deferral of its third and final reading until he could make representation to the Secretary of State for the Colonies, Lord Ripon. Ripon subsequently studied the document and agreed that it contravened their rights as British subjects and refused its passage. Encouraged by this victory, in 1894 Gandhi founded the Natal Indian Congress, hoping to organise active, peaceful resistance to the array of laws and ordinances being used to repress his compatriots. But the doughty Europeans were not done yet. Another measure, Act 17, was enacted in 1895. This, it could be argued, was more of a change to contracts of employment than rights as subjects of the Crown. It required indentured Indians to either return home when their contract expired, agree to an extension or pay £3 for a license granting them leave to remain in the colony.[21]

Then the Legislature reconsidered its franchise bill, and this time it was beyond the writ of the Secretary of State to veto. It was successfully passed as the innocuously named Act 8 of 1896, and was followed by another attempt to pass an Immigration Restriction Bill. But this legislation was still within the gift of the Secretary of State, and again considered too overtly racist. The Australian colony of New South Wales had previously had similar legislation refused for the same reason, so Natal proceeded to tweak its wording to make it more tolerable, even though its intention was identical This was made clear when it was debated in the Legislative Assembly on 25 March 1897, one member candidly reiterating the rationale for such a measure:

> ... we think that a large addition to the Indian population will be a cause for difficulty, not only in the present as regards competition, but also in the future as regards political conditions in the colony ...[22]

The British were naturally aware of the clamour in the white-governed colonies to keep them European. They were looking forward to greater self-government, and did not envisage sharing power with Blacks, Asians or any other races they considered to be a challenge. But the position remained that overt discrimination could not be tolerated. So when the premiers of the self-governing colonies met at the Colonial Office in London in July 1897 to celebrate Queen Victoria's jubilee, Secretary of State Joseph Chamberlain again took the opportunity to clarify his government's position:

> I wish to direct your attention to certain legislation which is in process of consideration, or which has been passed by some of the Colonies in regard to immigration of aliens, particularly of Asiatics [including Indians] ... [although] we quite sympathise with the determination of the white inhabitants of these Colonies which are in comparatively close proximity to millions and hundreds of millions of Asiatics that there shall not be an influx of people alien in civilisation ... in religion ... in customs ... we ask you to bear in mind the traditions of the Empire, which makes no distinction in favour of, or against race or colour ...[23]

Thus, in a somewhat veiled manner, Chamberlain had conceded that while the British government sympathised with the colonies, any legislation had to be couched in the most subtle language. When, following the debate in March of 1897, Natal presented a revised text of its Immigration Bill, it was finally approved, not because it aimed for less discrimination but because it now met Chamberlain's criteria. With his tacit connivance, they had devised so watertight a document that it cleverly failed to mention race at all but instead imposed educational, health, age and means testing provisions which only Europeans were likely to meet. Most significantly it included a fifty-word dictation test in English, immediately disqualifying any non-English-speakers. It proved so effective that it became the benchmark for similar legislation in sister colonies and, as circumstances permitted, was further tightened in 1900, 1903 and 1906.[24] Thus, without overtly breaking any established conventions, procedures or imperial legislation, the whites of Natal had secured their ends and relegated Indians to a permanent position of inferiority. By a cumulative aggregation of steps, their freedom of movement, employment and labour rights, and commercial and business interests had all been curtailed. As a disenfranchised community, they had also successfully been deprived of the legal means through which to channel their complaints or seek redress. It appeared that the Europeans had provided for every eventuality save that of outright repatriation, prompting Gandhi to pursue a campaign of passive resistance in an attempt to have the rules overturned. These steps were soon replicated by likeminded neighbours.

Principal among these neighbours was Britain's Cape Colony. Originally founded by the Dutch in 1652, it changed hands a couple of times before being finally annexed to Britain in 1806. By the 1890s its prime minister was the notorious Cecil Rhodes, founder of Rhodesia and an entrepreneur who had grown rich on South Africa's gold and diamonds. He was now keen to appease the colony's Afrikaner community, those families who remained after the Great Trek of 1836.[25] In 1891 they remained the most vocal among a white population of some 337,000[26] who, like in neighbouring Natal, objected to their Indian neighbours' growing economic and potentially political influence. Yet while there were 619,547 'native or coloured' non-Europeans in the colony,[27] still only 1,453 of these were Indians.[28] Nonetheless, they were perceived as the 'other' and deemed to be an increasing challenge to white dominion.

Consequently, in 1892 the legislature passed a Franchise and Ballot Act, which it believed would address the problem. Like similar measures taken in Natal, it could not yet be overtly racist in intent, and had to apply to all regardless of ethnicity. Therefore a measure that also removed some white voters from the electoral rolls could not possibly lead to charges of racial discrimination. Its key provisions, raising the property qualification from £25 to £75 and requiring voters to be able to write in English, were therefore to apply to all, but the Indians were not fooled. Appreciating they were the real targets for the legislation, an angry delegation travelled to London to protest, and Secretary of State Lord Ripon considered their appeal. His impartiality could not be doubted, having been embroiled in the notorious and highly divisive Ilbert Bill, and he was probably more approachable than many in his position. He examined the evidence and agreed that it was certainly suspect, but there was little that he could actually do other than convey his reservations to an unsympathetic Cape Government.[29] Property qualifications were a common feature of the franchise all over the Empire, and would not be entirely abolished by the UK until 1918, so the legislation would have to be allowed. Thus another of Britain's southern African dominions took its first tentative measures towards alienating subjects from the subcontinent.

Even beyond Britain's' immediate sphere of control, white-led and dominated states were looking to take similar steps. Cape Colony's neighbouring Boer republic of Transvaal sought to address the threat posed by growing numbers of foreigners, who it was feared would displace the simple farmers and destroy their quiet pastoral existence. Englishmen were unwelcome enough, but Indians were beyond the pale entirely, and came in for particular attention. So the Transvaal government drafted Law 3 of 1885 which proposed to exclude any 'persons belonging to any of the native races of Asia'[30] from enjoying citizenship and voting rights, land ownership or freedom of movement.[31] The British government objected, claiming that the law contravened Article 14 of the 1881 London Convention that had ended the First Anglo-Boer War, but there was little that could be done short of going to war again. So the Boers stuck to their guns and then in 1891, passed further legislation designed to 'provide against the influx of Asiatics',[32] and subsequent legislation restricted residency to two months without a permit, and denied the right to naturalisation, property ownership, or the operation of any business.[33]

Secretary of State for War Lord Lansdowne led Government condemnation of the Transvaal's actions. Tensions were already rising between the British colonies and the Boer republics, and this was seen as simply a further provocation which could not go unremarked. He stated unequivocally that 'among the many misdeeds of the South African Republic I do not know that any fills me with more indignation than its treatment of these Indians.'[34] Governor of Madras Lord Ampthill added his own comments to a chorus of disapproval when he claimed that the republic's Indians were now struggling 'for the maintenance of a right and the removal of a degradation'.[35] However sincere the outrage might have been, treatment of Indians was highly unlikely to have been among the motives for the conflict which erupted in 1899. The causes were land, gold, British rights in the Transvaal and Orange Free State, and their growing estrangement from British South Africa. Yet it now left most Indians in an invidious position. If they remained loyal to Britain they were inevitably going to alienate themselves even further from the Boers, but if as British subjects they fought alongside their white neighbours, they would be deemed traitors to the Crown. Gandhi, for one, instinctively sympathised with the Boers, seeing them as bullied underdogs, but nonetheless he believed that he still 'owed allegiance' to Britain,[36] and had a duty to serve his Queen-Empress. However reluctantly, this pacifist and non-violent campaigner for human rights offered his services.

True to his word, Gandhi began organising and training volunteers to serve as front-line medical orderlies in support of the British Army now pouring into the country. As Sergeant-Major Gandhi he commanded a 300-strong Volunteer Ambulance Corps, consisting of free and indentured Hindus, Muslims and Christians. His assistance was initially declined by the government, but as soon as the inadequacies of British medical provision were exposed he and his colleagues were thrown into the fighting. Often in harm's way, they found themselves in numerous engagements including, as Gandhi later recounted, 'the slaughter of British troops at Spion Kop [which] found us working within the firing line',[37] where they retrieved the wounded under fire and then carried or transported them many miles in rickety horse-drawn ambulances to the nearest field hospital. Their contribution to the eventual victory, however, earned them little more than some medals and the appreciation of the English-speaking colonists. Gandhi later recounted how 'our humble work was at the moment much applauded, and the Indian's prestige was enhanced. The newspapers published laudatory rhymes with the refrain, "we are the sons of Empire after all" ... '[38]

But having sided with the hated English, the Indians had earned the defeated Boers' utter contempt. They were now a marked community, the enemy within, and what little tolerance there had been for them had evaporated completely. Moreover, Sir Alfred Milner, the governor of the annexed Transvaal and now Orange River Colonies, was keen on reconciliation between the British and the defeated Afrikaners, leaving little inclination to protect their interests.[39] They soon discovered how much those early plaudits were actually worth and in 1907 a new Registration Law was passed, forbidding any new Indians from entering Transvaal and introducing a system of fingerprinting for those already living there.[40] This was followed in 1908 with measures banning Indians without licences from trading and making them liable to arbitrary expulsion.[41] In 1910, the four provinces of the now self-governing Union of South Africa, Cape, Natal, Transvaal and Orange River Colony not only had their own well-established immigration regulations to fall back on,[42] but rights to enforce even more stringent nationwide laws.

Shorn of even the thin veneer of Colonial Office protection, it was increasingly for the Government of India to try to ameliorate its people's plight abroad. Feelings were certainly high. Violet Markham insisted that the 'grievances affecting Indians themselves are a matter of very active concern in India today',[43] a fact highlighted by Annie Besant when she accused the South Africans of treating Indian migrants 'in the most abominable manner ... indentured labourers [are treated] worse than ordinary slaves ... their women are not safe, nor are their children.'[44] Their indignation was shared by Joseph Baptista, an Indian home ruler and politician from Bombay. He was particularly embittered by the short memories of the British: '[I]n the South African war, Indians stood by Englishmen and fought beside and shed their blood for them. What is their reward? Exclusion from the country or confinement in isolated places, subjected to regulations so odious it makes our blood boil.'[45]

In an attempt to improve relations, Gopal Gokhale paid a visit in October 1912, where he called upon the South Africans to adjust the 'conflicting claims of the European and Indian populations ... for justice and greater generosity in the consideration of these claims'.[46] His entreaties appeared to have made some impression, Prime Minister General Smuts responding that his attitude was 'perfectly reasonable',[47] while some progress was made in January 1914 when Gandhi secured an arrangement with Smuts whereby if he abandoned passive resistance the £3 annual tax would be abolished. Smuts also conceded that wives could accompany their spouses, and that a Certificate of Domicile would entitle the holder to enter the country freely.[48]

Yet behind this façade of conciliation there remained the granite-hard conviction that South Africa had to stay 'white'. The Afrikaner mindset was described perfectly by the East African Economic Commission, sponsored by the Governor of Kenya in 1919, which concluded that 'the self-governing states of the Union ... control Indian immigration with a view to ultimate exclusion',[49] a position Sir T. B. Sapru told General Smuts at the Imperial Conference of 1921 would lead to 'perpetual frictions' between the two countries.[50] Smuts, however, in spite of his cordial reception of Gokhale's proposals and apparently amicable arrangement with Gandhi, showed that at heart his sympathies with South Africa's Indians was only skin deep. He replied that as India was not yet constitutionally on a par with his country, its citizens really had no right to expect equal treatment.[51]

Despite the hostility of the whites, by 1926 South Africa's Indian community would grow to 302,000,[52] and as their numbers increased so did the amount of legislation. The South African government enacted a further twenty ordinances between 1919 and the Second World War, limiting economic activity, the right to own or live in certain areas, or the entitlement to enter to the country. The loss of British influence and ultimately the Statute of Westminster gave the South Africans even greater scope to pursue their racial policies, now almost completely unhindered by the British government. Even as late as April 1943, when imperial unity was being hailed as pivotal in the fight against fascism and militarism, the so-called Pegging Act was passed. It was designed specifically to limit the number of affluent Indians buying land from Europeans in the city of Durban,[53] a measure which the American consul in the city compared to 'the usual Jim Crow discriminations against negroes in our Southern States'.[54] Nor was this growing appetite for discrimination and segregation limited to Afrikaners.

There had been an Asian presence in East Africa for at least 300 years before the British arrived, and by the 1870s there were around 4,300 Indians settled along its coastal regions, having established themselves in trade with local Arabs.[55] They generally welcomed the stability that the British brought, which protected their commercial enterprises from pirates and also encouraged more entrepreneurs to make the journey from the subcontinent. British colonial administrator Bartle Frere travelled the region and in 1873 remarked upon 'the preponderating influence of Indian traders [who] if not the monopolist, are the most influential, permanent and all-pervading element of the commercial community'.[56] By the middle of the 1880s these push-pull factors would see their numbers swell by a further 2,500,[57] by which time the region's economic potential had caught the attention of British speculators. Sir John Kirk, who had accompanied David Livingstone on much of his travels in the region, later admitted that 'but for the Indians we should not be there now,'[58] but these newcomers were accompanied by a different set of principles and priorities. The British East Africa Company was chartered in 1888 charged with exploiting and developing commercial opportunities in the area. Further stimulated by the so-called 'Scramble for Africa', the intention was to open up for settlement the rich and productive hinterland which lay beyond the littoral. After a protectorate was established in 1895, more British colonists arrived to make their homes in what would later become Kenya and Uganda. But they were limited in the extent to which they could develop these vast tracts of real estate, which were largely inaccessible due to the long distances involved. It was soon realised that, just as railways had opened up great swathes of India to European capital and investment, the same technology could serve similar objectives in the nascent protectorate.

A plan began to germinate to drive a line from the coastal city of Mombasa, capital of the British East Africa Protectorate, deep into the heart of the territory, finally reaching Lake Victoria, discovered and named by Kirk's mentor Livingstone. The first stage of this massive undertaking, later known as the Uganda Railway, would require thousands of workers building bridges, cutting ravines and laying track all the way to its terminus 325 miles away in the town of Thika. Almost immediately though, the project faced its first hurdle: the perennial lack of willing local labour. With too few Africans prepared to undertake the back-breaking work, Kirk, now chairman of the enterprise, turned to India. Recruits were willing enough, and many borrowed from moneylenders or used all their savings to pay their passage,[59] hoping to repay their expenses from the fourteen pence a day they were promised in wages.[60] In 1896 the first boatload of 350 landed, but numbers rose quickly as the work progressed, to 4,000 a year later, and 13,000 by 1898. At its peak the railway employed some 20,000 labourers in all.[61] It was to prove a tough, arduous and dangerous project, earning it the epithet of the 'Lunatic Line', but thanks largely to the Indians who worked and died on the project, it was finally completed in 1901 and became operational two years later. While as many as two thirds of the labourers took the usual option to return home,[62] the rest, faced with few prospects in India, chose to stay and make their lives in the Protectorate. And at first they found themselves generally welcome.

In stark contrast to Natal and other colonies in southern Africa, plans had already been drawn up to encourage more permanent Indian settlement along the coast and the lowlands. Lord Lugard, later Governor of Nigeria, believed in the 'civilising effects' they would have on Africans,[63] as well as relieving some of the pressure of growing population in the subcontinent. To this end incentives of fifty acres of land were offered to anyone willing to make the commitment. They were told disingenuously that they would be establishing the 'America of the Hindu'[64] in the territory, a prospect which the whites had not as yet recognised as a challenge to their hegemony. This was in large part due to the nature of the land being set aside for the Indian colonists being poor, unproductive and challenging to work, much like that given to former labourers in Natal. In 1900 swampland around Nairobi, unwanted by the Europeans, was also leased to Indians, and by 1911 the total population in the Protectorate stood at 11,886,[65] outnumbering the British, of whom at this point there were just 3,000.[66] This was largely because they had different plans and white farmers were attracted to the bushlands and savanna beyond. They would acquire what would become known as the 'White Highlands', the cool and temperate climate considered ideal for Europeans and from which both Africans and Indians would be excluded.

In 1902 the Crown Lands Ordinance was passed confirming this policy, by which all land vacated and deserted by Africans was deemed to have reverted to the Crown, making available for sale or lease[67] up to 640 acres of cultivable land and 1,000 acres of freehold land.[68] This was all part of a strategy being pursued by men such as Lord Delamare, who had arrived in 1900 and soon became an influential voice among the minority white community. He was to lead a campaign to effectively usurp the native peoples and the Indians such that Kenya would become in his words 'a white man's colony',[69] and bring to an end any thought of a Hindu America. His position was enhanced by the foundation in 1902 of the grandly named 'Society to Promote European Immigration', which claimed that Indians were 'detrimental to the European settler'.[70] Delamare and his supporters went so far as to advocate that Indians be replaced by Africans altogether in the labour market and excluded from mainstream life. But he had his opponents even among the whites, particularly Kirk, who warned starkly that if they were to 'drive away the Indian ... you may shut up the Protectorate',[71] such was their value to its economy. Nonetheless, the same attitudes which prevailed in southern Africa were gaining currency among the whites in East Africa. Their numbers nonetheless remained painfully small and would not surpass 9,000 until 1921,[72] adding to their insecurity.

While the two camps set out their stalls the subjects of this heated debate appeared content to keep themselves to themselves and were showing little interest in politics. One senior administrator had observed in 1905 that 'one hears little of their grievances because they are nearly all [busy] making money.'[73] Their apparent apathy however was misleading, and as one indignity piled upon another they began to respond. Not only had they been excluded from the Highlands, but they faced increasing segregation in law, education, transport, restaurants, hotels and other public places. Slowly they emerged from their inertia, opening their own newspaper to voice their views in 1895,[74] and in 1900 established the Mombasa Indian Association. This was followed by a branch in Nairobi in 1906, and a year later the British East Africa Indian Association was formed. When the territory was granted a legislative council in 1906, leaders within the Indian community agitated for the right to full participation and representation. This proved too much for the white settlers, however, who expressed their opposition 'in the most emphatic way'[75] to the prospect of sharing power with anyone else.

Among those emerging from the margins of the Protectorate's political life was prosperous businessman Alibhai Jeevanjee who, following his arrival in Mombasa in 1890, secured the contract to provide the labourers for the railway. This proved a highly lucrative venture, the profits from which he decided to invest in businesses in the city. In 1901 he bought the Indian Bazaar in Nairobi and three years later reopened it as the 'Jeevanjee Market', but this success soon invited the envy and resentment of the whites. When a plague broke out in 1908 the cause was put down to insanitary conditions in his establishment as a pretext to open a whites-only European market in competition. Instead of submitting, and unwilling to be treated like a pariah, he threw himself into politics and succeeded in having himself appointed to the legislative council in 1909.[76] He wasted no time in using this platform to air his countrymen's grievances. He reminded his European critics that 'it is the Indian traders ... alone who have done the work of exploitation and development of the country's resources',[77] and not the privileged farmers living almost exclusively in the White Highlands.

His accusations predictably did little to endear the Europeans to his cause, and amid growing mutual hostility the decision was taken to try to identify the root causes of the growing estrangement between the two races. As a result the Sanderson Committee was established in 1910, tasked with investigating the situation and making recommendations. It took evidence from numerous leading lights in the territory, including Sir John Kirk, who firmly supported Jeevanjee's contentions, insisting that his compatriots were an indispensable asset. Such support was reinforced by evidence from writer on Africa and part-time administrator Sir Harry Hamilton Johnston, who explained to the committee that 'it is rather a scandal ... that 400 European farmers should have the power to monopolise the whole of ... British East Africa and exclude Indians'[78] when it was those Indians who had proven to be the backbone of the community. The commission agreed; the evidence was overwhelming. It concluded, 'The presence of a considerable number of Indian inhabitants has been and continues to be of material advantage to the British administration of the Protectorate.'[79]

Indeed, if evidence were needed that they were an asset, it was from the colony's growing affluence. Figures for the period 1912–13 would show that revenue had grown by 30 per cent since the Protectorate had been established, running at nearly £1,000,000, and that for the first time the British government had not needed to provide support in the form of grant-in-aid.[80] The farmers Hamilton criticised so scathingly, however, and the rest of the white community remained unmoved. Despite these hard facts, the legislative council passed an ordinance in 1915 further limiting where Indians could live, and with relations continuing to deteriorate Governor Henry Belfield commissioned a further report in 1917. Entitled 'The East African Economic Commission', it was ostensibly intended to be an economic study but when it reported its findings in 1919 it contained claims and allegations solely intended to blacken the Indians' reputation. It refused to recognise their contribution to the economy and the Protectorate's commercial success, and instead accused them of being organised 'to keep the African out of every position which an Indian could fill', of having an 'incurable repugnance to sanitation and hygiene' and of being an 'inciter to crime, since it is the opportunity afforded by the ever-ready Indian receiver which makes thieving easy'.[81] Furthermore, it proposed that 'the Railway and other Government Departments should as quickly as possible replace Indian employees by Europeans in the higher grades and Africans in the lower .... if the African Colony is to be ruled by Asiatics then the responsibility is on the Imperial Government for the result.'[82]

These vindictive calumnies were music to the ears of men such as Lord Delamare, who along with his cronies was demanding further restrictions. He also claimed that 'if Indians are to be allowed to steam in ... in unlimited numbers, it will scarcely be possible to localise them indefinitely in any one territory.'[83] This stream of obloquy was received in London with some consternation. The Colonial Secretary, Viscount Milner, condemned the accusations as 'deplorable'[84] and distanced himself from such gratuitous racism. But those who sympathised with the colonists tacitly supported their objectives. His own private secretary, Arthur Parkinson, sought to justify their attitudes:

> ... to the native 'Mzungu' (white man) is the master. The native sees the Indian ... in a lower position than the white man ... on the whole he despises the Indian, who is neither one of the ruling race nor of his own race ...[85]

Therefore, if Indians were granted greater rights the standing of the white community would be damaged in the eyes of the Africans. This could undermine its authority and possibly transform a currently passive native population into a troublesome one. It was therefore essential for good order and discipline that the status of the European population be maintained and even enhanced. Edward Northey, Belfield's successor as governor, shared such opinions. He saw through the 1918 Segregation of Races Act and the 1919 Municipal Corporation Ordinance, which cumulatively sought to deny Indians the civil and human rights taken for granted by the white population.[86] He also favoured further steps to exclude them from the civil administration, ostensibly on the grounds of Africanising the civil service,[87] further ramping up the tension. Matters came to a head in 1919 when a raft of proposals came to the attention of the Colonial Secretary. An electoral representation ordinance proposed a modestly reformed legislative council of eleven elected Europeans, but contained a clause that to qualify for the franchise voters now had to be at least twenty-five years old, and more explicitly, a British subject of European origin or descent.[88] This provoked outrage among Indians and prompted the hasty despatch in April 1920 of an angry delegation to London to reiterate their demand for 'absolute equality with the Europeans'.[89]

For the settlers, the most logical solution would be to prevent any further immigration into the territory. This proposal was received by the Secretary of State, now Lord Milner, who as we have seen had already stepped carefully in

South Africa so as not to tread on white toes. Nonetheless, in a memorandum of 21 May 1920 he refused the request on the familiar grounds that 'there must be no bar on the immigration of Indians'[90] – at least, nothing overt. He in fact looked more favourably on segregating the races, particularly with regards to keeping the Highlands white. When he was presented with proposals which would consign Indians to certain prescribed areas he came to the disingenuous conclusion that in reality 'there is no question here of discrimination ... the principle that in laying out of townships in tropical Africa separate areas should be allotted to the separate races is not only from a sanitary point of view, but also on grounds of social convenience the right principle.'[91] Once again, the tacit sympathy of the political class in London was conniving with the settlers in its colonies to marginalise non-whites.

By 1922 the protectorate had been upgraded to a colony, but faced a post-war recession. As it began to bite, another committee was formed to see what economies could be made to offset the downturn in trade. The subsequent report, authored by acting governor Charles Bowring, made a number of proposals aimed at increasing taxation through a rise in the hut and poll taxes. These measures fell upon the Africans, but although he was considered more sympathetic to the Indian community Bowring also looked to them to further reduce the expenditure of the government. He supported reducing the size of the civil administration, but instead of the Europeans, who earned as much as a quarter more than Indians, it was the latter upon whom the axe was to fall.[92] Yet when Milner's successor Winston Churchill spoke at the Kenya and Uganda Dinner on 28 January 1922, all he delivered was the mildest of rebukes, cautioning that 'natives and Indians alike, who reach and conform to well-marked European standards, shall not be denied the fullest exercise and enjoyment of civic and political rights.'[93] Increasingly the British government, in attempting to walk a tightrope of compromise and appeasement, was instead sending out mixed and confusing messages.

Churchill's admonishment also came at a time when settler anxiety was approaching its peak, and with it a resurgence in their assertiveness. Whereas the African population had dropped from 3,000,000 in 1911 to 2,483,000 in 1921, and the white population had increased from 2,736 to 9,025 over the same period, the number of Indians had doubled, from 11,816 to 22,731.[94] These statistics prompted increasingly strident demands to stem immigration, and a paranoid white community, fearful for the preservation of their white privilege, was also developing a siege mentality. Lord Delamare was one of those who had benefitted considerably from the lifestyle that the whites had created for themselves, and he had no intention of surrendering it in the interests of the natives or the Indians. On 10 May 1922 he addressed a meeting at the Parklands Club in Nairobi, calling upon his fellow Europeans to resist 'all Indian claims to fellow citizenship',[95] and if necessary to be prepared to resort to force. This outburst prompted representatives of the Indians to confront the new governor, George Coryndon, and demand that he 'prohibit such incendiary talk',[96] but instead Coryndon sought to downplay the seriousness of the situation.

In a telegram of 3 February 1923 he assured the new Secretary of State, the Duke of Devonshire, that the whites were not advocating 'any deliberate and real violence against Asiatics [but a refusal to] ... pay taxes, and ... [impose a] commercial and personal boycott against Indians'. However, when he added that they might also seize the 'Treasury, Armoury, railway, customs and telegraph offices with the same general object of paralysing the Government',[97] he was not drawing a particularly reassuring picture. Devonshire's options were nonetheless limited. Despite what could amount to the threat of a coup and a unilateral declaration of independence, Coryndon counselled that 'there is no possibility of triumph if force becomes [the] ultimate issue, however respectfully applied,'[98] because using native troops against the settlers was out of the question. Furthermore, he warned, any confrontation would only put Indians at further risk of 'outrages by Africans'.[99] A blockade was one solution he admitted, but as it would only serve to 'wreck the country economically',[100] that would be entirely counterproductive. The only really practical approach was to try to assuage the settlers' fears and attempt to appease them further.

Their greatest concern was clearly that of being 'swamped' by Indians. Segregation could go only so far, and with pressure mounting Lord Devonshire was being repeatedly asked by the governor to approve 'some stringent form of control of immigration',[101] but this of course could only be approved if it was in a form 'not involving racial discrimination'.[102] Exasperated by the impasse, on 21 February Lord Devonshire invited Coryndon to head a delegation to confer with him in London. Top of the agenda would be 'to discuss fully and frankly all questions' with a view to drafting a 'strengthened immigration law of general application', which he conceded was 'an essential part of any settlement'.[103] Such a meeting could not come a moment too soon. The colonists were impatient and in no mood to compromise. In July 1923 rumours circulated that there was a plot to kidnap the governor, declare independence unilaterally and secede from the Empire altogether[104] – not a prospect which was likely to be greeted favourably in London.

However, while the British government and the white settlers were in concave, Indian suspicions were mounting, and the president of the East African Indian National Congress accused Coryndon – and not without reason – of being 'hostile to Indian rights'.[105] Furthermore their interests were also the subject of growing concern by the Indian Legislative Assembly which had raised the issue several times in July 1923 alone.[106] In the meantime the discussions between Lord Devonshire and the settlers had produced a White Paper. Published in July, it essentially conceded to all the European demands. The British agreed to an immigration bill which again could not overtly discriminate against Asians but instead would use the tried-and-tested Natal template, employing economic qualifications to exclude any 'undesirables'.[107] This legal dexterity would produce legislation that would supposedly 'safeguard the interests of the African natives of the colony [and] implement the policy … relating to Indians in Kenya'.[108] Key to achieving this mendacious end was Clause A of Section 5, which entitled the Immigration Officer to refuse entry if the applicant was unable to produce visible means of support. In addition, if he was entering the colony as a labourer, his employer had to first demonstrate that 'he cannot obtain in the colony an employee for the work,'[109] and if that was the case then he was required to produce a certificate to that effect. Only then would the migrant be admitted into the colony.[110]

This subtle interpretation of freedom of movement seemed to satisfy the settlers, Coryndon hailing it as 'a sound and just settlement',[111] but that was not how the Indians interpreted it. Their outrage was then compounded by another discriminatory franchise bill, scheduled to coincide with elections in 1924. Although it conferred upon Indians the right to vote, they could do so only under a system of separate rolls, which allocated them five seats to the whites' eleven. Thus, irrespective of their numbers, they would be held in a permanent state of inferiority, their voice suppressed by a fixed and arbitrary voting arrangement. Subsequently they boycotted the general election of April 1924, and none of their five seats were taken up. Ironically the Government of India expressed its concern over the tide of events by warning that 'separate representation for the different communities will perpetuate and intensify racial antagonism',[112] while across India there were demonstrations in support of their compatriots. Unsurprisingly none of these protests served to change any minds in Lord Delamare's club. The unresolved tensions between the two communities would drag on through the 1920s and 1930s, by which time the Africans too were becoming more militant.

When there were calls for a merger of Kenya, Uganda and Tanganyika into a virtual federation with the longer-term ambition of achieving Dominion status and all that implied, the Indians were again in uproar. Such a step would leave the whites with practically free rein to duplicate the policies pursued by South Africa. The Moyne Commission was established in 1932 to investigate their concerns, but found that they had nothing to fear even if such a constitutional arrangement was to be implemented.[113] Unimpressed, in 1935 Indians and Africans formed the Labour Trade Union of Kenya, which provided a firmer platform for joint action against the Europeans. But this move simply aroused greater suspicion among the Europeans who in turn increased their own demands for greater self-government. However, with little sign of a meeting of minds, these divisive jealousies and antagonisms persisted throughout the 1930s.

In order to better understand and quantify the full extent of the tensions developing between the two races on the continent, Anglican priest Charles Freer Andrews travelled to Africa to see for himself. His findings made for interesting reading. He travelled, as he later wrote, 'from the midst of the strained racial attitudes at Nairobi to the calm and natural social atmosphere of Zanzibar [where] ... there seems to be no racial conflict at all.'[114] He also went to Mozambique and spoke to Portuguese colonists who informed him, in contrast to the settlers of British East Africa, that the Indians were 'industrious, law abiding [and] valuable to the African native ... we could not get on without them.'[115] Even in Rhodesia they appeared to be 'treated well ... have a right to free entry ... on a very simple educational test ... [which was] fairly and impartially administered ... [and] no single complaint of unfairness was brought to me.'[116] Clearly, the attitudes of Europeans towards the Indian population varied considerably, and from such accounts one might infer that the policies of the fiercely segregationist South Africans and the arriviste whites of East Africa were exceptional. In reality racial dogma was not confined to remote colonial enclaves, and all across the white-ruled empire the Indian diaspora experienced similar discrimination.

Towards the end of the nineteenth century small numbers of Punjabis had travelled to work in the logging industries of Canada's British Columbia. But even by 1905 their numbers were still very modest, and of those who had made the journey just forty-five had settled.[117] But as demand for their labour increased these figures leapt to 387 the following year, 2,124 in 1907 and 2,623 in 1908.[118] Warning bells began to sound and the same white fears of being 'swamped' were aroused as had consumed Europeans in southern and eastern Africa. In 1907, meetings opposing further immigration were held across the province, and premier Sir Wilfrid Laurier sent Deputy Minister of Labour William Lyon Mackenzie King to London to discuss the situation. He wanted authority to secure their repatriation, but failing that it was suggested that they might be persuaded to move on to British Honduras. Unfortunately when a delegation went to see their proposed new home, they politely declined to take up the offer.[119]

Faced with this impasse, the government decided that they could at least try to control numbers now entering the country. Mindful of the protocol forbidding discriminatory regulations, they contrived the Continuous Passage Act, which was passed in 1908. Its somewhat prolix wording stipulated that 'immigrants may be prohibited from landing or coming into Canada unless they come from the country of their birth or citizenship, by a continuous journey and on through tickets purchased before leaving the country of their birth or citizenship.'[120] At that time there were no direct routes to Canada from India, so its purpose was somewhat self-evident. Many migrants from the subcontinent travelled via Hong Kong, a route disqualified by the Act; likewise if the journey was from any other intermediate port of embarkation. Just in case this measure did not in itself achieve the objective it was followed by the 1910 Immigration Act, which required immigrants from the subcontinent to have at least $200 in their possession when they landed. Pointedly, those from anywhere else in the world were only required to have $25. Although its apologists tried to explain it as an economic and not racially motivated measure, few were fooled. As Annie Besant explained, the average Indian now:

> ... goes over [to Canada] ... they put burdens on him they do not put on other coloured men that are not under our famous Union Jack ... They allow the Japanese to travel through the country with a far smaller amount of money than any coloured citizen of the Empire can travel with ... [and] the coloured man's wife and children are not allowed to come and live with him.[121]

Another critic added that while 'a self-governing colony has the right to say who shall come across its borders, it has no moral right to impose petty restrictions on an educated man because his skin appears to be brown.'[122] Former missionary and Senator for Saskatchewan James Douglas went so far as to vilify such policies as 'un-Christian, un-British and ungrateful'.[123] The now familiar trope of hygiene was also deployed to justify such treatment, but an experienced ship's surgeon promptly disavowed this calumny. He testified that rather than being the dirtiest, he found most Indians 'especially the Sikhs, one hundred per cent cleaner in their habits and freer from disease than the European steerage passengers I had come into contact with'.[124] Nonetheless, despite the condemnation of those who recoiled from such laws, the new legislation appeared to achieve its ends, at least from the point of view of its proponents. In 1911 Canada admitted 11,932 Chinese, 2,986 Japanese but only one Indian.[125] Even the handful who secured admission were subjected to further petty bureaucracy and malicious restrictions. Hindus in Victoria were refused permission to construct a crematorium,[126] while others were prevented from registering to vote in the province despite meeting all the criteria.[127]

Then in August 1913 scurrilous and unfounded reports began to circulate, claiming that 100,000 Indians were to be brought into the country, while the aptly named Asiatic Exclusion League seized the opportunity to become prophets of doom. Most notable among them was journalist and author Agnes Laut, who revelled in making salacious and unfounded claims about an imminent *War of the Worlds*-style alien invasion.[128] It was into this McCarthyite atmosphere that the Japanese-owned *Kotamagata Maru* set sail from Hong Kong to Vancouver in January 1914. On board were 376 Sikhs, Hindus and Muslims. At first they were denied entry on the grounds that they had breached the Continuous Passage Act, and then that they did not possess $200, and finally that the authorities suspected that the group harboured nationalist agitators. But the passengers stood their ground, invoking their rights as British subjects while the ship rolled at anchor in a state of semi-limbo. But when the ship still refused to leave, a tug was despatched to push them out to sea, and when that tactic failed a Canadian warship was deployed to threaten them with even more extreme sanctions. Naturally, as soon as the story of the impasse leaked out journalists flocked to the scene to get as much sensationalist copy as they could. One Vancouver newspaper, *The Province*, called the arrival of the ship a 'Hindu invasion of Canada',[129] the sort of headline sure to stir up animosity and stoke the fears of concerned white Canadians.

The unseemly stand-off lasted for sixty days while lawyers for the two parties battled it out, and sympathetic Indians in Canada raised funds and staged protests against the government's policy. Eventually, after much negotiation the Canadians decided to allow just twenty passengers to enter the country, and the remainder were sent back, leaving Vancouver and returning to Calcutta in September 1914. But that was not the end of their tragic experience. Upon arrival, fighting broke out between their supporters and the police and in the ensuing riot nineteen passengers were killed. The entire episode left a bitter taste in the mouths of many liberal-minded Canadians who thought they held to higher moral standards. One, economist George Paish, regretted that 'the people of Canada ... are all settlers from foreign lands or the descendants of such settlers. We had fondly hoped that knowing all this they would recognise the consequent Imperial obligation upon them. We have been disappointed.'[130] Canada, however, proved to be far from alone in not feeling bound by its imperial obligations, as Indians in the antipodes were also finding out.

Visitors from the subcontinent had been a familiar sight in the Australian colony of New South Wales almost from its inception. Domestic servants were taken to Sydney in 1810, and after 1837 workers were being employed widely as labourers. Small numbers followed in the 1840s, including servants and traders, until in the 1850s further admissions were limited out of concern that white men were suffering from the competition. But by now they were quite a common sight throughout the colony, working as seasonal hands in the sugar cane and fruit industries, and some joined the thousands converging on the colony of Victoria following the discovery of gold there in 1851. They were followed by so-called Muslim cameleers, a small number of whom arrived from the North-West Frontier Province in the late 1850s and early 1860s, intending to apply their skills to the growing caravanserai trade, as European settlement moved further inland.[131] Nonetheless their numbers remained modest, as those that arrived were offset by others who returned home, and subsequently by 1857 only 277 'Hindoos' were known to be in the country.[132]

But when the transportation of convict labour to Australia began to slow, some colonies faced a serious problem. Within Queensland and South Australia in particular, the work to be done was typically hard and unyielding, and of a type snubbed by white and Aboriginal alike. The most logical solution was once again to turn to India, but both colonies were deterred from signing contracts with its government due to the stringent conditions it attached.[133] Finally, after much tough negotiating, the government of Queensland passed the Indian Coolie Act of 1862, which opened the way for limited Indian labour.[134] But it was a slow process, and not until the 1880s would the subject start to dominate Queensland politics. It then suddenly became a hot potato, one that aspiring and unscrupulous politicians grasped in order to advance their own interests. Manchester-born William Brookes was standing as Liberal Party candidate for North Brisbane, and at one hustings warned his audience that Indians risked introducing cholera, measles, smallpox and other pestilences into their community. But nothing caused him as much anxiety as the prospect of 'the permanent establishment within our territory of coloured labour',[135] concerns which undoubtedly resonated with his audience. He won the seat and held it for six years from 1882. But the separate colonies could only take their own independent decisions on immigration matters until 1901, and then subject to British approval. When federation offered the prospect of concerted action, politicians began to explore what measures could be taken to limit Asian immigration further. Prominent among them was Attorney General Alfred Deakin, who on 12 September 1901 called openly for

> ... the prohibition of all alien coloured immigration and more ... the deportation or reduction of the number of aliens now in our midst. The two things go hand in hand, and are the necessary complement of a single policy – the policy of securing a 'White Australia' ...[136]

Such rhetoric, however, did not reflect the actual situation in the country at that time, because although the 1901 census gave the population of Australia as 3,377,000,[137] only 800 Indians were registered in the entire commonwealth.[138] Nonetheless the seeds of fear were being sown, and in order to gauge the views of the average man-in-the-street, the *Melbourne Herald* undertook a special investigation. Its findings reflected a malignant undercurrent of hostility which seemed to vindicate Deakin's own attitude. Its subsequent report confirmed that 'to most people in Queensland the Pacific Islander is less obnoxious than the British Indian coolies who have been coming to Australia in gradually increasing numbers,'[139] but because 'they are British subjects ... it will not be found easy to refuse them admittance if they continue to come of their own accord.'[140] Many of those interviewed gave as their main concern fears for their livelihoods, worried that Indians would undercut wages and depress the market. Under the circumstances the *Herald* asked rhetorically, 'Is it wise to run the risk?[141] But men such as the Scottish-born Mackinnon Fowler, representing the Labor Party in the House of Representatives, was disgusted by such attitudes. He remained convinced that rather than being some kind of virus 'many of these people are at least our equal in all that goes to make up morality, or even intellectual or physical qualities,'[142] and were an asset rather than a liability. Such views were shared by Edward Foxall, liberal free trader and vocal opponent of the White Australia mentality. He was withering in his condemnation of a shibboleth which he regarded as 'beyond the pale of discussion',[143] and derided the 'careless claptrap oratory'[144] which underlay it. It was a stance especially difficult to fathom, he added, because the number of Asiatics, including Indians, was reducing rather than increasing.[145]

But Deakin's arguments won through and secured the passage of the Immigration Restriction Bill of 1901. Although he claimed it was primarily aimed at Japanese immigration he clearly had in his sights the feared Indian bogeyman. It sought by the crudest of measures to restrict entry into the country simply by giving immigration officers the authority to refuse admission on the grounds that they deemed the migrant to be 'undesirable'. One key clause duplicated Natal's legislation, and required immigrants to undertake a fifty-word dictation test in any European language, not necessarily English. Annie Besant seethed, bitterly resentful of the fact that 'an Indian going [to Australia] is given a passage in modern Greek to read and translate and if he cannot do it he is turned back,'[146] but like Canada's legislation it served its purpose. The Act was applied 1,359 times up to 1909 and resulted in only fifty-two would-be migrants being granted entry, and after 1909 none.[147]

Another issue brought to the fore by federation was the need to consolidate and codify the voting system, and Senator Richard O'Connor introduced a bill to provide for a Federal Uniform Franchise. This included extending the vote to all women, aboriginals and non-Europeans, which would have included Indians, anathema to White Australians. His bill naturally provoked uproar in the chamber, and heated debate followed which finally saw those clauses extending rights to non-whites deleted. Instead, the final text of the legislation included one which confirmed that 'no aboriginal native of Australia, Asia, Africa or the Islands of the Pacific except New Zealand',[148] would be permitted the right to vote. This was passed into law on 12 June 1902, followed by the Naturalisation Act of 1903, which made similar exclusions applicable to Asians.[149] Then in 1909 the decision was taken to create a uniform state pension. But this otherwise philanthropic act too was subverted to the cause of discrimination. Those who wanted the benefit limited to 'all natural-born British subjects of a white race'[150] rallied round Minister for Home Affairs Sir Littleton Ernest Groom, whose advocacy for the policy attracted huge support. Consequently those Labor politicians who condemned this approach as 'racial prejudice'[151] found themselves outfoxed. After all, for Groom and his supporters 'the general intention of our legislation is not to encourage Asiatics to remain in Australia,'[152] and if denial of the state pension served that end, then all to the good. Certainly, the cumulative effect of the measures introduced since federation seemed to have achieved what most White Australians sought. In 1911, the number of Indians in the county stood at 3,698, falling to 2,200 in 1921. A decade or so later they had fallen again to just 2,100,[153] all courtesy of a White Australia policy which remained on the statute books until 1973.

New Zealand, which Annie Besant called 'the only country that treats its coloured races decently [and] the only country under the British flag where justice is done to the original possessors of the land',[154] would also prove far from the paragon of virtue that she described. Discovered by Dutchman Abel Tasman in 1642, it was another 127 years before the English explorer James Cook arrived to begin charting its coastline, after which the country became increasingly exposed to European settlement. Early records describe two Muslim sailors arriving in 1796 aboard the *Saint Jean Baptiste*, and there were instances of sailors and sepoys deserting when East India Company ships hove to and collected supplies. In 1809 a Bengali was rumoured to have jumped ship ostensibly to marry a Māori woman,[155] but few others ventured so far south. There were nonetheless stories of another Indian making a home for himself with a Māori woman in the Bay of Islands in 1815, and another living on Stewart Island at around this time.[156]

It was not until the 1880s that steadier migration took place, mainly by independent traders and Indians who had completed their indenture contracts in Fiji and did not wish to return home.[157] In any case, census returns showed that only six Indian men were living in the country, three of whom were domestic servants working for a family which had moved from India to live in Canterbury.[158] It was not until the 1890s that noticeable migration took place, mainly Gujaratis and Punjabis who undertook a variety of jobs as labourers, farm workers, scrub cutters and drain diggers. There were also hawkers of fruit and vegetables and bottle collectors in a couple of the main towns such as Auckland and Christchurch. Nonetheless, only forty-six migrants originating from the subcontinent were recorded for 1896,[159] but even these pitifully small numbers were seen by many as a challenge to the 703,000 Europeans now living in the colony. Many saw New Zealand as the 'Britain of the South' and that was how they intended it to remain.

To that end, Lancashire-born Premier Richard Seddon sought to place into statute the Asiatic Immigration Bill. It was overtly intended to mirror Australia's whites-only platform, but it was deemed too explicit to pass muster in London.[160] Joseph Chamberlain, however, wrote to Seddon consolingly, 'I hope ... it will be possible for us to arrange a form of words which will avoid hurting the feelings of any of His Majesty's subjects, while at the same time it would amply protect the [Self-Governing Colonies] against any invasion of the class to which they would justly object.'[161] Once again, a colonial government applied itself to drafting a document which avoided 'hurting' anyone's feelings' while guaranteeing the exclusivity of their society. Concluding that the tried and trusted language test introduced in Natal fitted the bill, the Immigration Restriction Act of 1899 (No. 83) was drafted. It now stipulated that 'any person other than of British (including Irish) birth and parentage, when asked to do so by an officer appointed under this Act ... [who] fails to himself write out and sign ... in any European Language, an application form ... would be a Prohibited Immigrant.'[162] It was the prerogative of the official on duty to decide who he would request to take the test, of course, so if he only asked Indians,

Chinese or anyone else that he did not like the look of, there was little that could be done about it. After the bill received royal assent and was enacted, the *Government Gazette* nonetheless proudly announced on 8 August 1900 that 'an Act to Place Certain Restrictions on Immigration into New Zealand' was in operation.[163]

Yet the grounds for such hysteria seem all the more difficult to fathom when one looks at the 1906 census returns. This recorded that the population of New Zealand now stood at 888,578. There were not enough Indians in the country to justify their own category, but under that of 'other' religions it was revealed that there were 356 including nine Brahmins, one Hindu, seventeen Muslims and two Vedatists.[164] Nonetheless, author Sir Arthur P. Douglas, who visited the country in 1907, noted how 'New Zealand was determined to preserve her people from contamination through all who were deemed undesirable persons,'[165] and they appeared to be achieving their ends. For the whole of 1912 there had only been twelve applications for residency and in 1913 just sixty-six.[166] Yet in 1914 an Auckland headmaster still felt strongly enough to write to a newspaper warning that further Indian immigration 'would be a national calamity',[167] even though the 1916 census recorded that there were now only 181 Indians actually in the country.[168]

When increasing numbers of former indentured Indians from Fiji began to arrive, some politicians used them as an excuse to hype up a vision of a greater apocalypse. Prime Minister William Massey began calling for urgent measures to 'restrict as far as possible the immigrations of Hindu coolies to this country' before the Dominion was overwhelmed.[169] When 174 entered in the first six months of 1920 in addition to 193 during the previous twelve months,[170] Massey panicked and reiterated calls for the immigration rules to be updated. Furthermore, there did not appear to be much doubt about the cause of this influx of interlopers. The Returned Servicemen Association's official journal, *Quick March*, published highly racist, offensive and salacious articles in which Indians were referred to as 'a scummy lot' who spent their time 'buying the favours of Fijian women' and 'mugging up English sentences' in order to gain admission into the country.[171] Massey used such sentiments to argue that the proposed 1920 Act was 'the result of a deep seated sentiment on the part of the huge majority of the people of the country that this Dominion shall be what is often called a "white" New Zealand ... we have a perfect right to safeguard our immigration policy and be quite sure that the persons who will come and take up their residence here shall be people of whom we shall be able to approve.'[172]

These sentiments, and the implications for Indians were not lost on the Government in Delhi or in London. Viscount Milner wrote to the Government of New Zealand in April 1920 insisting that 'the Imperial Government could not accept the idea of denying the right of entry to British Indian subjects,'[173] but publications such as the *Wanganui Herald* of 22 November 1920 countered that 'we do not want to see New Zealand piebald just because it suits the British government.'[174] Consequently, the Immigration Restriction Amendment Act of 1920 was passed, and now required people 'not of British or Irish parentage' to apply for an entry permit,[175] bringing the prospect of an all-white New Zealand one step closer. Now each of the self-governing Dominions had the legislation in place which protected their special status, but at the cost of estranging and embittering those at whom it was directed.

At her presidential address to the Second Reform Conference in Bombay on 23 August 1921, Annie Besant virulently challenged this mindset. She urged the conference to pass a resolution 'in favour of the same status for European and Indian residents in the Dominions ... [as] the first recognition that Indians are citizens of the Empire in the real sense'.[176] Gandhi was more stark, warning that 'if ever India becomes lost to Britain and the British Empire, it will not be so much on account of questions of internal administration ... but on this question of treatment of Indians in the Colonies.'[177] But the Dominions were adamant, and were now actively collaborating with the British Government to ensure that their next tranche of settlers came only from the metropole. In 1919 the Overseas Settlement Scheme was established, while the Dominions organised similar initiatives to attract labour from the UK. They proved highly successful, luring around 86,000 British migrants to Canada, Australia, South Africa and New Zealand.[178] This scheme was followed by the Empire Settlement Act of 1922 and, keen to offload its surplus population, the British government set aside £3,000,000 a year for fifteen years for assisted passages.[179] The two schemes would ultimately facilitate the migration of nearly 2,000,000 individuals,[180] 400,000 of them Scots, a third of whom made the long journey to New Zealand.[181] By contrast, it was calculated that of the 13,000,000 square miles of British territory outside of India, special laws against Indians were in force in over 8,000,000 by 1928,[182] a statistic which underlines the determination of the white-run empire to treat Indians as 'the Other', quite undeserving of equality within their exclusive club. It is hardly surprising that Nehru had been so scathing about the dubious advantages of membership of the British Commonwealth.

Britain, however, for so long the final arbiter of Indian rights around the empire, had to practice what it preached, and passed little overt immigration legislation of its own. This was in large part due to the fact that it never experienced the same issues as many of the colonies, having no requirement for Indian labourers and little cause to restrict large-scale settlement. There was one exception, however. Thousands of lascars served on British ships, and although the timber, cotton, sugar and other commodities they helped carry into these islands were welcome, they were not. From 1823 the Merchant Shipping Act made it compulsory for shipowners to notify the authorities of any 'Asiatic sailors' among their crews,[183] and from 1855 employers were required to repatriate Indian sailors to their original ports of embarkation at the end of their contracts.[184] In 1858 the India Office also provided facilities to ensure Indian sailors were collected together and returned home, and in 1871, the Board of Trade instituted a system whereby lascar transfer officers were installed in all the main ports to prevent sailors absconding.[185] Such precautions seemed to do the trick. A census in 1931 indicated that there were just 9,243 Indians living in the UK, of whom 7,128 resided in England, and of these 2,000 were students.[186]

One exemplar of a more tolerant attitude, however, was unimpeachable: Queen Victoria herself. In 1887 she invited Indian servants into her household, among whom was Mohammed Abdul Karim. He taught his mistress Hindi and became one of her favourites, but in the process aroused resentment and jealousy among other members of the household. They plotted and connived at his removal, but the Queen refused to part with him. It was not until her death in 1901 that the hated interloper could be pensioned off and returned to India, where he died in 1909.

9

'A bulwark of British rule in India'

India's diaspora could nonetheless only observe from afar the continuing struggle for the freedom of their compatriots. Here the developing political situation had only served to reinforce the gulf between the Statute of Westminster of 1931 and the India Act of 1935. While the constitutional reforms introduced in the 1930s freed members of the British Commonwealth from their political ties with Britain, British India continued to languish under what remained effectively direct alien rule. Canada, Australia and New Zealand would take time to ratify the statute, but the Irish Free State, apart from the Union of South Africa arguably the least enthusiastic member, seized the opportunity with both hands. It exploited British concessions to become a republic in all but name with the oath of allegiance abolished, the post of Governor-General dispensed with, and the role of the British Privy Council ended. Finally, in 1937 it legally adopted the name Eire and its new constitution retained only the barest of legal links to the Crown consistent with continued membership.

Yet in India, neither passive resistance, direct action or violence had succeeded in mirroring Eire's achievements because, as Nehru had explained, legally their hands were tied. Then the crisis in Europe deepened and war appeared imminent. As in 1914, India would be embroiled in any subsequent conflict, with its rulers claiming to fight for freedom while denying the same rights to its own empire. This was a paradox which soon confronted nationalists with a serious dilemma, as Nehru explained in an interview with the *Times* newspaper in May 1939:

... a fascist world victory will be not only disastrous for the world as a whole but bad for our own freedom ... on the other hand supporting British Imperialism is obviously wrong policy for a country dominated by that imperialism ... if [the present British Government] was in favour of real democracy, its first function should be to introduce democracy in its empire ...[1]

This dichotomy became glaring when war was declared in September 1939 and Eire announced its neutrality, while the Union of South Africa only grudgingly announced its allegiance to Britain. Even Canada, Australia and New Zealand had the right to make up their own minds whether or not to throw in their lot with the metropole, but India had to follow the colonies and protectorates and go to war alongside Britain. Nehru and the other nationalist leaders were naturally outraged when Viceroy Lord Linlithgow did not deign even to consult them, but magnanimously offered to cooperate on condition that immediate self-government was granted and Indians allowed to participate in managing the war effort. However, Lord Linlithgow was an avowed imperialist who would have no truck with such outrageous demands. He saw the writing on the wall for the Empire if these demands were conceded and rejected the proposals outright. Instead, anticipating a Congress backlash, he imposed a state of virtual martial law through the Defence of India Act 1939 (No. 35), which was passed on 29 September. He also backdated it to 3 September to ensure any nationalist activity since the declaration would be covered. It was a catch-all piece of legislation echoing the punitive legislation of the past, and rendered anybody 'acting in any manner prejudicial to ... the efficient prosecution of the war',[2] liable to arrest and trial without right of appeal, and upon conviction to transportation for life or even death.

Nonetheless, to sweeten the pill Linlithgow was authorised on 17 October to announce that once the war was over the British government would embark in good faith on a consultative exercise with all parties to shape the country's future as a Dominion. To nationalists this was yet more jam tomorrow and did not address the immediate challenge of India being asked to participate in a war in which they were to be allowed no say. Consequently, following a meeting of the Congress Working Committee which was held between 17 and 31 October, the offer was rejected. Its members began resigning their ministries in the hopes of paralysing the government and forcing the British to the negotiating table. Anticipating the move and the violence which would inevitably follow, the Chiefs of Staff Committee met on 24 October and concluded that because 'we may be faced with a civil disobedience campaign in India in the near future, possibly supported and financed by Russia,'[3] all contingencies needed to be considered to maintain law and order, including invoking the Act and suppressing any signs of sedition. This unwelcome albeit fair prospect was, however, partly offset by two key factors: Congress did not enjoy unanimous support, and the All-India Muslim League opted not to follow their lead.

Instead, Jinnah saw the Congress resignations as an opportunity to reassert League influence, especially over the growing calls for a separate state, and on 22 December declared a 'day of deliverance and thanksgiving',[4] hoping to exploit the rift and galvanise Muslim opinion. The implications for deepening the divide between the two main nationalist parties prompted both Nehru and Gandhi to implore Jinnah to think again, but he was adamant. Jinnah's objective in setting himself and his party apart was explained to League members in Lahore at their 22–25 March 1940 conference. He made what was called the 'Lahore Resolution', 'and announced definitively that 'the Muslims are a nation according to any definition of a nation, and they must have their homelands, their territory and their state.'[5] He went on to insist:

> No constitutional plan would be workable in this country or acceptable to the Muslims unless it is designed on the following basic principle, that geographically contiguous units are demarcated into regions which should be so constituted, with such territorial adjustments as may be necessary, that the areas in which the Muslims are numerically in a majority, as in the North-Western and Eastern Zones of India, should be grouped to constitute 'independent states' in which the constituent groups should be autonomous and sovereign.[6]

But many non-League Muslims as well as Congress derided the idea, with the Muslim Congress leader Abul Kalam Azad mocking it as a 'meaningless and absurd' proposition.[7] Others criticised the double standards inherent in such a new state. Jinnah frequently rejected the prospect of a 'Hindu Raj' in place of a British one, but he saw no apparent contradiction in creating a Muslim state which would mean, as one critic explained, 'imposing, without even their consent and against their declared will, a Muslim Raj over forty five per cent of the population of Bengal, over sixty six per cent of the population of Assam, and jointly speaking, over forty eight per cent of the population of Bengal and Assam, who are non-Muslims'.[8] This was a truth that would later serve to haunt the new state, while in any case Partition would provide a national home for at best half their number, leaving millions more scattered throughout Hindu India, still leaving it with the world's third-largest Muslim population. The rift this exacerbated between Congress and the League was also grist to the mill for men like Churchill. Prime Minister since May 1940, he welcomed this further 'Hindu-Moslem feud' as a 'bulwark of British rule in India',[9] and in any case British policy remained fixed on the provisions of the 1935 Act which allowed only for a single federation, not separation. In a speech at the Foyle Luncheon Club, Secretary of State for India Leo Amery explained the alternative:

> Once broken up into separate independent entities India would relapse, as it did in the decline of the Mughal Empire, into a welter of contending powers, in which free institutions would inevitably be suppressed, and in which no one element would have the resources to defend itself against external attack whether by land or sea.[10]

Eminent British professor R. Coupland concurred. He articulated his arguments against partition in his book *The Future of India*:

> British India has preserved free trade between all parts of a region about half the size of Europe ... raw materials have been produced in one [area], manufactured in another, and the finished goods marketed in all, without having to cross and pay for crossing, a single customs barrier ... partition would throw India back to something like the state she was in after the Mughal Empire had collapsed and before the British Raj replaced it ... [instead] a United States of India might reasonably expect to rank in years to come among the great political units of the world ... she has the potential strength and wealth required to achieve it.[11]

Britain in any case had its hands full with Congress and did not need the added complications implicit in negotiating Partition. On 8 June 1940, Chakravarti Rajagopalachari, since 1937 the premier of the Madras Presidency, produced his own solution to the thorny problem. He proposed that the British simply declare India 'once and for all time free and independent, and then India would declare herself as a new-born ally on the side of England and France',[12] a prospect from which Churchill naturally recoiled. Others still called only for Dominion status, but he opposed even minor concessions let alone being asked to agree to independence overnight. In any case he had his hands full, with Hitler now on the other side of the English Channel and the country facing a life-or-death struggle for its very existence. As he telegraphed Linlithgow on 16 July:

> ... great difficulties in our agreeing upon a new constitutional declaration at the present time when invasion appears imminent, when the life of the Mother Country is obviously at stake, and when in consequence the thrashing out in Parliament of the issues involved in such a far-reaching departure is impossible ...[13]

Moreover, at the other end of the spectrum were the minorities and moderate nationalists who did not sympathise with the Rajagopalachari demand and whose rhetoric renewed fears of being sold out. As the Viceroy warned Amery, 'Indians who genuinely support the war effort would accuse us of again deserting friends and placating enemies,'[14] while the 'cooperation of non-Congress parties will be a real asset [and] ... commit us to nothing in future.'[15] It was proposed therefore that anti-Congress sentiments could be cultivated through an offer to expand the Viceroy's Executive Council, but only 'taking in ... non-official advisers from elements opposed to Congress' which might include League members. Linlithgow, however, thought this might be too provocative, warning it 'may only exacerbate the situation vis a vis Congress and ... tend ultimately to increased communal and party ill-feeling.'[16]

Warren Hastings faces the House of Lords on charges of corruption, 13 February 1788.

The Throne Room, Government House, Calcutta.

Overleaf: The Indian subcontinent around 1783, showing English-, French- and Dutch-controlled territories.

Government Buildings Calcutta.

Contemporary print, dated between 1850 and 1860, showing Indian labourers in Mauritius washing and praying.

European officers of the Madras Infantry, 1847.

Left: Madras cavalry and horse artillery officers, 1847.

Below: View of the Lucknow Residency taken some years after the Mutiny.

A satirical cartoon from an 1896 edition of American publication *Puck* concerning British colonies and interest from the other great powers. The legend reads, 'Greedy Johnnie: He has got a lot of good things – but how long can he keep them to himself?'

Victoria, Queen of an Empire on which the sun never set, until 1947.

Queen Victoria's Diamond Jubilee in 1897 marked the apogee of British power in India.

The Uganda Railway, or 'Lunatic Line', built at the expense of so many Indian labourer's lives.

Edward VII as Prince of Wales, displaying their 'kill'.

Dadabhai Naoroji, moderate
nationalist who sought
self-government through reform,
not revolution.

Famine victim, circa 1900.

Above: Member of the Volunteer Ambulance Corps, ferrying British wounded during the South African War.

Right: Spion Kop, Natal, South Africa, where Indians served alongside the British against the Boers in the South African War.

Above: The Delhi Durbar of 1903, held to celebrate the accession of Edward VII to the Emperorship of India.

Left: Annie Besant in 1906. A stalwart supporter of Indian self-government.

Indian labourers unloading rice-boats, Rangoon, Burma, 1907.

The Prince and Princess of Wales visit Rangoon Burma, 1906.

Left: Neuve Chapelle, one of the first battles of the First World War on the Western Front in which Indian troops were engaged.

Below: Plague Hospital, Bombay 1922. The other side of the Imperial coin.

Indian mosque, Nairobi, 1936.

Girl workers in a booming Bombay textile mill during the Second World War.

Lord Louis Mountbatten in 1943, prior to becoming the last Viceroy of India.

Some of the provincial governors were also wary. Assam, North-West Frontier Province, Orissa and Madras were more bullish, but the Governor of Sind Sir Lancelot Graham warned that 'you would be running a grave risk [of] ... alienating those [non-Congress Hindus] ... anxious to cooperate with you actively in the prosecution of the war.'[17] He also wondered, 'If you put yourself in the hands of the Moslem League, is there not a risk of your [the Viceroy] being interpreted as having accepted Pakistan?'[18] Churchill remained opposed too, preoccupied with maintaining the war effort, persuading the United States to help save the country and fending off the Germans. He nonetheless reluctantly approved a limited enlargement of the Viceroy's Executive Council and the establishment of a War Advisory Committee, reforms which he felt committed the British to nothing but which might reassure moderate opinion. These proposals would be included in a formal announcement clarifying the British government's longer-term strategy,[19] and on 8 August 1940 a statement was released which it was hoped would defer the issue:

> Last October His Majesty's Government made it clear that Dominion Status was their objective for India. They added that they were ready to authorise the expansion of the Governor-General's Council to include a certain number of representatives of the political parties, and they proposed the establishment of a consultative committee ... they hope that in this process new bonds of union and understanding will emerge, and thus pave the way towards the attainment by India of that free and equal partnership in the British Commonwealth which remains the proclaimed and accepted goal of the Imperial Crown and of the British Parliament.[20]

Congress's reaction to what they considered a damp squib was predictably negative. It ignored the Rajagopalachari proposals altogether, instead asking for nationalist cooperation now in return for something ill defined at some unspecified future date. But when they turned to Gandhi for guidance his response was equally disappointing. Instead of responding with rousing oratory to stir the masses, he appointed an emissary, Vinoba Bhave, to simply tour the country urging boycotts and non-cooperation. He was to tell villagers and city dwellers that it was 'wrong to help the British war effort with men and money ... the only worthy effort is to resist all war with non-violent resistance.'[21] Although Congress as a whole urged a more pro-active stance, this approach was hardly likely to energise the population into mass resistance but it was nonetheless deemed serious enough by the government to prompt the rounding up of ringleaders and prominent nationalists, including Nehru. Instead of being silenced, however, Nehru took advantage of the publicity that his arrest attracted, and in Gorakhpur Prison on 3 November 1940 he further clarified the Congress position:

> [We] have had a year of war government. The people's elected legislatures have been suspended and ignored, and a greater and more

widespread autocracy prevails here than anywhere else in the world
... [therefore] ... we must dissociate ourselves from this war and
advise our people to do likewise and not help in any way with money
or men ...[22]

Yet despite such passion, Congress appeared to be having had little impact
upon the wider public mood. We have seen how Nehru had long before
conceded that Congress at best enjoyed the confidence of half a million
grassroots activists at any one time, and the result of its call to action
appeared to underline the fact. On 29 November Delhi told Amery that
despite the Congress leadership's best efforts, 'there is still no real excitement
in most places,'[23] and rather than the hundreds of thousands of arrests that
might have been anticipated, late 1940 and early 1941 saw only 30,000.

But despite many key protagonists being in prison, the League standing
aloof from their boycott and the challenge to authority so far less than
expected, there was little let-up in pressure from those nationalists still
capable of voicing their opinions. A so-called Non Party conference was held
in Bombay in March 1941 under the chairmanship of Sir Tej Bahadur Sapru
which demanded a new Executive Council of entirely non-official members
with full responsibilities over the government, and for the British to give
a definitive time limit within which the country would be established as a
Dominion. Sapru visited Linlithgow on 7 April and presented him with a
copy of the demands, but the Viceroy was not very forthcoming. Amery
instead spoke in the House of Commons on 23 April, proposing that, in
view of the fact that the eleven former Congress provinces were de facto
without a government, the constitution be suspended under Section 93 of
the Government of India Act. In May Linlithgow held discussions with
representatives from other groups in order to gauge so-called moderate
opinion and demonstrate that it was not the British government blocking
progress.

Little of promise developed until in August 1941 the ambitious-sounding
Atlantic Charter was published, underwritten by US President Roosevelt
and his now loyal sidekick Winston Churchill. It was a document which
spoke highmindedly of, among other things, a bright new post-war world
in which, as Article Three pointed out, 'the right of all peoples to choose
the government under which they live' would be respected,[24] and granting
self-government and democracy to those who demanded it. But it was not
all it was held up to be, and the British government had no intention of
practising what it preached – especially towards India. Despite raising the
hopes of colonial peoples all around the world, Leo Amery dismissed it as
'meaningless platitudes and dangerous ambiguities',[25] to which Britain had
signed up mainly to placate the Roosevelt and secure further assistance in
prosecuting the war. He added that Article Three in particular 'was inserted
primarily as a reassurance that we are not out to democratise countries
that prefer a different form of government',[26] and certainly not to signal a

process of immediate decolonisation. Another hardened cynic, Sir James P. J. Grigg, Under-Secretary at the War Office, derided the entire document and all its promises as 'poppycock'[27] with no relevance to the realities of Britain's worldview. The widespread disappointment this utterance caused was shared by sympathisers in Britain. Labour MPs Rhys Davies, W. G. Grove and R. R. Stokes issued a document in which they argued that 'as Britishers we must, if our sincerity is to be believed, apply this principle to India and the Colonial Empire ... [but] the prime minister has categorically declared against this policy specifically excluding India, a statement which has been described by the premier of the Punjab as the biggest rebuff that India has ever received.'[28]

This sentiment also received a great amount of sympathy in the United States where public opinion had long been hostile to British imperialism. Its propensity to imprison nationalists was also proving to be a hard sell for diplomats in Washington. Having reached another impasse, Nehru's release was recommended by Lord Linlithgow in November 1941 as a gesture of goodwill. He admitted to Amery that 'his detention, however justified, was producing a bad effect in Left Centre in Parliament and doing harm in USA,'[29] but he remained 'absolutely opposed to a wholesale release of prisoners without a definite guarantee from Congress that civil disobedience will be called off'.[30] Churchill was also worried that 'the release of these prisoners will be proclaimed as a victory,'[31] and he advocated standing firm. Furthermore, Congress's campaign was still failing to stir the masses, and Linlithgow was able to report confidently that 'outside the United Provinces there was little public interest, and from May onwards figures [of arrests] began to drop rapidly ... by October 1st they were down to 5,600 ... [and] in spite of Mr Gandhi's appeal there has been no desire on the part of his released followers to invite a second imprisonment. The whole campaign has in fact, been a complete failure.'[32]

Still, matters could not remain in a state of limbo indefinitely. Jinnah was still arguing for his own state, but partition was something the British still refused to contemplate. In a speech discussing 'the Indian constitutional problem' at the Manchester Luncheon Club on 19 November 1941, Amery reiterated that even if some sort of Indian unity had not already existed, 'it would have to be invented'.[33] Nor was there any sign that Congress was going to be drawn on the matter. Instead, on 30 December 1941, the Congress Working Committee framed the so-called Bardoli Resolution, which reiterated the Rajagopalachari demand of the previous year. This simply entrenched positions and did not advance the question of India's future any further than it had been two years before, and on 8 January 1942, Amery broke from his usually diplomatic prose and launched instead into a scathing indictment of Congress. He condemned its 'ingrained conviction that it is the natural heir to the British Government in India and entitled to take over control both of legislative and executive power, unfettered by any limitations save such "safeguards" for the "minorities" as it has professed to be willing to grant',[34] while Linlithgow denounced the Bardoli Resolution as little more than 'a reiteration of the Congress demand for surrender by His Majesty's Government to Congress claims ... ignoring other parties and interests and their own obligations in the hope that they will get Congress support in fighting the war ... The Moslem League attitude, so far as I am aware, remains unchanged, with Jinnah apprehensive that His Majesty's Government will allow themselves to be stampeded by Hindus and Congress.'[35] Furthermore, he claimed that the Muslim leader was afraid Britain would continue to 'rule out Pakistan'.[36]

The government was also preoccupied with the possibility of external threats, with Japan having entered the war in December of the previous year and advancing upon Britain's colonies in Malaya and Burma. The Viceroy expressed anxiety that any 'further transfer of power would give marked encouragement to Quisling activity ... there is a large and dangerous potential fifth column in Bengal, Assam and Bihar and Orissa ... Potential of pro-enemy sympathy and activity in Eastern India is enormous.'[37]

Nonetheless, there was more encouraging news coming from other quarters, with Indian industry functioning well despite calls not to cooperate with the war effort. Some 1,250,000 tons of steel had been produced, while 7,000,000 army uniforms and nearly 4,000,000 boots were being manufactured every month. Furthermore, six ordnance factories were now in operation, and an aircraft factory in Bangalore was busy providing repair facilities. Amery was also delighted to report that 'the Ministry of Aircraft Production have placed an order for 400 gliders with the Indian firm of Tata.'[38] India's contribution to the war effort was not only to be quantified in material terms. As Labour's Lord Faringdon reminded his fellow peers:

> India has paid handsome dividends, and is paying handsome dividends, for anything which we may have done for her. It has incidentally been computed that in addition to the interest on something like £1,000,000,000 invested in India, in the form of pensions and in other ways, India pays annually something in the neighbourhood of £138,000,000 to this country. That is a substantial sum, and a sum which puts us under a very considerable obligation to India ...[39]

Between 1939 and 1946, the Government of India would spend astronomical sums, in consequence of which over 17,000,000,000 rupees was stored in the Bank of England, rising further to some 21,000,000,000 rupees by the war's end.[40] So, with Jinnah relatively compliant, Congress far less of a threat to the war effort than might have been feared and the majority of Indians willing to carry on as usual, matters might have coasted along comfortably. But the war with Japan, an event which completely revolutionised Anglo-Indian relations, was not going well. After the Imperial Japanese Army captured Singapore in February and then swept through Burma and Malaya, Linlithgow's apprehensions appeared to have been vindicated. Commander-in-Chief General Sir Claude Auchinleck painted a stark picture of the situation:

> [Natives show] little antipathy for [the] Japanese ... in Bengal left wing elements have professed readiness [to] support Japanese invaders [and there is a] ... danger active fifth column undoubtedly exists ... heavy exodus from East India industrial areas and Bombay, prompted by [the fear of] bombing ... expectation [of] rioting ... communal troubles [and] looting ... police forces ... inadequate ... danger to communications from sabotage ... Anti-war and defeatist rumours being spread especially [in] recruiting centres...[41]

But such reports sounded far too apocalyptic for Amery, who was hardly able to digest such dire news. Instead he telegrammed Linlithgow, asking for 'urgently your official criticisms or endorsement of [Auchinleck's] report and also your views on situation generally as it has developed since fall of Singapore'.[42] Much to Amery's relief, Linlithgow's response was far less pessimistic. He reported that 'industrial centres have not so far been appreciably affected,' although he expressed some concern over 'Axis broadcasts, alarmist rumours ... [and] irresponsible utterances from political speakers ... [the] withdrawal [of deposits] from savings banks and discharge of cash certificates ... and a tendency to hoarding'.[43]

Despite Linlithgow's evaluation, the fall of Singapore proved a disastrous blow to British prestige. G. W. Seabridge, editor of the *Straits Times* from 1928 until the island fell, was scathing, both regarding preparations for the invasion, and the manner in which it was confronted. He censured the civil administration for having 'cracked badly and [breaking] completely at some points. There was little cooperation with the services, and many indications of jealousy and fear that outsiders might poach on the preserves of the civil servant ... The extent to which obstructionists flourished was staggering.'[44] Seabridge also repeated 'many bitterly sarcastic references among the Asiatics to subjects of the Protecting Power who were concerned only with protecting their own skins and leaving the "protected" to face whatever might befall [them]'.[45] If this was the standard of leadership in Singapore, what confidence could there be that Europeans in Bengal, Assam and elsewhere might not simply fold and bolt?

Nonetheless, there were two sides to this coin, and if the nationalists were minded to use these reports as grist their mill, they were also reminded that Japanese invasion did not equate to benevolent liberation. Foreign Secretary Anthony Eden reminded the House of Commons how the 'Japanese at Hong Kong perpetrated against their helpless military prisoners and civil population, without distinction of race or colour, the same kind of barbarities which aroused the horror of the civilised world at the time of the Nanking Massacre of 1937 ... officers and men of the British army ... bound hand and foot and then bayoneted to death ... women, both Asiatic and European, were raped and murdered ... one entire Chinese district was declared a brothel.'[46] The prospect of being deserted by the British and left to the tender mercies of the Japanese was not therefore a reassuring prospect. Nonetheless, if forced to choose between British rule for the foreseeable future or the prospect of Japanese 'liberation' and the chance of freedom, the latter option might be more appealing. In that event, law and order could break down completely and the country descend into anarchy. Amery wired Linlithgow that 'with a [war] situation which must for some time ahead get worse instead of better, we cannot afford to delay our announcement of policy much further.'

Nonetheless, there were still many opinions and viewpoints which would have to be factored in before any renewed offer could enjoy popular acceptance. The Muslim Minister of Labour in the Viceroy's Executive Council, Firoz Khan Noon, warned, 'His Majesty's Government will be playing with fire if they establish a Hindu Raj in defiance of all the friendly elements who are responsible for great war effort of India at the moment.' He also hoped that 'His Majesty's Government will stand by their duty which involves protection of best interests of the people of India as a whole,'[48] and was convinced that this would have to include serious consideration of Jinnah's aspirations, while early in March a new Cabinet committee under the chairmanship of Clement Attlee was formed to decide upon the next steps. The government was also becoming increasingly fearful that the existing consensus might unravel and concerned about being overtaken by events. The war situation was continuing to deteriorate and the last thing that was needed now was an ungovernable India. Four days after the Japanese took Rangoon on 7 March 1942, the British announced that they were sending Leader of the House of Commons Sir Stafford Cripps with fresh proposals. Urged by his colleagues to show some willingness to compromise, on 12 March he outlined the Cabinet's latest plan to the House of Commons:

> Immediately upon the cessation of hostilities, steps shall be taken to set up in India ... an elected body charged with the task of framing a new constitution for India ... provision shall be made ... for the participation of the Indian States in the constitution making body ... the right of any province of British India that is not prepared to accept the new constitution to retain its present constitutional position, provision being made for its subsequent accession to it if it decides.[49]

But even before Cripps set off on his mission the proposals were condemned as mere cant and too little too late. At a meeting of the Communist Party's Central Committee on 14 March in Swansea, General Secretary Harry Pollitt ridiculed the offer, mocking the fact that 'India is belatedly and begrudgingly now to be wooed, by some magic formula, not as an act of justice and equity, but only because Japan is at the Gates.'[50] It was a view which reflected the nationalist position, and one Amery feared Gandhi might exploit, 'with [the] aim of compelling the British to withdraw from India ... we must be prepared for a movement instigated by Gandhi to defy the law of the land, and incidentally to obstruct the war effort.'[51] He therefore advocated preparing for the inevitable, insisting that 'even Gandhi cannot be permitted to flout the law of the land and must be treated like any other law-breaker.'[52] Bearing in mind Britain's now blemished world reputation he also suggested that 'it is highly important that opinion – particularly in America – should not be taken by surprise if repressive measures are forced on us, I am taking steps to warn His Majesties Representatives in Washington, Kuibyshev [at that time the alternative capital of the Soviet Union], and Chungking and the UK High Commissions in the Dominions.'[53] He also decided, however, that because 'any intervention on our part would merely stiffen Gandhi's attitude and might well present opponents or waverers to his cause ... we therefore propose to wait and see'.[54] As events were to prove, he would not have long to wait.

Cripps, accompanied by Attlee, arrived in Delhi on 22 March only to draw fire from all quarters. The Chamber of Princes put the British on notice that 'for any scheme to be acceptable to the States [it] must effectively protect their rights arising from the Treaties',[55] while Gandhi left him in no doubt that 'Congress would not accept the Declaration, owing firstly, to the provisions regarding the Indian States, and, secondly, those dealing with accession or non-accession of provinces.'[56] His meeting with Jinnah was equally unrewarding; he was 'mainly interested whether these Provinces [Bengal and Punjab] could have an effective right to opt out of the proposed Union',[57] and continued to demand his Muslim state.[58] Cripps also met Sikhs and representatives of the Depressed Classes, both of whom expressed reservations. The Sikh All Parties Committee was nervous for the Punjab's prospects should Pakistan be conceded, telling him that 'we shall resist by all possible means separation of the Punjab from an All-India Union'.[59] When he met Rajagopalachari, however, he appeared to have become more pre-occupied with semantics than practicalities. Congress did not like the term 'Dominion', he advised, with all the undertones of subservience that it implied. Should India choose to remain in the British Commonwealth it would want the new country to be known simply as a 'Free Member State'.[60] It was amid this flurry of conflicting and mutually incompatible demands that Sir Stafford attempted to mediate, but in doing so he committed such a diplomatic faux pas that he made matters worse.

On 29 March, Cripps confirmed that once it became a Dominion India 'will be completely free to remain within or go without the Commonwealth of Nations', and therefore 'to take all measures which are open to a sovereign state'.[61] He added furthermore that 'the moment the new constitution comes into force, the changeover takes place,'[62] and that Britain will have no further say in the nation's decisions. Although since the Statute of Westminster these were perfectly valid points, such a proposal simply threw the cat among the pigeons and sent moderate nationalists, minorities and most notably Jinnah into a tailspin. The admission confirmed their worst fears, that if power were handed over to a Hindu-dominated government all their aspirations would be subsumed by those of the majority community. Linlithgow warned that as a consequence of Cripps' statement 'all [the] minorities and Princes have ... been seriously upset'[63] by being side-lined in an attempt to succour Congress. In the meantime, Cripps compounded the felony when he appeared to imply that the Viceroy's Council might have the powers of a cabinet, with executive powers and the right to outvote the Viceroy.

Back in Britain, Churchill seethed. Cripps had wildly overstepped his brief and made undertakings far beyond any he could stomach. He was particularly appalled by the proposed changes to the council, which implied that any disagreement between its members and the Viceroy 'could arise in its most acute form if they were to demand [a] cessation of hostilities in India against [the] guns of His Majesty's Government'.[64] Congress was left with precisely that impression, and now demanded immediate control of the Indian Army, foreign affairs, and a much greater say over the budget, none of which Churchill would contemplate. On defence in particular the Viceroy insisted that 'it is not possible to take away from Commander-in-Chief the substance of Defence Portfolio as now held by him in order to entrust it to a representative Indian,'[65] while the latest incumbent to the post, General Archibald Wavell, confirmed 'it would not be possible to separate my dual function as Civil and Defence Member without causing complete dislocation.'[66]

When rumours of such a possibility leaked out they soon sounded alarm bells in other quarters, providing a revealing insight into the prevailing attitudes of many whites concerning the capabilities of even educated Indians. General Smuts reminded the Prime Minister that 'India is now key to our whole Empire's defence and putting that key in unskilled Indian hands may have fatal results for this war.'[67] Such sentiments chimed perfectly with Churchill's opinions. He insisted to the Viceroy that 'there can be no question of any convention limiting in any way your powers under the existing constitution ... if Congress leaders had gathered the impression that such a new convention is now possible, this impression should be definitely removed.'[68] Instead, a rather clumsy compromise was suggested and Congress was to be offered an insulting sop. An Indian minister could be appointed, 'with responsibility for demobilisation and post-war reconstruction, public relations, the coordination of fuel supplies, the provision of amenities for troops such as canteen facilities ... accommodation and social arrangements'.[69]

The reaction to the proposal was as could have been expected, so Cripps, assailed on all sides and resigned to the futility of his mission, cabled the Cabinet in London on 1 April that 'from all appearance it seems that Congress will turn down the proposals ... they are selecting the question of defence as their main platform for opposition ... the Muslim League ... will no doubt if Congress refuse also find some reasons for refusal as well,'[70] and this was precisely the outcome. Faced with London's offer, Nehru told a press conference on 25 April that 'if Sir Cripps thinks that the position in India has improved by his visit, he is grievously mistaken. The gulf is as great today than ever before ... it surprises me that the British Government could still talk in its old pre-war patronising language and try to pose to the world that it is a kind of arbitration in India.'[71] Gandhi also rejected the proposals, dismissing them as 'a post-dated cheque on a bank that was already crashing'.[72] In the middle of this melee was President Roosevelt's emissary to India, Colonel Louis Johnson. He believed Churchill's Machiavellian machinations were really behind the failure of the mission, confiding in the President that 'neither Churchill, the Viceroy nor Wavell desired that the Cripps mission be a success and ... in fact, were determined that it should not be.'[73]

So the Cripps mission had failed and they were back to square one. In the meantime, the Japanese threat to the borders of India was increasing at the worst possible time. Cripps was all too aware of the country's volatile state, warning that 'except in the Punjab and the North-West Frontier Province the present situation as to morale amongst the Indian and in many cases the European population is deplorable. The anti-British feeling is running very strong ... unrest is growing ... the outlook so far as internal situation goes is exceedingly bad and if we cannot persuade Indian leaders to come in now and help us we shall have to resort to suppression ... which may well get out of hand ... even though we use for this purpose a part of our frail military.'[74]

Moreover, on 11 April more bad news filtered through from Burma:

A serious problem has arisen ... in connection with the refugees who are trying to get into India. The Indian population of Burma in normal times is rather more than one million. Many of these, as well as European women and children left Burma before the sea route was closed, and since then and up to the end of March 35,000 Indians and 700 Europeans have passed over the route of the new road now under construction ... The Governor has reported that he is trying hard to avoid racial or class distinction ... [but] failure to evacuate a large number of Indians is bound to arouse an outcry ... the refugee problem is already becoming a first-class political problem in India – and according to one press correspondent has been influencing the attitude of the Congress Party towards the constitution proposals.[75]

Yet despite these dire developments, Amery refused to countenance any further offers, insisting that 'initiative must now come from Indians. We can hardly be expected after this rejection, to go chasing them again, or to send yet another emissary.'[76]

Such entrenched positions served only to make Congress even more uncompromising, and probably vindicated the British stand over changes to the Viceroy's Council and the defence portfolio. When the All-India Congress met in Allahabad between 29 April and 1 May it agreed a resolution stating that 'Japan's quarrel is not with India. She is warring against the British Empire ... if India were freed her first step would probably be to negotiate with Japan ... The AICC is therefore of the opinion that the British should withdraw from India ... the Committee appeals to Britain ... to let go her hold'.[77] Gandhi then wrote on 3 May that he was 'convinced the presence of the British is the incentive for Japanese attack', on 10 May adding demands for Britain's 'complete and immediate withdrawal from India'. In a press interview on 15 May he said Congress policy was 'to advise the British to leave the country, and if they do not do so force them to go by non-cooperation'.[78] Understandably, newspapers such as the *Times of India* and the *Eastern Times* condemned Gandhi's position, while the Muslim League journal *Dawn* predicted that his strategy could only result in the law of the jungle,[79] with Jinnah accusing Congress of simply trying to exploit the situation to force the British to 'establish a Hindu Raj'.[80]

Despite such opprobrium, Gandhi was unrepentant. He said in response to his critics that 'even if all the United Nations oppose me, even if the whole of India tried to persuade me I am wrong, even then I will go ahead.'[81] Lord Linlithgow, however, assured London that matters were still under control: 'I see no sign of any particular excitement in the country ... I doubt if response to an appeal for mass civil obedience by Gandhi would be in any sense wholehearted.'[82] Nevertheless, while 'neither His Majesty's Government nor I have any desire to take on Congress ... if Congress attitude forces us to take them on, we must be prepared to do so and with utmost vigour.'[83] That determination was soon to be put to the test. On 8 August, following a speech by Gandhi, Congress's call for Britain to simply hand over power was crystallized in one pithy phrase: 'Quit India'.

The premise was that unless the British resigned their posts and offices immediately and handed them over to Indians, the country would immediately be paralyzed and rendered ungovernable. Such a prospect was becoming increasingly likely as tempers frayed, so Amery moved quickly. Invoking the Emergency Powers Act, he implemented well-rehearsed plans to round up the senior leadership, issuing an 'Extraordinary Gazette Notification', charging Congress with being a 'totalitarian organisation'[84] and announcing that it was proscribed forthwith. The expected disorder followed, and on 18 August, ten days into the campaign, Wavell described a worrying situation, reporting how 'two Europeans were pulled from [a] train and killed ... RAF personnel mobbed in railway compartment and attacked ... serious rioting near Trichinopoly ... student hooliganism continues in Calcutta ... minor disturbances Dacca'.[85] By the end of the month a thousand were dead and three times as many wounded. By mid-

September 1942, 240 railway stations had been destroyed or seriously damaged, government offices and banks ransacked and set on fire, and 550 post offices and sixty-five police stations attacked, many destroyed.[86] Innocent Indians working for the government were also beaten up and some murdered, including forty-three railway employees and twenty-six government employees.[87]

Still Churchill refused to compromise, insisting that the violence 'did not represent the masses of the Indian people',[88] while Lord Linlithgow claimed that 'apart from a small coterie of ambitious politicians, there was precious little interest in any radical change in the system of government.'[89] By January 1943, in any case, it appeared that the rioters might well be running out of steam. One report asserted that 'the "Congress rebellion" has degenerated into spasmodic terrorist outrages ... [although] isolated sabotage incidents continue to occur.'[90] Despite sensing that the nationalist campaign was losing momentum, Gandhi announced from prison on 10 February 1943 that he was intending to embark on a hunger strike, prompting further boycotts and demonstrations. Then came a hint of a possible change of tack.

On 1 October 1943 Lord Linlithgow, having come to the end of his long tenure, was replaced by newly promoted Field Marshal Wavell. Having clashed with Churchill over Middle East military strategy, Wavell had been sent to command forces in the Far East. His previous experience as Commander-in-Chief of India was undoubtedly an asset, but unlike his predecessor the plain-speaking military man did not see eye to eye with Churchill. Despite some nationalist newspapers calling his appointment the continuation of existing policy 'with the additional touch of a military mind',[91] Wavell brought a more conciliatory tempo, telling a press conference, 'I am a sincere friend of India ... I am wholeheartedly in sympathy with her aspirations to political development.'[92] But, despite Amery's public assurances at a meeting of the East Indian Association on 26 October 1943 that it was for India to decide 'the constitution under which [her] destiny was to be carried forward in coming years',[93] Wavell was not convinced. He echoed Colonel Johnson's suspicions that 'the Cabinet is not honest in its expressed desire to make progress in India.'[94]

Furthermore, denied the plenipotentiary powers he would have needed to make any real inroads, he soon found his hands were tied, and when he suggested releasing all Congress prisoners and inviting them to a conference in Simla Churchill overruled him.[95] In recording his frustrations in his diary on 8 October he confirmed Churchill's intransigence: 'P.M. was menacing and unpleasant ... and indicated that only over his dead body would any approach to Gandhi take place. I think ... he is determined to block any political advance so long as he is in power.'[96] Faced by a veritable brick wall, all that was left to Wavell was 'continual hard work, and almost continual failure. No rest, no success.'[97] Instead, it was to be hoped that the two key nationalists might find a way forward.

Following his eventual release from prison on humanitarian grounds, Gandhi held a series of meetings with Jinnah between 19 and 27 September 1944. Gandhi appeared to finally accept the concept of Pakistan, but subject to conditions. Jinnah must first endorse all-India independence and cooperate in the formation of an interim government during a transition period. A commission would then be established at the end of the war and demarcate Muslim-majority areas in which referenda would be held with a view to creating a Muslim bloc.[98] This was not good enough for Jinnah, who rejected an offer that would, he said, leave him with little more than a 'bundle of contiguous areas',[99] resulting in 'a maimed, mutilated and moth-eaten' Pakistan.[100] The meetings ended in yet another impasse while the rest of the country, and particularly its armed forces, fought on against the King-Emperor's enemies.

10

'This is the last Indian Army order'

Much of the Raj's ability to prosecute the war against Japan and its Axis allies was predicated upon the unswerving loyalty and reliability of its Indian Army. By this stage in the war its ranks were serving in many theatres including Europe, Africa, the Middle East and closer to home protecting the subcontinent itself. They were also helping to maintain internal order, protecting British interests against rioters, terrorists and the more extreme elements of the Quit India campaign.

Much of the credit for this bond arose from a lineage that could be traced back to the earliest days of the East India Company. From small beginnings many fine regiments had earned numerous battle honours and been imbued with a tradition of excellence. Indian soldiers had indeed been an indispensable component of the Company almost from the day it needed to protect its first factory, but it was not until Major Stringer Lawrence arrived on the scene that an army in the modern sense came into being. When the French attacked Fort St George at Madras in 1746 its garrison consisted of only 150 Europeans and was totally outnumbered by the cannier French. It was consequently left with no choice but to cede a prized and highly profitable commercial asset for the want of a credible defence. This calamity prompted the Company to up its game, and the decision was taken to augment its European defenders with 2,000 Indians, the nucleus of what became known as the Madras Presidency Army,[1] to which Stringer added the Bombay Presidency Army in 1748.[2]

Stringer's work was further enhanced by Colonel John Abercron, who in 1754 began the process of amalgamating the European and Indian contingents with regular British regiments,[3] and the first regiment of Regular Native Infantry or sepoys, from the Persian *sipahi*, meaning soldier, was raised in 1757 after the Bengal Presidency Army was created.[4] It was christened the 'Lal Paltan' or Red Regiment and would be joined by such formations as the Punjab Regiment in 1759, and the Rajputana Rifles and the Rajputana Regiment, raised respectively in 1775 and 1778. Later the

129th Baluchis would be formed in 1844, followed by Coke's Rifles and Wilde's Rifles in 1849, and the Royal Garwal Rifles in 1887, all bound by honour to continue the traditions of their forebears. Many cavalry regiments too would go on to gain considerable renown, for example Skinner's Horse, founded by James Skinner in 1803, later to become the 1st Bengal Lancers and going on to fight in the Punjab, China and both the First and Second World Wars. There was the Deccan Horse, with a lineage going back to the 1790s, the Poona Horse founded in 1820, the Bengal Light Cavalry in 1797, the Scinde Horse raised in 1838, and Hodson's Horse, created in 1857.

While regimental structures along with their rules and regulations evolved slightly differently between the three armies, that of Bengal serves to illustrate the basic formation of an average infantry unit. Each was commanded by a lieutenant-colonel and divided into ten companies, to which was assigned two British and two native officers, an adjutant, interpreter and a quartermaster. There were 800 privates to each regiment, 120 non-commissioned officers – havildars and naiks – and twenty native commissioned officers – subedars and jemadars. In addition, there were two British sergeants and twenty-six British commissioned officers.[5] The first native cavalry regiment was raised in Bengal in 1796, modelled largely on those of Britain,[6] commanded by a colonel and two lieutenant-colonels. A regiment consisted of two wings, each under the command of a major, six or seven captains and twelve lieutenants, and the junior officers serving as adjutants, interpreters, quartermasters and so on, in addition to a surgeon and a veterinary surgeon. The rank and file comprised 400 *sowars*, a term originating from the days of the Mughals and meaning horse-soldier.

What motivated recruits to join any of the Presidency armies varied widely. Many were drawn by the desire to continue a martial tradition, others by regular pay, a wish to escape rural poverty or the promise of a secure pension after twenty years' service. Others were attracted by the prospect of adventure. Eleven-year-old Muslim Sake Dean Mahomed wrote in 1761 how he was lured to the colours because 'the notion of carrying arms and living in a camp could not be easily removed' and thus 'my fond mother's entreaties were of no avail … Her disappointment smote my soul'[7] as, like thousands of others, he made the army his new home. For their part, the Presidencies naturally sought to appropriate the fighting skills of men from predominantly warrior castes, Brahmins, Rajputs and Muslims – those it was believed would cut the mustard – but this was not always practicable. Consequently, in 1777 there were complaints of recruits to the Madras Army being 'low in size, low in caste, and very bad indeed',[8] but a later commander, General Harris, nevertheless insisted that although 'such men obtained in southern countries are much inferior to the northern recruits in caste, size and appearance … they are nevertheless hardy and thrifty'.[9]

The preference for higher-caste men persisted nonetheless, so that in 1839 it was necessary to issue a General Order instructing that 'all natives are eligible for enlistment without reference to caste, provided they are in other respects perfectly fit for service.'[10] By the 1850s this meant that on average the sepoy was 'rather a small man, but he is of an active make, and capable of undergoing great fatigue upon a slender diet'.[11] The Bombay Army's initial choice of recruits also could not have been further removed from the high warrior caste. It called largely upon the Mahars, so-called Untouchables, for whom life as a sepoy promised an escape from the drudgery and oppression of an otherwise unbearable life. At one time they constituted a fifth to a quarter of the army, although it also employed a significant force of British, Swiss and German mercenaries. Higher-caste Marathas also formed a significant proportion, being the Presidency's largest ethnic group, as well as Telegus, Jews and low-caste Hindus. Nonetheless, the Madras and Bombay Armies were relatively small bodies by comparison to Bengal, which maintained by far the largest army and implemented a much stricter recruitment policy.

The Bengal force chose its men almost exclusively from the higher castes, producing tight-knit units but also a culture of separateness, setting themselves apart from lower-caste soldiers, even those of higher rank. In 1855 Captain Rafter described his Rajput sepoys as 'born a soldier, and ... obedient, zealous and faithful'[12] but sharing a greater affinity with one another than those under whom they served. This sense of otherness manifested itself in various ways. Lt-General Sir Charles Napier complained how 'all the higher Hindoo [sic] castes are imbued with gross superstitions. One goes to the devil if he easts this; another if he eats that; a third will not touch his dinner if the shadow of an infidel passes over it; a further will not drink water unless it has been drawn by one of his own caste.'[13] Nonetheless, for the most part the British were prepared to entertain these foibles for the sake of morale and military cohesion. Lt-Colonel William Sleeman assured his fellow countrymen that when they were committed into action 'a braver set of men is hardly anywhere to be found,'[14] but they also possessed one further idiosyncrasy. They could refuse to serve overseas, or the Black Water – *Kala Pani* – as they referred to it,[15] because they claimed that by doing so they could forfeit caste completely. Although their superiors harboured a strong suspicion that this was simply a ruse because they did not want to be parted from their families for long periods, the refusal would prove increasingly irksome.

Pay was obviously a key incentive for recruitment, and at seven rupees, or roughly seven shillings a month, it was calculated to be double that which could be earned by the 'class of person from which they are generally drawn'.[16] A havildar could earn double that of a private soldier at fourteen rupees a month, and increments of between ten or twelve rupees a year were also the norm after sixteen and twenty years' service.[17] Nonetheless, it was no king's ransom, comparing poorly with a regular British private's fifteen rupees a month, and was much less than, say, a village carpenter who might expect to earn up to ten rupees or even a blacksmiths' twenty rupees a month from his labours. Moreover, Bengal sepoys had several deductions made to meet the cost of their uniform and equipment, food, laundry, the barber and even for baggage when their regiment was on the march, and particularly the much-resented and so-called off-reckoning system. Senior officers often exploited this arrangement to retain the difference between what the men contributed and what was actually spent, sharing the windfall among themselves and causing understandable animosity. Moreover, pay failed to keep up with the cost of living. Measured by the price of grain, costs doubled between 1796 and 1852, and while the village artisan could increase their prices to offset inflation, sepoy pay remained static. It stood at seven rupees or so from 1800 until 1895, and only then was it raised to nine rupees a month. In 1837 some attempt was made to ameliorate the more egregious aspects of their terms and conditions when pay and entitlements were rationalised across the three armies, and the number of years a sepoy needed to serve to qualify for a pension was reduced from twenty to fifteen. The pension too was increased from three to four rupees a month, but these measures did little to offset the financial burdens imposed.

Nor were low pay and deductions the sole cause for discontent. Men accustomed to loose-fitting cotton garments, ideally suited to the climate and their way of life, were squeezed into impractical uniforms and obliged to cope with unsuitable equipment. His tunic and trousers, designed for show and little else, were tight and constricting, making mobility all but impossible in the stifling heat. Balanced on their head for many years was the *shako*, a cumbersome headdress weighing between 2 and 3 pounds and nearly 9 inches in height. Not only did it cut into the head, it was such a nuisance that men had to keep one hand free to stop it slipping over their eyes or toppling off entirely when in action. Some were burdened with less troublesome forms of headdress but even these could cause issues. One was a round hat which too closely resembled that worn by Europeans and Indian converts to Christianity, a further affront to the highly sensitive Brahmins and Rajputs. The men also had to wear a knapsack made of painted cloth through which no air could penetrate to the back, crammed with often redundant kit and rubbing against flayed skin for hours on end. Knapsack and belt were held together by tight leather straps which clawed into the upper body, and from which hung ammunition pouches containing sixty rounds of ammunition. All together this made for a total weight of some 65 pounds to be lugged around in suffocating heat and dust.[18]

Most appalling of all perhaps was the tight leather stock. This evil device was tucked around the neck and secured with a brass clasp, designed solely for the purpose of maintaining an upright and soldierly posture. It had no practical application but, as Lt-General Napier explained, 'it prevents the free use of the musket in battle; and when taking to the bayonet, if the stock be not thrown away, the man is half strangled before closing in mortal strife.'[19] He suggested that whoever was responsible for inventing this horrendous object 'should be ranked for venomous imagination in tormenting his fellow creatures'.[20] Nonetheless, the device remained in use for many years. Their personal weapon was the British Land Pattern Musket or Brown Bess, in service from 1722 to 1838. Some 58½ inches long, these 0.75 calibre muzzle-loaded monsters added a further 10 pounds and 3 ounces to the sepoy's load, and he was expected to fire it at a rate of six rounds per minute while weighed down by the rest of his kit. It was topped with a 21-inch bayonet, an item of weaponry synonymous with the British style of close-quarter fighting, but which was also awkward and cumbersome.

Sometimes sepoys could only bear so much, borne down by these encumbrances day in day out as an indifferent officer class demonstrated no empathy for their suffering and discomfort. In the southern Indian city of Vellore in July 1806 emotions had been particularly strained for some time, and the sepoys needed just one more affront to set them off. Unpopular instructions had been issued requiring Muslims to trim their beards and adopt restyled turbans, and Hindus to dispense with caste marks while on duty.[21] Furthermore, Hindu soldiers had been ordered to wear the highly unpopular round hats, which the officers argued gave the men a more soldierly bearing but which the sepoys despised. Both took exception to these perceived slights on their religions and urged their officers to reconsider. After fruitlessly voicing their concerns the men lost patience and seized the fort, embarking upon an orgy of killing in which 200 Europeans and 350 of the mutineers perished. The arrival of cavalry and artillery from Arcot brought the insurrection to an end, but the incident served as a cautionary tale. In the event the Company held an enquiry into the incident and found the officers' coercion of the men unacceptable. The orders that provoked the mutiny were also cancelled, but relief from the constricting uniform regulations would be a long time coming. Perhaps even more galling than the dress regulations, however, was the frequent application of the iron discipline to which the average infantryman was subjected.

Each Presidency Army applied its own military law, but as in the British Army it could be severe and arbitrary. The lash was frequently employed as a means by which to impose the will of the Company, and although widely condemned by libertarians, reformers, philanthropists and even some officers, it would prove difficult to abandon. To one critic it was also very often entirely counterproductive. Captain Walter Badenach of the Bengal Army wrote in 1826 that 'the lash should disappear altogether from the native armies of India … it needlessly degrades individuals and hurts the feelings of the population.'[22] Such punishments could also have repercussions with respect to the highly contentious question of caste. Captain Badenach wrote, 'I have known regiments, nearly half of the rank and file of which were Brahmins … punishing those men before men of lower caste … [a practice which] degrades them beyond any European conception.'[23] This issue proved to be yet a further cause of rancour among the men, and although Governor-General Bentinck abolished corporal punishment in 1835 the experiment was deemed not to have worked, and it was claimed that discipline had deteriorated in the absence of the lash. It was reinstated in 1845 but was not supposed to be used with the same relish with which it had been applied in the past and was reserved only for the most serious infractions; terms of imprisonment were imposed for most crimes. Generally, however, ill discipline was not an issue of great concern, particularly in the Madras and Bombay Armies. Lt-General Sir Charles Napier asserted in fact that on the whole 'no army ever possessed better behaved soldiers than the sepoys.'[24] Certainly, compared to most European troops – renowned for carousing, drunkenness and violent behaviour – sepoys were exemplars of good behaviour. Most sent all but two rupees of their wages home every month anyway and did not have the money to spend on excessive entertainments such as prostitutes, alcohol and gambling.

Discipline aside, Company policy and simple prejudice also meant that equal opportunities for promotion were few and far between. Even for the more gifted recruits there was, as in the civil service, a glass ceiling which few could aspire to shatter. There were officer grades of a sort in the armies, later known as Viceroy's Commissioned Officers to distinguish them from the King's or Queen's Commissioned Officers in the regular British Army, and to distinguish them subalterns were known as jemadar, captains subedar and majors subedar major, but they did not carry the same seniority as their European equivalents. As early as 1817, Sir Thomas Munro, who served as Governor of Madras from 1819 to 1827, recognised the resentment this aroused. He later wrote that as a consequence 'no elevation of character can be expected among men who in the military line cannot attain any rank above subedar, [or] where they are as much below an ensign as an ensign is below the commander-in-chief.'[25]

This was a practice which also had implications beyond bruised egos. It led, Lt-General Napier explained, to 'the veteran [being] commanded by a fair-faced beardless ensign, just arrived from England with a gold laced cap hanging over his ear, but entirely ignorant of military matters'.[26] When some officers advocated the abolition of officer grades for Indians altogether, Napier was appalled. He protested that such a drastic step would destroy morale and 'blast the hopes of 200,000 armed men: for every soldier in the Indian Armies looks forward to be an officer'.[27] Nonetheless, senior commanders such as Lord Frederick Roberts, born in the country and having served in its army for forty-one years, would forever maintain that 'British leaders are essential to the success of Native soldiery,'[28] an attitude which would persist almost to the very end of the Indian Army in 1947 despite efforts at reform, which will be examined later.

Instead, British officers foolishly cultivated an air of superiority and even disdain for their native colleagues, rarely deigning to ask the opinion or advice of even the most experienced and knowledgeable subedar. This was to have serious consequences, because the Indian officer would repay the snobbery of his British colleague by keeping his counsel and rarely if ever sharing his knowledge and expertise. This communication vacuum was naturally very unhealthy, producing a chasm between European and Indian soldiers which would later prove almost unbridgeable. As Captain Badenach explained, 'the feeling of the native soldier to his European officer [means that] ... he has no great reliance on him till he has known him some time,'[29] but as British officers and in particular commanders grew increasingly distant and aloof from their men, the role as conduit that native officers could have performed would prove an even greater loss. Many, like the fresh-faced subaltern described by Napier, would be newcomers, unfamiliar with complex superstitions and caste distinctions and the other nuances of sepoy habit and tradition.

By the middle of the 1850s few officers could even speak their men's languages, and a virtual firewall had built up, preventing effective communication. Napier lamented how as a result 'more than one sepoy has been brought to trial for "insolence", his vehemence in vainly trying to make his officer understand having been misunderstood.'[30] If Europeans were too proud to seek the intervention of native officers, serious misunderstandings would inevitably occur. At Barrackpore in 1824, language barriers compounded serious misunderstandings over orders to prepare for service in Burma. These were misinterpreted by the sepoys who subsequently refused to embark on the journey because they thought they were being ordered to abandon their baggage to expedite the arrangements. Others convinced themselves that they were being ordered to go by sea rather than the longer land route which had been arranged for their benefit. The matter ended in a bloodbath when jittery officers ordered the artillery turned on them, killing hundreds completely unnecessarily.

Tensions were not helped by the fact that everyone lived in such close proximity. When not campaigning troops were accommodated in large cantonments, self-contained miniature townships which provided for nearly all the troops' material needs. They were situated primarily where they would be most likely to be called upon, for instance on the troublesome frontier, but there were permanent garrisons at such places as Kamptee and Sitabuldi in Nagpur, Meerut, Bangalore, Delhi, Calcutta and Barrackpore. Segregation was naturally strictly observed, with accommodation allocated according to rank and race. Officers received the best housing, the white troops barracks, and the sepoys occupied 'lines' well away from their European comrades. Their camp-followers had to content themselves with even less salubrious quarters, usually tents or some other rudimentary accommodation if there was insufficient room in the sepoy lines. Conditions varied, but the report of one inspection carried out at Kamptee and Sitabuldi described reasonably hygienic and healthy environments. Its author, Surgeon-Major J. L. Ranking, reported that 'each hut is detached from its fellow, and the courtyards are spacious. There is consequently more free circulation of air. The streets are wide and kept very clean.'[31] Furthermore, they benefited from 'screened bathrooms and privies', from which 'all excreta [is] removed daily, and every family is instructed to keep a vessel of dry earth mixed with ashes at the privy for use as a deodorant.'[32]

The sepoys were also quite content to be left to their own devices in their lines. Off duty they could ditch their hated uniforms and relax with like-minded compatriots dressed instead in their dhoti and cotton shirt. Their socialising was usually where they aired and shared their complaints, reverting to type because, as one Lieutenant Edward Martineau later remarked, 'we may make a grand mistake in supposing that because we dress, arm and drill Hindustani soldiers as Europeans they become ... European in their feelings and ideas,' concluding rhetorically with the $64,000 question, 'What do they talk about in their lines?'[33] This was one mystery which would be resolved in good time.

Otherwise, daily life on duty was monotonous and unyielding. The rarely varying routine began early with a bugle call to morning parade, which had to be attended in full uniform, kit and rifle. This was followed by the cleaning of weapons and accoutrements, drill and more parades where the men were assigned the day's duties. The evening heralded yet more drill and parades, followed by guard assignments. These invariably involved eight hours of tediously marching up and down outside stores and magazines, or protecting government offices and escorting treasure details and prisoners. These tasks were so pronounced in their unpopularity that in 1844 Henry Lawrence attempted to ameliorate their plight by suggesting to the Directors that such tasks should instead be assigned to 'invalids', only supported by regular troops if the need arose. He also recommended less drill and fewer parades, but for the most part his suggestions went unheeded. Nearly ten years later, a despairing Napier was still writing of 'frequent heavy duties [which] deteriorate discipline when the excitement of war is absent; and even when there is no fighting it wears out body and mind'.[34] The only diversion from such ennui and the tedium of life in the cantonment, therefore, was the peril and challenge of campaign.

Having increased in number from 9,000 in 1765 to 155,000 by 1808,[35] the sepoy had become indispensable in the Company's pursuit of its aims on the subcontinent. One early commentator testified to the fact that the 'Sepahees [sic] of the native army afforded numerous noble proofs of their fidelity and devotion,'[36] qualities increasingly put to the test in frequent wars. These included the expeditions mounted against recalcitrant rulers such as Hyder Ali of Mysore and his son Tipu Sultan between 1767 and the fall of Seringapatam in 1799. In this campaign sepoys from Madras and Bengal contributed 22,000 of the Company's total of 26,000 troops, without whom the subsequent victory might not have been possible. In 1817 sepoys from Bengal and Madras helped in the defence of the Nagpur Residency when its Maratha ruler turned against the British Resident. Once again they earnt accolades from the British, Colonel John Studholme writing years later how their performance in the engagement had crowned them 'with an immortal wreath of glory'.[37] Such plaudits came at great cost. Although many men took their wives and families with them to serve as cook and cleaner and provide for other home comforts, the practice had serious drawbacks. As one Captain Bryce explained, it meant that that the 'wife shares the hardships of war with her husband',[38] and these could be considerable and frequent.

By the early nineteenth century Russia had been expanding its own empire southwards, stoking fears among the British that the Russians would not stop until they had reached the very frontier of India itself. In 1814, and again between 1826 and 1828, Russia fought Persia and replaced Britain as the dominant power in that country. These manoeuvrings prompted President of the Board of Control Lord Ellenborough to fear Russia would use Afghanistan as a base from which to attack India. In order to forestall this, it was decided to usurp its ruler, Dost Mohammed, and install a puppet king, Shah Shujah. In October 1838 Governor-General Auckland created the 'Army of the Indus', in which the Bengal and Bombay Armies were to play a significant role. The Bengal Division of 9,500 men included Skinner's Horse, the 43rd Native Infantry and the 2nd Light Cavalry, while the Bombay Division contributed 5,600 men of the 19th Native Infantry and the Poona Light Horse. In addition, there were British Army regiments plus 6,000 Indian mercenaries, 38,000 camp followers – which included the sepoys' families – and 30,000 camels.

The invasion force set off in December and by April 1839 had entered Kandahar. Leaving behind a garrison to protect their flanks, the main force proceeded to Kabul, reaching the city in August 1839 and installing Shah Shujah on the throne. Dost Mohammed surrendered himself in November 1840 after a lengthy guerrilla war, but his son Akbar Khan remained at large to carry on resistance, ambushing and harassing troops, disrupting lines of communication and making the British presence in Kabul increasingly precarious. Throughout 1841 the situation continued to deteriorate, and the British were finally persuaded by Shah Shujah that tensions might be eased if they agreed to decamp to the cantonment outside of the city. This show of weakness emboldened the Afghans, who took up position in the heights above, from which they were able to fire down upon the exposed camp. With food, ammunition and medicines running out, on 6 January 1842, the commander accepted that their position was hopeless and that their only option was to cut their losses and try to make their way back to India. The remnants of the expedition now consisted of just 4,500 half-starved and diseased troops, 12,000 camp-followers and some of the officers' wives and families, all of whom now faced a 90-mile trek to Jalalabad. The trek home was to prove an unmitigated nightmare for British and Indian alike, as Lady Sale, wife of British officer Sir Robert Sale, later described in her diary:

> ... the evening and night were intensely cold: no food for man or beast procurable, except a few handfuls of bhousa [food grain], for which we paid from five to ten rupees ... the road is strewn with baggage; and ... numbers of men women and children are left on the roadside to perish ...[39]

As the retreat continued, the situation deteriorated further, the long column winding its way agonisingly slowly towards India under constant harassment from Afghan ambush which wore down their numbers. One unit, the eighty-strong Light Company of the 54th Native Infantry, had left Kabul thirty hours before, but had been reduced to just eighteen men.[40] Lady Sale saw sepoys having to burn 'their caps, accoutrements and clothes to keep themselves warm',[41] and under such circumstances it was inevitable that discipline began to dissolve. On one occasion her own tent was invaded by desperate sepoys and their camp-followers, trying to escape the bitter, gnawing cold and who 'tried to force their way, not only into the tent, but actually into our beds'.[42] Everywhere there were signs of men deserting and abandoning their positions, and as Lady Sale noted, 'discipline was clearly at an end. If asked why they were not with their corps, one had a lame foot, another could not find his regiment, another had lost his musket...'[43] Finally the column reached safety, but it was a humiliation which scarred British prestige for a long time.

The British did recover from the debacle, and the bitter experience did not deter them from taking their sepoys into further adventures. Having been stung by their injudicious foray into Afghan affairs, they decided that their interests might be better served by creating a deeper buffer between themselves and any renewed threat from Russia, real or imagined. This was a policy that created tensions with Sind, one of the candidates for the role. Lord Ellenborough, now Governor-General, ordered Major-General Napier to lead a punitive expedition into the country in 1843 to facilitate a change of mind. At Miani, 6 miles north of Hyderabad on the Indus River, the general with 2,800 Anglo-Indian troops met 20,000 Baluchistanis. They attacked and almost overran his position but were finally repulsed with the loss of a quarter of their men. Napier then went on the offensive, sweeping southward along the Indus, and on 24 March he attacked the capital Hyderabad. Although it had been reinforced, Napier's army still numbered just 6,000, but its artillery nevertheless enabled a successful assault on the city, securing its capture and bringing Sind under British control. Napier was rewarded with £70,000 and the governorship of the new province.

British concerns then turned to the Punjab, which had descended into chaos after the death of its leader, Ranjit Singh. The first conflict with the Sikhs emerged from a dispute over the Sutlej River areas of north-west India in 1845, and the British initially appeared to have bitten off more than they could chew, with casualties ominously high. At Mudki on 18 December they lost 900 men, among them Lady Sales' husband General Sale. At Ferozeshah on 21 December the British were again bested, Sikh artillery exacting a high toll before inexplicably beginning to withdraw. They were pursued by the British until finally, at Sabroon on 10 February 1846, the tables were turned and the Sikhs were finally crushed, leaving the way open for the occupation of Lahore and the end of the war. Nonetheless, discontent persisted, and several Sikh chieftains raised another rebellion against the British in 1848, but they were again defeated the following year. The fighting had also bankrupted the country, so two of its key provinces of Jammu and Kashmir were detached and sold to a Hindu nobleman, Golab Singh, for £750,000.[44] By now the sepoy of the Indian Army had earned a reputation unparalleled among any regiment of the regular British Army. Their leaders, especially generals such as Sir Charles Napier, increasingly acknowledged this and later a light-hearted ditty would reflect Britain's growing reliance upon their martial prowess:

> We don't want to fight
> But by jingo if we do,
> We'll stay at home and sing our songs,
> And send the mild Hindoo[45]

But behind this façade of stoic loyalty there was still unease among the ranks. Had Lieutenant Martineau eavesdropped, his curiosity as to what they discussed among themselves into the evening may have been satisfied. Ongoing dissatisfaction over uniforms, deductions, discipline and the boredom of garrison duty were compounded by more incrementally aggravating subjects. One emerged soon after the annexation of Sind and Oudh when it became clear that troops serving there no longer qualified for foreign service *batta*, a contentious system by which pay was topped up to cover the additional costs of serving away from home. The Company, looking for ways to save money, often sought excuses to reduce the amount or abolish it altogether, much to the chagrin of the men. Now that these two territories were no longer technically foreign, *batta* was withdrawn from men serving there. Such issues relating to pay often escalated, and ringleaders suspected of trying to provoke a mutiny were convicted and transported to the Andaman Islands, but even such severe reprisals failed to have an impact on the men's discontent.

In 1850 there were murmurings in the 'lines' arising from suspicions of forced Christianisation, perhaps understandable given the zeal with which missionaries were pursuing their calling. Consequently, the 66th Bengal Native Infantry rose up and tried to seize the fort at Amritsar, fearful that they were to be subjected to some demonic ritual. Their action, however, was put down ruthlessly and after its leaders were summarily dealt with the entire regiment was punished with disbandment and having its name stricken from the army rolls.[46] When the issue of foreign service was raised again it too would add to the grievances of the men. The Company had become exasperated that so many well-trained troops could not serve overseas, and Lord Canning was determined to resolve this issue. Ignoring the feelings of the sepoys, the General Service Enlistment Act of September 1856 was implemented, removing exemption to foreign service from any future recruits into the Bengal Army irrespective of caste. Yet another perceived slight was seen in the increasing recruitment of lower-caste soldiers from the recently annexed territories, interpreted as a deliberate affront to the fighting qualities of the staunchly conservative and status-conscious Brahmins and Rajputs.[47]

Sepoys were not immune from developments beyond the limits of their cantonments either, and they shared the unease of their countrymen towards the social, religious and educational reforms being implemented. Many if not all were interpreted as part of a series of gradual attempts to undermine their beliefs and force eventual conversion. The annexation of Oudh and Sindh also had repercussions for the sepoys recruited from there, who were anguished by the loss of their independence, the usurpation of their princes and the expropriation of land rights. With these developments, just one spark could ignite the powder keg. Such was the growing level of discontent that at one stage General Napier calculated that of the 50,000 men under his command, he had 'strong presumptive proof that 30,000 were mutinous'.[48] To add to an already dangerous situation, Many European troops had been transferred to fight in the Crimean War against Russia, leaving at best 40,000 to deal with any trouble among the Company's 300,000 Indian soldiers.[49] Still, discontent continued to simmer among the ranks, some turning to mysticism and the occult. Rumours were spread that the British would be turned out of the country on the centenary of the Battle of Plassey on 23 June 1857, and as conspiracies and agitation increased so did the deteriorating atmosphere in the barracks and garrisons.

As hearsay worked its way around, the most extraordinary claims were being made, including one that the flour they used for baking was contaminated with bonemeal. The introduction of new rifle cartridges could not have come at a less propitious moment either; suspicions abounded that the cartridges were greased with animal fat, anathema to Muslim and Hindu alike, and the British authorities could not disprove the rumours. Perhaps had relations between European and Indian officers been better, and communications with the men seething in their barracks more effective, what was to follow might have been nipped in the bud. Certainly the more adroit sensed that relations were deteriorating badly and became increasingly concerned that they were going to lose control. Lieutenant Martineau noted on 5 May 1857, 'I can detect the near approach of the storm, I can hear the moaning hurricane, but I can't say how, when or where it will break forth.'[50] The more perceptive among the European civilians also sensed something was wrong, and at Cawnpore in Oudh in late 1856 Elizabeth Sneyd noted with concern how the sepoys omitted their customary salute when she approached, instead remaining seated and seemingly mocking her 'appeared very ominous of evil'.[51] In Lucknow, Amy Haines was similarly disturbed by the deterioration in the demeanour of the natives, noting how they were behaving in an 'indecent' and 'abusive' manner.[52] So bad were the signs that her father decided to make arrangements for them to move out of town completely, detecting in the attitude of the natives 'the shadow of coming events'.[53]

Yet faced with complacency among senior commanders, there was probably little that could have been done anyway. Some officers tried to circumvent army red tape to warn the Governor-General directly that something was likely to blow very soon, but the general mishandling of the situation was to come home to roost. This vein of stubbornness was demonstrated by men such as Colonel Mitchell, in command of the military station at Berhampur, 90 miles to the north of Calcutta. He was a truculent man who cajoled and threatened his men with compulsory service in Burma or China if they refused to comply with his orders. General John Hearsey, commander of the 34th Bengal Native Infantry at Barrackpore, was more circumspect and tried to allay sepoy fears, but he was too late.

The toxic atmosphere had now reached its climax, and on 29 March sepoy Mangal Pandey finally took the law into his own hands. Dressed ostentatiously in his dhoti, in blatant disregard of regulations and possibly under the influence of drugs, he ran amok. He cut down his sergeant-major and when a British officer intervened he began to lay about him furiously too, calling upon his stunned comrades to join him and kill all the Europeans. Although they did not participate, his Brahmin caste protected him from any attempt to restrain him physically and they refused to interfere Failing to instigate an uprising, the crazed Pandey tried to commit suicide rather than be captured, but he only managed to wound himself. After a furious tussle he was finally subdued, placed under arrest and hospitalised to await a court martial. He was found guilty and sentenced to death, but when the time came for his sentence to be carried out he had still not recovered, so on 9 April 1857 he was ignominiously dragged to a banyan tree which served as a makeshift scaffold, and from this he was hanged.[54] Meanwhile, the disorder was spreading, and elsewhere similar mutinous activity was filling the ranks of the Bengal Army.

It was on 24 April at Meerut, 40 miles from Delhi, under the command of Major-General W. H. Hewitt, that the pressure cooker which had been building up finally exploded. Eighty-five upper-caste sepoys of the 3rd Bengal Light Cavalry repeatedly refused to use the new cartridge, and finally on 8 May they were arrested, court martialled and most sentenced to ten years imprisonment with hard labour. As part of their punishment the entire garrison of nearly 2,500 was paraded and ordered to witness their ritual humiliation as they were divested of their uniforms and placed in chains ready to be hauled off to prison. By the following day – a Sunday – tensions were at fever pitch. Rumours were circulating among the sepoys that the British were going to seize their weapons and make an example of them all, while the Europeans were in receipt of intelligence to the effect that the native troops were plotting to free the captives and mount an insurrection. The British, however, in their typically complacent way, and disdainful of the feelings of their men, failed to act. Instead, the officers and their families prepared for church while some of the British soldiers got ready to go into town. The sepoys then made their move. They freed the men from prison, broke into the arsenals and magazines, and started attacking the Europeans, leaving around twenty dead along with fifty loyal Indians.

Leaving Meerut in chaos, the rebels set off en masse for Delhi 40 miles away, collecting more men and supporters as they went. They then occupied the city and ostentatiously restored a rather bemused Mughal emperor Bahadur Shah II to the throne, and by nightfall on 11 May most Europeans who had not escaped had been captured or killed. The rebels also seized the city's main magazine, 3 miles outside the city, which gave them sufficient powder for up to three months. But instead of consolidating their advantage, the mutineers, civilians and emperor began to argue among themselves almost immediately.[55] It was soon evident that apart from a shared hatred of the British there was no common purpose, no unified strategy and no effective plan to prosecute the uprising. Nor was it universally welcomed by ordinary Indians or the wary princes, who had yet to show their hand. It would also soon become apparent that the uprising was almost exclusively a Bengali affair, and few if any troops from either of the other Presidency armies were participating. No Gurkhas and only two regiments of the Bombay Army mutinied, and thanks to Salar Jung's suppression of the attempted coup in Hyderabad, elements of the Madras Army were freed to deploy to the north. Having failed to elicit a popular uprising, the rebels' options were to become increasingly limited.[56]

As the rebellion started to unravel, the British recovered from the initial shock and hastily prepared to retrieve the situation. Instructions were issued for an expeditionary force to sail to India and crush the rebellion. The British organised a force to relieve Delhi, and on 14 September, 11,200 Anglo-Indian troops, of whom 7,900 were sepoys, stormed the city and took terrible vengeance on the defenders. Fuelled by alcohol, the relief force slaughtered mutineers and residents alike in a week-long orgy which produced a death-toll of over 600 before order was restored. Soon after the mutineers captured Delhi, two other communities, Lucknow and Cawnpore, were threatened. Forewarned by the conspiracies and sepoy activity in April, the British in Lucknow had the presence of mind to fortify the Residency. When news of the uprising spread the British in both towns were attacked and in Lucknow 1,800 British men, women and children and 1,200 loyal native soldiers and civilians were besieged by over 20,000 mutineers. In Cawnpore, where 240 men and 375 women and children took refuge, the mutineers were assisted by one of the few Indian princes to intervene, an embittered Nana Sahib. He besieged the Residency which nevertheless held out until 25 June, when supplies were depleted. Nana offered the besieged safe passage if they surrendered, and two days later the exhausted remnants of the garrison marched out. The rebels then opened fire, killing sixty men, and threw the survivors into a makeshift prison.

On 15 July, Nana Sahib received news that the British were marching on the city. In a panic, he had all the prisoners stabbed to death and their bodies thrown down a well. Two days later a relief force under Sir Henry

Havelock arrived, and, learning of the fate of the Europeans, he ordered the most savage and brutal revenge on any Indians the force encountered. He meanwhile set out for Lucknow, where he faced such strong resistance that he was twice forced to return to Cawnpore. Although on 25 September his force managed to battle its way into the Residency, it was too weak to get out again and had to be relieved. On 9 November, Commander-in-Chief of the army in India, General Sir Colin Campbell, finally marched on Lucknow with 5,000 men, entering the city on the 16th. He too found himself hard pressed to consolidate his gains so abandoned the town, which would not be liberated properly until March 1858. The eventual recapture of both towns, however, finally marked the beginning of the end for the mutiny, its civilian leaders evaporating and leaving the sepoys to fight on against increasingly hopeless odds. The British fought a ruthless campaign to pursue and pacify the rebels, employing brutal methods which finally brought the Mutiny, or First Indian War of Independence, to a conclusion. Peace was not officially declared until 8 July 1859, when Lord Canning proclaimed:

> War is at an end; Rebellion is put down; the Noise of Arms is no longer heard where the enemies of the state have persisted in their last struggle; the Presence of Large Forces in the Field has ceased to be necessary; Order is re-established; and peaceful pursuits have everywhere been resumed ...[57]

There is little doubt that the British victory was in very large part due to the loyalty of most sepoys, the mutineers having failed to galvanise popular support or secure the alliance of any important princes. A much relieved and grateful Governor-General awarded one notable ally in particular, the Nizam of Hyderabad, with gifts to the value of £10,000. He also praised his Diwan, Salar Jung I, lauding the 'courage and firmness with which he had discharged his duty to the Nizam and ... England'.[58] Nonetheless, the Mutiny and taught a salutary lesson on the perils of complacency and inertia. Having nearly lost India, many officers who had long criticised the structure of the three armies detected an opportunity to address their many shortcomings. Colonel John Studholme Hodgson was among those who acknowledged that it was 'apparent to the most superficial observer, that the present system of the native army requires some reformation to suit the altered state of things, and their changing aspect ... never was there an army ... whose moral and physical improvement been more neglected'.[59]

In July 1858, a royal commission was appointed under the chairmanship of Major-General Jonathan Peel, Secretary of State for War, to undertake a thorough review of the three armies and recommend improvements, and the committee submitted its findings in March 1859. One proposal was to simply disband the Indian Army altogether and defend the subcontinent exclusively with European soldiers, but this option was considered to be going too far, if only on account of the prohibitive cost.[60] The solution would have to be found by undertaking a profound internal restructuring, with one of the three Presidency armies in particular coming under intense scrutiny. Having been at the epicentre of the mutiny, the Bengal Army would not only face a severe reckoning for its actions, but it could never again be in a position to wreak such havoc. Having acknowledged the disproportionate dominance of a hardcore clique of high-caste sepoys within its ranks, the Punjab Committee, which had been formed to advise the Peel Commission, proposed a profoundly dramatic solution by which 'all races, Hindu and Mahommedan, of one province be enlisted in one regiment, and no others, and having thus created distinctive regiments, let us keep them so against the hour of need by confining the circle of their ordinary service to the limits of their own province and only marching them on emergency into other parts of the Empire, with which they will then be found to have little sympathy'.[61]

This new structure would be partly achieved by switching from the traditional recruiting grounds to include men whose reliability had been proven in the war, and who could confidently be depended upon in the future. Key among these would prove to be the loyal Sikhs of the Punjab. Consequently, although the province constituted only 10 per cent of the country's population, it would contribute 35 per cent of the Bengal Army by 1870[62] and around half by 1914. The Gurkhas, too, had long been appreciated for their loyalty. Sir Charles Napier had observed shortly before the Mutiny that 'in the Nepaul [*sic*] war of 1814 with inferior numbers they defeated British troops more than once; and acquaintance with them under arms in no way tended to diminish my opinion of their high character as soldiers.'[63] He saw them as an ideal counterweight to the Indian soldier because 'they have a dislike to the sepoys amounting to contempt,'[64] and believed that 'with 30,000 or 40,000 Goorkas [*sic*] added to 30,000 European troops, the possession of India will not "depend on Opinion", but on an Army, able with ease to overthrow any combination among Hindoos [*sic*] or Mahomedans, or both together.'[65]

The total size of the three Presidency armies and the ratio of European to Indian troops had clearly been another significant factor in the Mutiny getting out of control so quickly. In future, not only would no sepoy regiment consist of more than 600 men, the total strength of the three armies was cut to 135,000. This decreased the proportion of native to British troops to a maximum of two to one, ensuring there were sufficient European forces in station to respond effectively to any future disturbance. To guarantee this, 50,000 of the 80,000 British soldiers serving tours of duty in the country would be garrisoned in the Bengal Presidency, and 15,000 respectively in Madras and Bombay.[66] To further underpin European military predominance, Indian troops would no longer have access to artillery and the British would control all the arsenals and principal forts in the country. Further changes were proposed in 1879, whereby the three Presidency armies would be replaced by four regional corps in Bengal, Madras, Bombay and Punjab.[67]

The war also stalled any further serious talk of commissioning Indians until in 1884 Sir George Chesney, Member of the Military Department, again raised the prospect of opening 'a definitive military career to natives of the higher classes'.[68] His suggestion, however, met with an icy response from his colleagues although a compromise was mooted whereby units officered entirely by Indians might be organised.[69] But it was evident that the prospects for an Indian officer sitting alongside Europeans in the hallowed confines of the Mess posed all sorts of social problems. Thus when, in 1895, the three armies were finally merged – and renamed the British Indian Army on 1 January 1903 – the resulting force was still dominated by European officers. Nonetheless neither Congress, who had argued for admission of Indians to higher ranks since its inception, or men like Dadabhai Naoroji were deterred. He wrote to the War Office on the subject in 1900, but in its reply it reiterated that 'candidates for commissions in the British Army must be of pure European descent and must also be British born or a naturalised British subject.'[70] But Theodor Monson echoed the words of Lord Napier when he ruminated on a system whereby 'the youngest subaltern from England ranks above a veteran native officer ... no native of India can hope to rise in the British Army above what is in fact the rank of a non-commissioned officer'. Despite such logic, the stock response was frequently that 'our gallant native officers very rarely have the qualities required in the higher positions of military command.'[71] Nevertheless, to his credit, Lord Curzon had striven to make some progress when he created the Imperial Cadet Corps in 1901, to which the sons of princes and wealthier Indians could be admitted. Even so, they would have no right to command British troops or rise above junior rank, and by 1911 just seventy-eight had graduated.[72] Following his appointment as commander-in-chief, Lord Kitchener also founded the Staff College in Deolali in 1905, later moved to Quetta in 1907, in the hope of advancing Indians to more senior positions, but it would be another decade before serious steps were taken to improve the situation.

Meanwhile, the ordinary sepoy continued to serve as the Raj's main tool for power projection and the defence of British interests. Between 1859 and 1904 Indian troops were engaged in thirty-seven wars and expeditions, including Chinese wars in 1860 and 1900, the Bhutan War of 1864–65, the Abyssinian War of 1878–79 and the Afghan Wars of 1878–79 and 1879–80. Indian troops also served in the Egyptian War of 1882, the Third Burmese War of 1885 and an incursion into Tibet in 1890. There were twenty-seven minor expeditions as well, including the sending of troops to Malta and Cyprus in 1878, plus numerous skirmishes and confrontations along the fractious border with Afghanistan.[73] In one of these, on 12 September 1897, twenty-one sepoys found their isolated outpost at Saragarhi under assault by at least 10,000 tribesmen. Under the command of Havildar Ishar Singh, the men fought off a succession of assaults over several hours until they were inevitably overrun and massacred. They killed an estimated 180 of the enemy before they finally succumbed, and their action subsequently became a matter of intense pride and huge renown. Two memorials were constructed in their honour, one in Amritsar and another in Ferozepur, commemorating their gallantry and more generally honouring those generations of sepoys who died serving the Raj.

Sepoys also proved a vital component in dealing with internal disorder, serving in a policing role forty-six times between 1860 and 1879 and on sixty-nine occasions between 1899 and 1901.[74] And as we have seen they would prove increasingly indispensable as the nationalist movement gathered momentum. There was nonetheless one significant event in which their services were not welcomed. When war with the Boers broke out in 1899 and the Government of India was asked to reinforce the army in South Africa, it was only British troops that were wanted.[75] Although the rulers of Kashmir and Jodhpur offered troops and horses and opened a fighting fund,[76] there was no question of employing sepoys against white Boer farmers; the British considered breaking that taboo a provocation too far. The 'white' self-governing colonies, on the other hand, were welcomed, with the Australian colonies contributing a total of 20,000 volunteers, Canada 7,000 and New Zealand 6,500. Rhodesia, the Cape Colony and Natal also offered a total of 24,000 white volunteers to fight the Boers. Instead, 10,000 Indian men were assigned to a range of auxiliary and non-combatant roles, such as medical orderlies, farriers and blacksmiths, in transport, and as stretcher bearers and laundrymen. It was here of course that Mahatma Gandhi received his first inkling of the discrimination to which his compatriots were subjected, but he nonetheless served with distinction with his ambulance corps.

Combat against non-white adversaries continued to present no such trouble. Reacting to increasingly worrying rumours of Russian intrigue in Tibet, one Colonel Sir Francis Younghusband was despatched to the country in December 1903 to persuade the Tibetans to keep their distance from St Petersburg. Many of the 3,000 troops participating in the expedition were Indians, including men of the 23rd Sikh Pioneers and Pathans, ably supported by Gurkhas. The entire episode was nearly a repeat of the abortive invasion of Afghanistan sixty years before, but this time a calamity was averted, in no small part due to the fact that Indian troops had once again demonstrated their capacity to endure hardship in the most difficult environments. Eleven years later this growing reputation would be put to its greatest test.

By 1914, India possessed a large, battle-hardened and highly professional fighting force, whose 193,901 men[77] could be deployed swiftly almost anywhere they might be required. During July 1914, with the chances of war in Europe growing increasingly likely, Britain asked the Government of India what assets might be available for possible service on the continent. By now any qualms they might have had about using Indian troops against a European adversary had been largely dispelled, and in any case the situation was far too serious. The Indian government therefore offered two infantry divisions and a cavalry brigade almost immediately, with a third to follow shortly afterwards.[78] These having been eagerly accepted, once war broke out the Meerut and Lahore divisions, each numbering approximately 24,000, arrived in Marseilles during September and October 1914.[79]

Although referred to collectively by the French as 'les Hindus'[80] despite being predominantly Punjabi, they soon proved their worth. The 129th Baluchis saw action at Hollebeke, where a Victoria Cross was awarded to sepoy Khudadad Khan for operating his machine gun until his position was overrun. It was the first given to an Indian soldier since they had become eligible just three years earlier.[81] The 57th Sikhs fought at Neuve-Chapelle on 27–28 October alongside the 9th Bhopal Infantry,[82] where on 28 October Subedar Malla Singh was awarded the Military Cross.[83] Two more VCs were won at Festubert on 23–24 November, another posthumously on 10 March 1915 by Rifleman Gobar Singh Negi of the Royal Garwal Rifles, killed leading an attack against an enemy trench.[84] When the Germans first used poison gas in the Second Battle of Ypres on 22 April 1915, Indian troops were sent to hold the line. Jemadar Mir Dast of the 55th Coke's Rifles earnt a VC for his actions in retrieving soldiers who had been incapacitated. These and other contributions made by the Indian troops at this early and crucial juncture in the war did not go unrecorded, and Lord Curzon admitted that they had arrived in France just in time 'to save the cause of the Allies and of civilisation'.[85] At a parade at Chateau Mazingham on 25 November 1915 a message from King George V underlined their value:

> More than a year ago I summoned you from India to fight for the safety of my Empire and the honour of my pledged word on the battlefields of Belgium and France. The confidence which I then expressed in your sense of duty, your courage and your chivalry you have since then nobly justified ...[86]

Their achievements had nonetheless come at great cost, suffering in excess of 7,000 deaths, and many more wounded.[87] The decision was therefore taken to rest and resupply the men and reinforce their numbers, but no sooner had they arrived back in Marseilles to recuperate than they were ordered to the Middle East to join in the fight against Turkey. But this decision carried with it considerable risks, and the British had earlier appreciated that they needed to tread warily in the event the decision was taken to deploy Muslim troops against a sultan who, as caliph, was also their spiritual leader.[88] Memories of the Mutiny recalled the religious undertones of a conflict which nearly shook the Raj to its foundations, but such eminent bodies as the Anjuman-i-Islamia, or Mohammedan Association, came to the rescue. On 7 November 1914, a resolution assured the men that '[India's] Mohammedans have no sympathy whatever with Sublime Porte in the present trouble brought upon itself by its own reckless action at the instigation of Germany,'[89] and so Muslim troops could march into battle absolved of any accusations of treachery or blasphemy.

A further three VCs were won by Indian troops in the fighting which followed,[90] in conditions of immense difficulty and danger. Perhaps the single most notorious action in which Indian soldiers participated was Kut-al-Amara. Here they spent 143 days trapped and half-starved until the garrison was finally surrendered on 29 April 1916. Some 9,000 men, 6,000 of them Indians, were then left to the tender mercies of the Turks. Unfed and without water the men died like flies, and as one officer later explained, 'if our treatment was that meted out to honoured guests, then God help those who were to be treated as ordinary prisoners of war.'[91] This was arguably the costliest theatre of all, leaving 29,000 sepoys dead or wounded,[92] but it was sacrifice and dedication replicated elsewhere in the region. Another 15,000 were sent to the Dardanelles, where 1,400 were killed and 3,500 wounded.[93] In one particularly costly engagement, out of fifteen officers and 574 men of the 14th Sikhs who assaulted Sagir Dara on 4 June 1915, just three officers and 134 men answered the roll call at the end of the day.[94] There was also a 650-strong Mule Corps with 1,000 mules employed hauling supplies and ammunition across treacherous terrain under constant sniper and machine-gun fire.[95] These professional and doughty soldiers soon earnt the deep respect of their British, Australian and New Zealander peers. Elsewhere they played an equally vital role, and Britain's determination to protect the strategically important Suez Canal meant a further 30,000 troops served in Sinai and Palestine.[96]

But they faced arguably their most physically challenging campaigning in the alien environment of East Africa, where they fought German and colonial forces under General von Lettow Vorbeck.[97] The first contingent, the 29th Punjabis, arrived on 1 September 1914, followed by the main force from India a month later, but by September of 1915 they were spent, having suffered 600 killed, 653 wounded and over 400 captured.[98] Their losses in combat were exacerbated by the debilitating climate and diseases such as malaria which were endemic to the region. There was also a shortage of sheep or goat milk for cooking, which alone contributed greatly to a general collapse in morale. Combined, these factors so weakened, exhausted and ground down the men that a commission recommended they be recalled;[99] by the time they were finally withdrawn, a total of nearly 5,000 had become casualties.[100]

This tradition of service remained largely unbroken for the remainder of the war, but there were some notable exceptions. In Singapore in 1915, 850 men of the 5th Light Infantry were already in poor spirits, and their officers were doing little to improve discipline and morale. The mood was not helped when rumours began to circulate that instead of being sent to a relatively easy posting in Hong Kong they were to join in the fighting against Turkey. Their low morale was also exploited by a local Muslim coffee shop owner, Kassim Mansoor, a nationalist who was doing all he could to undermine morale further and to incite them to mutiny. Even the commanding officer of the captured German ship *Emden*, which they were guarding, was suspected of trying to sow discord, while Ghadr activists on the island were adding to frayed nerves. On 15 February 1915 matters got completely out of hand when a fracas degenerated into a full-blown mutiny and half of the men turned on the Europeans, first attacking officers and British troops in Alexandra Barracks and then spilling out into the streets of Singapore where they ran amok. Again, in the absence of coherent leadership, the mutiny turned into a shambolic free-for-all and the British were able to regroup and suppress the uprising, although ten days passed before the last of the mutineers were hunted down. By then the lives of forty-four British officers, soldiers and civilians, three Chinese and two Malays and fifty-six sepoys had been lost. Retribution was swift nonetheless, with thirty-seven of the ringleaders condemned to death[101] and another 165 men transported to the Andamans. Kassim, widely suspected of helping to foment the rebellion, was hanged.

Nonetheless, Indian soldiers' contribution to final victory galvanised renewed calls for root-and-branch reform of the army once peace returned. These had materialised from the recommendations that produced the 1920 Government of India Act, which had made provisions for a committee to 'enquire into and report ... upon the administration [and] the organisation of the Army in India'.[102] Under the chairmanship of Reginald Brett, 2nd Viscount Esher, and tactfully including two Indians, Major Sir Umar Hayat Khan and Sir Krishna Gupta, this committee seemed well placed to undertake such a task. Esher had been instrumental in seeing through successful reforms to both the British Army and the Allied command structure during the war, but he proved wildly out of kilter with the thinking of the government and especially the nationalists. Nonetheless, the committee submitted its findings on 22 June 1920 and they horrified many of its readers:

India has now been admitted into partnership with the Empire ... and it can no longer be regarded as a local force ... it must rather be treated as a part of an Imperial army, ready to serve in any part of the world ...[103]

This could not have been more at odds with popular opinion in India. Lord Chelmsford insisted that 'so long as India pays ... India must control its own army,'[104] and as for it being used as an auxiliary to the British Army, this was totally opposed by the Imperial Legislative Council and even members of his own committee. Most shocking of all to nationalists and liberals alike was that the army should cease to come under the authority of the Viceroy. Already, in March 1921, Sir Tej Bahadur Sapru spoke to the Legislative Council, and insisted that the Indian Army must henceforth be exclusively for 'the defence of India against external aggression and the maintenance of internal peace and tranquillity',[105] deployed elsewhere only 'for temporary defence purposes, or with the previous consent of the Governor-General in Council in grave emergencies'.[106] He received wide support, with Sir P. S. Sivaswami Iyer proposing fifteen resolutions rejecting the Esher Report in the Imperial Legislative Assembly.[107]

Nonetheless, although this proposal was accepted in principle, Esher's plans were soon overtaken by events, the interpretation of 'internal peace' and 'grave emergencies' proving to be somewhat elastic. In addition to operations in Waziristan in 1919–1920 and again in 1936–39, Indian troops served in Turkmenistan during the Allied intervention of 1918–1919 and the Third Anglo-Afghan War of 1919. During 1920–21 they were also deployed in Britain's Mandate of Mesopotamia, later renamed Iraq, where 24,000 men were despatched to suppress an uprising. In 1927 the British government asked for contingency plans to be drawn up for their possible deployment to protect the oilfields in the Persian Gulf, although it did now assure the Government of India that if they were used 'no financial liability' would be imposed on the Government of India.[108] In 1928 Indian troops were also despatched to Iraq for a second time, and to Singapore, demonstrating that Indian troops were not only in considerable demand but remained largely at the beck and call of the British.

The vexed question of commissions for Indian soldiers also emerged from the post-war deliberations. This had dogged relations since the earliest times, but the First World War proved beyond doubt that Indian soldiers were every bit as fit for command as their white colleagues, and in 1917 the Montagu-Chelmsford Report proposed that 'in recognition of the brilliant and devoted services of the Indian Army in the various theatres of war'[109] a 'considerable number of commissions [for Indians] should now be given'.[110] For reasons of simple practicality, these measures were essential. Most of the best public schools contained officer training corps, but the war put an end to many dreams of a lengthy career, as they had done in the civil service. Of the 3,000 Etonians who went to war in 1914–18, 1,157 had been killed,[111] and the death rate among officers was as much as 81 per cent. One in five of the students drawn from Oxford and Cambridge had been killed, and from King Edward VIII School 32.4 per cent of those who marched off to war in 1914 never returned. Among these casualties may have been men who would have served in the Indian Army, and the gaps created in the ranks of the officer class by their loss would have to be filled from other quarters. It was therefore decided that in future all Indians would be eligible to serve in the army, navy and air force and receive what would be called King's Indian Commissions and that 'no less than twenty five per cent ... should be given to His Majesties Indian subjects.'[112]

It was nonetheless easier to decide policy than to ensure it was implemented, and the first experiment proved a dismal failure. For reasons of culture, class or simple racism, the first attendees to go to the Royal Military Academy at Sandhurst proved almost to a man to be unprepared for the reception they received. So by March 1922, the Prince of Wales Royal Indian College had been established in Dehra Dun to prepare them before making the journey to the UK. This appeared to go some way to improving their chances of success at Sandhurst, as up to 1 January 1923 thirty-two commissions were granted.[113] This still proved too slow to keep up with the pace of constitutional change. At this rate there would still only be eighty Indians holding King's Indian Commissions by 1927–1928 compared to 7,000 British officers. So in June 1925 the Skeen Committee under the chairmanship of Lt-General Sir Andrew Skeen, Chief of the General Staff in India, was formed to find more creative ways of accelerating the process.[114]

Following its recommendations, the British government increased quotas to Sandhurst for the army, Cranwell for the Royal Air Force and Woolwich for the Royal Artillery. It was also agreed that India should now have its own military academy, and this was established at Dehra Dun in 1932. Among the first officers to graduate in 1935 was Lieutenant Mohan Singh, a young man with a calling and not content to play second fiddle to his white colleagues. We will encounter him again later, but as General Wilson had warned back in 1884, graduation into the officer class was only the first hurdle Indians needed to surmount before they could hope to be accepted as bona fide. As Claude Auchinleck, Commander-in-Chief of the Indian Army, later admitted, men like Mohan Singh found themselves subjected to 'differential treatment in respect of pay and terms of service compared with the British officer' and had to endure 'the prejudice and lack of manners by some ... British officers and their wives, [which] all went to produce a very deep and bitter feeling of racial discrimination in the minds of the most intelligent and progressive of Indian officers',[115] treatment that would come home to roost in a few years' time. Consequently, progress remained stubbornly slow, and by 1938 the total number of senior Indian officers would stand at just fifty-four.[116]

Notwithstanding the various skirmishes and campaigns in which it continued to be involved, peacetime also produced a smaller army, and many well-known regiments were disbanded, reorganised or merged. These included the Baluchis, Coke's and Wilde's Rifles, all regiments which had performed well in the war and had served with distinction. One factor did not change, however, and that was the makeup and demographics of its lower ranks, especially the percentage of men from the Punjab, North-West Frontier and Kashmir. These rose from 47 per cent in 1914 to nearly 60 per cent in 1930, while the Gurkhas had grown from 15 per cent to over 16 per cent.[117] These figures translated into the average percentage of Punjabi Muslims serving in the infantry as 27 per cent and the cavalry 14.28 per cent. Punjabi Sikhs constituted 16.24 per cent of infantry and 23.81 per cent of cavalry, whilst Jats formed 9.5 per cent of the infantry and 19.06 per cent of the cavalry.[118] But as the 1930s saw the rise of fascism in Europe and an increasingly dangerous militarist clique in Japan, Britain would again look to the subcontinent to provide the fresh cadres of men it needed to supplement the ranks of the British Army when war returned in 1939. This would soon be reflected in another call to arms for men to join the colours.

As a result, Secretary of State for India Leo Amery reported on 30 January 1942 that 'the expansion of the Army in India has been rapid ... between

May 1940 and September 1941 5,200 officers, of whom 1,400 were Indians, were recruited. The recruitment of Other Ranks in the same period included about 550,000 Indians of various ranks and kinds. On the 1st October 1941, the strength of the Army had reached a total of 820,000 ... by next month ... [there will be] 264,000 officers and Other Ranks in various theatres ... [of which] 58,000 in Malaya and 20,000 in Burma.'[119] He added that the authorities now had to draw increasingly upon volunteers who were not from the traditional martial classes 'with their long tradition of military service and loyalty to the Crown' but 'from many classes which were not enlisted ... before the war ... and thus have not the traditional military qualities and loyalty of the pre-war martial classes'. Instead they enlisted largely for 'the pay and material benefits' offered by the army. He also warned ominously that many Indian officers had been identified who 'look forward, honestly enough to the day when India will be independent of the British Raj'.[120]

There was a third factor, and one most likely to adversely affect the morale of the older veterans. On 2 March 1942, Acting Major-General R. M. M. Lockhart reflected upon the constitutional turmoil now threatening the country, warning that 'any indication ... of a fundamental change in the conditions in which he has accepted service – whether affecting his material prospects or his creed as a soldier of the British Crown, cannot fail to have at once an unsettling affect [and] induce hesitation to enlist and a reluctance to leave India for service overseas.'[121] This prompted Amery to add a rider to the effect that it was 'essential that senior officers should be instructed to make it quite clear to all subordinates that nothing is happening now that affects their position as the King-Emperor's troops'.[122] This could only be wishful thinking. We have seen how Congress had actively dissuaded recruitment, and indirectly put the mark of Cain on any man who defied their instructions. Many of those who took the King's shilling at this period in the country's history must have done so with a fear of the possible repercussions, torn, as Amery observed, between their loyalty to India and the need to feed their families.

The reservations voiced by both Amery and Lockhart would be largely vindicated when new recruits were sent into battle. *Straits Times* editor G. W. Seabridge observed that during the battle for Singapore 'some were disappointing; some gave themselves up to the enemy depressingly readily. Here the Japanese propagandists were at their most brilliant. By means of radio and pamphlets dropped from aircraft, they laboured the point that they were fighting only the white man; that the British were putting Asiatic troops in the front line as cannon fodder, while the white soldiers remained skulking in the background. They promised that any Asiatic soldier who gave himself up would go unharmed.'[123] As defeat followed defeat the tactic began to work.

Among those persuaded was Captain Mohan Singh, the young officer who had graduated from Dehra Dun to face the derision and hostility of white officers and for whom British defeat offered the chance to turn the tables. He had been captured earlier during the campaign on the peninsula, where he met Major F. Fujiwara, a Japanese intelligence officer charged with turning captured Indian soldiers. The Japanese had even sent men into the region before the war to establish contacts and organise the various anti-British groups already operating there. Later, in the words of Indian National Army historian S. A. Ayer, 'the fateful and historic meeting between Giani Pritam Singh [a member of the failed 1915 Ghadr conspiracy] and Captain Mohan Singh of the 1/4 Punjab Regiment, took place in the jungles near Jitra [in the Malayan peninsula]. Captain Singh and fifty others agreed to join an Indian National Army, and Singh was designated General Officer Commanding.'[124] Then, when Singapore was surrendered, the Indians in the garrison were segregated from their European counterparts and assembled in Farrer Park. Here they were placed under the care of Captain Singh who addressed them with those fateful words, 'I appeal to you to join the [Indian National] army.'[125] They were to form the nucleus of Azad Hind Fauj (the Indian National Army or INA), fighting alongside their new allies to free India by force.

Such dissent became contagious as Japan extended its reach and even produced bloody mutinies. On the tiny outpost of Christmas Island, a phosphate-rich outcrop south of Java, a small garrison of British and Indian troops armed with a single six-inch naval gun awaited developments. Two of the Indian contingent of some twenty-six men, havildars Mir Ali and Ghulum Qadir, had been listening in on Axis radio and learning about events in Malaya and Singapore. Already disenchanted with their situation, the bad news convinced them that their best chance lay in turning on the British and throwing in their lot with the Japanese, whose arrival they believed was imminent. Having persuaded enough of their men to join them, on the night of 10–11 March 1942 they struck, killing five of the British soldiers and throwing their corpses over the cliff into the sea. The remaining Europeans, including their commanding officer, were held captive. The mutiny was not wholeheartedly supported, though, and Lieutenant Muzzofar Khan managed to retain the loyalty of the rest of the sepoys and prevent the killing of the surviving Europeans. This proved a pyrrhic victory for the mutineers. The Japanese did not come for another three and a half weeks, and when they did arrive they did not appreciate the men's betrayal of their officers. Qadir and Ali were not lauded or thanked as they might have expected but assigned to clean-up details instead, an ignominious fate for two men who had staked so much on the amity of their perceived liberators.

Nor were they alone in their disillusionment. Similar demonstrations of Japanese disdain began to grate on Mohan Singh, who fell out with the Japanese over the role of the Indian National Army, its equipment and arms. At the end of 1942 he resigned his command in frustration and was promptly arrested and held until the end of the war.[126] Elsewhere, too, Singh's compatriots were coming to the conclusion that they had made friends not with liberators but even more ruthless conquerors than those they had displaced. For their part, the Japanese were growing impatient with the reluctance of many sepoys to renege on their oath to the King-Emperor, and resorted to coercion and compulsion, revoking their prisoner-of-war status and designating them voluntary collaborators subject to military law. When they remained recalcitrant, the decision was taken early in 1943 to transport them from Singapore to various isolated camps scattered across the Pacific. In one incident 500 members of the 2/12 Frontier Force Regiment and the 1st Battalion of the Hyderabad Regiment were sent in awful conditions to the Palau Islands, 600 miles north of New Guinea,[127] a journey which took a month in a packed and squalid ship. Half-starved and exhausted, they were then subjected to further brutal and degrading treatment in order to crush their will.

Less scrupulous about Japanese motives than Mohan Singh and thousands of other Indian soldiers was Subhas Chandra Bose. This former acolyte of Gandhi thought his chance had come with the war against Japan, and after fleeing India he made his way to Berlin and thence to Tokyo, where he willingly threw in with the enemy. Having established the Indian Independence League in Bangkok in June 1942, he presided over the creation of the INA in September. He had also authorised Singh's short-lived tenure as commander-in-chief of the army. Using his charisma and powers of oratory and persuasion he succeeded where Japanese brutality had failed, managing to persuade around 40,000 men to follow him. Those who saw action occasionally succeeded in gaining converts among loyal Indian troops. During the first British Arakan Offensive of 1942/43, INA troops convinced just under forty members of the 1/15th Punjab Regiment to defect, and during the Japanese Ha-Go campaign of 1944 some members of the Indian States Forces changed sides.[128] During the simultaneously mounted U-Go offensive in Assam, an outpost of the 3rd Gwalior Lancers also went over to the Japanese,[129] but these were the exceptions rather than the rule. Although they had agreed to serve they did so with little distinction, finding themselves not only indifferently led, under-equipped and short of supplies but also exposed to malaria, dysentery and malnutrition. Of the 7,500 INA soldiers actually deployed in the Ha-Go offensive, 2,000 were killed or incapacitated, mostly through starvation rather than combat.[130]

As it became clear that the Japanese were finally being pushed back, more and more men lost heart. Men of the Bose Brigade, named in honour of their venerable leader, handed themselves over to the British in July 1944,[131] and another 2,000 had surrendered by the end of March 1945.[132] Their contribution to the Greater South East Asia Co-Prosperity Sphere, as the Japanese grandly named their new order in the east, had therefore been negligible and little more than a chastening experience for those who participated. Their former comrades were in little mood to display any magnanimity, however. Captured British soldiers had often been abused by the INA, and loyal sepoys badly treated if they refused to join. Now the boot was on the other foot, and such was the hostility with which they were received that British commander General Slim had to issue orders to treat them as legitimate prisoners of war according to the Geneva Convention. Summary courts martial were instead set up in the field, in which twenty-seven were sentenced to imprisonment, and nine to death by hanging. Surprisingly, though, many of those who showed sufficient contrition were reinstated,[133] perhaps indicating a British reluctance to be seen as overly harsh.

The British were also keen to understand what motivated their erstwhile comrades to turn against them, and a Combined Services Directorate of Investigation Corps was formed to undertake interrogations of the 19,500 captured. They were categorised as White (men who only joined the Japanese under duress), Grey (those persuaded by Japanese propaganda or the promise of better treatment), and the incorrigibles, or Black, who joined willingly out of hatred for the British and a desire to throw them out by force of arms.[134] Some 2,565 were categorised as Black, and of these ninety were considered to have committed such serious war crimes that they had to be held to account.[135] Under normal circumstances they would have faced the death penalty, but moderate voices in the British government, aware that their days in the country were numbered, counselled tolerance towards men who if imprisoned would quickly be released, or if executed would become martyrs. Others, however, believed that what these men had done was so serious that the full weight of the law had to bear down upon them regardless of the developing political situation. There were also fears that serving soldiers, seeing mutiny going unpunished, would decide that they no longer felt bound to the oath, and these men were needed more than ever at this difficult time. Auchinleck, well aware of the state of the country and the consequences should the British be seen to engage in a witch hunt, wanted to follow a middle path. So although he supported courts martial in principle, he thought they ought to at least be convened by their peers to avoid any accusations of bias.[136] To the nationalists, naturally, these men were freedom fighters, among them Nehru. But his attitude was more nuanced, as he explained to the Associated Press in August 1945:

> I was of the opinion three years ago and am still of the opinion that the leaders and others of this [Indian National] army had been misguided in many ways and had failed to appreciate the larger consequences of their unfortunate association with the Japanese ... nevertheless they had put themselves on the wrong side and were functioning under the Japanese auspices ... [however] ... I would say that it would be supreme tragedy if these officers and men are liquidated by way of punishment ... their dominating motive was love for India's freedom ...[137]

Jinnah was equally sympathetic, and the League and Congress temporarily joined forces in their defence, providing them with counsel and legal support, and a compromise was finally reached whereby only the most egregious ringleaders would face trial. The first group would comprise Shah Nawaz Khan, P. K. Sahgal and G. S. Dhillon, followed by Abdul Rashid, Shinghara Singh, Fateh Khan and Captain Singh Munawar Khan Awan.[138] They were to be charged with 'waging war against the King-Emperor', murder and abetment to murder,[139] and their trials were scheduled to begin in the Red Fort in Delhi on 5 November 1945. They were to take place in a country that was deteriorating rapidly. Nor was the atmosphere any longer conducive to good order and disciple among servicemen well aware that the days of the Raj were numbered.

Early in 1946 barracks and installations around the country began to show signs of dissent. One of the most serious occurred in Bombay in February 1946 when men of the Royal Indian Navy staged a series of strikes, refusing to parade or work and complaining of bad food, low pay and being subjected to racist abuse. The number of mutineers grew to 3,000, and some began assaulting officers and destroying property. General Officer Commanding Lt-General Sir Robert Lockhart mobilised a battalion of Marathas to force the men back to their quarters, but this only inflamed the situation, with shots being exchanged. A squadron of Mosquitoes was then sortied in the hope of intimidating the men, but by 22 February the mutineers appeared to have taken over their ships completely and were training their guns on the city. Lockhart responded by having artillery directed back at them, but it was only on the 23rd when Gandhi and Nehru appealed to them to hand themselves in that they agreed reluctantly to surrender.

When news of the mutiny reached Karachi ratings there sought to emulate their comrades, those on board HMIS *Hindustan* ejecting their officers and setting in chain a series of similar actions on other ships. Then the dockworkers and other civilians turned out to show support and the local communist party became involved. The British responded with gunfire, and this finally persuaded the mutineers that they had made their point and an uneasy calm was restored. There were further expressions of sympathy elsewhere, such as at the signals training establishment at Jubbalpore later in February which, although peaceful and mainly motivated by grievances over food, pay and accommodation, was suppressed at the point of the bayonet. Neither the League nor the Congress could condone such action, but the implications were crystal clear. These mutinies, Nehru believed, showed 'in which direction the mind of the Indian Army is working'.[140] Nevertheless, the trials went ahead.

It had been decided that the charges of murder and abetment would now be dropped in an effort to assuage public opinion, but the main charge of making war on the King-Emperor remained. One of the accused, Shah Nawaz Khan, remained unrepentant. He told the court that 'this tribunal has no jurisdiction to try me. I had taken part in setting up Azad Hind Fauj for the liberation of my country and had given a pledge to ... die if necessary for the independence of India. I had to choose between India and the Motherland. Our choice fell on our country.'[141] Despite such impassioned rhetoric, the evidence under the terms of the indictment was irrefutable, and the men were duly found guilty but sentenced to the lesser punishment of deportation for life. This outcome did nothing to beguile those who remained convinced that the trials were a charade, the last of which were not concluded until May 1946.

Auckinleck had found himself under mounting pressure and did his best to placate nationalist opinion, seeking clemency for those officers who were given harsh sentences. Even though he played a prominent role in the wartime desertions, Mohan Singh was only cashiered and dishonourably discharged while the Christmas Island mutineers also found themselves the beneficiaries of the changing post-war environment. Seven had been captured at the end of the war and were tried in Singapore towards the end of 1947 and sentenced to death. By this time, however, both India and Pakistan were independent, and they used their influence to have their sentences commuted to life imprisonment. Eventually they were pardoned entirely, while one of the ringleaders, Mir Ali, escaped justice altogether, having eluded the authorities, never to be seen again. These episodes were a pitiful curtain call for an army that had remained overwhelmingly loyal to Britain throughout the war, but with Britain's time in India now approaching its end there was one final indignity it had to endure.

Ultimately the decision would be taken to partition India, and two new Dominions were to emerge, meaning that inevitably the institution established by Stringer Lawrence and honed by subsequent generals would face a similar fate. The British had somewhat naively hoped at first that the armed forces could remain intact and serve as the defence of both India and Pakistan, but Muslim leader Ali Jinnah, if not the Congress leadership, considered that this wildly optimistic solution struck at the heart of each nation's sense of sovereignty, and it was promptly shelved.

The prospect of separating an organisation which had served as a cohesive single unit for over a hundred years was a daunting one, and Auchinleck believed that it was well-nigh impossible. When the decision was initially put to him he warned starkly that 'the armed forces of India, as they now stand, cannot be split up into two parts each of which form a self-contained armed force,' and if attempted 'would take a period of several years ... and might be disastrous to the continued morale and efficiency of the Armed Forces'.[142] His Chief of Staff, Lord Ismay, also condemned the idea, calling it 'the biggest crime and the biggest headache',[143] but the decision had been taken and it had to be carried out. Publicly he had to sound positive, and confidently assured his subordinates that 'we shall, I hope, have no difficulty in achieving our common object which is to reconstitute the Armed Forces of India with the minimum of disturbance and delay and the maximum of efficiency in the equal interests of both Dominions.'[144] Two key points were conceded, however. One was that the division be delayed until after the Raj ended as it would be needed to maintain internal security, and would coincide with the forecast end of British rule in June 1948. Secondly, they would remain temporarily under Auchinleck's supreme command supported by two British generals, Sir Robert Lockhart for India and General Sir Frank Messervy for Pakistan. This it was hoped would at least ensure some short-term continuity, and allow time to tie up the inevitable and numerous loose ends. It was far from ideal, but it appeared to be the only solution that could be agreed upon and that would allow the division of assets to proceed with anything like the efficiency and speed required.

Accordingly, on 15 May 1947 orders were issued that the 'Indian Army should be allocated according to the territorial basis of recruitment and placed under the control of the respective governments,'[145] and in mid-June the Armed Forces Reconstitution Committee was formed to oversee the exercise. The logistical challenges were indeed immense and would have been hard enough to overcome if the two parties had been of a mindset to cooperate and work in harmony. Congress certainly was not inclined to do so, seeing Pakistan as having opted to secede from India and in so doing abrogating the rest of the country from any obligation to facilitate its decision.

Therefore the division of assets was made difficult not just insofar as the practicalities of sharing them but in that one country was loathe to part with the other's share. All ordnance and equipment was meant to be allocated on a ratio of thirty-six to Pakistan and sixty-four to India,[146] but India tried everything to hold on to as much as possible. All sixteen ordnance factories were in India, and only two incomplete installations in Pakistan. India, not being prepared to undertake the complexities of dismantling and removing such assets, only with the greatest reluctance undertook to pay 60,000,000 rupees so that Pakistan could build its own.[147] India also contained the officers' training college and Dehra Dun, in addition to other training establishments, whereas Pakistan was the home of the Staff College at Quetta, the Royal Indian Service Corps headquarters and several regimental training centres.[148] Such fixed assets were one factor to be resolved, but equipment was a further bone of contention, and here Delhi proved to be extraordinarily recalcitrant. Consequently, of the 300 trainloads of arms and other materiel to which Pakistan was entitled, only three were despatched, and they proved to contain just 5,000 pairs of boots and 5,000 mostly unserviceable rifles.[149] Such ruses proved to Jinnah, as he confided to Lord Ismay, that 'the Government of India ... were determined that Pakistan should not have her share,'[150] thus contributing to the mounting animosity which would very soon mar relations between the two countries.

By far the most painful and emotive aspect of the split was the need for officers and other ranks with divided loyalties to abandon regiments they had been proud to call their home. Each was provided with a form, and upon this he was required to indicate the country he now wished to serve. Officers and men who had perhaps fought alongside one another were to say farewell, and there were numerous occasions when final messes were the scenes of emotional parting ceremonies and toasts. Old and revered regiments such as Hodson's and Skinner's Horse, the Sikhs and the Dogras, the Jats, Pathans, and Madrassas would also have to serve new masters. Sometimes simple pragmatism succeeded where dogma would perhaps ordinarily have prevailed, and one Pakistani regiment, the 19th Lancers, offset its shortfall of Muslims by simply exchanging its Jat and Sikh soldiers from India's Skinner's Horse for its own Hindus.[151] There was also the prized regimental silver to be split up, the instruments for regimental bands, and all the other impedimenta which had been accrued over the years.

This process also further exposed the years lost when the Indianisation of the army had been neglected. By 1947 there were still only nine Hindu, five non-Muslim and four Muslim Lieutenant-Colonels, although one of the Muslims had achieved promotion to temporary colonel and one to acting brigadier.[152] The situation for Pakistan was inevitably worse. Against a requirement of 4,000 officers just 2,300 would emerge from the exchange, so that nearly 500 British officers had to be requested to remain in post until the shortfall could be met.[153] On the plus side, this also meant that some younger and less experienced officers found themselves with commands they would otherwise have had to wait years to secure.[154]

As Auchinleck had predicted, the exercise resulted in two quite mismatched armed forces. Pakistan ended up with 150,000 of the former Indian Army's 461,000 men while the balance remained in India. This roughly translated into Pakistan receiving six armoured regiments to India's fourteen, eight artillery regiments to India's forty and eight infantry regiments to India's twenty-one.[155] This outcome further undermined Pakistan, which had only thirteen serviceable Stuart light tanks and one week's ammunition in reserve.[156] Six Gurkha regiments were also shared between Britain and India through a tripartite agreement signed between India, Nepal and Britain, so that one tradition at least continued. Nevertheless, despite the immense difficulties he had been called upon to overcome, British Prime Minister Clement Attlee assured Auchinleck that 'the fact that the army held together as well as it did, that reconstitution went through so smoothly, and that India and Pakistan now have disciplined Armed Forces at their commands is clear proof of the real and lasting success of the work you did.'[157] On 14 August 1947, as if to draw a final line under its long association with the Raj, Auchinleck issued the following poignant instruction:

Discontinuance of Indian Army Orders – This is the last Indian Army Order.[158]

11

'I would rather be killed with bullets'

By the time the Indian Army was being wound up and its various regiments dispersed, the country was only gradually recovering from yet another traumatising experience. Food shortages which had started from the beginning of the war had progressed to full-scale famine by 1942/43, in which millions would die and many more would be forced to flee their homes and abandon their livelihoods. A destructive phenomenon at the best of times, it could not have come when the country was less prepared to confront it. The failure of the Cripps Mission and the Quit India campaign had hamstrung a government preoccupied with the war against Japan, and a devastating cyclone had just laid waste to great swathes of Bengal, ruining precious rice crops, wiping out villages and dispossessing millions of people in an ominous portent of the terrible disaster to follow.

But these militating factors were not alone to blame. Like so many ills which beset the country, they found their origins in the rigid administrative and commercial policies instigated by successive Directors of the East India Company and perpetuated under the rule of the Crown. They had in the process gradually created an underclass of permanently indebted and poverty-stricken Indians who were helpless in the face of natural disaster. Among the most damaging of the measures imposed by the British was to turn on its head a tried-and-tested strategy for ensuring healthy rice harvests and ameliorating the effects of shortages and failures. This was a two-fold protocol which involved planting up to three harvests a year, commencing with the *aus*, planted in the spring before the monsoon and harvested in the autumn. Then *aman* was sown in the monsoon period, during July to August, to be harvested in December, in a good year yielding three-quarters of the annual requirement. Some areas also had a third crop, planted even earlier in the year, which was harvested in the spring. This delicately balanced arrangement might in reasonable times be enough to see them through and leave enough to meet their overlords tax demands.

As might be expected in a subcontinent as vast as India with successive and frequently overlapping rulers, there was no uniform system of land revenue, until in 1538 Sher Shah decided upon a realignment of his domains. In deciding how much of his subjects' wealth to appropriate he applied a number of variables, including the land's fertility and the occurrence of natural disasters such as flood, cyclone or drought. These were designed to ensure an equitable outcome for both the farmer and his overlord. As later emperor Abu Akbar explained, 'there shall be left for every man that cultivates his lands as much as he requires for his own support, till the next crop be reaped, and that of his family for seed. This much shall be left him. What remains is land tax and shall go to the public treasury.'[1] This protocol was underpinned by the simple principle that no farmer should have to pay more than he could afford, and in exchange his master would ensure that should shortage or hunger threaten, he and his family would be looked after. For example, when famine hit Bengal in 1661 Emperor Aurangzeb organised relief efforts and arranged for surplus grains to be transported from the Punjab to meet the shortfall in Bengal,[2] an arrangement which survived largely intact until the British established themselves on the subcontinent. Once the British arrived, however, compounding the eradication of the country's industries and the imposition of punitive trading restrictions was the extortion of every penny possible through a range of crippling tax regimes.

When the East India Company started to become involved in collecting land revenue in the recently established Bengal Presidency in 1764, the previous system of checks and balances was largely abandoned. The priority was building up the bottom line through increasingly oppressive taxes, so when a two-year famine struck in 1770 it killed 10,000,000 people too poor to buy food.[3] Nonetheless, it was not the death toll which concentrated minds but the effect on earnings. In his report of 3 November 1772, Warren Hastings assured the Court of Directors proudly that 'notwithstanding the loss of at least one third of the inhabitants of the province, and the consequent decrease in cultivation, the net collections of the year 1771 exceeded even those of 1768.'[4] There was no reference to what efforts, if any, had been made to relieve the suffering of those affected, because as Macaulay admitted 'the business ... of the Company was simply to wring out of the natives a hundred or two hundred thousand pounds as speedily as possible,'[5] and the consequences for the ordinary peasant were of little concern.

Some attempts were made at reform nonetheless – not to better the lot of the peasant, but to extract more revenue. In Bengal, the so-called Permanent Settlement was introduced in 1793 which it was hoped would rationalise the system of evaluating and collecting land tax. A key element in trying to improve upon the Mughal system was to assign to the zamindars who collected the tax hereditary ownership of the land. In return for a fixed annual rent, they would theoretically become its trustees, ensuring that it remained productive and efficiently farmed. But in making this change the Company further shattered the dynamics which had previously governed the collection of tax. Unlike the previous system whereby a cultivator or landowner surrendered a proportion of his crops in cash or kind, he was now compelled to pay a fixed sum based on projections and estimates of the land's value. This was irrespective of the actual outturn of his fields. As a report assessing the new system bluntly concluded, 'they have to pay as much when crops fail as when they succeed.'[6]

Compounding the shortcomings of the Permanent Settlement, which was in force in the north of the country, a not dissimilar *ryotwari* system was applied in the south, where peasants were nominated to act as collectors. This inevitably led to massive disparities, with some areas adopting annual rent revisions, others fixing the tax for a number of years, and others entering into covenants with the landowners who paid a set amount in perpetuity.[7] Whatever system was applied, they were inflexible and unyielding to prevailing conditions because, as one critic later remarked, in order to meet these demands the farmer had either to 'submit to each renewed assessment, or to leave his ancestral fields and perish'.[8] Consequently, in order to pay the tax and keep hold of his land, he turned increasingly to moneylenders, and if he defaulted he became landless and the property fell to his creditor,[9] producing an almost permanent downward spiral of indebtedness and poverty. Often, 80 per cent of the peasantry were in debt at any one time and their account with their moneylender could never be paid off.[10]

Land tax was not the only burden which weighed upon the peasant; there was the equally invidious Salt Tax. In 1759 the Company had come into possession of land near Calcutta where salt works were operating. In 1764, having taken control of all revenues in Bengal, the Company made the sale of salt the preserve of officers of the Company. Seeing its commercial potential, rents were doubled, transit charges imposed and contracts issued for producers, or *malangas*, to deliver the commodity to salt depots which became the sole distributors. The malangas then sold the salt to agents at a fixed price, initially two rupees a maund with a tax of 1.2 rupees to 1.8. rupees.[11] In 1772 the Company started selling leases to the highest bidders, who were contracted to deliver the salt at a fixed price. Dublin-born politician Philip France was among those appalled by the practice and condemned what he called the venality of 'monopolising the necessity of life, whether for the advantage of the Government or of individuals',[12] but such protests were lost in the clamour to extract more profit. In the event the system fell victim to inevitable and rampant corruption and its management returned to the Company in 1780,[13] but even under stricter Company administration it remained subject to severe criticism.

A parliamentary committee of 1783 concluded that 'even if the monopoly of this article was a profitable concern, it should not be permitted,'[14] but it was far too lucrative to be abandoned willingly. Instead, in deference to government scrutiny minor reforms were instituted. Agents governed by a controller were placed in charge of different elements of the process to provide some oversight and this process remained more or less intact with a few changes until 1947. Nonetheless the monopoly became such a burden on ordinary Indians that smuggling was widely practised to evade the oppressive duties. By the early nineteenth century the practice became almost industrial in its nature and a 500-mile 'Salt Barrier' from Attock to Berar, consisting of a deep impenetrable hedge of thorny bushes manned by a small army of 8,000 men, had to be erected as a deterrent.[15] Together, the Salt Tax and the exactions from land revenue contrived to grind down the life of the peasant to such an extent that the famine of 1770–1772 would prove to be only the precursor of mounting suffering.

In 1785 a harrowing eyewitness account described how in Dacca famine had 'reduced its inhabitants to the lowest depths of misery and distress ... parents were forced to sell their children, and many hundreds of them were disposed of'.[16] In Bombay in 1803, the Customs Master wrote of 'mothers [who] sold their children and themselves to escape perishing from want; young women gave themselves up to prostitution, lived as mistresses with strangers ... or abandoned themselves to the guidance of procuresses,'[17] and in 1813 the Indian Law Commissioner reported that in Agra men were forced to sell their wives and children 'for a few rupees ... and even for a single meal'.[18] As the decades rolled by and with no respite the same stories repeated themselves, an eyewitness watching in 1833 as 'hundreds of half-starved, helpless wretches thronged the suburbs and streets of Calcutta ... offering themselves and their children for sale for a few measures of rice'.[19] Yet while this litany of suffering was played out the Company's coffers continued to fill. Revenues had increased from £800,000 in 1793, to £1,600,000 by 1832–33,[20] and by the 1850s accounted for 10 per cent of Company income.

A direct correlation between the existence of the Company and the prevalence of famine is most discernible when one appreciates that whereas there were two recorded famines in the eleventh century, one in the thirteenth, three in the fourteenth, two in the fifteenth and three in the sixteenth centuries,[21] during the Raj, in addition to constant hunger formed out of poverty, there were famines or serious shortages recorded in 1769–70, 1783–85, 1791–92, 1803, 1813, 1833, 1837–38, 1860–61, 1865–67, 1868–70, 1873–74, 1876–77, 1889, 1892, 1896–1897 and 1899–1900.[22] These occurred in places as far afield as Bengal, Punjab, Rajputana, the Deccan, Orissa, Bihar, Madras, Bombay and the United and Central provinces. The total number of deaths is difficult to calculate accurately but just one estimate of 15,000,000 equates to the eradication of an average European country.[23] The primary cause was of course grinding, persistent poverty, because no meaningful attempt had been made to ameliorate the ryot's lot, and since the Company first began its regime of unremitting demands one British commentator, William Digby, conceded that cultivators continued '[to] live for one-third of the year on advances from moneylenders'.[24] This was confirmed by a Public Works Commission which in 1853 reported that the average Madras ryot 'lives from hand to mouth ... [and] rarely sees money except that obtained from the *chetty* [moneylender] to pay his *kist* [instalment of Government revenue]'.[25]

As the years passed the same tragic stories were repeated. In Bengal alone between 1892 and 1896 over 50,000 acres had been sold to moneylenders and as much again to non-peasant purchasers, rising to 120,000 acres by 1899–1900, while nearly 300,000 acres were under mortgage.[26] In 1896 a blacksmith in the Punjab mortgaged a small plot of land for £2 at 37 per cent interest and by 1906 the debt had reached £33,[27] an impossible sum to pay back. Labourers were even worse off because their wages were often fixed by local custom or contract and were not adjusted for changing conditions.[28] Moreover, some were paid in kind, with free board and lodging, clothing or some additional grain,[29] keeping them in a permanent state of dependency. Their lives were made even more tenuous when European fashion created a demand for blue dye, which planters in India attempted to satisfy by increasing the cultivation of indigo. This meant that less food was grown, and although farmers were reluctant to switch, an enquiry in 1861 concluded that '*ryots* are not at liberty to devote what lands they chose to the cultivation of indigo, but their best land', reducing them to the status of 'working cattle ... not men reconciled to labour by their gains'.[30] One witness, W. H. Elliott, officiating magistrate of the Burdwan Division of Bengal, testified that 'I have never yet heard of one instance in Bengal of a ryot gaining substance by the cultivation of indigo.'[31] The Honourable Ashley Eden, magistrate, collector and salt agent for Cuttack, told the commission established to look into the industry that 'indigo cultivation is in no instance the result of free agency, but always compulsory,'[32] while one of those forced to cultivate the plant, Panji Mullah, later admitted, 'I would rather be killed with bullets and have my throat cut, than sow indigo.'[33] Nonetheless, he and many thousands of others could not refuse, due to their indebtedness to zamindars. This hold allowed them to:

> send for the ryots, and command them to take the planters money, and pay their arrears. The ryots might object that the planter would only advance the money on their entering into contracts to plant indigo at prices less remunerative than rice, and which would perhaps not leave them land enough to grow rice for themselves, or not to give them enough money both to buy rice and pay rent.[34]

This state of virtual bondage meant they 'never get out of the planter's books ... once in them',[35] until 'the weak and the poor, who form the great mass of the population should be made weaker and poorer for the benefit of a small body of men [the planters]'.[36] They were also mistreated and exploited on a par with indentured labourers and sepoys, planters and mill owners routinely resorting to 'acts of violence [which frequently] occasioned the death of natives'.[37] Fear and intimidation meant they could act with impunity, and often in collusion with the police and the magistracy. Even if a sympathetic ear could be found, 'the planter tells us that whoever goes to the magistrate will have his house pulled down and be turned out of the village,' one victim of the system, Kulin Mundal, later explained.[38] Finally, the peasants had enough and began to organise against the planters and their lackeys, a strike breaking out in February and March 1859 when thousands combined and refused to grow the hated crop. There were violent confrontations and although it never developed into an outright rebellion it frightened the Europeans, especially after mobs fell upon the indigo factories at Mollahat, Lokenathpur and Chadupur. Governor-General Lord Canning later conceded that such was the ferocity of the rebellion that 'it caused me more anxiety than I have had since the days of Delhi ... '[39] But it served some purpose, Lord Canning admitting that he was 'thoroughly convinced that the condition of the people of Bengal cries out loudly for amendment, and that amendment is in a great degree in the hands of the government'.[40] The subsequent Commission of Enquiry concurred, concluding that 'the whole system is vicious in theory, injurious in practise and radically unsound.'[41] Yet despite such condemnation its findings fell far short of what the evidence justified, and no new laws were recommended for the protection of the peasants or punishment of the planters.

Increasingly, nonetheless, voices were being raised by public figures urging that something be done to improve the peasants' lives, particularly for the abolition of the Salt Tax. But the British government remained unrepentant. In 1869, by which time the tax was yielding £5,176,000 a year, Secretary of State for India Lord Argyll maintained that 'on all grounds of general principle, salt is a perfectly legitimate object of taxation ... if they [the Indians] are to contribute at all to the expenditure of the State, it must be through taxes levied upon articles of universal consumption.'[42] Sir John Strachey, who held various posts in the Government of India, shared the Secretary of State's mindset. He asserted in December 1877 that 'there is certainly no reason in the condition of the agricultural classes why they should not bear their share of any necessary fresh taxation for the purpose of protecting themselves and the country against famine [because] ... when famine is at its height the mass of the people receiving relief are field labourers, petty ryots and artisans. Very few priests, and lawyers and schoolmasters and people with fixed incomes actually demand Government relief, although they may feel sorely the pressure of famine prices.'[43] So it stayed, rising ever more until by 1881–82 it was contributing £6,809,000 to the government's coffers.[44]

These attitudes were in part due to a conviction that the peasants' condition was largely due to their own fecklessness. The Secretary of State for India in 1877, Lord Salisbury, exposed his complete lack of understanding of the situation when he told a meeting in Bradford somewhat glibly that 'the only true remedy against famine and scarcity is the frugality of the people. The people ought in years of plenty to make money enough to lay up against times of famine.'[45] Such attitudes informed the prevailing opinion that if only the ordinary Indian saved more and better managed his budget he would be able to withstand the lean times, but prolific author and nineteenth-century polymath John Dacosta was among those who railed against this myopic attitude. He maintained that 'the drought of 1876 and 1877 [in Western India] found the agricultural population so impoverished, and so denuded of the means of tiding over the season of scarcity that, notwithstanding the millions of public money which were expended for their relief, an appalling amount of death ensued, and the bulk of the surviving cultivators has remained in a chronic state of indebtedness and debilitation.'[46]

Nearly twenty years later, nothing had changed, as *The Pioneer* in 1893 explained, 'all the persons of the labouring classes, and ten percent of the cultivating and artisan classes, or forty five percent of the total population, are insufficiently clothed, or insufficiently fed, or both,'[47] a total of approximately 70,000,000 people.[48] The taxes which the peasants went hungry to pay went in large part to fund the canals, the water from which, as we have seen, farmers also had to pay for to irrigate their land. Having been promoted as a silver bullet to eradicate famine, this fallacy was soon demolished by its harshest critics. In 1878 Dacosta pointed out that 'the irrigation schemes already tried have failed to yield the results they were intended to produce,'[49] citing in particular the famines which 'desolated the Doab in 1860–61 and 1869 ... the canal has not afforded the immunity contended for'.[50] He shared the conviction that lifting them out of perpetual debt was a much more plausible solution than canals,[51] and advocated establishing a uniform annual land tax across the entirety of British India, rather than making annual and often arbitrary evaluations.[52] He cited as one example the Bombay Presidency where the demand 'was so excessive that, within three or four years, a considerable number of cultivators who had previously been in a prosperous condition were ruined, their farms were abandoned, a large amount of agricultural capital was irretrievably destroyed, and in spite of the extreme severity of the collectors, increasing difficulty was experienced in the recovery of the revenue'.[53]

Painfully slowly such arguments led to some action, and in 1880 a Famine Commission was established to identify the causes of famine and shortage and how best to address them. A key recommendation – counterintuitive considering the debt and poverty that already existed – was to extend loans to farmers for the purchase of seed and cattle.[54] But this time the money would be advanced on much more favourable rates than might be expected from usurers – around 6 per cent – with average repayment periods of between seven and twelve years.[55] Uptake of the scheme saw 206,380 rupees distributed between 1880 and 1891,[56] and steps were also taken to lower the rate of the revenue demand. But as Viceroy Lord Lansdowne conceded, this could only be 'a temporary reparation, as at the same time it has involved a serious and continuously increasing loss to the State Exchequer'.[57] He concluded that the best remedy to break this vicious circle was 'the further extension of the system of advances to cultivators ... the introduction of a greater element of elasticity into our revenue system [and] ... measures for restricting the right of land transfer'.[58]

But these steps alone could not address the underlying problems, and in 1883 the commission also produced the so-called 'Famine Code', which laid down a system of early warnings of coming shortage so that the necessary steps could be taken in advance. Measures to prevent hoarding and controlling prices were included in the plan in addition to special government projects and relief programmes which would provide peasants with an income. The code also provided for remission of taxes and the free distribution of seed for the following year's planting.[59] A famine relief fund was also created, but this came in for much criticism, as Dadabhai Naoroji explained in January 1897 when he condemned it as 'nothing more or less than a means of taxing the starving to save the dying. This fund does not rain from heaven, nor does the British Exchequer give it. If the government spend say, £5,000,000 on the present famine they will simply squeeze it out of the poverty-stricken surviving taxpayers who would in turn become the victims of the next drought.'[60] Instead, he insisted, 'the British Exchequer should pay the whole cost of both saving life and restoring the stricken people to their normal industrial condition and wants'[61] – not an approach likely to appeal to men like Lord Salisbury.

Yet while Indians went without the country was exporting vast amounts of foodstuffs to feed the metropole, and by 1886 it was supplying nearly a quarter of its needs.[62] Furthermore, due to the country's own internal market, food which could have fed the needy of one province was often exported to another, simply to raise much-needed revenue. Henry Hyndman described a situation whereby 'though famine was seen to be coming upon [Orissa] in 1865, food stuffs were exported from the province in order to get money to meet the Government demand' and 'during the year 1877 the North West Provinces exported grain ... to Madras and England, though 300,000 people, according to thoroughly trustworthy testimonials, died in those provinces of starvation during that period.'[63] Hoarding in lean times in the expectation of inflationary pressures also exacerbated shortages. Noted Sanskrit scholar Ernest Wood believed that 'even in the worst times there is no scarcity in the famine stricken districts. At the very worst time in the Gujerat famine of 1900 it was shown by official returns that there was sufficient grain to last for a couple of years in the hands of grain dealers.'[64]

Together, such practices naturally created shortages where supplies were needed most and pushed up prices further. Consequently the average price of rice, wheat, jowar, bajra, ragi, gram and barley would rise by 37 per cent between 1901 and 1905, by 91 per cent between 1905–1910 and 93 per cent between 1911 and 1914.[65]

An obvious solution was to simply outgrow demand, creating permanent surpluses which might keep prices down and make it unnecessary to hoard and sell in times of need. Montgomery Martin calculated optimistically that 'if all the wasteland of India were cultivated ... India might sustain in comfort 400,000,000 people and become one of the wealthiest regions of the earth,'[66] but Sir James Caird, British agriculturalist and chair of the Famine Commission, challenged this hypothesis, claiming that on the contrary all the good land in India had by now been taken.[67] This was in part due to the fact that the most fertile land was competing increasingly with more lucrative produce which, like indigo, was seen as a more attractive proposition than wheat or rice. In 1900 495,000 acres of tea had been planted, and this would increase to 636,000 by 1915,[68] by which time India would be supplying 71 per cent of all the tea consumed in the UK.[69] This was big business, leaving peasant farmers with the least profitable land with which to try earn a living. The soil on which they struggled had also become poorer and less productive after generations of overuse and outmoded farming practices. Henry Hyndham observed that 'fallows have ... ceased in India, rotation of crops is at best very imperfect, and the supply of manure from bullocks de-pastured in wastelands has all but disappeared.'[70] Agricultural wheat output in India was subsequently estimated to be just thirteen bushels per acre compared with sixteen in the USA, twenty-two in Canada, and thirty-two in England.[71]

Strong, healthy livestock with which to undertake the more onerous aspects of farming and provide rich sources of fertiliser may have been a godsend to overworked farmers, but they were too few and too weak to make much of a contribution. William Digby's investigations revealed not only that 'during [1890] among a population of 140,000,000 in British India ... there were only 90,750,065 animals (including cows, bulls, buffaloes, ponies, mules, donkeys, sheep and goats) ... Australia, with only 4,000,000 of population, had 113,550,831 animals.'[72] If the same ratio of animals was applied to India there should have been nearer to 2,628,000,000 animals,[73] but numbers did not tell the whole story either. Alfred Deakin observed that although the proportion of cattle in Bengal was double that in the UK, 'they could not be trusted to perform one half of the work, not merely because they are small, they are ill-fed.'[74] Basically farmers could not afford to feed them properly, so they proved more of a hindrance than any source of relief. Hyndman revealed that in Orissa alone, 'fully seventy five per cent of the cattle died' of starvation and exhaustion.[75] At one time upwards of a million perished through contracting rinderpest, the most virulent disease known to affect cattle,[76] and even in times of extreme distress religious orthodoxy prohibited their slaughter for meat or to put them out of their misery. It was evident that no single solution could address the multitude of factors dogging the lives of India's peasants, although Lord Curzon thought there was one answer. Addressing the Viceregal Council on 28 March 1901 he expounded his theory that 'what a prudent government endeavours to do is to increase its non-agricultural sources of income. It is for this reason that I welcome ... the investment of capital and the employment of labour, upon railways, canals, in factories, workshops, mills, coal mines, metalliferous mines, and on tea, sugar and indigo plantations.'[77]

But as we have seen, Curzon's promise to drag India out of its pre-industrial torpor would take some time to be realised. The First World War heralded the long-awaited industrial boom but poor harvests due to lack of rain and heavy floods persisted well into the 1920s and 1930s.[78] In 1935 and 1936 the high level of the Ganges caused a flood which was especially disastrous to Mursishabad, Nadia and Jessore, destroying the crop in Aman and delaying the sowing of the winter crops.[79] Yet in spite of the evidence, there persisted a blinkered refusal to acknowledge that poverty lay behind it all and a determination that modern technology would save the day. In 1932 Victor Alexander John Hope, later to become Viceroy Lord Linlithgow, published a thirty-two-page pamphlet entitled *The Indian Peasant* in which he claimed that 'modern means of transportation have eliminated the risk of famine. Bad harvests inevitably inflict grievous hardships upon the cultivator, and seasons of dearth still unhappily lead to heavy mortality among the cattle; but the risk to man of perishing by starvation has been definitely removed.'[80] His audacious overconfidence was completely turned on its head by a survey in 1933 which revealed that rather than hunger being eradicated, only 22 per cent of Bengalis were well nourished and 31 per cent remained badly nourished. In India as a whole the statistics were only slightly less distressing, at 39 per cent and 26 per cent respectively.[81] Compounding the situation was a population expanding at an alarming rate. That of Bengal alone had increased from 42,000,000 in 1901 to 60,300,000 by 1941, a rise of 43 per cent, of whom 90 per cent were eking out a living in one of 84,000 poverty-stricken villages. There was also a large urban population of 6,000,000, two-thirds of whom were living in Greater Calcutta working in war industry.[82]

But with demand for food increasing, the harvests continued to disappoint. In 1940–41 there was only between a quarter and half as much produce as the previous year, forcing Bengalis to break into their reserves.[83] This in turn meant that by the end of 1942 most of the 1941–42 harvest had already been exhausted, and hopes of any improvement was shattered by a highly destructive seed blight that struck some areas, reducing yields by 50 per cent.[84] In normal times, Bengal might have been able to obtain relief from elsewhere in the country, but in Rajasthan poor rainfall and crop failures exposed nearly a quarter of its population to shortages, meaning there was none to spare for anyone else. Similar problems were experienced in the Punjab, the Central Provinces, Bihar and Orissa. Their governments responded by invoking their rights under the Government of India Act of 1935, holding back from export and reserving stocks for their own populations. Taken together such measures were creating, in the words of renowned entomologist M. Afzul Husain, 'independent food kingdoms',[85] which became increasingly insular and looked to their own interests before those of the country as a whole. Inevitably hoarding increased under pressure of supply, and Defence of India regulations had to be put into effect to force traders to desist and release their stocks.[86]

Even if there had been an appetite in other provinces to assist Bengalis, valuable engines and rolling stock, as well as repair facilities and personnel which may have undertaken relief operations, were now assigned instead to the war fronts in the Middle East. The problem was exacerbated further when war broke out with Japan and fear of invasion led to a scorched earth policy to obstruct and delay the enemy advance. Rail lines were torn up, roads rendered unusable and crucial stocks of rice actually destroyed to deny them to the Japanese. Nearly every boat along coastal Bengal was also requisitioned or rendered inoperable, with 1,613 taken by the military, nearly 8,000 wrecked and 40,000 moved outside of the so-called 'Denial Zone'.[87] This left only a fraction for distribution of any relief in a province heavily dependent upon its rivers for transport, while efforts were further hampered by the Japanese advance, which threw 30,000 Bengalis out of their homes.[88]

The proximity of the Japanese to Bengal had also drawn huge numbers of troops to the region, and their demands placed additional strain on supplies. In 1940–41 military purchases accounted for 88,000 tons of foodstuffs, and in 1942–43 this had soared to 312,000 tons.[89] This would obviously put even greater pressure on prices, and despite the Defence of India regulations being invoked hoarding persisted. Bengal's government therefore issued a Food Grains Order in May 1942 prohibiting stockpiling while it tried to offset price hikes by opening its own grain shops. These efforts were accompanied by a series of price control conferences between 1940 and 1943 to discuss what further steps might be taken, but M. Afzul Husain found them to be little more than talking shops. He despaired that the delegates were too concerned with provincial autonomy to acquiesce in meaningful joint action, and consequently 'they caused not a stir, till the situation was out of hand.'[90] Meanwhile, as the authorities talked the retail price index continued to rise exponentially, from 100 in 1939 to 246 by the height of the crisis.[91] These factors alone were enough to blight efforts to control the deteriorating situation, but then Mother Nature decided to throw in her lot when one of the most destructive cyclones for many years hit the province on 16 October 1942. Shortly afterwards, Secretary of State Leo Amery described its devastating effects to the House of Commons:

A heavy cyclone from the Bay of Bengal passed over the Districts of Midnapore and Twenty Four Parganas [a group of villages or subdivision of a district] on 16th October. It began about 7.00 a.m. and lasted twenty four hours. A tidal wave, in places twenty-six feet high, penetrated over ten miles inland. Approximate estimate of persons killed is 11,000; seriously affected 550,000; partially affected one million; cattle killed, 75,000; huts destroyed, 700,000; area affected, 3,000 square miles ... the difficulties of relief work are intensified by lack of roads, flooding, damage to telegraph lines and also the civil disobedience movement which continues to obstruct government workers ... our troops did all in their power to assist the villages ...[92]

The Governor of Bengal, Sir John Herbert, immediately opened a relief fund to which the King and Queen, the Bank of England and other bodies subscribed. But it was soon evident that it would take more than hard cash to recover rice fields swamped with saltwater and exposed to the destructive properties of the *helminthosporium oryzae* fungus which now also infected rice paddies with brown spot disease. Coming at the moment when so many other factors were conspiring to torment the country, it had an impact of almost biblical proportions. The Government of India consequently felt compelled to make its first direct approaches to London asking for help. Britain was by now totally engaged in a war on many fronts, and key to fighting the conflict was the availability of shipping to supply armies in the field as well as keep the metropole fed. It would therefore be a considerable addition burden to divert resources, so on 13 February 1943 Viscount Frederick Leathers, Minister of State for War Transport, laid out the options:

> ... apart from an existing military requirement (which we were already meeting) of some 15,000 tons a month, India asked for 200,000 tons of cereals by end April. The request was referred by the Shipping Committee to the Lord President's Committee who decided that an additional 40-50,000 tons should be provided out of tonnage which would otherwise have been available to the UK Import Programme. The Committee also considered that by economies and by diverting shipping based in India or under Indian control, an additional 80,000 tons could be provided. I have already made the necessary diversions to cover 46,000 tons for February and March loading, apart from 27,000 tons on military account. Owing to the failure of India to supply Ceylon with rice we have had to ship wheat and flour, totalling 130,000 tons, from Australia in the last few months ...[93]

But time was of the essence. In April Amery warned, 'The [rice] harvest just completed was a sad disappointment, and thus means that the outlook for the last months of this year is an anxious one. Rice prices in Bengal are alarmingly high but efforts are being made to meet the situation by imports from surrounding Provinces. Steps are being taken preparatory to the introduction of rationing ... other measures are [the] reduction of the bran percentage extracted from wheat, prohibition of the polishing of rice, closer control of speculative operations ... propaganda against hoarding and for economy.'[94] In June, the government appointed respected Professor of Economics Sir Theodore Gregory as chair of the Food Grains Policy Committee (India) to investigate and report upon the crisis. But his analysis of the situation would take some time to filter through, and urgent action was needed. Optimistic 'food drives' were conducted throughout June and July, designed to further ferret out and expose any hoarders, but although the 1,000,000 tons thereby uncovered sounded substantial it was a drop in the ocean compared to what was needed, especially shared out among 10,000,000 families, or 56,000,000 people,[95] while all the time the situation was becoming more critical all over the country.

At the end of July, the Shipping Committee had some disquieting news, admitting to the War Cabinet that 'there is likely to be a deficit for the fiscal year 1943–1944 of the order of 1,350,000 tons' exacerbated by the fact that '[producers] continue to hold stocks in the anticipation of an increase in prices [and] fear of Japanese invasion ... India Office state that it should be realised that famine conditions are already reported as having begun to appear in some parts of India ... Travancore, Cochin and Bengal.' Finally, 'consideration [of meeting all Indian demands] would necessitate a comprehensive review of requirements and tonnage prospects extending far into 1944 ... 500,000 tons for India between September – February would require additional 80,000 tons of shipping a month from UK and North America.'[96] There were also fears that the situation would have serious knock-on effects in other areas. Amery stated unequivocally that 'unless the requirements of the Government of India are substantially met [there would be] a reduction in munitions manufacture and supplies ... [refusal of] all exports of foodstuffs to Ceylon [and] Persian Gulf ... famine conditions ... civil disturbances ... subversive activities' and finally, and perhaps most seriously for the British Government, 'plans for future operations based on Indian theatre jeopardised and the whole concept of India, not only as a source of supplies but as a base for operations, may have to be reconsidered.'[97]

By September 1943 news was becoming increasingly dire, as Amery reported:

[In Bengal and Assam] famine conditions are now rife ... In Chittagong, ARP [Air Raid Precaution] personnel have had to take over the daily removal of corpses from streets and houses. In Dacca the poor are living on what rice water they can get, *since even the rich are unable to obtain rice* [author's italics]. Cholera, smallpox and starvation are causing hundreds of deaths daily in the surrounding villages ... Such conditions are not confined to the north-east. A British Resident on a [rubber] estate in Mysore writes that it is dangerous to walk through the estate now as they are having trouble over food ... many estates in Travancore have had to stop working owing to supplies of rice being insufficient to feed their labour ... in the Calcutta area there have been numerous strikes ... workers' demands in all cases has been centred around the supply of food ... and when this demand has been met the situation has rapidly returned to normal ... On existing evidence it appears strikes are influenced by purely economic and not political motives ... [98]

Although the government believed the disruption was not politically based, as news of the famine spread Azad Hind Fauj and its Japanese sponsors did try to make political capital out of the situation. On 14 August, Axis radio broadcast from Berlin that 'the Indian Independence League at Bangkok has decided to enlist the help of Japan, Thailand and Burma to export rice to India and thus improve the situation ... if the British Government approve the proposal and give an undertaking that the food so sent will not be reserved for military consumption or exported from India. This gesture of the League is expressive of the sympathy of Indians in East Asia and their desire to relieve the suffering of their brethren. If the British do not accept this generous offer they will be betraying their true intentions.'[99] Some nationalists inside India also sought to exploit the situation to stir up public opinion against the government, charging it with culpability, a lacklustre approach and simple neglect, while the government countered with accusations that the non-cooperation movement was making matters worse and exploiting the situation for its own ends.

While the bickering went on Amery reported on 22 September that 'arrangements for 30,000 tons of wheat from Australia have so far been made, and for 5,000 tons from the US', but 'the year leading up to the main rice harvest about Christmas lies before us with singularly little reason to anticipate improvement in the situation before its end. Over India as a whole there has not been much change in the food position; it is still one of grave anxiety ... meantime the Central Government has been taking such steps as are open to it to meet the day to day situation. Bombay City started rationing in May [and] similar plans are being put into operation for seventy of the larger cities ... Bengal is still the main danger spot.'[100] He was also concerned that, 'even if all promised supplies of foodstuffs come through, I envisage a large death-toll throughout the province from starvation ... coupled with endemic malaria during the next three and a half months. Though famine is not officially declared conditions are those of famine for the landless labourer in many areas and the normal wreckage of population which subsists on charity ... '[101]

However, 'so far there has been no widespread disorder [but] … the worst point is yet to come … for the next three months the people have to depend upon the old crop. These months are always difficult and this year they have to be faced from a bad start … Last year's grow more food campaign has been intensified and where 8,000,000 additional acres were brought under food crops last season, 12,000,000 will be brought under food crops this year … other long term measures are expected to emerge from the committee which has just reported … I understand it not only recommended the importation of 1,000,000 tons of grain annually until normal conditions are re-established, but strongly urges the necessity to import at once 500,000 tons to afford, so to say, the springboard from which to launch its long-term policy with prospect of success … '[102] Viceroy-designate Lord Wavell had no sooner been appointed to the post than he was bombarded with demands from the War Cabinet. With the war now at a critical phase they impressed upon him to make 'every effort … even by the diversion of shipping urgently needed for war purposes, to deal with local shortages'.[103]

Then a ray of hope appeared when in late October the Prime Minister of Canada offered 100,000 tons of wheat if the British could arrange the necessary shipping. However, despite the War Cabinet's instructions to Wavell, Amery had to admit that 'there was no hope of shipping anything like the full 100,000 tons from North America, even over a long period … the most that could be hoped for was a few shiploads.'[104] Thus, a tantalising offer was to go begging because of a lack of ships, but there was another issue to consider. If the news leaked out, it would be a gift to nationalist propaganda, especially 'if the Canadian Government publish this offer and we have to inform the Government of India that the wheat cannot be shipped.'[105] He therefore urged that 'all possible means of giving at any rate some effect to it should be explored',[106] but this was easier said than done, and the revelation came alongside increasingly bad news from Bengal. Here, '9,448 malnutrition cases were admitted to hospital between 15 August and the 15 October, of whom 2,757 died. About twice as many deaths have been accounted for outside the hospitals in Calcutta. Reliable figures elsewhere cannot be obtained but an informed guess puts the death toll at 2,000 a week for Bengal as a whole in mid-October.'[107]

Meanwhile, rationing and price controls were to be imposed in Calcutta, and orders for the use of army transport had also been approved. The 'Provincial and Central Governments hope to get through the critical period between now and the winter rice harvest [which] should be in the market in January … [it] is reported to be in good condition and measures are being taken to purchase as much as possible on behalf of the Government.'[108] Yet the issue remained one of shipping and although 'His Majesty's Government have been able to provide shipping for … imports of food grains from overseas between now and the end of the year … the problem of imports is entirely one of shipping … [especially as] operational and other claims throughout the world make it exceedingly difficult to find sufficient shipping suitably placed, and there is no free tonnage which can be switched to such a purpose without affecting other needs of the United Nations war effort.'[109]

Although it was constantly reiterated that lack of ships was the main obstacle to progress, critics in London were convinced there was still more that could be done. Socialist MP for Edinburgh East Frederick Pethwick-Lawrence made an impassioned speech as Leader of the Opposition in the House of Commons on 4 November 1943:

> If this terrible death rate had occurred in any one part of the British Isles, the member who sat for that locality would have been vociferous in demanding that something should be done ... if there has been a lack of imagination in handling this problem, lack of initiative, any failure to take full cognisance of the facts and bring the best remedy to bear, we in this House are ultimately responsible, and we cannot shirk that responsibility ... I think that our Government in India ... must take a substantial share of the blame for what has taken place.[110]

But the government fought back. Amery blamed the provisions of the Government of India Act of 1935 for allowing the provinces to act arbitrarily and against the common interest. This was due to the fact that 'Agriculture and Food are in the Provincial field' and 'for the Government of India to invade the field of Provincial responsibility would ... have been not only unconstitutional ... but actually illegal'.[111]

But if the Viceroy was wary of asserting himself others were not. At the Fourth Food Conference in October its president, Sir J. P. Srivastava, finally laid his cards on the table. He, like Amery, was frustrated by the lack of cooperation between provinces and warned them sternly that if they did not act collegiately and coordinate their activities more effectively the Government of India would 'exercise whatever degree of superintendence and control at every stage may be necessary, or to invoke the use of whatever powers are essential to ensure success'.[112] For his part Lord Wavell was directing army resources to the worst-affected districts, and between November 1943 and April 1944 troops covered 836,000 miles to deliver 70,000 tons of supplies.[113] In addition, by November 1943 Bengal had 6,625 food kitchens set up, and another 55,000 victims were being looked after in destitute homes and camps.[114]

Nonetheless more still needed to be done, and Amery was increasingly strident in his calls for assistance, as in this statement from 4 November:

> It is now clear that I must ask the War cabinet to consider the question of additional imports without waiting for the end of the year ... [because] the rice harvest will not reach the market until January ... and ... [we] need to show hoarding farmers in Punjab and Bengal if they do not release supplies they will be replaced from elsewhere ... authorities

in Bengal unable to cope with current cereal supplies. Supplies coming from areas also in need in Bombay and Malabar States ... immense public pressure in India for more help from overseas. If our refusal of the offer of 100,000 tons of wheat from the Canadian Government becomes known, it will be desirable to show that adequate quantities of wheat are being shipped instead from other sources...[115]

He added that the minimum amount of shipping that 'will give them a fighting chance (as distinct from a good prospect) of extracting supplies and restoring confidence is an assurance of 50,000 tons per month for twelve months and authority to make an announcement that this has been promised ... [otherwise, agreement that] ... there should be loaded for India from Australia 50,000 tons of wheat before the end of 1943 additional to the 80,000 tons requested, and 50,000 tons of wheat in January 1944, and a further 50,000 tons in February 1944; and question of how much Iraqi barley can be made available after 130,000 tons has been sent'.[116]

By November, things did appear to be improving, with Amery now reporting that 'progress made with the aid of the army, both in transporting food supplies from Calcutta to outlying districts and in distribution to the more remote villages from these centres ... Rice harvest expected to be 4,000,000 acres larger than 1942 ... Every prospect of a large crop in Bengal, which has been unofficially estimated as likely to bring the total rice supplies of the Province to 11,000,000 tons as against 7,000,000 tons last year ... in order to relieve the pressure on the Bengal markets the Government of India has agreed to supply from outside Bengal the needs of Calcutta City and its industrial suburbs, of which the requirements are expected at 650,000 tons for the year.'[117] Matters were somewhat better in Bombay and the Deccan districts too, as they received 'a well-distributed monsoon with the result of a normal millet crop ... in Travancore and Cochin the position is difficult and will remain so during December until the Madras rice crop begins to move out ... state-wide rationing is being introduced ... the Government of India expect to improve supplies during 1944 and the States will receive about 20,000 tons of imported wheat. In Madras the rice and millet position is generally satisfactory. Nearly all the famine camps have been closed and the labourers are now employed on normal agricultural work. Rationing in Madras is successful and is to be extended to towns in Malabar and to certain districts.'[118]

In spite of such progress, Wavell was shocked by the manner in which the Government of India Act was being employed. In early 1944, having seen things for himself, he felt compelled to insist that 'by whatever means, the responsibility for control of the food situation in Bengal must be taken out of the hands of the Minister,'[119] whom he had concluded was corrupt and inefficient. Wavell accused him of having made 'little or no progress ... only touching fringe of vast health problem ... fear present harvest will go underground or get into unscrupulous dealers ... there is much graft and knavery ... no confidence in the Ministry and [officials] believe Bengal will starve itself again next summer ... although Muslim League may kick, especially in the Eastern Districts of Bengal, there will be many political elements in favour'.[120] Not only was this another damning indictment of the 1935 Act, but it also appeared to vindicate some of the reservations expressed in the Statutory Commission of 1928. Corruption and graft were rife, and instrumental in exacerbating the plight of ordinary Indians. Nonetheless, whether it was politic to enter into open conflict with a provincial government at this time was perhaps open to question, particularly as it appeared the crisis was finally turning a corner.

It was now possible to report that 'during December the import of food grains into Bengal, coupled with the assistance of transport and distribution given by the army, has effectively secured the Province from food shortage for the time being. [However] problems of post-famine nutrition will continue for some time to come. The main rice crop ... would probably suffice to cover requirements of the Province for the crop year to 1944 ... Elsewhere in India the food situation has been generally satisfactory. The Punjab Government has reluctantly agreed to apply rationing and price controls from next autumn's crop and the Sind Government are acting upon the direction of the Central Government that they shall introduce rationing in the Province.'[121] Also by this time, Gregory's analysis was available, and seemed to contain a startling admission. He recommended that 'India must cease, for the duration of the war, to be a net exporter of food: no exports should be permitted unless such exports are fully compensated by imports,'[122] laying bare the fact that at such a critical time food was still being sent overseas. In any case, there was certainly no cause for complacency; quite the contrary. Another investigation cautioned in the strongest terms:

> Attempts by HMG to prove on the basis of admittedly defective statistics that we can do without help demanded would be regarded here by all opinion – British and Indian – as utterly indefensible ... carry over from year to year unknown. The problem is that cultivator's stocks are less now than pre-war ... population increase from 1938-39 to 1943-44 inclusive must be of order of 30,000,000, justifying increase in consumption of order of 4,000,000 tons over consumption of 1938-39 ... since it is known that His Majesty's Government is not prepared to help India, and I do not see how the fact can be concealed since amount of grain imports is a question closely studied, I fear that all our work at control of past months, which has had considerable success, will be lost, prices of grain and of all other commodities will rise, and situation may pass out of control...[123]

With the war against Japan now reaching a critical stage, concerns that India's role in the war might be compromised by the famine resurfaced. As a consequence, British Chiefs of Staff Field Marshal Alan Brooke, Chief Air Marshal Charles Portal and Admiral of the Fleet Andrew Cunningham found themselves drawn into the debate. They concluded that 'the provision of wheat for India is therefore a military requirement of strategic importance ... a possible means by which shipping can be found to meet this requirement is by making a corresponding reduction in the revised "SEXTANT" allocation of tonnage for military maintenance programs.' This could, they believed, be done through 'an overall reduction in maintenance programs ... [which] should amount to some eight sailings a month or say twenty-five ships over the quarter. If an equivalent allocation were made to carry wheat from Australia to India, some 200,000 tons could be imported without interfering with other approved programs.' Furthermore, such an initiative 'might enable some further advantage to be taken of the Canadian offer of wheat [by adding it to ships sailing from North America to India]'.[124]

With that possible solution added to the mix, thoughts also turned to the supposed 'special relationship' between Churchill and President Roosevelt, which was meant to open doors closed to lesser mortals. Therefore, on 24 April the War Cabinet asked Home Secretary Herbert Morrison to draft a communication from the Prime Minister to Roosevelt in the hope that he may 'help us with shipping to carry grain to India',[125] but the US President's response was disappointing. Revealing the much-lauded partnership as something of a sham, Amery reported that a 'negative reply having been received from President Roosevelt, the Prime Minister directed that the matter should again be considered in the Indian Food Grains Committee'.[126] This disappointment simply brought them back to square one, as 'Committee agreed [there was] no possibility of finding further shipping for imports of food grains to India unless this would be found out of shipping already allocated for military purposes.'[127] The low priority Washington gave to the problem was underlined by the fact that it would not be until March 1946 that President Truman despatched former president Herbert Hoover on a factfinding mission. This was followed by the American Famine Mission led by agricultural economist Theodore Schultz. It was only upon his return to the United States that he recommended 750,000 tons of wheat be despatched to India,[128] by which time the immediate crisis was over. In any case, according to Viceroy Wavell, Hoover had conceded that 'India had done all she could about food.'[129] There was little hope of help from that quarter. The British were on their own.

Instead, in August 1944, Sir Henry French, Permanent Secretary to the Ministry of Food, was asked to lead a mission to India and investigate the situation. He visited Sind, Delhi, Bombay, the United Provinces, Madras, Punjab and, critically, Bengal. His conclusions were damning. He agreed that the Government of India Act of 1935 made it impossible for Delhi to impose its views on any single province, and that there was an almost complete lack of empathy by one part of the country for any other. As a result rationing was 'unequal, uneven, and does not reflect local need'.[130] He accused officials of presiding over a 'widespread system of graft', with bribes paid to give priority on railways to private goods over relief supplies, something Wavell had already exposed. He also discovered that despite the best efforts of the government the black market was rife, making 'administration by British standards almost impossible'.[131] Like Wavell, he singled out Bengal for particular criticism, concluding that 'the arrangements in the Province ... are on the one hand inadequate ... and on the other hand are such as do not secure the best results from ... the senior and qualified officers now available.'[132] On a more practical level he concluded that 'the food grains requirements of India should be kept under constant review, and modifications either up or down should be made in the import programme in accordance with the best estimates which can be framed of future requirements. This is approximately the procedure which has been adopted during the last twelve months.'[133]

The Fifth All-India Food Conference was held in Delhi a few months later, and appeared considerably more upbeat. The earlier admonitions and threats seemed to be working and it was able to report a 'marked increase in confidence and cooperation between the administrations ... basic ration of 1lb of cereals per diem for each adult; examination of diets, increase in production of eggs, poultry, fish, milk, quicker and more even movement of food grains, organisation of markets, increased production and use of manures, improved supply of agricultural implements, machinery and material ... Grow More Food Campaign, nutritional education, supply of agricultural machinery'.[134]

Nonetheless, they were not entirely out of the woods. Two weeks later Amery was still warning that 'the food situation in March gave rise to some anxiety. Supplies to markets in the wheat growing Provinces dried up some weeks before the new harvest with the result that a heavy strain was thrown on the Central Food Department to meet outstanding liabilities for rationed cities and other deficit areas during the following two months. There is some fear that the resources at their command may not fully suffice to meet demands until the new crop comes on the market.' It was not possible to meet the Government of India's Request for an emergency supply of 50,000 tons of wheat in May to fill this gap.[135] Even by June the situation was patchy, but at last Bengal was seeing light at the end of the tunnel: 'Indian wheat harvest good in Punjab, United Provinces, not so in Sind. Rice position in Bengal improved enough to be able to release 100,000 tons to deficiency areas and for Ceylon.'[136] By November 1944, about 460 towns and municipal areas were brought under rationing, covering 42,000,000 people; by October 1946 some 771 towns and rural areas comprising 150,000,000 people would be rationed. But the black market continued to flourish. Even Nehru had to concede that blame for the deaths arising from the disaster could not be laid only at Britain's door. He later calculated that 'black marketeers made a profit of 1000 rupees for each of the 1,500,000 people who died during the Bengal famine.'[137]

There has also been considerable speculation over the role Winston Churchill played in the famine. He has been charged at worst with wantonly ignoring pleas for assistance and actively encouraging the deaths for his own political advantage, or at best with failing to grasp the seriousness of the situation. But as inadequate as he may have been, the steps taken by the government to alleviate the distress in Bengal and elsewhere do not chime with accusations of callous inaction. Nonetheless, controversy surrounds the decision by the British government not to seek assistance from the United Nations Relief and Rehabilitation Administration. This was surprising on one level insofar as India was a founder member when it was established in November 1943 and had contributed 80,000,000 rupees to its coffers.[138] As its role was to provide relief 'upon the liberation of any area [occupied] by the enemy [including] food, clothing, shelter [and] the resumption of urgently needed agricultural and industrial production',[139] it would have seemed tailor made to go to India's aid. Churchill was apparently adamant that the orbit of the organisation did not extend to India; after all, it had neither been occupied nor liberated. Nonetheless his stance understandably enraged nationalists, most notably J. J. Singh, an Indian businessman who chaired the influential India League of America. He was reported in the *New York Times* of 27 November 1943 to have proposed that unless aid was forthcoming India ought to resign her seat on the UNRRA Council in protest.[140] Furthermore, he urged the US Congress to withhold its contribution to the organisation's budget unless India was included in its aid program.[141]

Nevertheless, Churchill held his ground and assistance to India remained outside of its remit. It may well have been that in the midst of a struggle with the nationalists he did not want to lose face by admitting that Britain was unable to protect and feed India on its own. To seek assistance from outside would be the thin end of the wedge, and before long America and the United Nations would claim the right to involve themselves further in Indian affairs. He was certainly very aware that Britain was losing its grip on the country, and for this reason perhaps the findings of the Famine Enquiry Commission, established under the chairmanship of Sir John Woodhead in 1944, proved controversial. It blamed food shortages, hoarding, a failure to control prices and transport and, as had Wavell and French, laid much of the responsibility on the shoulders of the provincial governments and their corrupt practices. Nationalists rejected these claims, accusing the commission of a whitewash and of being more concerned with exonerating the British than determining the root causes of the catastrophe. Certainly, the official version was accompanied by a so-called Minority Report authored by M. Afzul Husain, who wrote a minute of dissent criticising the government. Perhaps it was no coincidence, then, that Woodhead ordered all the evidence amassed by the commission destroyed after the report's publication.[142]

Nevertheless, for all the shortcomings inherent in their response to the famine, the evidence does not support the oft repeated contention that the British callously and deliberately stood by and let people die. Food did exist, and the government made strident efforts to drive out the hoarders and black marketeers, but as Nehru conceded they remained a considerable obstacle to relief efforts. There can be little doubt, furthermore, that the simultaneous presence of war and a devastating cyclone added further to the insurmountable challenges faced by the authorities. Strident efforts were made to secure additional shipping, to seek the assistance of the US and to import more food. Notwithstanding these mitigating arguments, however, it was entirely due to decades of British policy that the dire physical and economic condition of ordinary Indians had rendered them unprepared for the devastating situation into which they were plunged.

It was perhaps simple justice, therefore, that the days of the Raj were coming to their inevitable conclusion.

12

Patience, Cooperation, Stability

The famine was only one of a multitude of challenges faced by the British during the war, but the approach of peace did not bring very much relief. Massive challenges remained, and with Britain arguably weaker and poorer than at any time in its recent history, it was necessary to take stock and decide upon priorities. India was just one among many hot potatoes that remained to be addressed, and from the point of view of all but the most diehard imperialists it could not be resolved soon enough. Yet despite everything – non-cooperation, the Quit India campaign, the war, the famine – the country was relatively quiet as the war entered its closing stages. For the first time since the resignation of Congress, ministries in six out of the eleven provinces were functioning more or less as intended under the Government of India Act of 1935, and for the most part were cooperating with the war effort and famine relief.[1] Nonetheless, Viceroy Wavell was among those desperate for negotiations to recommence, having urged Churchill that despite the situation being more or less under control 'the present government cannot continue indefinitely or even for long'[2] unless strenuous efforts were made to break the political deadlock. But having failed to persuade Jinnah to abandon his demands for Pakistan, he decided to try a different tack.

Wavell took the bull by the horns and invited the political leaders to Simla for a conference on 25 June 1945, proposing another reformed Viceroy's Council, but comprised entirely of an equal number of Hindus and Muslims. Only the posts of Viceroy and Commander-in-Chief would still be in British hands. He was soon enlightened as to the extent of the issues which prevented any rational discussion, however. Jinnah immediately insisted that only the League should have the right to appoint its Muslim members, a demand which Congress rejected, and as had been largely anticipated, the conference ended in abject failure with the parties as far apart as ever. A crestfallen Wavell admitted in his journal afterwards that, as a result of yet another impasse, 'so ends my attempt to introduce a fresh impetus and a fresh spirit into Indian politics.'[3] His efforts were not made any easier by the fact that, even now, Churchill remained obdurately opposed to concessions. While he and his supporters remained at the helm nothing of material significance was likely to be placed on the table. But then the political landscape changed completely when the self-proclaimed 'anchor'[4] keeping India British fell from office following a landslide Labour victory in the British general election of July 1945. A British public, thankful to Churchill as a war leader and saviour, did not share the same confidence in him as a peacetime leader. Having denounced his former wartime deputy as 'the quiet little man and his quiet little voice sweeping away our position in India',[5] the old warhorse was forced to take a back seat. With socialist and anti-imperialist Clement Attlee installed as prime minister, Britain's posture changed overnight and the nationalists were encouraged to up their game. Wavell, however, was concerned that the new administration might prove too radical and hasty to reach a solution, 'bent on handing over India to their Congress friends as soon as possible'.[6] But Attlee would prove not to be the pushover some believed.

The new prime minister had also tired of the nationalists' tactics. He had come to the conclusion, he said, 'that there was a great deal of happiness for them [Congress and the League] asking for everything, and putting down everything that was wrong in India to British rule ... and then sitting pretty ... I concluded the thing to do was to bring them right up against it and make them see they'd got to face the situation themselves.'[7] He was convinced that they now had to take responsibility and play a constructive role in the transfer of power. This could only occur if they accepted the consequences of their actions, and to this end he announced that elections to the Central Legislative Assembly and Indian provinces were to be held between December 1945 and January 1946. Furthermore, the constant wrangling about the country's future would have to come to an end. A Constituent Assembly was also to be created, and it would debate the shape of the country's future.

But when the results of the elections to the Legislative Assembly secured Congress fifty-nine of the 102 seats and the League all the Muslim constituencies, a reinvigorated Jinnah saw another chance to seize the initiative. He insisted once again that the elections had fortified his mandate to pursue the solution he had been advocating since 1940, and on 6 December he called upon 'His Majesty's Government to declare their resolution to the establishment of Pakistan'. He added that 'it is high time that the British Government applied their mind definitely to the division of India and the establishment of Pakistan and Hindustan, which means freedom for both ... [not] slavery for Mussulmans and complete domination of the imperialistic caste Hindu Raj.'[8] When the results of the provincial elections gave Congress 90 per cent of all the non-Muslim seats and the League 87 per cent of Muslim seats, he was beside himself. With the bit now between his teeth, he declared a Day of Victory on 11 January 1946, announcing that the results established the League as the definitive and unquestionably sole representative of all of India's Muslims. On 9 February he demanded once again that 'the Government should, without any further delay, make a clear declaration of its policy accepting Pakistan as the only solution to India's constitutional problem ... we cannot agree to any arrangement which postulates an all-India government whether interim or permanent.'[9]

Attlee was nonetheless ambivalent. By 1943 he had concluded that for the 'Westminster Model' to work the 'minority [had to] accept the will of the majority', and Jinnah's demands made that possibility highly questionable. The problem was, Attlee admitted, 'that no community will trust the other to play the game without a referee'[10] – the role Britain had been playing, rightly or wrongly, for three centuries. Others shared his reservations. A certain Professor Friedrich, who had also been studying the problem, agreed that 'there is not a single modern state which has not, at one time or another, forced a recalcitrant [minority] national group to live under its authority,'[11] implying that Muslim fears of a Hindu Raj were quite valid. So far, so good as far as Jinnah was concerned. However, Attlee did not necessarily view Jinnah's Pakistan as the obvious answer because the task of creating two new states was stymied by the fact that India's 'communities are so intermingled'.[12] This dichotomy was evident when he addressed the House of Commons on 15 March. He assured the MPs that while his government was 'very mindful of the rights of minorities, and minorities should be able to live free from fear ... we cannot allow a minority to place a veto on the advance of the majority'.[13] But how could he solve this conundrum? He would seek to do so through a rather awkwardly contrived halfway house whereby a federal system divided the country into three, with the Hindu provinces, the Muslim provinces and the states exercising considerable autonomy, with a weaker centre responsible only for such matters as defence and foreign affairs. Alternatively, only a greatly truncated compromise version of Jinnah's Pakistan would be established, sitting alongside an Indian union.

Armed with these the ill-starred compromises, another Cabinet mission was despatched comprising Lord Pethwick-Lawrence as Labour Secretary of State for India, Sir Stafford Cripps and First Lord of the Admiralty A. V. Alexander. Arriving in March 1946, its remit was to form a representative Viceroy's Council, present the compromise solution and establish a Constituent Assembly to allow alternatives to be thrashed out. But if they hoped to reconcile the irreconcilable, they would soon be disabused. The proposals for a federation predictably fell at the first hurdle, with even Nehru forced to accept that 'if you examine Pakistan in that diluted and restricted aspect it becomes so difficult of constitution as a state that it is almost inconceivable.'[14] Jinnah predictably also dismissed the idea out of hand, but his and Nehru's were not the only voices that demanded to be heard in designing the new India. There remained the princes, the minorities and other interest groups who feared being overwhelmed in the clamour to arrive at a solution. The princes will be covered in more detail later, but a more immediate problem proved to be the zamindars, representatives of whom Wavell met on 15 April, and who wanted protections for the privileges they had enjoyed under the British. Wavell listened to them patiently enough, but later concluded that 'they had nothing to say, except that they had always been loyal to the British and now wanted protection.'[15] Sikh leader Tara Singh, too, had considerable reservations and 'launched into a declamatory jeremiad on the wrongs and oppressions of the Sikhs and their need for an area completely their own, which is impossible'.[16] To these demands were added those of Congress Muslims, Jews, Christians and a raft of others. Exasperated and disheartened, the Viceroy and his mission members could see that the only way to advance matters was to make the Constituent Assembly a reality and let the various views and demands be debated there.

Elections were held in July and August 1946, providing 208 Congress and 73 Muslim seats, with others set aside for the various minorities. But having participated in the election, the mercurial Jinnah immediately demanded a separate Constituent Assembly to define a Pakistani constitution and backed up his call with a day of direct action. Held on 16 August 1946, it began peacefully enough, with various marches and demonstrations and the displaying of black flags, but it soon descended into intercommunal violence. Calcutta witnessed some of the worst scenes, allegedly incited by League Chief Minister H. S. Suhrawardy. Muslims attacked Hindu-run shops, and inevitably the Hindus retaliated, the mayhem continuing for four days before troops restored some semblance of order.

Faced with this constant anarchy, the British government – Wavell in particular – was fast losing hope. The Viceroy confided to his diary on 9 September, 'I despair of ever being able to make these Indian politicians see sense or lessen the tensions between the communities.'[17] On 28 September he further complained, 'It is weary work negotiating with these people, it takes weeks or months to make any progress on a point which ordinary reasonable men would settle in an hour or so.'[18] His deputy private secretary, Ian Scott, shared his despair, concluding that 'our only course is to get out of India as soon as possible, and leave her to her fate, which must be civil war.'[19] Wavell's weariness was not helped by reports that the violence was spreading. On 16 October he was informed that there had been nearly 1,500 casualties in Bombay, 360 of them fatal. No-go areas were being established, and despite some 6,000 arrests the situation was showing little sign of improvement.[20]

In the midst of all this pandemonium the Constituent Assembly held its opening session on 6 December, but it soon fell prey to the old arguments, demands and counter-demands. As Wavell became ever more convinced that 'Congress is not interested in making a constitution under British auspices, only in consolidating their power,'[21] he turned his mind to securing 'the safest and most dignified withdrawal possible'.[22] In January 1947 he proposed handing the two sides an ultimatum. Unless they broke the log-jam he would begin pulling out all British troops and abandon the country to its fate. He suggested a deadline of March 1948[23] and gave the plan the codename

Operation Ebb-Tide. The inevitable consequences of such a strategy prompted members of his staff to rename it Operation Madhouse,[24] which more accurately reflected the view of the startled Cabinet in London, where it was condemned as 'a policy of scuttle unworthy of a great power' and prompted questions about Wavell's continued employment.[25] Nonetheless, when news of the plan leaked out it actually appeared to concentrate the minds of some nationalists. Congress Party leader Maulana Azad balked at the prospect and told Field Marshal Montgomery, who was in India at the time, that he did not want to see British troops withdrawn in the middle of a serious crisis.[26] Jinnah admitted that he feared civil war if they did so.[27] The field marshal was left convinced that much of the stalling and prevarication was therefore bravado, and 'whatever they said in public, the political leaders of both parties were equally desirous for the continued presence of British troops in India.'[28]

But how long would the British want to hold the line between the two? Although Wavell's proposal was a non-starter in the way he had framed it, the British had indeed had enough of presiding over endless bickering while thousands died. The Cabinet mission having failed, a deadline for British withdrawal would indeed be set regardless of whether the warring parties could come to an agreement, and on 10 February 1947 Attlee outlined his plans in the House of Commons. Although couched in rather more diplomatic language than the doughty soldier had proposed, the message was essentially the same:

[While] it has long been the policy of successive Governments to work towards the realisation of Self-Government in India ... it is with great regret that His Majesty's Government find that there are still differences among Indian parties which are preventing the Constituent Assembly from functioning as it was intended that it should. It is of the essence of the plan that the Assembly should be fully representative ... His Majesty's Government wish to make it clear that it is their definite intention to take the necessary steps to effect the transference of power into responsible Indian hands by a date not later than June 1948 ... if it should appear that such a constitution would not have been worked out fully before [that time] ... His Majesty's Government will have to consider to whom the powers of the Central Government in British India should be handed over on due date, whether as a whole to some form of Central Government for British India, or in some areas to existing Provincial Governments, or in such other way as may seem most reasonable and in the best interests of the Indian people ...[29]

This was arguably the most unequivocal statement of policy yet uttered by a British prime minister. It was an unmistakable guarantee that the British were leaving irrespective of whether the League, Congress or any of the other parties could reach an agreement. It was also evident that at this pivotal moment someone was needed at the helm with energy and drive, and Wavell was clearly at the end of his tether. On New Year's Day 1946 he wrote, 'I very much doubt whether my brain power or personality are up to it.'[30] He later went on, 'I have tried everything I know to solve the problem of handing over India to the people, and I can see no light.'[31] Attlee decided instead to call upon the King's engaging and charismatic cousin and friend Lord Louis Mountbatten to see through the final end of the Raj. Although suspected by some critics of having been over-promoted due to his royal connections, he had successfully served as Supreme Commander in South East Asia and had well-proven leadership qualities. He inspired loyalty, confidence and trust, and a reputation for managing to achieve consensus. These were priceless qualities for the onerous task which confronted him, and on 18 March 1947 Attlee left the Viceroy-designate under no illusions as to what was required:

> It is the definitive objective of His Majesty's Government to obtain a unitary government for British India and the Indian States, if possible within the British Commonwealth ... [however] ... there can be no question of compelling either major party to accept it.[32]

Although Wavell agreed that 'Dickie's personality may perhaps accomplish what I have failed to do,'[33] Mountbatten felt that the appointment was something of a poisoned chalice. He was being asked to succeed where successive predecessors had failed and felt that 'the odds are we shall end up with bullets in our backs.'[34] Nonetheless, he was left in little doubt that he had a huge task ahead of him, and had massive expectations to meet. The *New York Tribune* had remarked that 'Attlee's announcement that the British were determined to withdraw from India whether or not a constitution could be agreed upon by the Indians is a truly momentous event ... The British might easily have lingered on in India, playing off Hindu against Muslim, prince against peasant presiding over a tense and costly stalemate in the interests of imperial prestige ... instead ... the British people ... have taken on a new dignity and a new moral strength.'[35] These sentiments were shared by the *Cincinnati Enquirer*, which concluded that 'they have tried hard to get the factions to join in drafting a single constitution. Agreement has proved impossible. It is logically the responsibility of the Indians to find the basis for unity within their own number.'[36]

The challenge confronting Lord Mountbatten was enormous. On their arrival, he and his staff encountered 'the people rioting, the Princes falling out among themselves, the entire Indian civil service and police running down, and the British ... left sceptical and full of foreboding'.[37] The scale of the challenge was made even more apparent once he started to meet the nationalists. It was hoped that his urbane charm and disarming manner – Auchinleck had referred to him as 'pretty Dickie'[38] – would work where Wavell's more workmanlike manner had floundered. He certainly started off promisingly when he assured Nehru that 'I want you to regard me not as the last Viceroy winding up the British Raj, but as the first to lead the way to the new India,'[39] in response to which the equally cultured veteran nationalist told him, 'Now I know what they mean when they speak of your charm being so dangerous.'[40] The Viceroy also met Gandhi, with whom he was 'deeply impressed',[41] but the opaque Jinnah proved to be almost impenetrable, 'haughty and aloof',[42] and after meeting him for the first time Mountbatten remarked tersely, 'My God he was cold.'[43] Having seen the gulf separating the key players, he quickly came to the conclusion that 'the June 1948 time limit, far from being not long enough, is already too remote a deadline,'[44] with the violence getting worse with every passing day. Furthermore, Mountbatten concluded that an agreement to create a unitary state under these circumstances was impossible and therefore Jinnah's demands had to be taken more seriously.[45]

In Calcutta, the violence was intensifying exponentially, with the Punjab also fast becoming a bloodbath. It appeared that the prediction of its chief minister, Sir Sikander Hyat, that the prospect of Pakistan had become 'an invitation to the Punjabi Muslims to cut the throat of every Hindu *bania* [moneylender]'[46] was becoming all too real. Furthermore, there were some 20,000 Europeans in the province, many thousands of whom lived in outlying and isolated areas, and all were at risk. Although a situation report stated reassuringly that 'it is clear from what the Governors have to say, that by far the greater part of the subcontinent is calm and quiet and ready to accept any reasonable solution,'[47] these two areas were the epicentres of a growing anarchy which could spread and infect the rest of the country. They also happened to be where the brunt of any potential physical division would be implemented should Partition secure British assent, made even worse by Hindu suspicions that Mountbatten was moving on the prospect. These fears prompted the *Hindustan Times* to warn on 26 April 1947:

> [If] the Muslim majority areas are allowed to constitute themselves into separate sovereign states, we have no doubt the Union will not stand in the way of Britain establishing contacts with those states ... however ... the Indian Union will consider it a hostile act if there is any attempt by Britain to conclude any treaty or alliance involving military or political clauses ...[48]

Nonetheless, despite such veiled threats the rising violence only served to strengthen Mountbatten's resolve. Accompanied by his wife Edwina, he embarked upon tours of the areas which would constitute any new state, starting with Peshawar in the North-West Frontier Province on 28 April. There he saw for himself the urgency of the situation when he encountered 30,000 demonstrators outside the town. They were calling for 'Pakistan Zindabad' and threatening to march on Government House. Somewhat counterintuitively, Governor Sir Olaf Caroe suggested to a dubious Viceroy that perhaps they should drive out to meet the demonstrators. Despite understandable reservations Mountbatten agreed, and incredibly after a tense few moments the crowd, like Nehru, warmed to the couple and started chanting 'Mountbatten Zindabad' as he waved back at them.[49] Encouraged by his reception, the following day he travelled to Rawalpindi in the Punjab, where Governor Sir Evan Jenkins whisked him off to see the extent of the violence and destruction. They encountered 'devastation ... as thorough as any produced by firebomb raids in the war',[50] according to his aide-de-camp Alan Campbell-Johnson.

In the meantime, preliminary plans for partitioning the country were being looked at and on 3 May Lord Ismay, Mountbatten's chief of staff, presented them to the Cabinet in London. They were approved in principle but nevertheless they still diverged from Jinnah's demands. Instead of simply being handed over, Punjab, the North-West Frontier Province, Sind and Bengal would have the right to decide whether to join India or Pakistan, and the Princely States could also choose which new Dominion they would join. Congress still remained to be persuaded, but when Mountbatten showed the plan to Nehru on 11 May he rejected it out of hand, condemning it as 'connivance at Balkanisation'.[51] Then on 22 May Jinnah increased his own demands by insisting upon a thousand-mile 'corridor' linking the two wings of Pakistan, prompting Nehru to insist that such an idea was 'completely unrealistic and indicates he [Jinnah] desires no settlement of any kind'.[52] His brief honeymoon over, Mountbatten was now being confronted with the same brinkmanship that hobbled Wavell. He flew to London for further discussions, from which Attlee circulated a memorandum reinforcing the Viceroy's dire prognosis:

> Since his arrival in India Lord Mountbatten has had a prolonged series of meetings with the leaders of Congress and the Muslim League and has also conferred with the representatives of the Sikhs. His conversations have convinced him that there is no prospect of acceptance of the Cabinet Mission's Plan or of a union of India on any other basis. He is also convinced that a very early announcement of His Majesty's Government's intentions as to the manner in which power will be transferred in 1948 is essential if widespread and uncontrollable criminal disturbances, especially in the North-West Frontier Province and the Punjab, are to be avoided ...[53]

At least one other apparently insurmountable hurdle had finally been overcome when on 21 May 1947 India's 'anchor', Churchill, finally resigned himself to the inevitable. He wrote to Attlee assuring him that 'the Conservative Party will agree to facilitate the passage this session of the legislation necessary to confer Dominion Status upon ... India.'[54] With the old warhorse now on side, this just left the recalcitrant nationalists to win over and Mountbatten returned to the conference table where he had to try to surmount the growing enmity and distrust. With pressure mounting more fevered discussions churned over the same arguments and the same objections over which the parties seemed incapable of reaching conclusions. Then finally, on 3 June 1947 the Viceroy, through twisting arms, offering compromises and making promises, produced the Mountbatten Plan. Through gritted teeth the main parties accepted the creation of two new states, the Dominions of India and of Pakistan, with a boundary commission tasked with demarcating the lines of partition. For their part, the Princely States would have to opt to join one or other of the new countries. The following day, Mountbatten held a press conference and explained the plan. He confirmed that acceptance of Dominion status meant exactly the same freedoms as were now exercised by countries such as Australia, Canada and New Zealand, and as confirmed by the 1931 Statute of Westminster. It represented, he confirmed, 'absolute independence in every possible way, with the sole exception that the member States of the Commonwealth are linked together voluntarily' by accepting the British monarch as head of state.[55]

He then dropped a bombshell that almost set the room alight. So far, everyone had assumed that the original 1948 deadline remained in place, but he instead announced that it was to be drastically brought forward to midnight on 14 August 1947. Montgomery, writing in his diary on 24 June, conceded that 'the division of India ... at such a speed raises terrific problems. These can only be settled satisfactorily by the closest cooperation between the two new Dominions. Failing this, there will be the most awful chaos and much bloodshed.'[56] Attlee's private secretary, Leslie Rowan, shared such reservations but the Prime Minister knew that the time for delay had passed. He had long held that the sooner the whole affair was resolved the better, and instructed him to 'accept [the] Viceroy's proposal'.[57] He duly proceeded to put the wheels in motion, drafting a brief bill of only sixteen pages and twenty clauses.

It would take just six weeks to end 350 years of British rule, the bill passing through its various stages in the Houses of Parliament and receiving somewhat undignified royal assent in the House of Lords tucked between the 'South Metropolitan Gas Bill' and 'The Felixstowe Pier Bill'.[58] Gandhi too had by now accepted that 'partition was not the decision of the British ... but if both of us – Hindus and Moslems – cannot agree on anything else, then the Viceroy is left with no choice.'[59] Russia's *Red Star*, however, perceived some Machiavellian ulterior motive behind the plan, claiming that it was 'nothing but an attempt to retain India as an important integral part of the British Empire ... the ... plan will inevitably lead to the political and economic weakening of India ... The partition does not affect the feudal power of the Princes who have always supported British domination.'[60] This was a minority view, however, with almost unanimous endorsement elsewhere, especially among those who had struggled for so many years to see Indian independence become a reality. Sadly, this did not help the worsening situation on the ground.

On 27 June it was reported that 'the situation in Lahore and Amritsar gives ground for grave concern. The violence takes the form of scattered and widespread arson and stabbings carried out by cloak and dagger techniques ... throwing fireballs through windows and skylights ... almost impossible to catch in the act.'[61] Lahore in particular contained all the ingredients for a serious flashpoint, with its 500,000 Hindus, 100,000 Sikhs and 600,000 Muslims all baying for one another's blood. The various communities were crowded together within the 17-mile wall of Akbar, or the old city, with 300,000 Muslims and 100,000 of the town's Hindus and Sikhs living cheek by jowl. Amritsar was just as dangerous, home to 6,000,000 of India's Sikhs and its temple and shrine. Unless the plans were carried through promptly it was only a matter of time before there was civil war. The threat of escalating violence resulted on 17 July in the formation of the Punjab Boundary Force under the command of Major-General T. W. Rees. But because Nehru refused to allow British troops to be used, there were only 55,000 Indian troops available to try and prevent wholesale slaughter. It would play a well-meaning but hopeless role in trying to stem the violence until it was unceremoniously disbanded on 29 August.

In the midst of this turmoil, the various parties had now to confront the issue of the new borders, and where they should be fixed. This was bound to produce endless wrangling and further deadlock, so leaving it to Hindus and Muslims to decide for themselves was clearly hopeless. Only an impartial arbiter with impeccable credentials could hope to command the trust of both sides and make the decisions for them. The suggestion for this approach also came from a surprising quarter. On 27 June 1947, the Viceroy's Council 'accepted with surprising speed and unanimity Jinnah's proposal that British lawyer Sir Cyril Radcliffe should be invited to serve as chairman of the Punjab and Bengal Boundary Commissions with a casting vote on both'.[62] Fortunately for the man to be offered this onerous task, all parties agreed to abide by whatever was decided, and a forty-eight-year-old barrister who had never visited the subcontinent would decide its fate. To guarantee he could not be influenced in any way, he would be secluded in an isolated cottage on the Viceregal estate beyond the reach of any official or politician, including Mountbatten. His purdah would last until the task was complete, and then he would depart as anonymously and as unmarked as he came.

In an almost surreal endgame to a drama which had been 350 years in the making, Radcliffe arrived on 8 July and was given five weeks to delineate the 2,000 miles of what would become the border between West Pakistan and India, and the 2,500-mile frontier between East Pakistan and India. But although he was supposed to have been assisted by four Indian judges, they became so fearful of being blamed for the outcome that they resigned before the job started. So Sir Cyril was largely on his own, guided only by outdated maps and the vaguest understanding of the economic and social consequences of his decisions. His was undoubtedly a Herculean task, and one which many felt was simply impossible. Jurist, politician and scholar Bhimrao Ramji Ambedkar was among them:

> It would be impossible to demarcate on the north west of our Indian Empire a frontier which would satisfy ethnological, political and military requirements. To seek for a zone which traverses easily definable ethnological features; which does not violate the ethnic considerations by cutting through the territories of closely related tribes; and which at the same time serves as a political boundary is utopian.[63]

Nonetheless this was what Sir Cyril was going to have to try to achieve, poring over maps and charts, referring to atlases and studying ethnographic, economic and religious records. By 9 August it was rumoured that he was ready, but Mountbatten did not want any of the so-called awards being made public before independence had been delivered. The inevitable anger and disappointment might risk 'destroying at one stroke the whole symbolic significance of freedom'[64] that was in the delicate process of being finalised. If news escaped of the now definitive borders, the violence that was already impossible to control would probably become still worse. It was reasoned that the psychological effects of independence might instead serve to ameliorate any anger and disappointment; in any case, nothing could be allowed to mar the pomp and ceremony which must inevitably accompany the end of the Raj.

So arrived 14 August 1947, the great day that would provide the template for the next twenty-five years of decolonisation, during which the Union Flag would be lowered in more than fifty territories. First Lord Louis Mountbatten, the quintessential Englishman from the same royal house which had presided over ninety years of India's constitutional evolution, attended the independence ceremony in Karachi, where Jinnah took the oath of office as its first Governor-General and addressed the newly formed Pakistan Constituent Assembly while thousands cheered and celebrated outside. Meanwhile, the Indian Constituent Assembly met with due solemnity at 11.00 p.m. in the Constitutional Hall in Delhi, and shortly before midnight Nehru spoke these immortal words:

> Long years ago, we made a tryst with destiny, and now the time comes when we shall redeem our pledge, not wholly or in full measure but very substantially. At the stroke of the midnight hour, when the world sleeps, India will awake to life and freedom ... the appointed day has come – the day appointed by destiny – and India stands forth again, after long slumber and struggle, awake, vital, free and independent. The past clings on to us still in some measure and we have to do much before we redeem the pledges we have so often taken. Yet the turning-

point is past, and history begins anew for us, the history which we shall live and act and others will write about ...[65]

Later the following morning, the Congress flag which had been adopted by the Indian Constituent Assembly on 22 July as the new Indian national flag was raised above the Lahore Gate of the Red Fort in Delhi for the first time. Mountbatten's assistant Alan Campbell-Johnson watched as it was slowly drawn up the flagpole, and then noticed how, quite poignantly, 'just as the flag was unfurled light rain began to fall and a rainbow appeared in the sky, matching the saffron, white and green of the flag.'[66] Behind the scenes, with somewhat less decorum, servants swept through the former Viceroy's House in their haste to remove and eradicate every symbol of the Raj that could be dismantled or removed, including cutlery, plates, soap and even the matchboxes upon which the Viceregal Seal was stamped.[67] In London, the proceedings in India represented King George VI's swansong as King-Emperor. His mother, George V's widow Queen Mary, lamented how for 'the first time Bertie wrote to me a letter with the "I" for Emperor of India left out ... very sad'.[68]

Amid the euphoria in Lahore and Delhi and the pathos in London there were rather more pragmatic problems still to be settled. Radcliffe's territorial awards were transmitted to the nationalist leaders as soon as possible on 16 August, while scores of officials in numerous committees and subcommittees under Muslim lawyer Chaudhuri Mohammed Ali and Hindu lawyer H. M. Patel met to share out the intellectual, financial and logistical assets of the two countries. Like the division of the Indian Army, however, there would be considerable scope for pettiness and spite, and India would do all in its power to ensure that as little as humanly possible found its way to its neighbour. India and Pakistan had between them war debts of around £5,000,000,000 and bank deposits and gold reserves which were supposed to be allocated, like the army, on a pro rata basis. There was naturally much haggling over which country was entitled to which share, but it was finally agreed that Pakistan would get 17 per cent of the cash in the bank and the sterling balances in exchange for taking responsibility for the same percentage of the former Empire's national debt. A roughly similar proportion of moveable assets would remain in India, and Pakistan would expect to receive the balance. But that would prove easier to promise than deliver and Mountbatten had to force the new Indian Government to send Pakistan the £30,000,000 in cash that it was owed.[69]

The divorce also involved the allocation of the most trivial of items, from official limousines to desks and paperclips. The now defunct Food and Agriculture Ministry contained 425 desks, 85 large tables, nearly 1,000 chairs, 56 hat pegs, 130 bookshelves, 4 iron safes, 20 table lamps, 170 typewriters, 120 fans, 120 clocks, 110 bicycles, 600 inkstands, 3 staff cars, 2 sets of sofas and 40 chamber pots, all of which was supposed to be shared,[70] while the Lahore Police had to find some way to divide their stocks of puttees, turbans, rifles, staves, and even the last of the band's trombones.[71] There were arguments over the books in libraries, road and rail repair tools, and even the Taj Mahal, which the Pakistanis wanted dismantled and reassembled in their new state. Widows and retirement pensions were another cause for animosity,[72] and even the allocation of government printing presses proved a bone of contention. All six were in Delhi, and India blankly refused to share any with Pakistan; only one of them was capable of printing postage stamps and currency. Deprived of their own facilities, the Pakistanis therefore had to overprint Indian rupees with 'Pakistan' until they could produce their own currency. The former trappings of British Imperial power also faced an ignominious fate. The Viceregal train was allocated to India and the private carriages of the former Commander-in-Chief went to Pakistan.[73]

While politicians and bureaucrats quibbled over trombones and printing presses, people were still suffering and dying in the bloodshed which intensified after the Radcliffe awards became public. Realising that they now lived on the wrong side of the Partition line, tens of thousands were moving, and in the process railway stations, border points, open fields and villages became flashpoints where each exacted fearful revenge on the other. In Bengal, the new British High Commissioner to India reported that 'Calcutta, which had been remarkably peaceful for a period of three weeks, has been the scene of renewed communal trouble.'[74] Feeling that his warnings over many years had now been firmly vindicated, Churchill remarked cynically, 'What about the deaths of half a million people in India? Enjoying democratic freedom?!'[75] Elsewhere, however, too exhausted and traumatised to engage in any further slaughter, groups simply ignored one another, as Campbell-Johnson reported after flying over the Punjab to assess the situation. He witnessed the pitiful sight of 'Sikh and Muslim refugees … moving almost side by side in opposite directions … they pushed forward obsessed only with the objective beyond the boundary.'[76]

In the midst of this turmoil and the preparations for the big day, there remained the unresolved and highly vexed question of the Princely States. With the Cabinet Mission Plan a dead letter and Partition an accepted fact, it was almost taken for granted that they would chose to accede either to India or Pakistan on a simple ethnic basis. But this was not necessarily how the princes saw it. Two of the largest, Hyderabad and Kashmir, loyal allies in peace and war and with legally binding treaties going back over a century, felt they had the same rights as the two new emergent states. After all, in 1942 the government had assured them that 'the fulfilment of treaty obligations to the States remains an integral part of His Majesty's Governments policy … these treaties will only be altered by negotiation and agreement.'[77] But these and the safeguards contained in the 1919 and 1935 Acts were by now empty promises, a point Nehru was anxious to make clear. His views on the princes remained unchanged, and he made no bones about it, reminding them starkly that 'they could not be left out simply because the British Government had entered into treaties with certain persons who were dead long ago,'[78] reiterating this stance on 5 March 1946 when he warned pointedly that 'you cannot yoke together a bullock with a swift horse. There is no difference between the people of the States and the people of the Provinces. Their future is one.'[79]

The fact that their options were narrowing was confirmed by Wavell on 12 May 1946 when he said, using somewhat opaque language, that although 'there was no intention on the part of the Crown to initiate any change in their relationship with the Crown ... without their consent ... it was at the same time stated that the Prince's consent to any changes which might emerge as a result of negotiations would not be unreasonably withheld.'[80] In other words, they either went along with what was agreed with Congress and the League or they were on their own and could not look to London for help. This was firmly reinforced by Section 7 of the Indian Independence Act, which stipulated unambiguously, if in somewhat prolix prose, that 'as from the appointed day ... the suzerainty of His Majesty over the Indian States lapses, and with it, all treaties and agreements in force at the date of the passing of this Act between His Majesty and the rulers of Indian States, all functions exercisable by His Majesty at that date with respect to Indian States, all obligations of His Majesty existing at that date towards Indian States or the rulers thereof, and all powers, rights, authority or jurisdiction exercisable by His Majesty at that date in or in relation to Indian States by treaty, grant, usage, sufferance or otherwise.'[81]

Nonetheless, neither the nationalists nor the British wished to alienate the princes unnecessarily. Each sought to allay their deeper fears by assuring them that their accession would be largely symbolic. Their vestigial rights would be left intact, with Nehru explaining how 'the rulers of the big States can continue to be constitutional heads,'[82] and even though the rulers of the petty kingdoms and small states might be absorbed, their rulers would find little change to their lifestyles because 'we are prepared to pension them off.'[83] Furthermore, Sardar Patel, who headed the States Department, assured them that the Instruments of Accession they would be asked to sign would ensure that 'their autonomous existence would be scrupulously respected.'[84] Even Mountbatten joined in the conspiracy, assuring them, 'I am not asking any state to make any intolerable sacrifice of either its internal autonomy or independence.'[85]

But as the date of independence approached, gentle persuasion gave way to increasingly veiled threats. Mountbatten advised the princes to dismiss any notions that they might coexist as pockets inside foreign states, and warned that the Instrument of Accession 'was a political offer from the Congress which was not likely to be repeated'.[86] Finally, when the Nawab of Bhopal ventured to ask what the likely consequence of such an attempt might be, the Viceroy is said to have lifted up a large paperweight, slammed it down on the table and exclaimed, 'God help it!'[87] Such dire warnings started to have the desired effect. At a reception a couple of days later one prince was overheard saying, 'There's no need for him to work on me. I'm signing tomorrow.'[88]

By 1 August, only Hyderabad, Kashmir and Junagadh held out, but their stubbornness would have consequences every bit as dire as Mountbatten warned. For the rest, they, like the former provinces of British India, were now effectively absorbed into either one of the new states. Their work done and their task seemingly complete, the last few British civil servants finished tying up whatever loose ends remained from their point of view and packed their bags for home.

In spite of decades of bitter acrimony, obfuscation, delay, deceit and bloodshed, the final parting of the ways was achieved with surprisingly little ill will. Perhaps it was with a collective sigh of relief that against all the odds the seemingly impossible had been achieved, and when the First Battalion of the Somerset Light Infantry (Prince Albert's) finally departed India on 28 February 1948, it did so without rancour or malice. As Congress member and lawyer K. M. Munshi conceded magnanimously, 'No power in history but Great Britain would have conceded independence with such grace.'[89]

13

'The decent living of the common man'

Sir Cyril Radcliffe had made the best fist he could under the rushed circumstances of his brief commission, but he received precious little thanks for his efforts. Moreover, Britain's departure left behind more loose ends than may have been anticipated, and with both states dissatisfied and in no mood to concede another inch, the future looked bleak. Each had sacrificed territory they later regretted having given up, and their mutual animosity was not helped by the fact that Pakistan inevitably came off worse. Lahore for example, had been almost entirely dominated by Hindu and Sikh traders and businessmen, but they had been driven out by the bloodletting, seeking new lives in India. Their absence meant that by 1950 only a little over a quarter of the city's productive capacity had been restored, and a similarly grim picture was painted across the Punjab as a whole. Britain's first High Commissioner to India, Sir Terence Shone, reported how 'the economic life of both East and West Punjab has been completely upset by the recent communal disturbances ... It is too early yet to estimate the money value of the economic loss which will result from the tremendous upheaval but there is little doubt that it will be immense.'[1] It was a prognosis that would affect Pakistan far more negatively than its new neighbour. The partition of the Punjab had also severely ruptured traditional patterns of trade and communications so that, for example, many of the head waters supplying the intricate river and canal systems in Pakistan's half of the Punjab were now in India and under its control.

The situation was similarly grim in Bengal, subjected to a partition far more profound than that of forty years previously. Its capital, Calcutta, served as the commercial and industrial hub of the Indian Empire, but being overwhelmingly Hindu, with a population of 1,531,512 against 497,535 Muslims,[2] it was inevitable that the city would become part of Indian West Bengal. It also meant that whereas the pre-Partition province had contained 33 per cent of India's industry, post-Partition East Bengal would retain just 2.7 per cent,[3] an outcome its last British governor predicted would turn it into 'the greatest rural slum in history'.[4] In order to ameliorate the logistical and practical consequences of partition, Lord Mountbatten had at least persuaded the new governments to agree transitional 'Standstill' arrangements to ensure that essential services and utilities could be maintained until more permanent adjustments were possible. But these could only be very short-term measures and did nothing to address Pakistan's long-term problems. In addition to losing its share of the industrial capacity of the country, Pakistan was left with only a fraction of the physical infrastructure that had been constructed under the Raj at such crippling expense. Only 4,913 out of a total of 18,077 miles of road and 7,112 miles of the former empire's railway lay within its borders.[5] Its very government apparatus, too, needed rebuilding practically from scratch. Of 550 members of the old Indian Civil Service, only 100 were Muslim, and of these six opted to stay in India. Furthermore, Pakistan's share of the military assets left it woefully ill prepared for the considerable tests it would soon confront.

Significant fault-lines were quick to open between the two nations. Jinnah had taken it for granted that Kashmir would form part of his new country, being overwhelmingly Muslim as well as strategically and economically indispensable. However, as its ruler Hari Singh was Hindu, Kashmir-born Nehru was equally determined that it should accede to India. The squabbling that had preceded independence simply continued afterwards, and it was soon evident that all sides were too intransigent to agree any sort of compromise. Indeed, such was the impression Jinnah left on Lord Ismay that he concluded glumly that 'it is impossible to see how war, or something very like it, between the two countries can be avoided for much longer.'[6] He was to be proven right, and with discussions having reached an impasse Jinnah sought to impose a fait accompli, conniving in the infiltration of Pashtun tribesmen from the North-West Frontier into the territory.

This penetration, beginning on 22 October 1947, soon sounded alarm bells and Hari Singh appealed to India for assistance. But Nehru also saw an opportunity to settle the matter and responded that he would only come to his aid if Kashmir immediately signed an Instrument of Accession. A desperate Hari Singh did so, and on 26 October Indian troops were duly airlifted into Srinagar charged with repelling the invasion. From here they slowly pushed the irregulars back to their starting point, but inevitably these forward units locked horns with regular Pakistani forces. Thus the two new Dominions, sharing the same sovereign and British Commander-in-Chief, now allowed their pent up frustrations and animosity to explode into open warfare. Their ill-matched armies fought one another in an inconclusive conflict which would grind on for over a year. By the time a fragile ceasefire was brokered by the United Nations in January 1949, Pakistan held roughly a third and India two-thirds of the disputed territory. Pakistan agreed to withdraw all its forces and India to maintain only enough to keep the peace while a referendum was arranged to decide its future. But no plebiscite materialised; Pakistan objected, declared the ceasefire invalid, and the scene was set for decades of dispute over the territory.

The division of the subcontinent also left Jinnah, as many had predicted, with little more than a patchwork of ethnic groups united only by a common religion. It was far from being in any sense a lapidary construct. As well as occupied Kashmir, he presided over Sindh, the North-West Frontier Province, Balochistan, West Punjab, East Bengal and a smattering of small Princely States. The four provinces that constituted the western wing were disparate enough, but the addition of a fifth, crazily separated by over a thousand miles of unfriendly Indian territory, would prove tragic. Spread over the same distance as London to Rome, their people had little in common except their shared faith. Rice-eating Bengalis speak a Sanskrit-based language; the wheat- and corn-consuming Punjabis, Sindhis, Balochistanis and Pathans communicate in Persian-Arabic and Indo-Iranian tongues. Bengalis hail from an ancient South East Asian heritage and look there for their art, literature, music and poetry; wider Pakistan leans towards Persia and Arabia for its cultural inheritance. Its people live either in freezing mountains, valleys, low-lying plains or arid deserts, while Bengalis live among many rivers and streams surrounded by dense and lush vegetation. For the vast majority of the existence of the British Indian Empire these two distinct cultures were completely ignorant of one another. Yet in 1947 they suddenly found themselves arbitrarily joined and expected to coalesce as two long-lost brothers. Instead, like Jonathan Swift's Liliput and Blefuscu, they immediately found themselves at odds, destined to endure twenty years of infighting and eventually bloody divorce. Underpinning this enmity was the shameless chauvinism practised against Bengalis by the Punjabis, willingly abetted by the Pathans and Sindhis, a sense of superiority whose genesis lay in the attitude of the country's founder.

Jinnah appeared to start off with the best of intentions, but it was to prove a short-lived honeymoon. Initially, he sought to demonstrate his secular credentials by including a Hindu and Shia and Ahmadi Muslims in his first Cabinet, but although the country had adopted the Westminster model of government in principle it soon proved incompatible with Jinnah's personal style of leadership. He used his position as Governor-General more like the office of an executive president, and in the process rendered the prime minister, his Cabinet and even the legislature increasingly superfluous. Honoured as *Quaid-e-Azam*, or father of the nation, a cult of personality had enveloped the man and made him almost infallible in the eyes of West Pakistanis. His point of view reflected this narrow support base, and when in March 1948 the question of the official national language became the subject of heated discussion his bias was evident. Constituting 54 per cent of the country's population of 75,000,000, East Bengalis felt it natural that Bengali and Urdu should at the very least share equal standing as the national tongue. However, many Urdu and Sindhi speakers associated Bengali with the strong influence of Hindi, something which did not sit well at all with their concept of a Muslim state. Jinnah himself was a native of Sindh, and the son of Gujarati-speaking parents, but was fluent in neither Urdu, Sindhi or Gujarati. As a British-trained barrister he was eloquent and well-versed in English. Nonetheless, there was widespread disappointment when he declared that 'there can be only one state language' and that it 'can only be Urdu'.[7]

It was soon evident too that only those speaking the language could expect to secure senior employment in the civil service and the military. Bengalis thus became increasingly resentful towards the Urdu-speaking and pro-Pakistani Biharis, who had fled to East Bengal following partition and who were favoured in employment and promotion. In Sindh, as well, Urdu-speaking refugees had chosen to settle after fleeing the partition of Punjab. Soon disparagingly labelled 'Mohajirs', or emigrants, despite constituting just 3 per cent of the population they would fill 21 per cent of government appointments and a disproportionate number of posts in the army.[8] There was also a knock-on effect in education and other areas of public life, provoking anger and resentment. Throughout the country, demonstrations were staged protesting the discriminatory nature of Jinnah's edict, which continued after his death from tuberculosis in 1948. The language issue and other concerns inspired politicians in East Bengal to found the Awami League in 1949, hoping thereby to counter the domination of the Muslim League. Under the leadership of Sheikh Mujab-ur-Rahman it would fight a long and often perilous struggle to safeguard Bengali interests as the Punjabis tightened their grip and became increasingly authoritarian. Jinnah's successor as Governor-General, Khawaja Nazimuddin, had further muddied the waters by reiterating in 1952 that Urdu was and would remain the only official language. When the Awami League proceeded to orchestrate protests the government responded with an outright ban on all public meetings. These draconian measures served only to escalate tensions, and in one incident the police, spooked by angry crowds, lost control and opened fire, killing a number of demonstrators.

In this febrile atmosphere, the Constituent Assembly was working on the new constitution. It was a broadly accepted principle that the Government of India Act of 1935 would be superseded by one creating an Islamic republic, but the form it should take was hotly debated. Bengalis wanted to retain the provincial autonomy conferred under the 1935 Act, leaving a relatively weak centre to exercise responsibility for foreign affairs and defence. But this did not chime with the ambitions of the Punjabi landlord class. They wanted a powerful centre from which they could more easily manipulate the levers of power and keep the provinces on a tight rein, particularly Bengal. The omens were not propitious when in 1948 the government revoked much of the fiscal autonomy over tax and revenue the provinces had enjoyed since 1935,[9] a measure compounded in 1951 when the Constituent Assembly published its draft proposals. These provided for such a highly centralised system that *The Pakistan Times* warned it would confer 'dictatorial powers' on any future federal government.[10] Nevertheless, when a compromise second draft followed in 1952 offering a looser federation, it was likewise rejected by the landowning aristocrats. A perfect storm was brewing, and discontent in the armed forces was also to prove pivotal.

In 1951 the so-called Rawalpindi Conspiracy led by General Akbar Khan was exposed. Its ringleaders, smarting from the stalemate of the Kashmir war, and resentful that British officers were still serving in the army, were further angered by what they perceived as the vacillating premiership of Liaquat Ali Khan. He had been in office since independence, and although overshadowed both by Jinnah and his successor Khawaja Nazimuddin, found himself blamed for the country's woeful condition. Although the coup was crushed, the ensuing turmoil saw Ali Khan assassinated, and in 1953 Governor-General Sir Malik Ghulam used the prevailing chaos as a pretext to dismiss Khawaja Nazimuddin, who had succeeded as prime minister. When, in 1954 the United Front won the East Pakistan elections and demanded greater autonomy the Central Government responded by dismissing the administration and imposing direct rule by its governor.

Relations further deteriorated when in 1955 Prime Minister Mohammed Ali of Bogra announced the so-called 'One Unit' system, which merged the separate provinces of West Pakistan into one bloc, and East Bengal, now officially renamed East Pakistan, as the second bloc. This move was clearly designed to further entrench Punjabi domination over all the other ethnic groups and neutralise the Bengalis. It naturally met with resistance, with the Awami League leading the opposition, and in 1954 the Constituent Assembly was urged to overrule the decision. A bill was subsequently passed which would have reversed the policy, but Ghulam retaliated by having the assembly prorogued. Meanwhile, with the connivance of General Ayub Khan, communications with London were severed to shield the outside world from what was effectively a coup. When legal action was pursued the assembly was dissolved completely and a more compliant body created instead. This produced the long-awaited republican constitution, which was adopted in 1956, delivering the centralised government the Punjabi elite had demanded, but as some small consolation Bengali was now recognised as the country's second official language. If the new constitution was supposed to bring closure to the country's woes, it failed. In 1958, confronted by continued unrest, President Iskander Mirza declared martial law. But such was the growing instability that within the year he was usurped by a regime headed by General Ayub Khan, and this would prove even more despotic.

These developments left East Pakistan increasingly isolated and excluded from mainstream political decision making, many Bengalis complaining that they had simply exchanged the 'British Raj' for a 'Punjabi Raj'. They were also suffering economically and socially from a Punjabi regime which unashamedly exploited the East to enrich the West. Most particularly Bengal lost much of the income from its jute manufacture, which would grow from just 2 per cent of total export revenues in 1952 to 46 per cent by 1970.[11]

This drain on their wealth saw Bengali living standards deteriorate year on year. In 1949–50, for example, the average gross national income for West Pakistan had been 338 rupees against 287 rupees in East Pakistan, but by 1969–70 the gap had widened even further, to 537 and 331 respectively.[12] West Pakistan also monopolised development funding, and for most of the post-independence period East Pakistan received just 20 per cent, rising only slowly to 36 per cent by 1969–70.[13] In education too East Pakistanis found themselves short-changed. In 1958 a plan was submitted to mandate education for children between the ages of six and eleven, but when subsequent proposals to construct more schools were announced, 42,500 were earmarked for West Pakistan and only 4,000 for East Pakistan. In fact, the number of Bengali primary schools actually declined by 902 between 1947 and 1971.[14]

In the meantime, Ayub Khan stirred the pot further when he proceeded with plans for even greater administrative centralisation, overseeing the introduction of a new constitution in 1962 which replaced universal suffrage for the election of both the president and the legislature with a system of electoral colleges. The president also became both head of state and head of the executive with the right to appoint and dismiss governors. Echoing the long-defunct Colonial Laws Validity Act, the new constitution also made any proposed laws repugnant to Islam null and void. Then came the disastrous war over Kashmir with India in 1965, bringing further discontent which the government attempted to head-off by convening an All-Pakistan Conference in Lahore in February 1966. The Awami League delegates seized the opportunity to take with them a list of six demands which they presented to the conference. These included proposals for a federation based on the Lahore Resolution of 1940, an end to capital flight from East to West Pakistan and greater oversight of central government expenditure. Furthermore, they wanted control of their own local armed forces. West Pakistan and opposition parties in the East naturally rejected these demands out of hand, seeing them as one step from complete secession. But having captured the imagination of the Bengali people, this morphed into the Six-Point Movement, gathering pace as meetings, demonstrations and strikes were held throughout the province. This manifestation of popular unrest further worsened relations between the two halves and rattled the central government into a clumsy reaction.

In 1967 an alleged plot was uncovered in which Sheikh Rahman and thirty co-conspirators were accused of seeking Indian support for East Pakistan's independence from West Pakistan. They were arraigned in what was called the Agartala Conspiracy Case, but the show trial provoked such a violent backlash that it had to be abandoned. The subsequent fall-out finally brought about Ayub Khan's resignation and he was replaced by General Yahya Khan. Khan proceeded to impose martial law in an attempt to restore order but he also held out an olive branch, scrapping the One Unit System and undertaking to hold democratic elections. When these materialised in

1970, Sheikh Rahman swept the board on his Six-Point platform, handing him a mandate to deliver the wholesale reform that had been demanded for years.

Yahya Khan promptly reneged on his promises, and in an effort to stoke up trouble Biharis and pro-Pakistan Bengalis began attacking Awami League members. When they fought back, the army was primed to exploit the violence as a pretext for brutal intervention. By March 1971 most Awami League activists had been forced into exile in neighbouring India, whose government had been watching developments. It has since been speculated that the claims made against Sheikh Rahman were justified because the clampdown in Bengal prompted Delhi to secretly assist the Bengalis, providing military training so that they could return home to fight a guerrilla war against Pakistani forces. Then Indian airspace was closed to the Pakistanis, seriously disrupting communications between East and West. By December 1971 intelligence reports were suggesting that Pakistan was planning retaliation, but when they launched an attack India swiftly achieved a crushing victory, and by 16 December all Pakistani forces in Bengal had been forced to surrender. Rahman was then installed as president of the new sovereign state of Bangladesh, serving briefly until his assassination in 1975.

The world's newest state had inherited a shattered economy and an infrastructure ruined beyond recognition, in large part due to the deliberate and vindictive actions of the Pakistan Army. Communications and transport were wrecked, bridges destroyed, and waterways blocked. Over 6,000,000 homes had been destroyed and nearly 1,500,000 families deprived of their livelihoods. As many as 3,000,000 people had been killed in the fighting, among them the ill-starred Biharis upon whom Bengalis wreaked bloody revenge for their perfidy. Many fled to an unwelcoming Pakistan, where their reception was lukewarm at best. The war was also cited as a major factor in inadequate responses to a series of devastating cyclones, floods and famines which killed another 5,000,000 between 1971 and 1988.

Bangladesh became a byword for poverty and hunger, images of starving children regularly filling television screens as the new nation struggled to extricate itself from an economy in the doldrums and problems which often appeared insurmountable. There were also separatist movements to overcome in the Chittagong Hill Tracts, where tribesmen sought to exploit the situation to achieve their own independence. Moreover, in spite of the long road they had travelled in order to extricate themselves from a loveless marriage, independence saw a descent into the very one-party state its leaders had ostensibly fought against. A succession of hard-line and ultimately unsuccessful military dictatorships followed, and it would not be until 1990 that something like democratic civilian government was restored. There still proved to be a long uphill road to climb, and so-called caretaker governments were deemed necessary to ensure fair play in elections. When the Awami League abolished this practice in 2008, however, it left itself open to accusations of intimidation and fraud. In response, opposition parties boycotted the 2014 election, allowing the Awami League to sweep the board and claim a mandate to push through their policies, many of which have resulted in it being categorised by the Economist Intelligence Unit as a 'Hybrid Regime', just one step above an authoritarian state.[15]

Economically, the country has fared far better. It has thrived as a major manufacturer and exporter of jute, which alone in 2018 realised an income of £125,000,000,[16] with the UK becoming the third-largest export market for Bangladeshi products, worth £2.5 billion in 2017–18, nearly 10 per cent of its total exports. Although 80 per cent are still knitted and woven garments and leather and jute goods, Bangladesh is also diversifying into frozen food, IT and engineering.[17] The country is also becoming an increasingly lucrative market for Britain. Following a 119 per cent growth in bilateral trade since 2007, the UK exported £450,000,000 worth of goods and services in 2013 alone,[18] helping to deliver an average GDP growth of 8 per cent.[19] In addition the country has been in receipt of British aid, which has increased from £170,000,000 in 2018–19 to £192,000,000 in 2019–20, most of which is invested in projects designed to battle endemic poverty and ill-health.[20] Nonetheless, India easily outstrips the UK as a trading partner, with exports to Bangladesh standing at £7.3 billion for 2018–19 whilst reciprocal exports to India lag somewhat behind at £800,000,000.[21] India has also extended credit worth £38 billion to Bangladesh for infrastructure development, including roads, railways, shipping and ports.[22] Such statistics are impressive, but the footprints of both the UK and India are slowly being eclipsed by that of China, which has also ploughed billions into the country. In 2020 Beijing granted tariff exemptions to 97 per cent of Bangladeshi products[23] and signed a joint venture initiative to generate 500 megawatts of renewable energy.[24] In total, it has been calculated that China has so far invested a total of £30 billion in Bangladesh as it seeks to further extend its own economic and political reach in the region.[25] Ordinary Bangladeshis nonetheless remain poor. Some 60 per cent of the population still live below the poverty line according to World Bank estimates, indicating that they have yet to share in the national economic revival which has been experienced in recent years.

The war's outcome left West Pakistan further humiliated and traumatised. When the new state of Bangladesh was officially recognised by other Commonwealth states it resigned its own membership, leaving the regime more isolated and friendless than before. Furthermore the success of Bangladesh encouraged similar agitation in other provinces. Sindh had shared Bengali discontent with Punjabi and Mohajir domination for decades, and also demanded concessions. Wisely, however, instead of repeating the mistakes over Bangladesh the government took a more accommodating line, recognising Sindhi as an official language, improving educational opportunities and opening up more government posts. This was largely at the expense of the now expendable Mohajirs, who found their two decades of privilege coming to an end. Nonetheless, conciliation has not always been the course followed when addressing aggrieved populations, as can be seen in Balochistan.

The situation in Balochistan has been aggravated by the fact that Afghanistan has disputed the territorial integrity of the province since the days of the Raj, having grudgingly signed an agreement in 1893 to demarcate the 1,510-mile border with British India. This left restless Pashtun tribesmen on both sides of the frontier, and resulted in regular demands from Kabul for it to be rationalised in their favour. Successive Afghan regimes have also been complicit in frequent disturbances, and Pakistani operations into Balochistan had to be undertaken from as early as 1948. Ever since then there have been inconclusive forays into the province to disarm and pacify the tribesmen. As recently as 2017 renewed Afghan claims on the territory were lodged, and the area remains volatile and dangerous.

In the meantime, the ongoing tensions with India over Kashmir have required constant vigilance along the line of control, leading to further conflicts in 1965, 1999 and 2002. Pakistan has sought to strengthen its hand by maintaining a substantial nuclear arsenal in addition to conventional forces, and possesses both tactical and ballistic nuclear missiles capable of delivering payloads to a range of up to 1,200 miles.[26] This has required prodigious amounts of the nation's denuded treasure to be committed to defence, and Annie Besant would have balked at the £8.75 billion or 3.6 per cent of GDP that is now committed to it annually.[27] Nor are the country's ambitions limited to the military sphere. Since 1961 the Space and Upper Atmosphere Research Commission (SUPARCO) has spent millions on the development of satellites, sending its first rocket into space in 1990 with the assistance of China. The government recently announced that it hopes to launch a manned flight by 2022, with a budget of around £34,000,000 for 2019–20.

While billions are expended on the military and space programmes, it is primarily foreign aid which addresses Pakistan's enduring and endemic poverty. As of 2017, according to Britain's Department for International Development (DFID), nearly a third of Pakistanis live in poverty, over 22,000,000 children do not go to school and half the population cannot read or write. Moreover, 44 per cent of under-fives are malnourished and one in eleven children die before their fifth birthday.[28] Statistics on wealth distribution are equally stark, with figures suggesting that the top 10 per cent of the population earn nearly 28 per cent of national income, and the bottom 10 per cent subsist on just over 4 per cent.[29] In an attempt to address this situation, DFID earmarked £302,000,000 in aid, half of which was allocated to health and education, while Official Development Assistance (ODA) subscribed a further £17,000,000 to assist in fighting terrorism and other threats to the country's stability. It is nevertheless unsurprising that with the country spending billions on arms and adventures into space, questions have been asked. Perhaps the answer lies partly in the need to prevent a country seen as vital in the so-called war on terror from becoming a failed state, but perhaps less altruistic is the prospect of stimulating improved trade. This stood at £2.9 billion in 2017, of which an albeit modest £1.1 billion was British exports to Pakistan, but it is hoped this can be further stimulated with £400,000,000 provided by the UK export agency UK Export Finance. The early indications are positive, with Pakistan exports to the UK taking the shape of textiles, garments and steel;[30] this is perhaps encouraging for a state which many expected to fail within a few months.

A succession of coups followed the loss of Bengal, staged by men intoxicated by the lure of high office. Zulfikar Ali Bhutto came to power in 1971, and he was overthrown in 1977 by Muhammad Zia-ul-Haq. Zia's regime was marked by an era of tyranny which only ended when his plane exploded in the air in August 1988, killing everyone on board. He was replaced by Ishaq Khan, whose promised elections were won by Benazir Bhutto and the Pakistan People's Party. She was succeeded by Nawaz Sharif, but another army coup was staged in 1990, and after some instability General Pervez Musharraf seized power in 1999. He survived until 2008 when a form of democracy was reimposed and elections returned. The struggle to achieve stability has not been helped by the constant battle between secularism and militant Islam, which has sought to create a vacuum which it can fill for its own ends. This threat is partly to blame for the existence of arcane blasphemy laws, while those who commit so-called 'honour killings', rape children and target women, gays, minorities and transgender people often escape justice entirely. Fear of reprisals has also suppressed free speech, leaving the country with a score of just 4.25 out of 10 for human rights and respect for democracy.[31] Little wonder that in the view of many observers it is as volatile and unstable in the 2020s as when Governor-General Ali Jinnah took the oath of office in August 1947.

India may have been better placed to join the comity of nations as an independent state than Pakistan, but the assassination of Mahatma Gandhi in 1948 by a member of the ultra-nationalist Hindu Rashtriya Swayamsevak Sangh or RSS, was an early sign that India remained racially and ethnically divided. A country of 275,000,000 Hindus, 70,000,000 Untouchables or Dalits, 50,000,000 Muslims, 7,000,000 Christians, 6,000,000 Sikhs, 100,000 Parsis and 24,000 Jews, speaking over 19,000 different languages or dialects, prompted the nation's founders to forge ahead with plans to establish a robust constitution around which all religions and ethnicities could coalesce. Jawaharlal Nehru and his supporters had long advocated that this could be achieved only through the creation of a secular, socialist republic, which naturally precluded any continuance of political and constitutional ties with the UK. Alladi Krishnaswamy Iyer, one of the nine-member Constituent Assembly Drafting Committee, explained that the new constitution therefore had to provide for 'a democratic government on the basis of adult suffrage [that will] bring enlightenment and ... promote the well-being, the standard of life, the comfort and the decent living of the common man'.[32]

However, there remained a strong body of opinion, particularly among the princes, minority groups and more conservative elements within Congress, which favoured membership of the British Commonwealth. The only plausible compromise would be to secure continued participation without the obligation of retaining the British monarch as head of state. This, however, was impossible under its current constitution. A precedent of sorts had been set by Eire, which had employed constitutional sleight of hand to become a pseudo-republic by the close of the1930s. But when the decision was taken in 1949 to severe all connection with the Crown its membership was swiftly terminated without too much regret on anyone's part. India, however, was a different proposition. Its departure might encourage others such as Pakistan and Ceylon to follow suit. Burma would achieve independence outside the organisation, so there were good grounds to fear that it might disintegrate completely unless some compromise could be reached. Early adjustments were already in train, and in 1947 the prefix 'British' was dropped, and there was established a Commonwealth Relations Office with its own Secretary of State. Furthermore, the term Dominion was to lapse and be substituted instead by the more egalitarian 'Member of the Commonwealth of Nations'.

Nonetheless, the role of the Crown remained a sticking point, and this vexed question left the British government in something of a dilemma. Attlee did not want to use coercion or compulsion to keep India, and insisted that 'we want no unwilling partners in the British Commonwealth,'[33] but any decision to amend the rules to allow a republic to remain a member would require a huge leap of faith. Such a change would also have to be unanimous. Staunch monarchists in Canada, Australia and New Zealand might well veto the idea, although South Africa, already loosening its own ties, would doubtless welcome it. It was therefore decided to convene a special conference, attended by all the interested parties, to try and resolve the matter. The heads of government met in London in April 1949, and finally, after much debate and discussion, the conference bowed to the inevitable and it was agreed that the Statute of Westminster should be completely revised to accommodate members with republican constitutions.

The new protocol for future membership was made public in the London Declaration of 28 April which announced that henceforth 'the continuing acceptance of the King as the symbol of the free association of its independent member nations and as such the Head of the Commonwealth' would be the only criteria for membership.[34] It was naturally a bitter pill for many in the establishment to swallow, but even the die-hard imperialist Churchill felt that the concession had to be made. He confided to sceptical Conservative peer Lord Salisbury, 'I have no doubt that it is our duty to do all we can to make a success of the new system.'[35] In response to General Smuts' fears that South Africa would follow suit, he asked rhetorically, 'Would I rather have them in, even on these terms, or let them go altogether?'[36] George VI was allegedly less magnanimous. He had already surrendered the prestigious title *Ind Imp* and was now not even wanted as a king. Hearing of the declaration, the somewhat crestfallen monarch was said to have remarked, 'So now I'm just an "As Such!"' Nevertheless, India had got its way, and on 26 January 1950, the anniversary of the momentous day in 1930 when the Congress flag was first raised and independence declared, India officially became a republic with continued membership of a reformed and revitalised Commonwealth of Nations.

Having declared the country's status as an equal member of the Commonwealth, Nehru proceeded to establish India on the wider world stage. In October 1946 he had already declared that 'our natural position in world assemblies is going inevitably to be one of leadership of all the smaller countries of Asia,'[37] and confirmed in March 1948 that 'we are going to count more and more in the future.'[38] Such ambitions even seemed to extend to neighbouring Ceylon. On 9 October 1946, Nehru told the 'Youth of Lanka':

> Lanka and India are so closely connected that they must inevitably be associated with each other politically and otherwise in future ... for Lanka this connection is vital [but] she must be perfectly free to choose ... culturally, racially and linguistically Lanka is as much part of India as any province ... [but] it is ... economic and political considerations that point inevitably to a closer union. Lanka's trade must of necessity be largely with India, any attempt to look elsewhere will produce instability and insecurity ...[39]

Nonetheless, Nehru's vision was not to compete with the United States, Britain or the Soviet Union. He saw India as a non-aligned state, acting as a pivot around which smaller nations could operate free of the influence of the major world powers. But first he would have to put his own house in order. High on his agenda were those Princely States which had so far omitted to accede to India, and who now had to be taken to task. We have seen the fate of Kashmir, but Junagadh and Hyderabad were yet to be confronted. As early as October 1947 Lord Ismay reported that 'Mr Nehru said that although Junagadh was legally entitled to accede to Pakistan, the Government of India were not prepared to accept this accession, owing to the geographical complications caused by the fact the other Kathiawar States and Junagadh were inextricably interlaced. Thus, there were Junagadh islands in Indian territory and Indian islands in Junagadh territory.'[40] The solution proved relatively simple: India imposed a blockade on the state, and by 7 November 1947 this had succeeded in its intention and the inevitable followed. Hyderabad too had resisted the blandishments of Mountbatten and the assurances and veiled threats of Delhi. Of all the Princely States, perhaps this was the most contemptible in the eyes of the Indian nationalists; vast, rich, spoiled, despotic and, despite all the achievements of Sir Salar Jung I and his successors, still relatively politically backward. Nonetheless the Nizam continued to disregard Gandhi's advice that he 'come in on the side of Congress otherwise, when I am gone ... Nehru will have no patience with you'.[41] Indeed, Nehru had given the Nizam fair warning when on 10 April 1946 he noted:

> Two years ago ... [the Nizam stated he] depended on the British for protection and therefore British overlordship should continue ... Well, it is certain enough now that the British will quit India. What then of his protection and what of independence in the State? [42]

Declining to take this broadest of hints, the Nizam tried to buy time, sticking to his guns and refusing to budge. On 29 November 1947 he agreed to a Standstill Agreement and promised that he was not going to accede to Pakistan. Then, in an extremely ill-judged act of bad faith, the Nizam funded Pakistan's dispute with India over Kashmir[43] and recklessly sponsored a renegade militia called the Razakars who ruthlessly intimidated pro-accession activists in his own state. With patience wearing thin, on 14 June 1948 the Indian government presented a draft Treaty of Accession to the Nizam and demanded that the Razakars be disbanded. The Nizam continued to prevaricate, all the time holding out the prospect that he might simply go it alone as a separate sovereign nation affiliated neither to Pakistan nor to India. Infuriated by his intransigence, the Indians employed the same tactic as they used against Junagadh and imposed a blockade. Once all access by road, rail and air had been cut off, and nothing could get in or out, the Nizam grudgingly resumed half-hearted negotiations. When they again broke down in September 1948, Delhi ordered its troops to invade. Faced with a fait accompli, the Nizam signed the Act of Accession and was compensated with a handsome annual pension of £400,000.

A programme of integration and consolidation of the smaller Princely States was also implemented. Shortly after 1947, some of the larger ones had been instituted as provinces in their own right, and when the republican constitution of 1950 came into effect further reforms were initiated. Previously, Part A states had been defined as former provinces of British India and Part B the former Princely States, while Part C were elements of both. There were also Part D territories, namely the Andaman and Nicobar Islands, but this unwieldy arrangement ended with the States Reorganisation Act of 1956, which created only states or territories. In the meantime, there had been growing demands for states to be reorganised on a linguistic basis, and this also gave Nehru the chance to exact sweet revenge on the troublesome Nizams of Hyderabad. In 1954 this once grand fiefdom, the largest and richest in the country, ceased to exist after being dismembered and assimilated into three neighbouring states.

By the time of the 1956 Act similar changes had been made to state boundaries, changing beyond all recognition the political map which had defined British India. The princes continued as titular rulers within the new republic for several years, but as the country advanced they were seen as increasingly anachronistic relics of the past. After two decades of idle retirement at the Indian taxpayers' expense, the late 1960s saw the Privy Purse come under intense scrutiny and despite their vehement opposition, Prime Minister Indira Gandhi used her victory in the 1971 elections to annul their privileged status entirely.[44] Nehru also sought to eliminate the age-old caste system and religious barriers, and in October 1945 he assured his soon to be fellow citizens that 'the future government of free India must be secular in the sense that the Government will not associate itself directly with any religious faith but will give freedom to all religions to function.'[45] Consequently, India officially became a secular state and laws to protect the Untouchables were passed soon after independence, while tribes living lifestyles unchanged since before the Mughals also had their traditions guaranteed. Quota systems to improve access to education and government posts were implemented, while a person's caste, legally at least, was to become a social category and not a religious stigma or political millstone.

Despite Nehru's best endeavours, serious fault lines persisted and continue to dog national politics to this day. Terrorist attacks were staged in Mumbai in November 2008 by the Islamist *Lashkar-e-Taiba*, and there have been ongoing confrontations with left-wing Maoist rebels in Andhra Pradesh. More serious has been the persistent issue of the Punjab, with generations of Sikhs failing to reconcile themselves to a future as part of the republic. In 1980 the Khalistan Movement was founded to demand a separate sovereign state, becoming increasingly violent until in 1984 Indira Gandhi ordered military action to be taken against the insurgents. Their spiritual home being the holy shrine of the Golden Temple in Amritsar, the rebels believed themselves to be inviolable, but the complex was stormed by the army in a bloodbath reminiscent of General Dyer's excesses in 1919. In retaliation, Gandhi was murdered by her own Sikh bodyguards, provoking a vicious backlash in which thousands more Sikhs were murdered. In disgust, prominent Sikhs returned their honours, resigned their positions in public life or their commissions in the armed forces. Then in 1986 there were further acts of terrorism, possibly incited by the Pakistan secret service, but this time the government response provoked wholesale mutinies in the army. Six hundred men of the 9th Battalion of the Sikh Regiment turned on their officers and the Sikh Regimental Headquarters was the scene of bloody reprisals by recruits who stormed the armoury and marched on Amritsar. In clashes reminiscent of 1857, loyal troops had to be called upon to suppress the mutineers using artillery to pound them into submission.

Meanwhile, Delhi had moved to eliminate the French and Portuguese enclaves scattered around the coast, those few remaining vestiges of European occupation persisting on the subcontinent despite the end of the Raj. French Pondicherry and Portuguese Dadra and Nagar Haveli were absorbed in 1954 and Goa and Diu would be fully integrated by 1961 after a brief fight. A more intractable problem arose when in the 1950s Communist China began insisting that the so-called McMahon Line be renegotiated. This referred to the treaty that had been concluded in 1915 to delineate the border with Tibet, and which China claimed had been signed under duress. Initially Nehru dismissed their demands, insisting that the integrity of the frontiers could not be compromised, but in 1954, as a sign of good faith, he relinquished the extra-territorial rights in Tibet inherited from the British. These concessions did not go far enough for Beijing, and frictions persisted.

In 1962 Chinese troops occupied the Aksai Chin Plateau bordering Indian-occupied Kashmir, provoking immediate protests from Delhi in the United Nations. Nehru also retaliated by establishing military posts in other disputed areas, and following further border incidents open warfare broke out in September of that year. Only when China faced the prospect of Russia, Britain and the United States backing India did it withdraw, while in 1964 insurgents in Arunachal Pradesh sought to exploit the stalemate to carve out an independent state of their own. Despite the ceasefire, there were further confrontations between India and China in the Nathu La border region in 1967 and it has remained a running sore between the two heavily armed neighbours ever since. Even as recently as June 2020 further clashes occurred in which Indian soldiers were killed, prompting crowds to take to the streets demanding retaliation. Britain's relations with neighbouring Nepal left behind other unresolved issues which have recently re-emerged. In 1816 an agreement between Britain and the mountain kingdom had ceded territory to the East India Company, and Kathmandu has demanded the return of the territory. Delhi has resisted these calls, resulting in a stand-off which has yet to be resolved.

Furthermore, in spite of its non-aligned status the country has not been shy about performing military actions all across the region. There has been intervention in the Indo-Seychelles war of 1986, the Maldive Islands coup of 1988, and a Sri-Lankan civil war which lasted from 1983 to 2009. Here the Indian Government effectively broke Nehru's non-intervention promise when troops were committed to the country to subdue the Tamil rebels. These commitments have all contrived to transform the country into the powerful regional player Nehru had predicted, but they have also placed great pressures on Indian finances. By 2018, 2.1 per cent of GDP or £46 billion was being dedicated to defence,[46] a financial burden exacerbated by the country being a nuclear armed state. An expensive space program has also been pursued since the late 1960s, with the first satellite successfully launched in April 1975. This achievement was followed in April 2019 by the launch of the EMISAT rocket, although a subsequent moon landing attempt failed. The cost of these adventures has understandably come in for considerable criticism, the Indian taxpayer footing the bill to the tune of £1,200,000.

Nonetheless, whereas Pakistan has been stretched in maintaining her defensive capability and space programs, India is more than capable of absorbing the cost of such commitments. Taking as an example West Bengal, its receipt of the lion's share of the former presidency's industry served as the basis for years of exponential growth. By 2016–17 it could boast a GDP of

£125 billion,[47] investing £800,000,000 in the construction of 4,000 miles of railway and a 9,000-mile fibreoptic network. There are 200 industrial parks covering 20,000 acres for the manufacture of textiles, chemicals and food processing; it produces 20 per cent of the country's minerals and sits on coal reserves estimated to total 31 billion tonnes. And this is for the fourth-largest economy in India. Other states also compete for inward investment, luring businesses with tax breaks and subsidies. These measures were enhanced in 2017 when the national government replaced several state and federal taxes with a single goods and services tax.

Yet as laudable as such progress has been, it is argued that not enough of this wealth has found its way to the very poorest. In 2003 approximately 47 per cent of the population was still living below the poverty line, and over half of under-fives were malnourished. Life expectancy for men was only sixty-two years and for women just sixty-four.[48] Nearly 71,000,000 Indians are reportedly still living in poverty, and a third of its children are said to be suffering from debilitating lung problems due to pollution and substandard housing.[49] Yet the top 10 per cent of the country hold 77 per cent of the national wealth, and 1 per cent hold 73 per cent.[50] While they sit on billions of rupees, millions more languish in debt to pay for medical treatment, just as their forbears lived in perpetual obligation to Chettiar moneylenders and the zamindar. In 2020 it was reported that there was a shortage of 800,000 teachers and 75 per cent more classrooms were needed in a woefully underfunded system which receives just 4.4 per cent of government spending. It is not surprising that critics maintain that money lavished on the military and space programs could be better spent.

Drought and famine also exacerbate the plight of the ordinary ryot, and although the number of deaths has been low compared to the great famines of the past, hunger persisted as a feature of everyday life long after independence. In Bihar in 1966–67, for example, it was reported that the average calorie intake for a little over a quarter of the population was just 1,800 a day against a recommended average of 2,450.[51] Further shortages followed in 1973 and 1982 and returned in 1990, 1997, 2004, 2011 and 2015, and then the shattering effects of Covid-19 in 2020–21 added to the miserable plight of the ordinary citizen. Lockdown deprived millions of the means to make a living and in response Delhi had to provide subsidised rice, wheat and pulses to those in most need.[52] Indeed, such were the devastating effects of the pandemic on India that the government, as in the worst famines of old, became overwhelmed and needed to accept assistance from without, notably the United Kingdom. Such challenges are exacerbated by a population that has grown relentlessly since Partition. In the 1970s a desperate programme of semi-compulsory sterilisation was implemented in an attempt to reverse the trend. Through a combination of coercion and incentives 2,700,000 sterilisations allegedly took place during 1974–1975, and 8,300,000 between 1976–1977.[53] Nonetheless today's population, standing at 1.353 billion, is over a billion higher than in 1947. It is hardly surprising that hunger, poverty and inequality has become an insurmountable problem which successive governments have sought to resolve.

For long after independence these challenges fell to a series of Congress administrations, mostly consisting of the 'old guard' of the nationalist movement. But when Jawaharlal Nehru died in 1964 and was succeeded as prime minister by Lal Bahadur Shastri, his passing served to expose the somewhat shallow pool of talent from which the country's leadership had been drawn for so many years. A distinctly British-educated and Westernised class had filled the void left by the Raj and created its own aristocratic elite. This convention continued when Shastri died shortly after assuming office and Nehru's daughter Indira Gandhi was accepted as the natural successor. But her premiership also underlined the inherent weakness of rule by one party. Serious political instability began to rise to the surface, along with accusations both of creeping authoritarianism – highlighted by the controversy over mass sterilisation – and even election fraud. In the mid-1970s Indira Gandhi was taken to the High Court where she was found guilty of vote-rigging and barred from office. Rather than step down she declared a state of emergency, during which mass arrests, press censorship, the suspension of elections and arbitrary rule by decree became common. Her actions caused a split in the Congress Party, and in 1977 she was thrown out of power by a non-Congress coalition. Nonetheless, despite the odds she succeeded in achieving re-election in 1980, and after her murder secured the family dynasty through her son Rajiv, who in turn was assassinated in 1991.

This pattern was not broken until the emergence in 2014 of Narendra Modi, who swept the Congress Party out of office after ten years in power and a total of fifty-five in all since 1947. Born in 1950 to a Gujarati tea merchant, Modi espoused a nationalist credo of an entirely different persuasion to his predecessors. He joined the RSS as a youth and became dedicated to extreme Hindu nationalism, working his way through the ranks of the party and becoming Chief Minister of Gujarat in 2001. His deep religious and political convictions saw him implicated in violence against Muslims, and in 2002 accused of complicity in Hindu retaliation to the murder of RSS supporters. He became so infamous for his strident and uncompromising views that he was banned from both the US and the UK for a time. Unfazed by such unpopularity, he put his mind to gaining power nationally, and finally achieved his aim as head of the Bharatiya Janata Party or BJP.

Modi began to put his cherished Hindu nationalist agenda, or Hindutva, into action almost at once. Beginning with the old adversary Pakistan, he broke the fragile peace in Kashmir and ordered troops into the territory on 11 August 2019. He then revoked its special status and forbad its Muslim population to observe Friday prayers. Then their schools were closed and access to the internet was severed. Pakistan's Prime Minister, Imran Khan, claimed that thousands had also been arbitrarily detained, beaten and tortured as the Indian troops ran amok, but India countered with accusations of Pakistani complicity in terrorist activity and threatened to flood the territory with Hindu settlers. Policies towards Muslims within India proper also came in for radical reform, and building upon an election promise to address the longstanding issue of illegal immigration, he sponsored the Citizenship (Amendment) Act, which became law in 2019. Despite the Muslim population of the country having grown from 50,000,000 in 1947 to 200,000,000 today, the law only granted citizenship to non-Muslim residents. Muslims were rendered effectively stateless, rounded up and detained in camps to await processing, existing in miserable conditions not unlike the wretched 'lines' of colonial days. This was accompanied by plans for construction of a temple on the site of a mosque in the city of Ayodhya which had been destroyed by Hindu fanatics in 1992.

Many of the country's 28,000,000 Christians have also witnessed a surge in attacks on churches, pastors and their congregations. They are frequently assaulted by mobs of RSS, who consider any religion other than Hinduism as un-Indian and therefore fair game, turning on its head the narrative of secularity which Nehru framed in 1946. Often the victims are left with life-changing injuries, and in 2019 alone there were 329 associated acts of violence recorded, in many cases carried out in full view of the police.[54] Caste distinctions have also re-emerged, with reports of Jat landowners beating lower-caste Dalits for refusing to work on their farms and instead taking better-paid and relatively safer jobs in factories. Those left on the land continue to live desperate lives on the margins, an existence made more difficult by government measures. Farm bills aim to scrap fixed price guarantees for crops in government markets and allow large private corporations to decide prices. Such has been the anger engendered that even the otherwise usually sacrosanct Republic Day was disrupted in 2021 by angry farmers demonstrating against their conditions. Such have been the emotions of those concerned that the matter had to be adjudicated upon by a rather more impartial and sympathetic Supreme Court. Their dire condition is no better illustrated than by the continued and pervasive existence of the moneylender, profiting by the need to bridge the widening gap between income and outgoings and increasingly pushing farmers into debt. In the face of government intransigence farmers have been driven to strike, to mount demonstrations, and in many cases to commit suicide.

Another target for the new regime has been the English language. A cornerstone of Indian education since Macaulay, in 2020 it was removed as a mandatory subject in primary schools because, although spoken by just 0.02 per cent of the population, it was seen by the BJP as another lingering reminder of British colonialism. At the urging of the Modi government, school syllabuses will instead concentrate on teaching 'ancient Indian knowledge', a move seen by the burgeoning middles class as a retrograde step. Many still maintain that a command of English is essential for securing employment in an increasingly competitive environment. Many among the highly educated and articulate middle class have consequently been galvanised in opposition to Modi and his policies.

Modi's response to such dissent has not been to seek consensus, however, but to suppress free speech. On 2 April 2018, there were echoes of the notorious Press Acts of British India when the guidelines for Press Information Bureau Accreditation underwent a radical rewrite. If a reporter 'misrepresents' or writes copy critical of the regime it is interpreted as 'fake news', and its author is threatened with a six-month suspension of accreditation. A second 'offence' risks a year and a third infraction a lifetime ban.[55] It has been further rumoured that an increasingly supine judiciary has contemplated applying Section 124a of the Indian Penal Code to journalists, making them subject to charges of 'sedition', punishable by life imprisonment, if they write any copy hostile to the government. These steps have lately been interpreted as part of a general trend of intolerance, with a survey of press freedom undertaken by media watchdog Reporters Without Borders placing India at a lamentable 136 out of 180.[56] Such threats have led to many newspapers and individuals imposing self-censorship out of fear of finding themselves in a prison cell or worse. In September 2017, journalist and BJP critic Gauri Lankesh was gunned down and killed outside her home, allegedly by members of the RSS.[57]

It might appear trite to draw comparisons with the austere and often intolerant rule of the Viceroys of old, but one cannot help but see similarities. This may in part have motivated present-day Indians to join those compatriots who had fled the country's shores during the days of the Raj. Its growing reservoir of highly skilled graduates has led to suggestions that the country's surplus, with some 37 per cent unemployed, could provide a second tranche of skilled workers who might take their resourcefulness overseas. Half the swiftly growing population is estimated to be under the age of twenty-six, and it is natural for the ambitious and industrious to look beyond their own borders. They will be joining an estimated 28,000,000 so-called Persons of Indian Origin who now live throughout the world and who, it has been estimated, send home over £60 billion in remittances, perhaps redressing somewhat the centuries during which such sums had travelled in the opposite direction.

Nonetheless, they are following in the wake of Indians, Pakistanis and Bangladeshis who have themselves enjoyed mixed fortunes since 1947. Once scattered around the British Empire as indentured labourers, traders and businessmen, their fates frequently depended upon the political, cultural and racial leanings of their respective hosts. After the reoccupation of Malaya, for example, Indian influence never recovered and following the establishment of Malaysia in 1957 the climate of nationalism undermined the position of poorer Indians in particular. A major factor in their decline was the failure to take up the offer of citizenship which was made upon independence, and subsequently they had to obtain work permits to secure employment,[58] putting them at a distinct disadvantage when competing with native Malays and other foreign workers. The move from rubber to tea and oil palm was also traumatic,[59] compounded by an inability to adapt to changing conditions. Furthermore, there was an understandable propensity for ethnic Malays to dominate the government, leading to accusations of discrimination in their favour. By 1969 a fragile 'understanding' between Malays, Chinese and Indians had come under considerable strain, resulting in riots and many deaths. Nonetheless, Indians continued to fare worst of all, and consequently, even though today up to 2,000,000 ethnic Indians live throughout Malaysia,[60] some 7 per cent of the total population,[61] they now contribute only 2 per cent of the nation's wealth.[62] They are often found eking out a living on the margins of Malaysian society, although following Malaysia's economic transformation, which began in the 1970s, a fresh tranche of educated Indians have been lured to the country, welcomed for their entrepreneurial and technological acumen.

South Africa's despised Apartheid Laws affected Indians as well as native Africans, and successive governments imposed incremental restrictions upon the country's Asian community. Although classified by the white-dominated state as being entitled to more rights than the indigenous population, they were nonetheless left in no doubt they were considered little better than their forbears. The longer-term impact of life in an increasingly racially segregated society came as a result of the Group Areas Act of 1950, which moved them from districts reserved for whites. In 1952, the Population Registration Act designated Indians as 'coloured', entitling them only to inferior education, living standards and housing. Their lot started to improve slightly in the 1960s, when their 'permanent status' was recognised and they had their own Department of Indian Affairs. It was not until the 1970s, however, that university education improved, and only in the 1980s that some limited voting rights were conferred. They were also exempted from the so-called 'homelands' which were being established and to which many Black South Africans were consigned. Nonetheless, many Indians became involved in the anti-Apartheid movement, progressing through the ranks of the African National Congress, and when the system was finally brought to an end in the 1990s they were rewarded with job preferment and positive discrimination for career opportunities.

The changes which followed the end of white rule encouraged a fresh wave of immigration from India, Pakistan and Bangladesh and a realignment of their relationship with the new Black majority government. This has resulted in claims that some of the newcomers have been complicit in the alleged corruption of politicians such as Jacob Zuma, charges which once again threaten the fragile truce that had been secured between the two communities. Likewise, when Uganda and Kenya moved to independence in the 1960s, South Asians were caught in the midst of an African resurgence. Having long looked upon their communities with envy and jealousy, independence presented an opportunity to 'settle scores'. From Uganda, due to the despotic and psychotic rule of the madman Idi Amin, thousands of Indian, Bangladeshi and Pakistani holders of British passports were arbitrarily expelled in 1972. Dominating 90 per cent of the nation's business, they also contributed the same percentage of the tax revenue. Almost as a direct consequence, the country's already ailing and mismanaged economy collapsed completely as businessmen, entrepreneurs and doctors disappeared from the scene. Kenya proved equally hostile towards its Asians, and it too witnessed an exodus in the 1960s as their continued presence in the country became increasingly untenable. Nonetheless, approximately 100,000 still live in Kenya and 14,000 or so in Uganda, and the Ugandan government in particular has made numerous attempts to lure others back.

Canada's attitude to non-whites slowly adapted to the realities of a post-imperial world, but migration from the Indian subcontinent was slow at first, gaining momentum only in the 1970s, by which time 23 per cent of today's community had arrived, followed by a further 23 per cent between 1981–90 and 45 per cent between 1990 and 2000.[63] By 2001 there were 700,000 people of East Indian extraction, 2.4 per cent of the entire population, of whom 67 per cent were born in India, Pakistan, Bangladesh or East Africa. Ironically perhaps considering the events of a century before, 84 per cent have made their homes in Ontario and British Columbia,[64] around a third Sikhs, another third Hindu and 17 per cent Muslim. Today, people from the subcontinent constitute one of the nation's largest non-European ethnic groups, the tenth-largest diaspora in the country, and some have reached among the highest political offices in the land as government ministers. On 28 May 2018, in a timely expression of reconciliation, Canadian Prime Minister Justin Trudeau made an official apology on behalf of his country over the *Kotamagata Maru* episode, hoping that finally the memory of their humiliation could be laid to rest. This new inclusiveness prompted 82 per cent of those asked in a survey to agree that they felt a sense of belonging to Canada.[65]

Australia too discovered a change of heart following years of excluding non-whites from the country. By 1981 the number of Indian-born Australians was 41,657,[66] many of whom were highly trained doctors, teachers, computer programmers and engineers.[67] Today they are among the highest-educated of all migrants to Australia, with over half possessing a Bachelors' degree or higher.[68] They were nonetheless slow to appreciate the appeal of the so-called lucky country, and only a quarter arrived prior to 2001.[69] The 2011 census, however, revealed that their numbers had grown to 295,362, double the number in 2006. The state of Victoria has become home to the largest community at 111,787, followed by New South Wales with 95,387.[70] Of these, 139,631 were Hindu and 55,312 Sikh.[71]

Indian Fijians increased their numbers and their political influence on the islands to such an extent that ethnic Fijians' fears of being outnumbered and outvoted gathered momentum. Independence in 1970 removed the restraining influence of the British, and in 1977 when an Indian majority gained power it was prevented from forming a government.[72] Nine years later an Indian-led coalition came into office and prompted a military coup which produced a new constitution preventing anyone but ethnic Fijians from holding the premiership.[73] Fearing becoming an underclass, Indian Fijians responded by leaving in growing numbers to start a new life elsewhere.[74] The result was a steady decline which saw the loss of 700 teachers, 60 per cent of all lawyers, half of all doctors and a quarter of all trained civil servants. By 2018 just 37.5 per cent of the population was recorded as being of East Indian descent.[75] Many took advantage of the changes in attitude which informed New Zealand's immigration policies following the Second World War, and today Indian Fijians constitute one of the fastest-growing ethnic groups in the country. The fourth-largest language in New Zealand is now Fiji Hindi,[76] and by 2018 there were 221,916 migrants living in the country.[77] The extent to which attitudes have changed in the former Dominion, once so determined to keep out Indians at all costs, is perhaps no better demonstrated than by the appointment in 2006 of the first Governor-General of Indian extraction, Anand Satyanand.

Today the Indian percentage of the population of Mauritius stands at around 68 per cent of its 1,270,000 people and the island's cultural, economic and political profile almost exclusively reflects this. Indian dialects contribute to the creole spoken by 85 per cent of the islanders,[78] but also the Hindi, Tamil, Marathi and other tongues taught in schools. Most Hindu celebrations are public holidays, and the cuisine, arts and music are heavily influenced by the traditions brought over by indentured servants. Relations with India, by virtue of physical proximity and shared culture and values, are extremely close and they cooperate widely in economic and defence issues. Mauritius was also the only country outside of South East Asia to send a representative to witness Narendra Modi's swearing-in ceremony as prime minister, and he reciprocated by making a state visit to the island in 2015. But one stark reminder of the old days remains. The capital, Port Louis, is the site of the infamous Immigration Depot, or Aapravasi Ghat, built in 1849 to process immigrant labour either for work on the island or as a transit point to elsewhere in the Empire. It remained in use until the end of the indenture system in the 1920s and has since become a UNESCO World Heritage site and popular tourist attraction.

The Indian experience in the Caribbean has been equally successful on the whole, where the descendants of indentured servants in places such as Trinidad, British Guiana, Jamaica and elsewhere largely succeeded in making good lives for themselves. There are now estimated to be at least 2,500,000 Indo-Caribbeans, and many islands commemorate their presence with annual national heritage and 'Indian Arrival Days'. In Guyana, formerly British Guiana, Indians constitute 43.5 per cent of the mixed population of just 773,000. Cheddi Jagan, one of the country's most famous sons, was born of indentured servant parents and went on to help secure the country's independence from Britain in 1966. Nevertheless, some racial tensions have emerged over the years between Indo and Afro-Caribbeans, particularly in Guyana, but politicians of all stripes acknowledge that to garner votes from such relatively small pools of electors they need to foster racial harmony rather than exploiting differences. It has largely been the case that communities with large Indian populations have tended to distance themselves from the British connection. Guyana, Trinidad and Tobago and most recently Barbados have adopted republican constitutions, while islands such as Jamaica, Grenada and St Lucia have so far retained the British monarch as head of state.

Inevitably, the UK has seen generations from the subcontinent make homes and thrive in the former metropole since the end of the Second World War. Today there is hardly a high street without an Indian restaurant to serve as a constant reminder of how culinary tastes alone have been transformed. From around 15,000 in 1947, numbers increased considerably as demand for labour in Britain's industrial heartlands drew workers to the textile mills of Bolton, Blackburn, Manchester and Lancaster. Inevitably there was a culture clash as their numbers grew, from 21,000 in 1951 to 55,000 a decade later, reaching 250,000 by 1971.[79] Their 'exotic' dress, 'strange' mannerisms and cooking raised eyebrows among their hosts, while the newcomers found British habits equally shocking. The use of toilet paper instead of water and bathing instead of showering were two of many traits that appalled conservative and traditional-minded newcomers.[80] Similarly a strong work ethic, a desire to get on and a thirst for education set them apart from many British contemporaries. Those who stayed introduced the phrase 'Desh Pardesh', roughly translated as 'home from home',[81] into the British lexicon as increasing numbers changed the demographic and ethnic character of the nation. They also created subcategories: those that came either as 'Direct Migrants', straight from the Indian subcontinent, or 'Twice Migrants', those driven from former British East African colonies such as Uganda but whose status entitled them to reside in the United Kingdom.

But increasing immigration came at a time of corresponding decline in Britain's industrial economy. The great mills and factories which had drawn Punjabis, Sikhs and others were closing by the 1960s and rendering thousands jobless. The poorly educated rural workforces who had once worked in them found themselves unemployed as well as unwelcome. As their communities declined, a sense of ghettoization developed, especially as employment prospects for Asians were much worse than for their white counterparts. This is reflected in the near 20 per cent unemployment rate among South Asian Muslims even quite recently.[82] Their growing numbers also prompted demands for stricter controls, especially with migration from other parts of the former Empire increasing at the same time. The independence of colonies also brought into question the right to unrestricted entry into the UK, and in 1962 Indian migrants fell within the purview of the first Immigration Act, which was strengthened further in 1968.

Finally, over a hundred years after the first Indians exercised their inalienable right to move freely throughout the British Empire, the door was hove to, bringing an end to one of the most dynamic and dramatic chapters of British involvement in the subcontinent. There have inevitably been issues over the years, raised by those who question the very notion of a multi-racial, multi-ethnic, pan-religious Britain. Racial tensions were a major problem in the 1950s and 1960s, stirred by the rhetoric of politicians such as Enoch Powell, and the expulsion of the Ugandan Asians by Idi Amin provoked heated debates throughout this period. The 9/11 terrorist attacks in 2001 and the invasions of Iraq and Afghanistan provoked retaliation, with home-grown terrorists among those seeking retribution. Nonetheless, the success of the experiment has far outstripped any doubts of its value to British society.

This is clear in the increasing contribution from South Asians in British politics, with many holding high offices such as Attorney General, Chancellor of the Exchequer and Home Secretary. Priti Patel and Sajid Javid are well-known figures in British politics, as indeed is Chancellor Rishi Sunak, grandson of 'Twice Migrant' Punjabis who migrated first to East Africa and then to the UK. He in particular has been touted as a future prime minister. Many others sit in the House of Lords and the opposition front bench. Party leader Kier Starmer added to his shadow cabinet following his election and this brought the total number of spokespersons from Indian backgrounds to five, including Valerie Vaz, sister of Keith, the first MP of Goan extraction to be elected to the Commons in 1987. There is also Lisa Nandy, who stood against Starmer in the leadership hustings following the resignation of the incumbent Jeremy Corbyn. But those in whose footsteps the modern generation have trod have not been entirely forgotten either. In 1995 a street in Dadabhai Naoroji's former constituency of Central Finsbury was renamed in his honour, and a plaque now proudly adorns Finsbury Town Hall, commemorating his election in 1892. Mancherjee Bhownaggree, who was re-elected to parliament in 1900, died in London in 1933 and was buried in Brookwood Cemetery in Surrey. While his gravestone rather modestly makes no mention of his role in changing attitudes towards India at the turn of the twentieth century, he would no doubt be pleased that the former capital of the British Empire has in Sadiq Khan a former MP and incumbent mayor who is the product of Pakistani origins.

The British Armed Services, too, now has among its ranks the descendants of some who once fought in the former Indian Army. Along with the RAF and Royal Navy, approximately 1,000 Hindus, 450 Muslims and around 150 Sikhs now serve in various arms of the British Army. There have also been considerable relaxations to once strict dress and hair regulations, with beards and long hair permitted, in addition to the wearing of religious headdress. Jatinderpal Singh Bhullar, the first Sikh Guardsman to perform in the Queen's Birthday Parade, or Trooping the Colour, was allowed to do so wearing a turban. Muslims are permitted to pray five times a day, observe Ramadan and have their own halal rations. Indeed, the famous Battle of Saragarhi is now proudly commemorated annually on 12 September as a sign not only of Britain's respect for those men who died all those years ago but also those who serve today, and the prospect of forming a Sikh regiment has even been mooted. There are growing numbers of non-commissioned and commissioned officers from Asian backgrounds, although they are all still very much outnumbered by the 3,500 Gurkhas who remain an integral and indispensable part of the modern British Army.

It is equally arguable that the direct benefits Britain gleaned from its 350-year relationship with the Indian subcontinent continue to pay dividends in the form of trade and other exchanges and collaborations, albeit on a far more equitable basis. In 2018 trade with India was worth £21.9 billion, up 17 per cent on 2017, with UK exports 39 per cent higher than the previous year, and imports from India worth £12.7 billion, up 5 per cent on 2017.[83] Britain also invested £19 billion in India up to 2016, 8 per cent of all inward foreign investment. Of this, £4.8 billion was invested in chemicals, £3.2 billion in drugs and pharmaceuticals and £2.5 2 billion in food processing.[84] The number of Indian companies doing business in the UK has also grown, from 800 in 2018 to 842 in 2019, with a combined turnover of £48 billion. Of this investment, 35 per cent is in technology and telecoms, 15 per cent pharmaceuticals and chemicals, and 16 per cent engineering and manufacturing.[85] This last feature is particularly significant because one of the key components of Indian investment has been in steel, undertaken by none other than the firm Tata. Created originally through the zeal of its founder and the sponsorship of Viceroys Hardinge and Curzon, it has grown into one of the world's biggest multinational concerns. In 2007 it acquired Corus, formerly British Steel, and the site in Port Talbot in Wales, for which it paid £6.2 billion.[86] Britain cannot afford to rest on its laurels, however. The United States has emerged as India's largest trading partner by far, with bilateral trade worth US$88.75 billion in 2019–20, and India enjoying a healthy trade surplus of US$16.86 billion.[87]

Overall, this change in equilibrium has proven to be of particular benefit to an India slowly approaching the status of a superpower. Nehru's vision, shared soon after independence, also serves to underline the constant changes in the relationship between India and the United Kingdom. The former has long since shed its position as supplicant to the latter, but for how long the United Kingdom can avoid having the tables turned upon it entirely is perhaps a matter for continued speculation.

Notes

1 There shall be perpetual friendship

1. H.M. Hyndman, The Bankruptcy of India, An Enquiry into the Administration of India under the Crown, p. 1
2. Durant, Will, The Case for India, p. 5
3. British and Foreign State Papers, 1817-1818, Compiled by the Librarian and Keeper of the Papers, Foreign Office, p. 944
4. Hermione de Almeida and George H. Gilpin, Indian Renaissance: British Romantic Art and the Prospect of India, p. 228
5. Henry Jeffreys Bushby Widow Burning, A Narrative, p. 13
6. Ibid p. 22
7. Edward Thompson, Suttee – A Historical and Philosophical Enquiry into the Hindu Rite of Widow-Burning, p. 57
8. Ibid, p. 36
9. Ibid, p. 54
10. Ibid, p. 54
11. Ibid, p. 39
12. Ibid, p. 62
13. Ibid, p. 62
14. Ibid, p. 57
15. Ibid, p. 67
16. Ibid, pp. 70-72
17. Ibid, p. 71
18. Professor A. Berriedale Keith, Speeches and Documents on Indian Policy, 1750-1921, Volume One, p208
19. Thompson, p. 78
20. Ibid, p. 79
21. Ibid, p. 81
22. Ibid, pp. 122-123)

23. D.R. Banaji, Slavery in British India, p. 226
24. Slavery and the Slave Trade in British India; with Notices of the Existence of these Evils in the Islands of Ceylon, Malacca and Penang, drawn from Official Documents, p. vi
25. Ibid, p. 26
26. Ibid, pp. 91-10)
27. Banaji, pp. 13-14
28. Banaji, pp. 50-53
29. Slavery and the Slave Trade in British India; with Notices of the Existence of these Evils in the Islands of Ceylon, Malacca and Penang, drawn from Official Documents, p. 28
30. Banaji, p. 334
31. Ibid, p. 73
32. Slavery and the Slave Trade in British India; with Notices of the Existence of these Evils in the Islands of Ceylon, Malacca and Penang, drawn from Official Documents, p. 2
33. Ibid, p. 72
34. Banaji, p. 404
35. Harald Fischer-Tine and Michael Mann (Ed.) Colonialism as Civilising Mission, Cultural Ideology in British India, p. 33
36. James Hutton, A Popular Account of the Thugs and Dacoits: The Hereditary Garotters and Gang Robbers of India, pp. 13-14
37. Ibid, pp. 64-65
38. Ibid, p90
39. Ibid, p85
40. Nancy Gardner, Social Legislation of the East India Company, Public Justice versus Public Instruction, p. 49
41. Ibid, p. 51
42. B.D. Basu, History of Education in India, p. 85
43. Ibid, p. 88
44. Mihir Bose, The Magic of Indian Cricket, p. 55
45. Basu, p.161
46. Valentine Chirol, Indian Unrest, p. 209
47. Arthur Berriedale Keither, A Constitutional History of India, 1600-1935, p. 226
48. Thompson and Grant, History of British Rule in India, p. 153
49. Cotter J. Morrison, Macaulay, pp. 29-30
50. Shaunagh Dorsett and John McLaren, Legal Histories, p. 218
51. Arthur Bryant, Macaulay, p. 62)
52. Dorsett and McLaren, p. 218
53. Romesh Dutt, India in the Victorian Age, p. 243
54. Lajput Raj, Unhappy India, p. 403
55. Chunder Dutt, pp. 30-31
56. Hyndman, p. 29
57. Ibid, p. 29

58. Montgomery Martin, British India: Its recent Progress and Present State, p. 29
59. Hyndman, p. 123
60. Dutt, p. 206
61. Ibid, p. 206
62. Ibid, pp. 206-207
63. Ibid, p. 203
64. Ibid, p. 184
65. Ibid, pp. 184-185
66. Ibid, p. 225
67. Royal Proclamation 1 November 1858
68. legislation.gov.uk
69. S.N. Sen, History of Modern India, p. 110
70. Montgomery Martin, p.293
71. Dutt, p. 425
72. Ibid, pp. 426
73. Hyndman, p. 137
74. Theodore Monson, Imperial Rule in India, being an Examination of the Principles Proper to the Government of Dependencies, p. 22
75. Ibid, p. 27
76. The Ilbert Bill: A Collection of Letters Speeches, Memorials, Articles etc, p. 13
77. Ibid, p. 14
78. Ibid, p. 46
79. Dabhadhai Naoroji, Poverty and UnBritish Rule in India, pp. 182-183
80. Sir William Wedderburn Allan Octavian Hume, C.B. Father of the National Congress, 1829 to 1912, p. 1
81. Proceedings of the First Indian National Conference on the 28th, 29th, 30th December 1885, held at Bombay, p. 3
82. Chirol, p. 158
83. B.S. Nagi, Child Marriage in India, p.8
84. Ibid, p. 10
85. Padma Anagol-McGinn The Age of Consent Act (1891) Reconsidered: Women's Perspectives and Participation in the Child Marriage Controversy in India, South Asia Research Vol.12, No.2
86. An Appeal to England to Save India from the Wrong and Shame of the Age of Consent Act, 25 April 1891
87. Ibid
88. Muhammed Shabir Khan Tilak and Gokhale: A Comparative Study, p. 36
89. Hyndman, p. 123
90. Government of India Despatch of 26 October 1892, quoted in Simon Commission Report of 1926
91. Monson, p. 17
92. Ibid, p. 20

93. *Daily Mail*, 22 June 1897

94. thehindu.com, India and the Last Jubilee Queen, Dinyar Patel, 16 June 2012

2 'Settle a new branch of the nation in the strong places of India'

1. Hon. Alfred Deakin, Irrigated India, An Australian View of India and Their Irrigation and Agriculture, p. 143

2. Chunder Dutt, India in the Victorian Age, p. 166

3. Dr G.S. Dhillon, Canal System of the Punjab Region, pp. 6-7

4. Robert B. Buckley, The Irrigation Works of India and their Financial Results, p. 1

5. Nirmal Tej Singh, Irrigation and Soil Salinity in the Indian Sub-Continent, Past and Present, p. 86

6. Deakin, p. 232

7. Robert B. Buckley, p. 6

8. Ian Stone, Canal Irrigation in British India, p. 21

9. Deakin, p. 265

10. Ibid, p. 266

11. Stone, p. 21

12. Deakin, p. 266

13. Dutt, p. 356

14. Deakin, Ibid, p. 143

15. Buckley, p. 312

16. Ibid, p. 312

17. John Dacosta, Facts and Fallacies Regarding Irrigation as a Prevention of Famine in India, p.7

18. Deakin, p. 279

19. Ibid, p. 145

20. Ibid, p. 302

21. Buckley, p. 317

22. Working Paper 209, Capital 'Development' and Canal Irrigation in Colonial India, Patrick McGinn, Institute for Social and Economic Change, 2009, p. 18

23. Stone, pp. 2-3

24. Dacosta, p. 2

25. Kartar Lalvani, Bloomsnury, The Making of India: The Untold Story of British Enterprise, p. 124

26. Robert Burton Buckley, p. 309

27. Ibid, p321

28. Valentine Chirol, Indian Unrest, p. 255

29. British Imperial Railways in Nineteenth Century South Asia, Laxman D. Satya, Economic and Political Weekly, November 22 2008, p. 69

30. Hena Mukherjee, The Early History of the East Indian Railway, p. 69

31. Hyde Clarke, Colonization, Defence and Railways in Our Indian Empire, p. 159

32. Ibid, p.148
33. Quoted in Indian Railways as connected with the Empire in the East, William P. Andrew CIE, W.H. Allen and Company London, 1884
34. Laxman D. Satya, British Imperial Railways in Nineteenth Century South Asia, Economic and Political Weekly, November 22 2008, p. 70
35. Ibid
36. Hyde Clarke, Ibid, p. 177
37. Minute dated 20 April 1853, quoted in Indian Railways: Rates and Regulations, N.B. Mehta, P.S. King and Sons Ltd, London 1927
38. Hyde Clarke, Ibid, p. 50
39. Ibid, p. 124
40. Ibid, pp. 124-125
41. Ibid, p. 125
42. Ibid, pp. 126-127
43. Montgomery Martin, p. 34
44. Ibid, p. 245
45. G. Huddleston, The History of the East India Railway, p.12
46. G.S. Khosla, A History of Indian Railways, p. 59
47. Nalinaksha Saryal, Development of Indian Railways, p. 46
48. H.M. Hyndman The Bankruptcy of India, An Enquiry into the Administration of India under the Crown, pp. 65-66
49. The Railway Mania: Fraud disappointment expectations, and the modern economy, Andrew Odlyzko, School of Mathematics, University of Minnesota, 2012, p. 2
50. Montgomery Martin, p. 253
51. Hena Mukherjee, The Early History of the East Indian Railway, p. 75
52. Nalinaksha Saryal, p. 45
53. Khosla, p. 28
54. Ibid, p.26
55. Hyde Clarke, p. 226
56. Montgomery Martin, p. 34
57. Saryal, p. 202
58. Ibid, p. 214
59. Ibid, p. 44
60. Ibid, p. 202
61. Ibid, p. 192
62. Montgomery Martin, p. 254
63. Nalinaksha Saryal, p. 45
64. Ibid, p. 45
65. Dr Sir Zia Uddin Ahmad, Indian Railways, p. 2
66. Uddin Ahmad, p. 1
67. H.M. Hyndman, pp. 107-108
68. William Digby, Prosperous British India: A Revelation from Official Records, p. 112
69. H.M. Hyndman, pp. 65-67

70. Uddin Ahmad, pp. 7-8
71. Digby, p113
72. Montgomery Martin, p. 256
73. Satya, p. 71
74. Montgomery Martin, p. 255
75. Laxman D. Satya, p. 71
76. Hena Mukherjee, p. 118
77. Satya, p. 71
78. Huddleston, pp. 161-163
79. Ibid, p. 242
80. Ibid, p. 244
81. Ibid, pp246-248)
82. Dadabhai Naoroji Poverty and UnBritish Rule in India, pp. 171-172
83. Mukherjee, p. 109
84. Khosla, pp. 59-60
85. Montgomery Martin, p. 255
86. Ibid, p255)
87. Saryal, p59)
88. Montgomery Martin, p. 255
89. Saryal, p. 130
90. Chandrika Prasada Tiwari The Indian Railways, Their Historical, Economical and Administrative Aspects, p. 151
91. Ibid, p141
92. Saryal, p. 57
93. Ibid, p. 130
94. Satya, p. 75
95. Ibid, p. 75
96. Ibid, p. 75
97. Ibid, p. 73
98. Saryal, p. 130
99. Ibid, p. 214
100. Tiwari, p. 134
101. Naoroji, p. 61
102. Ibid, p. 61
103. Tiwari, p. 51
104. Ibid, p. 67
105. Ibid, p. 53
106. Savel Zimand, Living India, pp. 184-185
107. Durant, Will, The Case for India, p. 37
108. Tiwari, p. 73
109. Ibid, p. 72
110. Ibid, p. 73
111. Ibid, p. 89
112. Ibid, p. 75
113. N.B. Mehta, Indian Railways: Rates and Regulations, p. 52

114. Tiwari, p. 88
115. Satya, p. 74
116. Ibid, p. 74
117. Ibid, p. 74
118. Mukherjee, p. 120
119. Satya, p. 74
120. Ibid, p.74
121. Hyndman, p. 112
122. Ibid, p. 38
123. Saryal, p. 59
124. Khosla, p. 46

3 'Great traffike for all sorts of spices and drugges'

1. G.A. Nateson, Speeches and Writings of Annie Besant p. 242
2. P.R. Ramachandra Rao, Decay of Indian Industries, p. 14
3. Ibid, p. 18
4. Early Travels in India 1583-1619, ed. William Foster CIE, pp. 8-9
5. Ibid, p. 13
6. Savel Zimand Living India, p. 30
7. Bhownaggree, Mancherjee, M., The Constitution of the East India Company, p. 10
8. Romesh Dutt, The Economic History of India Under British Rule, from the Rise of British Power in 1757 to the Accession of Queen Victoria in 1837, p. 2
9. Mancherjee, p. 12)
10. Zimand, p. 31
11. Montgomery Martin, British India: Its recent Progress and Present State, p. 1
12. Ibid, p. 6
13. Ibid, p. 6
14. Zimand, p. 31
15. Rao, pp. 75-76
16. Ibid, p. 27
17. Dutt, p. 256
18. Ibid, p. 276
19. William Bolts, Considerations on India Affairs, pp. 191-192
20. Karl Marx, writing in the New York Herald Tribune of 25 June 1853 and article under the heading 'British Rule in India'
21. Rao, p. 14
22. Karl Marx, writing in the New York Herald Tribune of 25 June 1853 and article under the heading 'British Rule in India'
23. H.M. Hyndman, The Bankruptcy of India, An Enquiry into the Administration of India under the Crown, p. 26
24. Dutt, p. 258

25. Ibid, p. 276
26. B.D. Basu, The Ruin of Indian Trade and Industries, p. 143
27. Ibid, p. 131
28. Montgomery Martin, pp. 275-276
29. Hyndman, pp. 75-76
30. William Digby, Prosperous British India, a Revelation from Official Records, p. 89
31. Dutt, p. 262
32. Digby, p. 89
33. Rao, p. 102
34. Jadunath Sarkar, Economics of British India, p. 142
35. Ibid, p. 142
36. Dutt, p. 263
37. S.N. Send, History of the Freedom Movement in India, pp. 10-11
38. J. Ramsay MacDonald, The Government of India, pp. 156-167
39. Digby, pp 234-345
40. Sarkar, p. 150
41. Ibid, p. 302
42. Sarkar, p. 304
43. The Emancipation of India, A Reply to the Article by the Rt. Hon. Viscount Morley OM, on 'British Democracy and Indian Government in the Nineteenth Century and After', for February 1911, by H.M. Hyndman, The Twentieth Century Press Ltd, London 1911, p10
44. House of Commons, 24 June 1858. Quoted in Poverty and UnBritish Rule in India, Dabhadhai Naoroji, p. 279
45. Sarkar, pp. 327-330
46. Radhakund Mookerji, Indian Shipping: A History of Seaborne Trade and Maritime Activity of the Indians from the Earliest Times, p. 81
47. Ibid, p. 212
48. William Taylor Money, Observations on the Expediency of Shipbuilding at Bombay, for the service of His Majesty and of the East India Company, p. 39
49. Ibid, p. 59
50. Ibid, p. 70
51. William Digby, p, 88
52. Mookerji, p. 200
53. Digby, p. 114
54. Mookerji, p. 81
55. Builders of Modern India: V.O. Chidambaram Pillai, R.N. Sampath and Pe.Su Mari, p44
56. Ibid, p. 43
57. Ibid, pp 43-48
58. Digby, p. 88
59. Syed Hossain Bilgrami, B.A. and C. Wilmott, Historical and Descriptive Sketch of HH the Nizam's Dominions, vol. 1, p. 399

60. Naoroji, p. 54
61. Rao, p. 14
62. Ibid, p. 43
63. Ibid, p. 56
64. Bilgrami and Wilmott, p. 399
65. Nateson, p. 328
66. Dutt, p. 287
67. Report of the Coal Mining Committee, 1937 Volume One, Delhi, Manager of Publications, 1937, p. 9
68. Sarkar, p. 197
69. Sarkar, p. 197
70. BV Narayanaswamy Naidu, Indian Trade, p. 34
71. Peter Mathias, The First Industrial Nation: An Economic History of Britain, 1700-1914, p. 319
72. Raj, p. p380-381
73. Summary of the Principles Measures of the Viceroyalty of the Marquess of Lansdowne in the Department of Revenue and Agriculture, December 1888 to January 1894, Office of the Superintendent of Government Printing India, Calcutta, 1894, p. 42
74. Ibid, p. 48
75. Lovat Fraser, Iron and Steel in India: A Chapter from the Life of Jamshedji Tata, p. 16
76. Ibid, p. 53
77. Ibid, pp. 52-53
78. Ibid, p20)
79. Sarkar, p. 190
80. Sarkar, p. 190
81. Digby, p. 10
82. Sarkar, p. 195
83. Digby, p. 109
84. Naidu, p. 37
85. Ibid, p. 37
86. Sarkar, pp. 359-362
87. Summary of the Administration of Lord Hardinge of Penshurst, p. 36
88. Ibid, p36
89. Sarkar, p. 367
90. Ibid, pp. 365-366
91. Fraser, p. 97
92. Summary of the Administration of Lord Hardinge of Penshurst, p. 67
93. Ibid, pp. 36-37
94. Ibid, p. 37
95. Pramathanath Banerjee A History of Indian Taxation, p. 218
96. Nateson, p. 333
97. Banerjee, pp. 221-234

98. Ernest Wood, An Englishman Defends Mother India, A Complete Constructive Reply to Mother India, p. 411
99. Chunder Dutt, India in the Victorian Age, p. 216
100. Mancherjee, p. 187
101. Dutt, p. 115
102. John Dacosta, The Financial Situation in India, As Expressed in the Budget Statement for 1886-87, p. 8
103. Lajpat Rai Unhappy India, p. 344
104. Dutt, p. 115
105. MacDonald, p. 150
106. Dutt, p. 115
107. The India List and India Office List, 1905, Harrison and Sons Limited, London, 1905
108. Montgomery Martin, p. 176
109. Digby, p.
110. Montgomery Martin, p. 176
111. DE Wacha Recent Indian Finance, p. 9
112. Dutt, p. 214
113. Hyndman, p. 56
114. Ranbir Vohra, The Making of India, A Historical Survey, p. 91
115. MacDonald, p. 148
116. Sarkar, p. 284
117. Durant, Will, The Case for India, p. 18
118. Dutt, 1904, p. 219
119. Montgomery Martin, p. 195
120. Sarkar, p. 138
121. Nateson, pp. 301-303
122. Ibid, p. 301
123. Ibid, p. 303
124. Banerjea, p. 14
125. Hyndman, p. 40
126. Dutt, 1904, p384
127. Ibid, p247
128. Ibid, pp. 255-257
129. Ibid, p. 548
130. Dutt, p. 604
131. Raj, 1928, p. 368
132. Naoroji, p. 260
133. M. Anees Chishti, Committees and Commissions in Pre-Independence India, 1836-1947: Vol.2, 1882-1895, p. 226
134. Naoroji, p. 322
135. Chishti, p. 227
136. John F. Riddick The History of British India: A Chronology, pp. 83-84
137. Chishti, p. 2
138. Chishti, p. 240

139. Dutt, 1904, p559
140. Chishti, p. 250
141. Nateson, p. 355
142. Ibid, p. 334

4 'The pivot of our empire'

1. William Digby, Prosperous British India: A Revelation from Official Records, pp. 288-289)
2. The Times, 3 December 1898
3. David Gilmour, Curzon, p. 245
4. Geoffrey West, The Life of Annie Besant, p. 224
5. Theodore Monson, Imperial Rule in India, being an Examination of the Principles Proper to the Government of Dependencies, p. 78
6. Mahmud Husain (ed.), A History of the Freedom Movement, p. 6
7. Ibid, p. 14
8. Ibid, p. 15
9. John S. Hoyland, Gopal Krishna Gokhale, His Life and Speeches, p. 133
10. Husain, p. 14
11. Harold Nicolson, King George V: His Life and Reign, p. 87
12. The Indian Demands: A Symposium on the memorandum of the Nineteen and Speeches at the Congress and Moslem League on their scheme of self-government for India, introduction by G.A, Nateson, p. 7
13. D.N. Banerjee, Partition or Federation? A Study in the Indian Constitutional Problem, p. 80
14. Ibid, p. 80
15. Mary, Countess of Minto, India, Minto and Morley, 1905-1910, p. 7
16. Ibid, p. 30
17. Naoroji M. Dumasia, The Aga Khan and His Ancestors, p. 97
18. Minto, p. 30
19. Ibid, p. 99
20. Patrick Jackson, Morley of Blackburn: A Literary and Political Biography of John Morley, p. 393
21. Minto, p. 97
22. Husain, p. 24
23. Chirol, Indian Unrest, p. 96
24. E. Major, Viscount Morley and Indian Reform, p. 133
25. Mary, Countess of Minto, Macmillan, p. 255
26. Colonialism as Civilising Mission, Cultural Ideology in British India, Ed. Harald Fischer
27. Minto, p. 122
28. Major, pp. 244-245
29. Minto, p. 332

30. Major, p. 78
31. Sir William Wedderburn, Allan Octavian Hume, C.B. Father of the National Congress, 1829 to 1912, p. 130
32. Major, p. 46
33. Minto, p. 212
34. Major, p. 114
35. John S. Hoyland, Gopal Krishna Gokhale, His Life and Speeches, p. 159
36. Khan Syed Sirdar Ali, The Life of Lord Morley, p. 251
37. Arthur Berriedale Keith, A Constitutional History of India, 1600-1935, p. 237
38. Press Act 1910
39. Nateson, p. 439
40. J. Ramsay MacDonald, The Government of India, p. 226
41. Major, p. 127
42. Nicolson, p. 167
43. Summary of the Administration of Lord Hardinge of Penshurst, Viceroy and Governor-General of India, November 10, 1910 – March 1916, pp. 14-15
44. Arthur Berriedale Keith, Halcyon Press, p. 234
45. Husain, p. 54
46. *Waikato Times*, 27 December 1912
47. Summary of the Administration of Lord Hardinge of Penshurst, p. 16
48. Ibid, pp. 18-19
49. Budheswar Pati, India and the First World War, 1914-1918, p. 7
50. Lt. Col. Dr Shyam Narain Role of the Indian Army in the First World War, p. 9
51. K.L. Gauba, Hyderabad or India, p. p44-45
52. Ibid, pp. 44-45)
53. Pati, pp. 23-24
54. Narain, p. 119
55. Ibid, p. 119
56. F.W. Perry, The Commonwealth Armies, Manpower and Organisation in Two World Wars p. 85
57. Narain, p. 6
58. Pati, p. 8
59. Narain, pp 7-8
60. Brian Lapping, End of Empire, p. 65
61. Nateson, p. 273
62. G.A, Nateson, The Indian Demands: A Symposium on the memorandum of the Nineteen and Speeches at the Congress and Moslem League on their scheme of self-government for India, p. 52
63. Narain, p. 11
64. Francis Robinson, Separatism Among Indian Muslims: The Politics of the United Provinces Muslims 1860-1923

65. Palavi Bhatte, Transnational Ghadr Movement: A Diasporic Dimension, p. 166
66. Summary of the Administration of Lord Hardinge of Penshurst, p. 21
67. Husein, p. 178
68. The Indian Demands, Nateson, p. 77
69. Ibid
70. Ibid, p. 43
71. Ibid, p. 48
72. Kailash Chandra, Tragedy of Jinnah, p. 23
73. Ibid, pp. 23-24
74. Ibid, pp23-24
75. Nateson, Speeches and Writings of Annie Besant, p. 39
76. Lloyd George, War Memoirs, p. 1045
77. Simon Commission Report on India (India Statutory Commission) Volume 1, Report of the Indian Statutory Commission, Volume 1 p. 2
78. Ibid, p. 4
79. Eugene F. Irschick, Politics and Social Conflict in South India, the Non Brahmin Movement and Tamil Separatism, 1916-1929, p. 97
80. Husain, pp. 138-139
81. Ibid, pp. 138-139
82. Geoffrey West, The Life of Annie Besant, p. 240
83. Kaushik Roy The Indian Army in the Two World Wars, p. 339
84. M.K. Gandhi, An Autobiography: or the Story of My Experiments with Truth, p. 348
85. Geoffrey West, p. 241
86. Larry Collins, Dominique Lapiere, Freedom at Midnight: The Electrifying Story of India's Struggle for Independence, p. 459

5 'That remarkable man, Sir Salar Jung I'

1. L.S.S. O'Malley, The Indian Civil Service:1601-1930, p.228)
2. Ibid, pp. 4-5
3. Ibid, pp. 4-5
4. Ibid, p. 9
5. Dabhadhai Naoroji, Poverty and UnBritish Rule in India, p. 244
6. H.M. Hyndman, The Bankruptcy of India, An Enquiry into the Administration of India under the Crown, p. 32
7. Suresh Chandra Ghosh, The Social Condition of the British Community in Bengal: 1757-1800, p. 83
8. O'Malley, p. 236
9. J. Ramsay MacDonald, The Government of India, p. 99
10. Lajput Raj, Unhappy India, p. 429
11. Chunder Dutt, India in the Victorian Age, p. 193
12. Ibid, p. 186
13. O'Malley, p. 206

14. Professor A. Berriedale Keith, Speeches and Documents on Indian Policy, 1750-1921, Volume One, p. 273
15. Montgomery Martin, British India: Its recent Progress and Present State, p. 176
16. O'Malley, p. 208
17. Hyndman, p. 134
18. MacDonald, p. 101
19. O'Malley, p. 209
20. Queen Victoria's Proclamation, 1 November 1858
21. Ranbir Vohra, The Making of India, A Historical Survey, p. 93
22. O'Malley, p. 209
23. Hansard, vol. 185, p839, quoted in Poverty and UnBritish Rule in India, Dabhadhai Naoroji, p. 356
24. O'Malley, p. 211
25. V.B. Mishra, Evolution of Constitutional History of India, p. 32
26. Surendranath Banerjea, A Nation in Making, p. 31
27. Ibid, p. 31
28. Ibid, p. 32
29. Ibid, p. 29
30. Ibid, p. 29
31. Hansard, 23 August 1883, quoted in Poverty and UnBritish Rule in India, Dabhadhai Naoroji
32. Banerjea, p. 33
33. P. Rajeswar Rao, The Great Indian Patriots, p. 67
34. Banerjea, p. 41
35. Chander S. Sundaram, Indianisation, the Officer Corps, and the Indian Army, p. 39
36. Banerjea, p. 44
37. Ibid, p. 44
38. MacDonald, pp. 104-105
39. O'Malley, p. 216
40. Ibid, p216
41. Vohra, pp. 92-93
42. O'Malley, pp. 219-220
43. Ibid, p. 217
44. Theodore Monson, Imperial Rule in India, Being and Examination of the Principles Proper to the Government of Dependencies, p. 142
45. timesofindia.com
46. hindustantimes.com
47. qz.com
48. William Digby, Prosperous British India: A Revelation from Official Records, p. 114
49. B.D. Basu, History of Education in India, p. 165
50. O'Malley, p. 196
51. Ranbir Vohra, p. 92

52. David Turner, The Old Boys: The Decline and Rise of the Public Schools, p. 171
53. O'Malley, p. 222
54. Ibid, p. 251
55. Ibid, p. 253
56. Simon Commission Report on India (India Statutory Commission) Volume 1, Report of the Indian Statutory Commission, Volume 1 – Survey, p. 46
57. Wood, Ernest, An Englishman Defends Mother India, A Complete Constructive Reply to Mother India, p. 426
58. MacDonald, p. 106
59. O'Malley, p. 151
60. Ibid, p. 223
61. Will Durant, The Case for India, p. 26
62. M. Fathulla Khan, A History of Administrative Reforms in Hyderabad, p. 20
63. John F. Law, Modern Hyderabad (Deccan), p. 141
64. Ibid, p. 141
65. R. Paton McAuliffe, The Nizam, the Origin and Future of the Hyderabad State, p. 42
66. K.L. Gauba, Hyderabad or India, p. 34
67. Sarajoni Regani, Nizam-British Relations, pp. 214-219
68. Syed Abid, Whither Hyderabad, p. 8
69. Syed Hossain Bilgrami, Historical and Descriptive Sketch of HH the Nizam's Dominions, p. 139
70. M. Fathulla Khan, p. 24
71. Ibid, p27
72. Ibid, pp. 33-34
73. Law, p. 33
74. Sarajoni Regani, p. 292
75. Syed Hossein Bilgrami, A Memoir of Sir Salar Jung I, pp. 20-21
76. Law, p. 33
77. Ibid, p. 36
78. Macmillan's Magazine, Volume 79, Issue 473, March 1899 pp. 390-400
79. Bilgrami, p. 25
80. M. Fathulla Khan, p. 60
81. Bilgrami, p. 27
82. Gauba, p. 52
83. Bilgrami, pp 28-29
84. Ibid, p. 34
85. Law, p. 141
86. Dr Santosh Jaganath, A History of the Nizams Railways System, p. 31
87. Barbara N. Ramusack, The New Cambridge History of India, p. 109
88. Imperial Gazeteer of India, 1909, p. 61

89. Ibid, p. 74
90. Ibid, p. 76
91. Bilgrami, and Wilmott, p. 117
92. Bilgrami, p. 45-46
93. Jaganath, p. 31
94. Khan, p. 66
95. Ibid, p. 66
96. Bilgrami and Wilmott, p. 383
97. Imperial Gazeteer of India, 1909, p. 4
98. Ibid, p. 30
99. Syed Abid, p. 77
100. Ibid, p. 79
101. R. Paton McAuliffe, p. 52
102. Bilgrami, p. 66
103. Imperial Gazeteer of India, 1909, p. 66
104. Ibid, p. 52
105. Ramusack, p. 109
106. Ibid, p. 194
107. Ibid, p194
108. Syed Abid, p. 92
109. Gauba, p. 52
110. (Imperial Gazeteer of India, 1909, p. 53
111. Law, p. 51
112. Ibid, p. 51
113. Imperial Gazeteer of India, 1909, p. 54
114. Digby, p. 96
115. Law, p. 31
116. Syed Abid, p. 15

6 'Striving to bring about a revolution'

1. K.C. Wheare, The Statute of Westminster and Dominion Status, p. 22
2. Parker Thomas Moon, Imperialism and World Politics, pp. 302-308
3. Simon Commission Report on India (India Statutory Commission) Volume 2, Report of the Indian Statutory Commission, Volume 1 – Survey, p. 223
4. Ibid, p134)
5. Dabhadhai Naoroji, Poverty and UnBritish Rule in India, p. 192
6. Savel Zimand, Living India, p. 214
7. Nateson, pp. 471-472
8. Ibid, p. 434
9. Ibid, p. 435
10. James Morris, Farewell the Trumpets, p. 299
11. Hansard, House of Lords Debates, 5 April 1916, vol. 21, cc604-22
12. Ibid

13. The Journal of the Royal Society of Arts, no.3, vol. LXXI, Friday August 3, 1923, p. 645
14. Asiatic Review, vol.19, no.57, January 1923
15. The 1924 Exhibition Catalogue
16. L.C.B. Seaman, Post Victorian Britain: 1902-1951, p. 210
17. Jabez T. Sunderland, India in Bondage: Her Right to Freedom, p. 65
18. Seaman, p. 211
19. Report of the Reforms Enquiry Committee, 1924, p. 1
20. Ibid, p. 2
21. Ibid, pp. 34-35
22. Ibid, p. 35
23. Ibid, p. 2
24. Lajput Raj, Unhappy India, p. 467
25. Ibid, p. 468
26. Report of the Reforms Enquiry Committee, 1924, p. 201
27. Ibid, p. 203
28. Ibid, p. 2
29. Ibid, pp. 108-115
30. A.A. Ravoof, Meet Mr Jinnah, p. 98
31. Wheare, p. 28
32. Simon Commission Report on India (India Statutory Commission) Volume 1, Report of the Indian Statutory Commission, Volume 1 – Survey, p xvi
33. Chandra, p. 51
34. Important speeches of Jawaharlal Nehru: Being a collection of most significant speeches delivered by Nehru from 1922 to 1946, p. 141
35. Simon Commission Report on India (India Statutory Commission) Volume 1, Report of the Indian Statutory Commission, Volume 1 – Survey, pp. 137-137
36. Ibid, p. 200
37. Ibid, p. 200
38. Ibid, p. 198
39. Ibid, p. 198
40. Ibid, p. 25
41. Ibid, pp. 26-27
42. Ibid, p. 30
43. Ibid, p. 225
44. Ibid, p. 226
45. Ibid, pp. 28-29
46. Harold Nicolson, King George V: His Life and Reign, p. 506
47. Important speeches of Jawaharlal Nehru, p. 88
48. Ibid, p. 57
49. Ibid, p. 56
50. Ibid, pp. 154-155
51. Ibid, p. 129

52. Shabnum Tejani, Indian Secularism, A Social and Intellectual History, 1890-1950, p. 187
53. Ibid, p. 187
54. Will Durant, The Case for India, p. 156
55. Ibid, pp. 158-159
56. Michael Silvestri, Ireland and India, pp. 62-63
57. ibid
58. Documents on Irish Foreign Policy, difp.ie
59. Wheale, p. 131
60. Ibid, p. 127
61. 1931, New Zealand, Imperial Conference 1930, Summary of Proceedings, National Library of New Zealand, p. 12
62. J.M. Kenworthy, India: A Warning, p. 106
63. Chandra, p. 63
64. Kenworthy, p. 103
65. Ravoof, p. 92
66. R. Coupland, The Future of India, p. 177
67. Ravoof, p. 94
68. Elizabeth Surriyeh, Sufis and Anti-Sufis: The Defence, Rethinking and Rejection of Sufism in the Modern World, p. 136
69. Kenworthy, p. 110
70. Kailash Chandra, p. 69
71. Ibid, p. 76
72. Coupland, p. 176
73. Ibid, p. 176)
74. Chandra, p. 64
75. Wheale, p. 145
76. Syed Abid, Hasan, preface
77. Nicolson, p. 509
78. Kenton J. Clymer, Quest for Freedom: The United States and India's Independence, p. 9
79. Ravoof, p. 108
80. Criminal Law Amendment Act, 1932, Act No.23 of 1932
81. Important speeches of Jawaharlal Nehru, p. 97
82. Hugh Toye, The Springing Tiger: A Study of the Indian National Army and of Netaji Subhas Chandra Bos, p. 282
83. Kenworthy, p. 47
84. Important speeches of Jawaharlal Nehru, p. 89
85. Kenworthy, p. 27
86. Chandra, p. 133
87. Ravoof, p, 94
88. Philip Zeigler, Mountbatten: The Official Biography, p. 350
89. Martin Gilbert, Churchill: A Life, p. 507
90. Ibid, p. 538
91. Chandra, p. 139

92. Important speeches of Jawaharlal Nehru, pp. 300-301

7 'A new slave trade'

1. S.B. de Burgh-Edwardes The History of Mauritius: 1507-1914, p. 72
2. John Scobie, Hill Coolies, A Brief Exposure of the Deplorable Condition of the Hill Coolies in British Guiana and Mauritius, and of the Nefarious Means by which they were induced to Resort to these Colonies, p. 7
3. Ibid, p. 25
4. Ibid, p. 28
5. Ibid, pp 14-15
6. Ibid, p. 7
7. David Northrup, Indentured Labour in the Age of Imperialism: 1834-1922, p. 124
8. History Today, Volume 36, issue 4, April 1986, Basdeo Mangru
9. Scobie, p. 19
10. Northrup, p. 99
11. Edward Jenkins, The Coolie, p. 198
12. Scobie, pp. 14-15
13. Shiu Prasad, Indian Indentured Workers in Fiji, pp. 12-13
14. Scobie, p. 19
15. Ibid, p. 26
16. Daniel Hart, Trinidad and the other West Indian Islands, p. 121
17. Scobie, pp. 14-15
18. Hart, pp. 84-86
19. Jenkins, p. 280
20. Hart, p. 71
21. Jenkins, p. 289
22. Ibid, p. 233
23. Hart, p. 66
24. Prasad, pp. 19-23
25. Jenkins, pp. 288-289
26. de Burgh-Edwardes, p. 87
27. Ibid, p. 87
28. Caribbeanatlas.com, The Experience of Indian Indenture in Trinidad: Arrival and Settlement, Sherry-Ann Singh, Department of History, University of the West Indies, St. Augustine, Trinidad and Tobago
29. Prasad, p. 2
30. Lanka Sundaram, Indians Overseas, p. 117
31. Jenkins, p. 244
32. Ibid, p. 244
33. Scobie, p. 27
34. Philippa Levine, (Ed.) Gender and Empire, The Oxford History of the British Empire, Companion Series, p. 144

35. Thirty Years Mission Life in Jamaica: A Brief Sketch of Reverend Warrand Carlile, Missionary at Brownsville, By One of His Boys, p. 83

36. An Account of the Island of Mauritius and its Dependencies, by a late official resident, published by the author, p. 119

37. John D. Kelly, A Politics of Virtue, Hinduism, Sexuality and Counter Colonial Discourse in Fiji, p. 31

38. An Account of the Island of Mauritius and its Dependencies, p. 100

39. Edgar Mayhew Bacon and Eugene Murray Aaron The New Jamaica, pp. 99-100

40. Herbert Theodore Thomas, The Story of a West Indian Policeman: or Forty Seven Years in the Jamaica Constabulary, pp. 388-389

41. Hart, p. 66

42. Jenkins, p. 240

43. Hart, p. 71

44. Northrup, p. 135

45. Jenkins, p. 365

46. Ibid, p. 367

47. Sundaram, p. 100

48. Hart, p. 90

49. Dr Rebecca Tortello old-jamaica-gleaner.com, Pieces of the Past, Out of Many Cultures, The People Who Came, The Arrival of the Indians

50. Jamaica, Painted by A.S. Forrest, Described by John Henderson, p. 138

51. de Burgh-Edwardes, p. 72

52. Ibid, p. 73

53. Colonial Reports: Annual, No. 1731, Annual Report on the Social and Economic Progress of the People of Mauritius, 1934, p. 7

54. Ibid, p. 4

55. Sundaram, pp. 124-125

56. Ibid, p. 126

57. economist.com 2 September 2017, The Legacy of Indian Migration to European Colonies

58. L.E. Neame, The Asiatic Danger in the Colonies, p. 23

59. K.A. Neelakandha Aiyer, Indian Problems in Malaya, A Brief Survey in Relation to Emigration, p. 102

60. M.K. Gandhi, An Autobiography: or the Story of My Experiments with Truth, p. 295

61. S.A. Waiz, Indians Abroad, 2nd Edition, p. 559

62. Paul Kratoska, Ed., South East Asia Colonial History, Vol. III, High Imperialism (1890s-1930s), p. 180

63. Michael Adas, The Burma Delta: Economic development and Social Change on an Asian Rice Frontier, 1852-1941, p. 58

64. Ibid, p. 60

65. Medha Chaturvedi, Indian Migrants in Myanmar: Emerging Trends and Challenges, India Centre for Migration, p. 12

66. Adas, p. 85

67. Chaturvedi, Senior Fellow, India Centre for Migration, Ministry of Overseas Indian Affairs, p. 19
68. Ibid, p. 9
69. Ibid, p. 16
70. Kratoska, p. 179
71. Ibid, p. 179
72. Chaturvedi, p. 16
73. Ibid, p. 12
74. Ibid, p. 19
75. Kratoska, p. 179
76. Dr V. Suryanarayan Southasiaanalysis.org, South Asia Analysis Group, Paper No. 3523, 26 November 2009, The Indian Community in Maynmar
77. Geerken, Hitler's Asian Adventure, p. 122
78. Paul Kratoska, The Thailand-Burma Railway, p. 109
79. Chaturvedi, p. 23
80. R.O. Winstedt Malaya, The Straits Settlements and the Federated and Unfederated Malay Straits, p. 121
81. Winstedt, Malaya and its History, p. 7
82. J.F.A. McNair, Prisoners Their Own Warders, p. 39
83. (Winstedt, Malaya, The Straits Settlements and the Federated and Unfederated Malay Straits, p. 123
84. McNair p. 62
85. Ibid, p30
86. K.S. Sandhu and A. Mani, (Eds) Indian Communities in Southeast Asia, p. 156
87. Aiyer, p. 5
88. Ibid, p. 12
89. Christopher Sellers and Joseph Melling, Dangerous Trade, Histories of Industrial Hazard Across a Global World, p. 28
90. Aiyer, p. 23
91. Mohd. Taib Osman, (Ed.) Malaysian World View, Southeast Asian Studies Program, Institute of South east Asian Studies, Singapore, p. 150
92. Sandhu and Mani, p. 152
93. Osman, p. 150
94. Sellers and Melling, p. 28
95. Sandhu and Mani, p. 155
96. Ibid, p. 155
97. Ibid, p. 156
98. Osman, p. 151
99. Sellers and Melling, p. 22
100. Sandhu and Mani, p. 159
101. Aiyer, p. 6
102. Ibid, p. 19
103. Ibid, p. 20

104. Ibid, p. 28
105. Prakash C. Jain, Racial Discrimination Against Overseas Indians, p. 96
106. Sellers Melling, p. 29)
107. Ibid, p. 28
108. Ibid, p. 26
109. Ibid, p. 26
110. Ibid, p. 29
111. Aiyer, pp 57-58
112. Sellers and Melling, p. 29
113. Sandhu and Mani, pp. 195-196
114. Sundaram, p. 71
115. Jain, p. 102
116. Aiyer, p. 41
117. Sandhu and Mani, p. 208
118. Aiyer, p. 35
119. Osman, p. 151
120. Sandhu and Mani, p. 154
121. Jain, p. 116
122. Ibid, p. 103
123. Sandhu and Mani, p. 214

8 'Provide against an influx of Asiatics'

1. Elphick & Davenport (eds), Christianity in South Africa, p. 286
2. Rodney Ragwan, Vision in Progress, Framing the Portrait of Indian Baptists in South Africa, p. 127
3. Michael West, Indian Politics in South Africa: 1860 to the Present, South Asia Bulletin, vol. 7, p. 98
4. J.N. Uppal, Gandhi: Ordained in South Africa, p. 46
5. West, p.99
6. sahistory.org.za
7. Ragwan, p. 128
8. L.E. Neame, The Asiatic Danger in the Colonies, p. 17
9. Uppal, p. 50
10. Neame, pp. 32-34
11. Ibid, p. 47
12. Violet R. Markham, The South African Scene, p. 368
13. Lanka Sundaram, Indians Overseas, G.A. Nateson, p. 162
14. Neame, p. 27
15. Ibid, p. 27
16. Elphick & Davenport (eds), Christianity in South Africa, p. 286
17. sahistory.org.za
18. Markham, p. 368
19. Uppal, p. 27

20. M.K. Gandhi, An Autobiography: or the Story of My Experiments with Truth, p. 82
21. Jonathan Klaaren, From Prohibited Immigrants to Citizens, The Origins of Citizenship and Nationality in South Africa, p. 20
22. Ann Curthoys, Marilyn Lake (eds.) Connected Worlds, History in Transnational Perspective, p. 220
23. Proceedings of a Conference Between the Secretary of State for the Colonies and the Premiers of the Self-Governing Colonies at the Colonial Office London, June and July 1897, 31 July 1897, pp. 13-14
24. Julie Fry and Peter Wilson, Better Lives: Migration, Wellbeing and New Zealand, p. 12
25. Robert I. Rotberg, The Founder: Cecil Rhodes and the Pursuit of Power, p. 450
26. J. Scott Keltit, The Statesman's Yearbook, p. 170
27. Ibid, p. 170
28. Ilsen About et al (eds.) Identification and Registration Practices in Transnational Perspective, p. 185
29. Uppal, pp. 51-52
30. Klaaren, pp. 21-22
31. Ibid, pp. 21-22
32. Ibid, p. 27
33. Ibid, p27
34. Neame, p. 59
35. Markham, p. 330
36. Uppal, p. 152
37. Gandhi, p. 157
38. Ibid, p. 157
39. Klaaren, p. 22
40. Markham, p. 369
41. Klaaren, pp. 26-27
42. Ibid, p. 47
43. Markham, p. 371
44. Speeches and Writings of Annie Besant, pp. 259-260
45. The Indian Demands: A Symposium on the memorandum of the Nineteen and Speeches at the Congress and Moslem League on their scheme of self-government for India, pp. 141-142
46. Markham, p. 376
47. Ibid, p. 372
48. David Hardiman, The NonViolent Struggle for Indian Freedom: 1905-1919, p. 104
49. S.A. Waiz, Indians Abroad, p. 2
50. Ibid, p. 328
51. Ibid, p. 386
52. Ibid, p. 380

53. George Singh, The Asiatic Act, The Asiatic Land Tenure and Indian Representation Act of South Africa, A Brief Summary of its Background, Terms and Implications, p. 24

54. Thomas Borstelmann, Apartheid's Reluctant Uncle: The US and Southern Africa in the Early Cold War, p. 30

55. Sana Aiyer, Indians in Kenya, pp. 22-23

56. Jain, p. 138

57. Aiyer, pp. 22-23

58. Sundaram, p. 134

59. Robert R. Gregory Quest for Equality, p. 7

60. Anna Greenwood, Harshad Topiwala, Indian Doctors in Kenya – 1895-1940: The Forgotten History, p50.

61. Ibid, p. 50

62. Aiyer, p. 5

63. Jain, p. 138

64. Aiyer, p. 34

65. Ibid, p. 23

66. Ibid, p. 42

67. Re-Distribution from Above, The Politics of Land Rights and Squatting in Coastal Kenya, Karuti Kanyinga, Nordiska Afrikainstitut, Research Report No. 115, Uppsala, 2000, p. 37

68. Jain, p. 143

69. Aiyer, p. 35

70. Jain, p. 146

71. Aiyer, p. 43

72. Jain, p. 146

73. Greenwood &Topiwala, p. 64

74. Gregory, 1993, p. 22

75. Marjorie Ruth Dilley, British Policy in Kenya Colony, 2nd Edition, p. 142

76. Parliament of Kenya, The National Assembly, History of the Parliament of Kenya, Fact Sheet No. 24, The Clerk of the National Assembly, Nairobi, 2017

77. Aiyar, p. 22

78. Ibid, p. 44

79. Sundaram, p. 134

80. Sara Abdullah, Kenya at the Crossroads, p. 114

81. Waiz, pp. 3-4

82. Ibid, pp. 4-5

83. Ibid, p. 4

84. Greenwood & Topiwala, p. 66

85. Robert M. Maxon, Struggle for Kenya: The Loss and Reassertion of Imperial Initiative, 1912-1923, p. 166

86. Greenwood & Topiwala, p. 67

87. Dilley, p. 148

88. Ibid, p. 23

89. CP99 (23), Cabinet, Indians in Kenya, Memorandum by the Secretary of State for the Colonies, 3, February 1923, CAB24/158
90. Ibid
91. Ibid
92. Greenwood & Topiwala, p. 66
93. CP99 (23), Cabinet, Indians in Kenya, Memorandum by the Secretary of State for the Colonies, 3, February 1923, CAB24/158
94. Waiz, p. 218
95. Ibid, p. 6
96. Ibid, p. 10
97. CP99 (23), Cabinet, Indians in Kenya, Memorandum by the Secretary of State for the Colonies, 3, February 1923, Telegram from the Governor of Kenya to Secretary of State for the Colonies, CAB24/158
98. Ibid
99. Ibid
100. Ibid
101. Ibid
102. Ibid
103. Christopher P. Youe, Robert Thorne Coryndon, Proconsular Imperialism in Southern and Eastern Africa, 1897-1925, p. 169
104. Hansard, HC Debates, 25 July 1923 vol. 167, cc541-94
105. Youe, p. 171
106. Dilley, p. 175
107. Youe, p. 172
108. The Official Gazette of the Colony and Protectorate of Kenya – Special Edition – Vol XXV, No. 914, Nairobi, November 23, 1923
109. Ibid
110. Ibid
111. Youe, p. 173
112. Jain, p. 149
113. Ibid, p. 153
114. Waiz, p. 43
115. Ibid, p. 45
116. Ibid, pp. 45-46
117. Sundaram, p. 126
118. Ibid, p. 127
119. Waiz, p. 650
120. 1908 Continuous Passage Act
121. Speeches and Writings of Annie Besant, 3rd ed, p. 261
122. Neame, p. 7
123. Waiz, p. 663
124. Ibid, p. 659
125. Ibid, p. 659
126. Ibid, p. 662
127. Ibid, p. 664

128. Ibid, p. 664
129. Palavi Bhatte, Transnational Ghadr Movement: A Diasporic Dimension, Kyoto University Research Information Repository, February 2013, p. 168
130. Waiz, p. 671
131. Philip Jones and Anna Kenny, Australia's Muslim Cameleers, p. 153
132. James Jupp, The Australian People, An Encyclopedia of the Nation, p. 431
133. Myra Willard, History of White Australia Policy to 1920, p. 101
134. Alexander E. Davis, Rethinking Australia's International Past, p. 84
135. Brisbane Courier, 18 August 1883
136. National Museum of Australia
137. Australian Bureau of Statistics
138. Jupp, p. 432
139. A White Australia, the Kanaka Labour Question, *Herald* Investigation, Melbourne 1901, pp8-9
140. Ibid
141. Ibid
142. Geoffrey Partington, Making Sense of History, p. 133
143. Colorphobia, An Exposure of the "White Australia Fallacy", Gizen-no-Teki, 1903, p. 2
144. Ibid
145. Ibid
146. Speeches and Writings of Annie Besant, p. 242
147. National Museum of Australia
148. Federal Franchise Act 1902, 'Disqualification of Coloured Races'
149. Nahid Kabir, Muslims in Australia, Immigration, Race relations and Cultural History, p. 75
150. John Murphy, A Decent Provision: Australian Welfare Policy, 1870 to 1949, p. 99
151. Ibid, p. 101
152. Ibid, p. 99
153. Jupp, p. 432
154. Speeches and Writings of Annie Besant, p. 263
155. rnz.co.nz
156. teara.govt.nz
157. Om Prakash Dwivedi, Rodopi, Tracing the New Indian Diaspora, p. 124
158. teara.govt.nz
159. Ibid
160. parliament.nz
161. Proceedings of a Conference Between the Secretary of State for the Colonies and the Premiers of the Self-Governing Colonies at the Colonial Office London, June and July 1897, 31 July 1897, p. 14
162. Immigration Restriction Act No.83 1899
163. Jennifer S. Kain, Insanity and Immigration Control in New Zealand and Australia: 1860-1930, p. 102)

164. Statistics New Zealand, 3.stats.govt.nz, Results of a Census of the Colony of New Zealand Taken for the Night of the 29th April 1906

165. Sir Arthur P. Douglas, The Dominion of New Zealand, p. 286

166. P.S. O'Connor, Keepin. g New Zealand White: 1908-1920, Article for the University of Auckland, p48

167. Ibid

168. Auckland City Labour Market Research Report, Migration and Auckland City, Mattia G. Barbera, February 2010, p13

169. O'Connor, p. 47

170. New Zealand Parliamentary Debates, First Session, Twentieth Parliament, Legislative Council and House of Representatives, 197th Volume, Comprising the Period From August 6 to September 24 1920, Wellington, by Authority, Marcus F. Marks, Government Printer, 1920, p905

171. O'Connor, pp48, 54-55

172. New Zealand Parliamentary Debates, First Session, Twentieth Parliament, Legislative Council and House of Representatives, 197th Volume, Comprising the Period from August 6 to September 24 1920, Wellington, by Authority, Marcus F. Marks, Government Printer, 1920, p905

173. O'Connor, p. 60

174. Ibid, p. 62

175. Auckland City Labour Market Research Report, Migration and Auckland City, Mattia G. Barbera, February 2010, p13

176. (Speeches and Writings of Annie Besant, p. 462

177. Jain, p. 150

178. exodus2013.co.uk

179. Tanja Bueltmann, Scottish Ethnicity and the Making of New Zealand Society, 1950-1930, p. 29

180. Stephen Constantine, Emigrants and Empire, British Settlement in the Dominions between the Wars, p. 1

181. Bueltmann, p. 29

182. Savel Zimand, Living India, p. 188

183. Ian R.G. Spencer, British Immigration Policy since 1939, The Making of Multi-Racial Britain, p. 5

184. Ibid, pp5-6

185. Ibid, p. 6

186. Census of India – Volume I, J.H. Hutton

9 'A bulwark of British rule in India'

1. Important Speeches of Jawaharlal Nehru, being a collection of most significant speeches delivered by Jawaharlal Nehru from 1922 to 1946, p. 71

2. W.P. (41) 274, 19 November 1941, War Cabinet Conclusions 115 (41) of 17 November 1941. Minute 4(2) CAB 66/19

3. War Cabinet, Chiefs of Staff Committee, Visit of Dominion Ministers, Review of Strategic Situation, 24 October 1939, CAB 66/3

4. Dr Saroja Sundararaja, Kalpaz, Kashmir Crisis, Unholy Anglo-Pak Nexus, p. 72

5. Ibrahim M. Abu-Raki,The Blackwell Companion to Contemporary Islamic Thought, p. 179

6. D.N. Banerjee, Partition or Federation? A study in the Indian Constitutional Problem, p. 16

7. B.R. Nanda,Road to Pakistan: The Life and Times of Mohammed Ali Jinnah, p. 282

8. Banerjee, p. 27

9. Christopher Thorne, Allies of a Kind, p. 62

10. Banerjee, p. 99

11. Ibid, pp. 113-117

12. Telegram from Viceroy to Secretary of State for India dated June 10, 1940, CAB66/10

13. Memorandum by the Secretary of State for India, 20 July 1940, WP (40) 272, CAB 66/10

14. Telegram from Governor-General to Secretary of State, dated July 4, 1940, 1223-S CAB66/10

15. Ibid

16. Telegram from Governor-General to Secretary of State dated July 5, 1940 1245-S, CAB66/10

17. Telegram from Governor-General to Secretary of State dated July 4, 1940 1218-S, relating opinion of Governor of Sind, CAB66/10

18. Telegram from Governor-General to Secretary of State dated July 14, 1940 1225-S, relating opinion of Governor of Sind, of 3 July, CAB66/10

19. WP (40) 294, July 30 1940, War Cabinet India, Memorandum by the Prime Minister. Telegram from the Prime Minister to the Viceroy dated July 28 1940 CAB 66/10

20. Banerjee, pp. 128-131

21. Richard L. Johnson, Gandhi's Experiments with Truth: Essential Writings by and About Mahatma Gandhi, p. 41

22. Important Speeches of Jawaharlal Nehru, being a collection of most significant speeches delivered by Jawaharlal Nehru from 1922 to 1946, p. 74

23. Telegram from Government of India Home Department to Secretary of State for India, dated 29 November 1940 CAB66/14

24. Clause 3 of the Atlantic Charter

25. Thorne, p. 61

26. Ibid, p. 61

27. Ibid, p. 62

28. The Atlantic Charter A Criticism, Parliamentary Peace Aims Group (Members of the Labour Party), House of Commons, 1941, p. 4

29. Telegram from Viceroy to Secretary of State for India, dated November 1, 1941. WO (41) 271, CAB 66/19

30. Telegram from Governor-General to Secretary of State for India, dated November 12, 1941, WO (41) 271, CAB 66/19

31. Telegram from Prime Minister to Viceroy, dated November 21, 1941, WO (41) 271, CAB 66/19
32. India: Release of Satygrahi Prisoners. Memorandum by the Secretary of State for India, covering further telegrams from the Viceroy, WP 942), CAB 66/19
33. Banerjee, p. 100
34. War Cabinet, The Indian Political Situation, Memorandum by the Secretary of State for India, WP (42) 42, CAB66/21
35. Telegram from the Viceroy to Secretary of State for India, dated 21 January 1942, WO (42) 43, CAB 66/21
36. Telegram from the Viceroy to Secretary of State for India, dated 21 January 1942, WO (42) 43, CAB 66/21
37. Telegram from the Viceroy to Secretary of State for India, dated 21 January 1942, WO (42) 43, CAB 66/21
38. War Cabinet, India's War Effort, Memorandum by the Secretary of State for Indian, 30 January 1942, WP (42) 54, CAB 66/21
39. Hansard: House of Lords Debate, 3 February 1942, vol. 121, cc 582-638
40. Food Crisis, Inflation and Political Control in Punjab (1940-1947), Sukhdev Singh Sohal, Journal of Punjab Studies, vol.20, 2013, p. 256
41. Telegram from Commander-in-Chief India to War Office, 3062/G 14/2, 15 February 1942 CAB66/22
42. Cypher telegram from Secretary of State to Viceroy dated 19 February 1942 WS 18514/18222, CAB66/22
43. Telegram from Governor-General to Secretary of State for India, 26 February 1942, CAB66/22
44. WP (42) 177, CAB66/24, April 25 1942, War Cabinet, Report on the Fall of Singapore
45. Ibid
46. WP (42) 264, CAB66/25, June 22 1942, War Cabinet, Treatment of War Criminals, Annex No.5 Extract from Parliamentary Debates (House of Commons), March 10, 1942 Hong Kong (Japanese Barbarities)
47. Telegram from Secretary of State for India to Viceroy, dated 28 February 1942, WP (42) 106, 2 March 1942, CAB66/22
48. Telegram from Viceroy to Secretary of State for India, dated 28 February 1942, No.481-S, CAB66/22
49. Banerjee, p. 131
50. WP (42) 132, 3 April 1942, War Cabinet Communist Party, Statement made by Mr Harry Pollitt on 14 March and circulated by the Communist Party. Speaking on behalf of the Central Committee of the Communist Party in the Brangwyn Hall Swansea on Saturday March 14th, CAB66/23
51. WP (42) 255, CAB66/25, 16th March 1942, War Cabinet, Policy to be adopted towards Mr Gandhi, memorandum by the Secretary of State for India
52. Ibid
53. Ibid

54. Ibid
55. R. Coupland, The Future of India, p. 145
56. WP (42) 283, July 6 1942, War Cabinet Report on Mission to India, Memorandum by the Lord Privy Seal, CAB66/26
57. Ibid
58. Coupland, p. 83
59. Ibid, p. 83
60. WP (42) 283, July 6 1942, War Cabinet Report on Mission to India, Memorandum by the Lord Privy Seal, CAB66/26
61. Banerjee, pp. 94-95
62. Coupland, OUP, 1944, p. 156
63. Telegram from Viceroy to Secretary of State for India, 5 April 1942, CAB66/23
64. Telegram from Viceroy to Secretary of State for India, 6 April 1942, 912-S, CAB66/23
65. Telegram from Viceroy to Secretary of State for India, 6 April 1942 No.9128, CAB66/23
66. Telegram from Commander-in-Chief India to the War Office, 6 April 1942 8230/C, Private for Prime Minister from General Wavell, CAB66/23
67. Telegram No.607 from General Smuts to Prime Minister, 4 April 1942, CAB6623
68. Brian Lapping, End of Empire, p. 87
69. Telegram from Viceroy to Secretary of State for India, 6 April 1942, 919-S, WP (42) 149, CAB66/23
70. WP (42) 138, 1st April 1942, War Cabinet India, Telegrams exchanged between the Lord Privy Seal and the Prime Minister, CAB66/23
71. Important speeches of Jawaharlal Nehru. p. 221
72. Y.G. Bhave, The Mahatma and the Muslims, p. 45
73. Arun Chandra Bhuyan, Quit India, p. 30
74. WP (42) 138, 1st April 1942, War Cabinet India, Telegrams exchanged between the Lord Privy Seal and the Prime Minister, CAB66/23
75. Evacuation of Indians from Burma, memorandum by the Secretary of State for Burma, 11 April 1942, WP (42) 160, CAB66/23
76. Bhuyan, p. 34
77. WP (42) 255, CAB66/25, 16th March 1942, War Cabinet, Policy to be adopted towards Mr Gandhi, memorandum by the Secretary of State for India, Appendix II, All-India Congress Committee War resolution May 1st 1942, original draft of Congress War Resolution as put to Working Committee on 27 April
78. WP (42) 255, CAB66/25, 16th March 1942, War Cabinet, Policy to be adopted towards Mr Gandhi, memorandum by the Secretary of State for India, Appendix III, Recent Utterance of Gandhi
79. Bhuyan, 1975, p48)
80. Ravoof, p. 152

81. Bhuyan, p. 56
82. WP (42) 271, CAB66/26 Policy to be adopted towards Mr Gandhi, Telegram from Governor-General to Secretary of State for India, June 28 1942
83. WP (42) 271, CAB66/26 Policy to be adopted towards Mr Gandhi, Telegram from Governor-General to Secretary of State for India, June 28 1942
84. Bhuyan, p. 65
85. Telegram from C-in-C India to War Office (18 August 1942) No.19842/1, WO 208/761A
86. Bhuyan, p. 80
87. Ibid, p238)
88. Thorne, p. 236
89. Ibid, p. 356
90. WP (43) 40, January 25, 1943, War Cabinet Report for the Month of December 1942 for the Dominions, India, Burma and the Colonies and Mandated Territories, CAB66/28
91. Coupland, p. 11
92. Ibid, p. 11
93. Banerjee, p. 131
94. S.N. Sen, History of the Freedom Movement in India, p. 309
95. Ronald Lewin, The Chief, Field Marshal Lord Wavell, Commander-in-Chief and Viceroy, 1939-1947, p. 288
96. S.N. Sen, History of Modern India, p. 309
97. Lewin, Farar, p. 288
98. GS Chhabra, Advanced Study in the History of Modern India, Vol. III (1920-1947) pp. 167-168
99. Sen, p. 208
100. Menon, p. 163

10 This is the Last Indian Army Order

1. Lt-Col E.G. Phythian Adams The Madras Soldier, 1746-1946, p. 7
2. Syed Hussain Shaheed Soherwordi, Edinburgh Papers in South Asian Studies No.24 (2010), The Punjabisation of the British Indian Army, 1857-1947 and the Advent of Military Rule in Pakistan, School of History and Classics, University of Edinburgh, p. 2
3. Ibid, pp. 2-3
4. Colonel John Studholme Hodgson, Opinions on the Indian Army, p. 36
5. Kim A. Wagner, The Skull of Alum Bheg, p. 15
6. Indiandefencereview.com, 10 April 2018, Sumit Walia
7. Michael H. Fisher, Migration, A World History, p. 81
8. H. Dodwell, Sepoy Recruitment in the Old Madras Army, pp. 19-20
9. Ibid, p. 37
10. Ibid, p. 15

11. Captain Bryce, Our Indian Army, p. 13
12. Ibid
13. Lt-General Sir Charles Napier, Defects, Civil and Military of the Indian Government, p. 29
14. Lt-Col. W. Sleeman, Rambles and Recollections of an Indian Official, p. 189
15. The Marquess of Anglesey, A History of the British Cavalry, p. 134
16. Bryce, p. 20
17. Wagner, 2017, p. 16
18. Napier, p. 243
19. Ibid, p. 244
20. Ibid, p. 244
21. Pythian-Adams, p. 77
22. Captain Walter Badenach, Inquiry into the State of the Indian Army, p. 106
23. Ibid, p. 109
24. Napier, p. 233
25. Pradeep P. Barua, Gentlemen of the Raj, Prauger, p. 5
26. Napier, p. 255
27. Ibid, p. 257
28. David Omissi, The Sepoy and the Raj, p. 103
29. Badenach, p. 30
30. Napier, pp. 239-240
31. Report Upon the Military Cantonments of Kamptee and Seetabuldee, Surgeon- Major J.L. Ranking, 1869, p. 52
32. Ibid, p. 51
33. Wagner, p. 20
34. Napier, p. 233
35. Omissi, p. 3
36. Studholme Hodgson, p. 37
37. Ibid, p. 40
38. Bryce, p. 23
39. Lady Sale, A Journal of the Disasters in Afghanistan: 1841-1842, Vol II, pp. 7-10
40. Ibid, p. 27
41. Ibid, p. 14
42. Ibid, p. 27
43. Ibid, p. 11
44. Chunder Dutt, India in the Victorian Age, p. 17
45. Arnold P. Kaminsky, The India Office 1880-1910, p. 110
46. Wagner, p. 24
47. Pythian-Adams, p. 77
48. Napier, p. 60
49. Pythian-Adams OBE, Superintendent Government Press, p. 78
50. Andrew J. Rotter, Empires of the Senses, p. 53
51. Ibid, p. 54
52. Ibid, p. 54

53. Rotter, p. 53
54. Vinayak Savarkar, The Indian War of Independence of 1857, p. 89
55. Ibid, p. 89
56. Ibid, p. 89
57. Christopher Hibbert, The Great Mutiny, India 1857, p. 389
58. Syed Hossain Bilgrami, B.A. and C. Wilmott, Historical and Descriptive Sketch of HH the Nizam's Dominions, vol. 1, pp. 116-117
59. Hodgson, pp. 7-8
60. Omissi, p. 8
61. Tan Tai Yong, The Garrison State, p. 52
62. Ibid, p. 55
63. Napier, p. 29
64. Ibid, p. 29
65. Ibid, p. 30
66. Soherwordi, p. 4
67. Barua, 2003, p. 3
68. Ibid, p. 6
69. Ibid, p. 6
70. Dabhadhai Naoroji, Poverty and UnBritish Rule in India, p. 441
71. Theodore Monson, Imperial Rule in India, Being and Examination of the Principles Proper to the Government of Dependencies, p. 143
72. Soherwordi, p. 23
73. Speeches and Writings of Annie Besant, pp. 296-297
74. Soherwordi, p. 15
75. Captain Harold Maurice Grant, History of the War in South Africa: 1899-1902, Compiled by the Direction of His Majesty's Government, Vol. VI, p. 673
76. Edgar Sanderson, The Fight for the Flag in South Africa: A History of the War From the Boer Ultimatum to the Advance of Lord Roberts, p. 94
77. Lt. Col. Dr Shyam Narain Saxena, Role of the Indian Army in the First World War, Bhauna, pp. 117-118
78. F.W. Perry, The Commonwealth Armies, Manpower and Organisation in Two World Wars, p. 85
79. Paul Kendall, The Battle of Neuve-Chapelle: Britain's Forgotten Offensive, p. 12
80. Ibid, p. 20
81. Allan Mallinson,1914: Fight the Good Fight, Britain, the Army and the Coming of the First World War, pp. 495-496
82. Saxena, p. 2
83. Martin Gilbert, The First World War, p. 95
84. Saxena, pp. 21-22
85. Ibid, p. 17
86. Ibid, p. 32
87. Gilbert, p. 245
88. Saxena, p. 52

89. Pati, p. 19
90. Saxena, p. 58
91. E.W.C. Sanders, In Kut and Captivity: With the Sixth Indian Division, p. 319
92. Gilbert, p. 245
93. abc.net.au
94. Saxena, p. 40
95. abc.net.au
96. Saxena, Bhauna, Prakashan, pp. 84-85
97. Pati, p. 30
98. Saxena, p. 71
99. Ibid, pp. 72-74
100. Ibid, p. 188
101. Gilbert, pp. 130-131
102. Report of the Army in India Committee 1919-1920, p. 4
103. Ibid, p. 13
104. Barua, p. 91
105. Saxena, p. 127
106. Saxena, p. 27
107. Barua, p. 90
108. Ibid, p. 91
109. East India Constitutional Reforms, Report on Indian Constitutional Reforms to both Houses of Parliament by Command of His Majesty, HMSO London, 1918, p. 261
110. Ibid, p. 263
111. List of Etonians who Fought in the Great War MCM – MCMXIX
112. Saxena, p. 127
113. Ibid, p. 130
114. Zimand, Living India, p. 194
115. Philip Warner, Auchinleck: The Lonely Soldier, The Truth about Britain's Foremost Commander, pp. 249-250
116. B.R. Ambedkar, Pakistan or Partition of India, p. 69
117. Ibid, p. 65
118. Ibid, p. 66
119. WP (42) 54, War Cabinet, India's War Effort, Memorandum by the Secretary of State for India, 30 January 1942, CAB 66/21
120. WP (43) 197, May 10 1943, War Cabinet, Subversive attempts on the loyalty of the Indian Army, Memorandum by the Secretary of State for India, CAB66/36
121. WP (42) 107, 2 March 1942, War Cabinet Indian Policy Memorandum by the Secretary of State for India, covering a note by Major-General R.M.M. Lockhart, CIE, MC, CAB 66/22
122. War Cabinet, Indian Policy memorandum by Secretary of State for India, 8 March 1942, WP (42)116, CAB66/22
123. WP (42) 177, CAB66/24, April 25 1942, War Cabinet, Report on the Fall of Singapore

124. S.A. Ayer, Story of the INA, p. 30
125. Ibid, p. 33
126. Ibid, p. 39
127. Lord Russell, The Knights of Bushido, p. 141
128. Daniel Marston, The Indian Army and the end of the Raj, p. 124
129. Perry, p. 119
130. Marston, p. 125
131. Ibid, p. 124
132. Ibid, p. 126
133. Harkirat Singh, The Indian National Army Trial and the Raj, p. 38
134. Ibid, pp. 39-40
135. Ibid, p. 50
136. Warner, pp. 249-250
137. Important speeches of Jawaharlal Nehru: Being a collection of most significant speeches delivered by Nehru from 1922 to 1946, pp. 159-160
138. Singh, p. 50
139. Marston, p. 131
140. Important speeches of Jawaharlal Nehru, pp. 322-323
141. M.S. Gill, Trials than Changed History, From Socrates to Saddam Hussain, p. 190
142. Warner, p. 263
143. Philip Zeigler, Mountbatten: The Official Biography, p. 389
144. Warner, p. 269
145. Alan Campbell-Johnson, Mission with Mountbatten, p. 109
146. C. Christine Fair, Fighting to the End, p. 57
147. Ibid, p. 56.
148. Ibid, p. 56
149. Larry Collins, Dominique Lapiere, Freedom at Midnight: The Electrifying Story of India's Struggle for Independence, p. 340
150. Record of Conversation between Lord Ismay and Mr Jinnah at Karachi on 3 October 1947, DO 121/69
151. globalsecurity.org
152. Soherwordi, p. 28)
153. pakistanarmy.gov.pk
154. pakistanarmy.gov.pk
155. Fair, p. 56
156. pakistanarmy.gov.pk
157. Warner, p. 290
158. National Army Museum, NAM,1951-05-87-1

11 'I would rather be killed with bullets'

1. Summary of the Principles Measures of the Viceroyalty of the Marquess of Lansdowne in the Department of Revenue and Agriculture, December 1888 to January 1894, p. 16

2. Kali Charan Ghosh, Famines in Bengal: 1770-1943, p. 1
3. Romesh Dutt, K. The Economic History of India Under British Rule, from the Rise of British Power in 1757 to the Accession of Queen Victoria in 1837, p. 5
4. Ibid, p. 53
5. Dabhadhai Naoroji, Poverty and UnBritish Rule in India, p. 244
6. Summary of the Principles Measures of the Viceroyalty of the Marquess of Lansdowne in the Department of Revenue and Agriculture, December 1888 to January 1894, p. 16
7. John Dacosta, The Effects of Periodical Revisions of Land Tax in India, p. 3
8. Dutt, p.xi
9. Summary of the Principles Measures of the Viceroyalty of the Marquess of Lansdowne in the Department of Revenue and Agriculture, December 1888 to January 1894, p. 16
10. Jadunath Sarkar, Economics of British India, p. 93
11. Pramathanath Banerjee, A History of Indian Taxation, p. 253
12. Ibid, p. 254
13. Ibid, p. 252
14. Banerjee, p. 255
15. Ibid, p. 288
16. D.R. Banaji, Slavery in British India, p. 47
17. Ibid, p. 4
18. Ibid, p. 69
19. Ibid, p. 48
20. Banerjee, p. 226
21. William Digby, Prosperous British India: A Revelation from Official Records, p. 123
22. Kali Charan Ghosh, Famines in Bengal: 1770-1943, p. 3
23. Dutt, p. vi
24. Digby, p. 320
25. Dutt, p. 72
26. J. Ramsay MacDonald, The Government of India, p. 138
27. Savel Zimand, Living India, p. 171
28. Jadunath Sarkar, Economics of British India, p. 77
29. Ibid, p. 231
30. Reverend J. Long, Evidence Explanatory of the Indigo System of Lower Bengal, p. 12
31. Ibid, p. 15
32. Ibid, p. 62
33. Ibid, p. 56
34. Ibid, p. 82
35. Ibid, p. 17
36. Ibid, p. 14
37. Ibid, pp. 1-2

38. Ibid, p. 59
39. Subhas Bhattacharya, Digital South Asia Library, Social Scientist, V5 No.60 (July 1977) The Indigo Revolt of Bengal, p. 20
40. Montgomery Martin, British India: Its recent Progress and Present State, p. 291
41. S.N. Send, History of the Freedom Movement in India, p. 42
42. Banerjee, p. 285
43. H.M. Hyndman,The Bankruptcy of India, An Enquiry into the Administration of India under the Crown, pp. 69-70
44. Banerjee, p. 290
45. Hyndman, p. 67
46. John Dacosta, The Rt. Hon. Henry Fawcett MP on the Nationalisation of the Land, and the Land Question in India, p. 10
47. Digby, p. 83
48. Ibid, p. 85
49. John Dacosta, Facts and Fallacies Regarding Irrigation as a Prevention of Famine in India, p. 2
50. Ibid, p. 3
51. Ibid, pp. 10-11
52. John Dacosta, The Effects of Periodical Revisions of Land Tax in India, p. 3
53. John Dacosta, The Rt. Hon. Henry Fawcett MP on the Nationalisation of the Land, and the Land Question in India, p. 8
54. Summary of the Principles Measures of the Viceroyalty of the Marquess of Lansdowne in the Department of Revenue and Agriculture, December 1888 to January 1894, p. 23
55. Alfred Deakin, Irrigated India, An Australian View of India and Their Irrigation and Agriculture, p. 129
56. Summary of the Principles Measures of the Viceroyalty of the Marquess of Lansdowne in the Department of Revenue and Agriculture, December 1888 to January 1894, p. 16
57. Ibid, p. 16
58. Ibid, p. 28
59. Nalinaksha Saryal, Development of Indian Railways, p. 134
60. Dabhadhai Naoroji,Poverty and UnBritish Rule in India, p. 340
61. Ibid, p. 573
62. Laxman D. Satya,British Imperial Railways in Nineteenth Century South Asia, Economic and Political Weekly, p. 76
63. Hyndman, Swan, p. 60
64. Ernest Wood, An Englishman Defends Mother India, A Complete Constructive Reply to Mother India pp. 394-395
65. Sarkar, p. 245
66. Martin, p. 292
67. Hyndman, p. 162
68. Sarkar, p. 198
69. Ibid, p. 199

70. Hyndman, Swan, p. 61
71. Sarkar, p. 182
72. Digby, p. 106
73. Ibid, p. 107
74. Deakin, p. 117
75. Hyndman, p. 63
76. Summary of the Principles Measures of the Viceroyalty of the Marquess of Lansdowne in the Department of Revenue and Agriculture, December 1888 to January 1894, p. 36
77. Digby, p. 371
78. M. Azzizal Huque, The Man Behind the Plough, pp. 18-19
79. Ibid, p. 15
80. Richard Stevenson, Bengal Tiger and British Lion: An Account of the Famine of 1943, p. 15
81. Famine Enquiry Commission on Bengal, Chairman Sir John Woodhead, 1944, p. 7
82. Ibid, p. 5
83. Mark B. Tauger, The Indian Famine Crisis of World War Two, British Scholar, vol.1, Issue 2, March 2009, p. 177
84. Ibid, p. 178
85. Famine Commission Report, Minority Report, Minute by M. Afzul Husain, p. 194
86. Tauger, p. 187
87. Famine Enquiry Commission on Bengal, p. 5
88. Ibid, p. 25
89. Ibid, p. 18
90. M. Afzul Husain, in his Minute of Dissent to the Family Enquiry Commission chaired by John Woodhead, p. 198
91. Sukhdev Singh Sohal, Food Crisis, Inflation and Political Control in Punjab (1940-1947), Journal of Punjab Studies, vol.20, 2013, pp. 255-256
92. Hansard: House of Commons debate 21 January 1943, vol. 386, cc276-7
93. WP (43) 63, 13th February 1943, War Cabinet: Cereals for the Indian Ocean Area. Note by Minister of War Transport) CAB66/34
94. WP (43) 170, April 22 1943, War Cabinet Report for the Month of March for the Dominions, India, Burma and the Colonies and Mandated Territories, report by the Secretary of State for India. CAB66/36
95. Tauger, p. 183
96. WP (43) 345, 30th July 1943, War Cabinet, India's Requirements of Imported Food Grains, Report by the Shipping Committee. CAB66/39
97. WP (43) 349, 31 July 1943, War Cabinet, India's Requirement of Imported Food Grains, Memorandum by Secretary of State for India CAB66/39

98. WP (43) 393, 10th September 1943, War Cabinet, Indian Food Situation, Memorandum by the Secretary of State for India. CAB66/40

99. WP (43) 393, 10th September 1943, War Cabinet, Indian Food Situation, Memorandum by the Secretary of State for India, CAB66/40

100. WP (43) 411, 22nd September 1943, War Cabinet, Economic Situation in India, Memorandum by the Secretary of State for India CAB66/41

101. WP (43) 411, 22nd September 1943, War Cabinet, Economic Situation in India, Memorandum by the Secretary of State for India CAB66/41

102. Ibid

103. WP (43) 450 (Revised), 8th October 1943, War Cabinet, India, Note by the Prime Minister and Minister of defence. The attached Directive to the Viceroy-Designate has now been approved by the War Cabinet, CAB66/41)

104. WP (43) 493, 1st November 1943, War Cabinet, Canadian Gift of Wheat to India, Memorandum by Secretary of State for India, CAB66/42

105. Ibid

106. Ibid

107. WP (43) 495, 26th October 1942, War Cabinet, Report for the Month of October for the Dominions, India, Burma and the Colonies and Mandated Territories. CAB66/42

108. WP (43) 493, 1st November 1943, War Cabinet, Canadian Gift of Wheat to India, Memorandum by Secretary of State for India CAB66/42

109. Ibid

110. Hansard HC Debate, 4 November 1943, Vol. 393

111. Hansard HC Debate, 4 November 1943, Vol. 393

112. M. Afzul Husain, in his Minute of Dissent to the Family Enquiry Commission

113. Famine Enquiry Commission on Bengal, p. 62

114. Ibid, p. 72

115. WP (43) 504, 4th November 1943, War Cabinet, Shipment of Food Grains to India, Memorandum by Secretary of State to India. CAB66/43

116. WP (43) 504, 4th November 1943, War Cabinet, Shipment of Food Grains to India, Memorandum by Secretary of State to India. CAB66/43

117. WP (43) 584, 26th December 1943, War Cabinet, Report for the Month of November 1943 for the Dominions, India, Burma and the Colonies and Mandated Territories. CAB66/44

118. Ibid

119. WP (44) 18, 10 January 1944, War Cabinet India, Proposed Suspension of the Bengal Ministry and Assumption of Powers by the Governor under Section 93 of the Government of India Act, Memorandum by the Secretary of State for India. CAB66/45

120. Ibid

121. WP (44) 55, 25 January 1944, War Cabinet, Report for the Month of December 1943 for the Dominions, India, Burma and the Colonies and Mandated Territories, CAB66/46

122. Extract from Conclusion of Gregory Food Grains Policy Committee 1944 – Chapter 4, p519, CAB66/46

123. WP (44) 99, 11th February 1944, War Cabinet, Indian Food Grain Requirements, Report by the President of the Board of Education, CAB66/46

124. WP (44) 165, 18th March 1944, War Cabinet, Situation in India, Report from Chiefs of Staff. CAB66/48

125. WP (44) 228, 27th April 1944, War Cabinet, Indian Food Situation, Memorandum by the Home Secretary [Herbert Morrison] CAB66/49

126. WP (44) 351, 27th June 1944, War Cabinet, Shipment of Food Grains to India, Memorandum by the Secretary of State for India, CAB66/52

127. WP (44) 326, Government House Calcutta, 20 May 1944, addressed to WSC, from Governor or Bengal R.G. Casey, CAB66/51

128. Benjamin Siegal, Hungry Nation, p. 58

129. Penderel Moon, Wavell, The Viceroy's Journal, p. 251

130. WP (44) 562, 10th October 1944, War Cabinet, Indian Food Situation, Sir Henry French's visit to India, Memorandum of the Secretary of State for India, CAB66/56

131. Ibid

132. Ibid

133. Ibid

134. WP (44) 212, 1st April 1945, War Cabinet, Report for the Dominions, India, Burma and the Colonies and Mandated Territories, CAB66/64

135. WP (45) 264, 20th April 1945, War Cabinet, Report for the Month of March 1945 for the Dominions, India, Burma and the Colonies and Mandated Territories, CAB66/65

136. CP (45) 88, 26th July 1945, Cabinet, Report for the Month of June 1945 for the Dominions, India, Burma and the Colonies and Mandated Territories, CAB66/67

137. Important speeches of Jawaharlal Nehru: Being a collection of most significant speeches delivered by Nehru from 1922 to 1946, p. 248

138. M.S. Ventakataramani, Bengal Famine of 1943: the American Response, p. 63

139. The Agreement Creating the UNRRA, National Planning Association Pamphlets, 31-32, February 28 1944

140. *New York Times*, 27 November 1943

141. WP (44) 118, 19th February 1944, War Cabinet, Committee of Food Grain Requirements, REPORT, CAB66/47

142. Stevenson, p. 166

12 Patience, Cooperation, Stability

1. R. Coupland, The Future of India, p. 4
2. Penderel Moon, Wavell, The Viceroy's Journal, p. 97
3. Ronald Lewin, The Chief, Field Marshal Lord Wavell, Commander-in-Chief and Viceroy, 1939-1947, p. 235
4. Moon, p. 168
5. Martin Gilbert, Churchill: A Life, p. 877
6. Moon, p. 170
7. David Thomson, England in the Twentieth Century, p. 231
8. Extract from a statement by Mr Jinnah, dated 6 December 1945 CAB 127/136
9. Letter from Muhammed Ali Jinnah to Sir Richard Stafford Cripps, New Delhi, 9 February 1946 CAB 127/136
10. WP (43) 199, May 11, 1943, War Cabinet, The Application of Democratic Principles of Government, Memorandum by the Deputy Prime Minister, CAB66/36
11. Professor Friedrich, in 'The Crisis of the National State – 1943 -, quoted in the prologue of Pakistan or Partition of India, B.R. Ambedkar
12. WP (43) 199, May 11, 1943, War Cabinet, The Application of Democratic Principles of Government, Memorandum by the Deputy Prime Minister CAB66/36
13. Hansard, House of Commons debate, 15 March 1946, Vol.420, cc1413-761413
14. Important speeches of Jawaharlal Nehru: Being a collection of most significant speeches delivered by Nehru from 1922 to 1946, p. 256
15. Moon, p. 245
16. Ibid, p. 271
17. Ibid, p. 348
18. Ibid, p. 353
19. Ibid, p. 336
20. Ibid, p. 361
21. Ibid, p. 368
22. Ibid, p. 368
23. Lewin, p. 236
24. Nisid Hajari, Midnight's Furies: The Deadly Legacy of India's Partition, p. 65
25. Philip Zeigler, Mountbatten: The Official Biography, p. 353
26. Bernard Law Montgomery The Memoirs of Field Marshal the Viscount Montgomery of Alamein, p. 425
27. Ibid, p. 426
28. Ibid, p. 426
29. Hansard, House of Commons Debate, 10 February 1947, vol. 433, cc 1395-404
30. James Morris, Farewell the Trumpets, p. 480

31. Zeigler, p. 353
32. Ibid, p. 359
33. Moon, p. 419
34. Zeigler, p. 359
35. Roundup of American Press Reaction to Britain's decision to leave India, 28 February 1947, FO 371/63529
36. Ibid
37. Alan Campbell-Johnson, Mission with Mountbatten, p. 41
38. Philip Warner, Auchinleck: The Lonely Soldier, The Truth about Britain's Foremost Commander, p. 279
39. Campbell-Johnson, p. 48
40. Ibid, p. 48
41. Ibid, p. 57
42. Ibid, pp. 62-63
43. Ibid, pp. 62-63
44. Ibid, pp. 61-61
45. Ibid, p. 75
46. Brian Lapping, End of Empire, p. 93
47. Campbell-Johnson, pp. 74-75
48. Ibid, p. 82
49. Ibid, pp. 84-85
50. Ibid, p. 92
51. Ibid, p. 105)
52. Ibid, p. 112
53. CP (47) 158 Indian Policy: Memorandum by the Prime Minister, Cabinet Office, 22 May 1947
54. PREM 8/565 Handwritten letter from Winston Churchill agreeing to support Indian independence
55. Campbell-Johnson, p. 127
56. Montgomery, p. 457
57. Zeigler, p. 388
58. Larry Collins, Dominique Lapiere, Freedom at Midnight: The Electrifying Story of India's Struggle for Independence, p. 236
59. Campbell-Johnson, p. 128
60. Soviet Reaction to Partition, quoting Red Star, 31 July 1947, CAB 371/635/67
61. Campbell-Johnson, p. 148
62. Ibid, p. 144
63. B.R. Ambedkar, Pakistan or Partition of India, pp. 51-52
64. Campbell-Johnson, p. 177
65. Brian McArthur, Penguin Book of Twentieth Century Speeches, pp. 234-237
66. Campbell-Johnson, p. 190
67. Collins and Lapiere, p. 340
68. Morris, p. 492
69. Collins and Lapiere, p. 199

70. Ibid, p. 200
71. Ibid, p. 200
72. Ibid, p. 340
73. Ibid, p. 201
74. DO 142/259 Telegram, Internal Situation in India. Sir Terence Allen Shone, High Commissioner of the UK to India, to Viscount Addison, Secretary of State for Commonwealth Relations, 10 September 1947
75. Gilbert p. 877
76. Zeigler, p. 435
77. WP (42) 391, September 5, 1942, War Cabinet India, Indian States: Request by Chamber of Princes for Statement of Policy by HMG Memorandum by the Secretary of State for India, CAB26/28
78. Important speeches of Jawaharlal Nehru, p. 219
79. Ibid, pp 268-269
80. K.L. Gauba, Hyderabad or India, p. 92
81. Indian Independence Act 1947
82. Important speeches of Jawaharlal Nehru, p. 272
83. Ibid, p. 272
84. Gauba, p. 95
85. J.C. Aggrawal and S.P. Agrawal (Eds). Utterakhand, Past Present and Future, p. 54
86. Campbell-Johnson, p. 163
87. Gauba, p. 102
88. Campbell-Johnson, p. 168
89. Ibid, p. 193

13 'The decent living of the common man'

1. DO 133/60 Terence Allen Shone, Economic effects of the disturbances in Eastern Punjab, 31 October 1947
2. Ibid, p. 88
3. Ibid, p. 96
4. Larry Collins, Dominique Lapiere, Freedom at Midnight: The Electrifying Story of India's Struggle for Independence, p. 129
5. Ibid, p. 200
6. DO 121/69 Record of Conversation between Lord Ismay and Mr Jinnah at Karachi on 3 October 1947
7. Contributions to Asian Studies, Volume I, J.G. Arapura et al, Sponsored by the Canadian Association for South Asian Studies, p. 115
8. Stephen Philip Cohen, The Idea of Pakistan, p. 215
9. University of Oxford, Discussion Papers in Economic and Social History, No.63, July 2006, p8)
10. Maya Tudor, The Promise of Power, p. 180
11. en.banglapedia.org

12. University of Oxford, Discussion Papers in Economic and Social History, No.63, July 2006, p. 9
13. Ibid, p. 9
14. Ibid, p. 50
15. The Economist Intelligence Unit
16. globaltrademag.com
17. bhclondon.org.uk
18. gov.uk
19. diplomat.com
20. DFID Bangladesh Profile, July 2018
21. economictimes.com
22. economics.com
23. thehindu.com
24. thefinancialexpress.com.bd
25. atlanticcouncil.org
26. AlJazeera.com
27. AlJazeera.com
28. parliament.uk
29. nationsencylopedia.com
30. Doing Business in Pakistan: Pakistan Trade and Export Guide, 2018
31. thenews.com.pak
32. Dr S.H. Patel, The Constitution, Government and Politics of India, p. 32
33. David Thomson, England in the Twentieth Century, p. 232
34. Ibid, p. 234
35. Martin Gilbert, Churchill: A Life, p. 885
36. Ibid, p. 885
37. Andrew Kennedy, The International Ambitions of Mao and Nehru: National Efficacy, Beliefs and the Making of Foreign Policy, p. 147
38. Baldev Raj and T.V. Paul, India in the World Order: Searching for Major Power Status, p. 134
39. Important Speeches of Jawaharlal Nehru, p. 69
40. Record of conversation between Lord Ismay and Pandit [Jawaharlal] Nehru on 2 October 1947, DO 121/69
41. R. Coupland, The Future of India, p. 139
42. Important speeches of Jawaharlal Nehru, pp. 285-286
43. K.L. Gauba, Hyderabad or India, p. 122
44. Angma Dey Jhala, Royal Patronage, Power and Aesthetics in Princely India, pp. 86-87
45. Important speeches of Jawaharlal Nehru, p. 252
46. Institute for Strategic Studies
47. telecomlead.com
48. Democracy, News Media and Famine Prevention: Amarya Sen and the Bihar Famine of 1966-67, Thomas L. Myhrvold, June 2003, sas.upenn.edu
49. children.org
50. Oxfam.org)

51. Myhrvold, June 2003, sas.upenn.edu
52. cnbc.com
53. timesofindia.indiatimes.com
54. Sunday Telegraph, 16 February 2020
55. qz.com/India
56. hindustantimes.com, 27 April 2017
57. Ibid
58. nriol.com
59. nriol.com
60. Population by States and Ethnic Group, Dept. of Information, Ministry of Communications and Multimedia, Malaysia, 2015
61. Current Population Estimates Malaysia, 2014-2016, Dept. of Statistics, Malaysia
62. nriol.com
63. Statistics Canada, statcan.gc.ca
64. Statistics Canada, statcan.gc.ca
65. Statistics Canada, statcan.gc.ca
66. immi.gov.au
67. immi.gov.au
68. interstaff.com.au
69. immi.gov.au
70. immi.gov.au
71. immi.gov.au
72. refworld.org
73. refworld.org
74. refworld.org
75. indexmundi.com, Fiji Demographics Profile 2018
76. Stats.gov.nz
77. Stats.gov.nz
78. index.mundi.com
79. Tahir Abbas (ed) Muslim Britain, p. 23
80. Roger Ballard (ed) The South Asian Presence in Britain, p. 13
81. Ibid, p. 13
82. Abbas, p. 29
83. UK Trade in Numbers, February 2020, Department for International Trade, p. 7
84. pw.co.uk
85. economictimes.indiatimes.com
86. tatasteeleurope.com
87. economics.com

Glossary of Terms

India uses different terms to describe some units of weights and measures. For example, a lakh is a unit of 100,000 and a crore is 10,000,000. A maund is an ancient unit of weight approximating to between 11 and 37 kg or 25 to 82.3lbs.

The Indian numbering system is different to that in the UK, so for example 100,000 is written as 1,00,000 or one lakh, and 1,000,000,000 as 1,00,00,00,000.

Various systems are used throughout the book, particularly when quoting contemporary accounts. As it would be confusing to try to convert in such cases, the above will hopefully serve as a guide.

A rupee equals 192 pies, or 16 annas. 1 anna equates to 4 pice and 1 pice to three pies.

When quoting sterling amounts, the pre-decimal system is being applied, which existed until 1971. This consisted of pounds, shilling and pence, with twenty shillings or 240 pence to the pound, hence 1 rupee being equal to 1 shilling and sixpence. There were therefore approximately 15 rupees to the pound sterling, depending upon the exchange rate at any one time. The rupee was valued at around 1 shilling and sixpence upon independence in 1947, although it varied during the preceding period of British rule. For comparison, it is worth approximately 0.011 pounds sterling in today's values.

Place Names

The major cities of India, and those most frequently referred to in this text, have changed their names since colonial times. For clarity and consistency I have used the colonial names throughout. However, they are now known as follows:

Bangalore = Bengaluru
Baroda = Vododara
Benares = Varanasi
Bombay = Mumbai
Calcutta = Kolkata
Cawnpore = Kanpur
Cochin = Kochi
Madras = Chennai
Mysore = Mysuru
Pondicherry = Puducherry
Poona = Pune
Simla = Shimla
Trichinopoly = Tiruchirapalli

Indian Army Ranks

The Indian army used a ranking system different to that of the British. The following are the most frequently referred in the text, with their British Army equivalents:

Sepoy = Private
Lance Naik = Lance Corporal
Naik = Corporal
Havildar = Sergeant
Havildar Major = Sergeant-Major

Appendices

Appendix 1: Queen Victoria's Royal Proclamation 1 November 1858

... Now ... we do by these presents notify and declare that ... we have taken upon ourselves the ... government (of the territories of India) and we hereby call upon all our subjects within the said territories to be faithful and to bear true allegiance to us, our heirs and successors, and to submit themselves to the authority of those whom we may hereafter, from time to time, see fit to appoint to administer the government of our said territories, in our name and on our behalf.

And we, reposing especial trust and confidence in our right trusty and well-beloved cousin, Charles John, Viscount Canning, to be our first Viceroy and Governor-General in and over our said territories, and to administer the government thereof in our name ... ... subject to such orders and regulations as he shall ... receive from our Principal Secretaries of State.

And we do hereby confirm in their several offices, civil and military, all persons now employed in the service of the Honourable East India Company, subject to our future pleasure, and to such laws and regulations which may hereafter be enacted.

We hereby announce to the native princes of India, that all treaties and engagements made with them by or under the authority of the East India Company are by us accepted and will be scrupulously maintained, and we look for the like observance on their part.

We desire no extension of our present territorial possessions, and, while we will permit no aggression upon our dominions or our rights to be attempted with impunity, we shall sanction no encroachments on those of others.

We shall respect the rights, dignity and honour of native princes as our own; and we desire that they as well as our subjects, should enjoy that prosperity and that social advancement which can only be secured by internal peace and good government.

Firmly relying ourselves on the truth of Christianity, and acknowledging with gratitude the solace of religion, we disclaim alike the right and the desire to impose our convictions on any of our subjects. We declare it to be our royal will and pleasure that none be in any wise favoured, none molested or disquieted, by reason of their religious faith or observances, but that all shall alike enjoy the equal and impartial protection of the law; and we strictly charge and enjoin all those who may be in authority under us that they abstain from all interference with the religious belief or worship of any of our subjects on pain of our highest displeasure.

And it is our further will that, as far as may be, or subjects, of whatever race or creed, be freely and impartially admitted to office in our service, the duties of which they may be qualified by their education, ability and integrity duly to discharge.

We deeply lament the evils and misery which have been brought upon India by the acts of ambitious men, who have deceived their countrymen by false reports and led them into open rebellion. Our power has been shown by the repression of that rebellion in the field; we desire to show our mercy by pardoning the offences of those who have been misled, but who desire to return to the path of duty.

Our clemency will be extended to all offenders, save and except those who have been or shall be convicted of having directly taken part in the murder of British subjects. With regard to such the demands of justice forbid the exercise of mercy.

When, by the blessing of Providence, internal tranquillity will be restored, it is our earnest desire to stimulate the peaceful industry of India, to promote works of public utility and improvement, and to administer the government for the benefit of all our subjects resident therein. In their prosperity will be our strength, in their contentment our security, and in their gratitude our best reward ...

Appendix 2: Provinces of British India around 1900

Province of British India	Area (sq. miles)	Population	Chief Administrative Officer
Burma	170,000	9,000,000	Lieutenant-Governor
Bengal	151,000	75,000,000	Lieutenant-Governor
Madras	142,000	38,000,000	Governor-in-Council
Bombay	123,000	19,000,000	Governor-in-Council
United Provinces	107,000	48,000,000	Lieutenant-Governor
Central Provinces and Berar	104,000	13,000,000	Chief Commissioner
Punjab	97,000	20,000,000	Lieutenant-Governor
Assam	49,000	6,000,000	Chief Commissioner

Source: A. B. Keith (ed.), *Speeches and Documents on Indian Policy, 1750-1921*, Vol. I, London 1922, p. 382.

Appendix 3: Revenue of British India, 1878–79

Land Revenue	£22,500,000
Taxation	
Excise	£2.500,000
Stamps (Judicial and Commercial)	£3,000,000
Customs	£2,000,000
Salt	£7,000,000
Assessed Taxes	£1,000,000
Court and Registration fees	£250,000
Provincial Rates	£2,500,000
Total taxation	£18,000,000
Receipts other than taxation	
Sale of opium	£9,000,000
Productive public works	£7,000,000
Post Office	£1,000,000
Other	£7,000,000
Grand Total	£65,000,000

Source: Indian Famine Commission, p. 90. (Figures have been rounded.)

Appendix 4: Increase in population of India

Year	Population
1871	250,000,000
1881	254,000,000
1891	276,000,000
1901	280,000,000
1911	298,000,000
1921	299,000,000
1931	332,000,000

Source: Visaria and Visaria, 'Population (1757-1947)', p. 490.

Appendix 5: Annual government revenue surrender to railway shareholders

Year	Amount (£S)
1858–59	606,946
1859–60	796,872
1860–61	1,096,332

Year	Amount (£S)
1861–62	1,396,991
1862–63	1,541,140
1863–64	1,634,634
1864–65	1,553,936
1865–66	23,667
1866–67	684,002
1867–68	1,491,565
1868–69	1,651,504
1869–70	1,498,084
TOTAL	13,975,673

Source: N. B. Mehta, *Indian Railways, Rates and Regulations*, 1927.

Appendix 6: Starting fares in pies per mile on three selected railways

	Great Indian Peninsular Railway from 1853	East Indian Railway from 1854	Madras Railway from 1856
Passenger fares			
1st Class	24	24	18
2nd Class	10	9	9
3nd Class	3	3	4
Goods rates/ton			
Coal	–	7	–
1st Class	10	9	6.75
2nd Class	14	13.5	13.5
3rd Class	18	18	20.25
4th Class	20	27	–
5th Class	30	54	–

Appendix 7: Respective percentages of population engaged in agriculture and industry

	1871	1881	1891	1901	1911
Agriculture	56.2	40.4	61.0	61.03	72.5
Industry	13.1	–	15.4	12.0	11.3

Appendix 8: Comparative income from Land Revenue achieved in Hyderabad and British India, 1853 and 1881

Gross Land Revenue (Rupees) Collected in Hyderabad under Sir Salar Jung	Gross Land Revenue Collected (£) in British India
Collected in 1853	Collected in 1853
64,85,098	£16,190,000
Collected in 1881	Collected in1881
1,83,40,861	£
Increase of 1,18,55,763, or 260 per cent	Increase of £5,560,000 or under 25 per cent

Source: William Digby CIE, *Prosperous British India: A Revelation from Official Records*, 1901, p. 95.

Appendix 9: Increase in the Indian national debt (illustrative)

Year	Amount in Sterling (rounded to nearest £,1000)
1792	£7,000,000
1799	£19,000,000
1805	£21,000,000
1829	£30,000,000
1836	£33,000,000
1845	£43,000,000
1851	£55,000,000
1858	£69,000,000
1860	£100,000,000
1914	£307,000,000

Source: Lajpat Raj, *Unhappy India*, 1928.

Bibliography

Government Papers

CAB24/158 CP99 (23), Cabinet, Indians in Kenya, Memorandum by the Secretary of State for the Colonies, 3, February 1923

CAB 66/3 War Cabinet, Chiefs of Staff Committee, Visit of Dominion Ministers, Review of Strategic Situation, 24 October 1939

CAB66/5, Weekly Resume No.21 of the Naval, Military and Air Situation, 12 Noon January 18th to 12 Noon January 25th 1940, dated 25 January 1940

CAB 66/10 Telegram from Governor-General to Secretary of State for India, dated June 1, 1940

CAB66/10Telegram from Governor-General to Secretary of State, dated July 4, 1940, 1223-S

CAB66/10Telegram from Governor-General to Secretary of State dated July 4, 1940 1220-S

CAB66/10 Telegram from Governor-General to Secretary of State dated July 4, 1940 1218-S, relating opinion of Governor of Sind

CAB66/10 Telegram from Governor-General to Secretary of State dated July 5, 1940 1245-S

CAB66/10 Telegram from Governor-General to Secretary of State dated July 14, 1940 1225-S, relating opinion of Governor of Sind, of 3 July

CAB 66/10 Memorandum by the Secretary of State for India, 20 July 1940, WP (40) 272

CAB 66/10 WP (40) 294, July 30 1940, War Cabinet India, Memorandum by the Prime Minister. Telegram from the Prime Minister to the Viceroy dated July 28 1940

CAB66/10 Telegram from Viceroy to Secretary of State for India dated June 10, 1940

CAB66/14 WP (40) 476, 05.12.40, War Cabinet India, Question of Action Against Congress Party, Memorandum by the Secretary of State for India

CAB66/14 WP (40) 476, 05.12.40, War Cabinet India, Question of Action Against Congress Party, Memorandum by the Secretary of State for India

CAB66/14 Telegram from Viceroy to Secretary of State for India, dated 1 December 1940, 2589-S

CAB 66/19 WO (41) 271 Telegram from Viceroy to Secretary of State for India, dated November 1, 1941

CAB 66/19 WO (41) 271, Telegram from Governor-General to Secretary of State for India, dated November 12, 1941

CAB 66/19, W.P. (41) 274, 19 November 1941, War Cabinet Conclusions 115 (41) of 17 November 1941. Minute 4(2)

CAB 66/19 Telegram from Prime Minister to Viceroy, dated November 21, 1941, WO (41) 271

CAB 66/19, India: WP 942 Release of Satygrahi Prisoners. Memorandum by the Secretary of State for India, covering further telegrams from the Viceroy

CAB66/21 WP (42) 42 War Cabinet, The Indian Political Situation, Memorandum by the Secretary of State for India

CAB 66/21 WO (42) 43, Telegram from the Viceroy to Secretary of State for India, dated 21 January 1942

CAB 66/21 WP (42) 54War Cabinet, India's War Effort, Memorandum by the Secretary of State for Indian, 30 January 1942

CAB 66/21 WP (42) 54, War Cabinet, India's War Effort, Memorandum by the Secretary of State for India, 30 January 1942

CAB 66/21 WP (43) 89, War Cabinet, India's War Effort, Memorandum by the Secretary of State for India, 1 March 1943

CAB66/22Telegram from Commander-in-Chief India to War Office, 3062/G 14/2, 15 February 1942

CAB66/22 Cypher telegram from Secretary of State to Viceroy dated 19 February 1942 WS 18514/18222

CAB66/22 Telegram from Governor-General to Secretary of State for India, 26 February 1942

CAB66/24 WP (42) 177, April 25 1942, War Cabinet, Report on the Fall of Singapore

CAB66/22 WP (42) 106, Telegram from Secretary of State for India to Viceroy, dated 28 February 1942, 2 March 1942

CAB66/22 Telegram from Viceroy to Secretary of State for India, dated 28 February 1942, No.481-S

CAB66/22 WP (42)116, War Cabinet, Indian Policy memorandum by Secretary of State for India, 8 March 1942

CAB66/23 WP (42) 138, 1st April 1942, War Cabinet India, Telegrams exchanged between the Lord Privy Seal and the Prime Minister

CAB66/23 WP (42) 132, 3 April 1942, War Cabinet Communist Party, Statement made by Mr Harry Pollitt on 14 March and circulated by the Communist Party. Speaking on behalf of the Central Committee of the Communist Party in the Brangwyn Hall Swansea on Saturday March 14th

CAB66/23Telegram from Viceroy to Secretary of State for India, 5 April 1942

CAB66/23Telegram from Viceroy to Secretary of State for India, 6 April 1942, 912-S

CAB66/23 WP (42) 138, 1st April 1942, War Cabinet India, Telegrams exchanged between the Lord Privy Seal and the Prime Minister

CAB66/23 Telegram from Commander-in-Chief India to the War Office, 6 April 1942 8230/C, Private for Prime Minister from General Wavell

CAB66/23 Telegram No.607 from General Smuts to Prime Minister, 4 April 1942

CAB66/23 WP (42) 149 Telegram from Viceroy to Secretary of State for India, 6 April 1942, 919-S

CAB66/23 WP (42) 160, Evacuation of Indians from Burma, memorandum by the Secretary of State for Burma, 11 April 1942

CAB66/24 WP (42) 177, April 25 1942, War Cabinet, Report on the Fall of Singapore

CAB66/25WP (42) 255, 16th March 1942, War Cabinet, Policy to be adopted towards Mr Gandhi, memorandum by the Secretary of State for India

CAB66/25 WP (42) 255, 16th March 1942, War Cabinet, Policy to be adopted towards Mr Gandhi, memorandum by the Secretary of State for India, Appendix 1, Telegram 4494 from Government of India, Home Department, dated 7 June 1942

CAB66/25 WP (42) 264, June 22 1942, War Cabinet, Treatment of War Criminals, Annex No.5 Extract from Parliamentary Debates (House of Commons), March 10, 1942 Hong Kong (Japanese Barbarities)

CAB 66/22 WP (42) 107, 2 March 1942, War Cabinet Indian Policy Memorandum by the Secretary of State for India, covering a note by Major-General R.M.M. Lockhart, CIE, MC

CAB66/25 WP (42) 255, 16th March 1942 War Cabinet, Policy to be adopted towards Mr Gandhi, memorandum by the Secretary of State for India

CAB66/25 WP (42) 255,, 16th March 1942, War Cabinet, Policy to be adopted towards Mr Gandhi, memorandum by the Secretary of State for India, Appendix II, All-India Congress Committee War resolution May 1st 1942, original draft of Congress War Resolution as put to Working Committee on 27 April

CAB66/25 WP (42) 255, 16th March 1942, War Cabinet, Policy to be adopted towards Mr Gandhi, memorandum by the Secretary of State for India, Appendix III, Recent Utterance of Gandhi

CAB66/26 WP (42) 271, Policy to be adopted towards Mr Gandhi, Telegram from Governor-General to Secretary of State for India, June 28 1942

CAB66/26 WP (42) 283, July 6 1942, War Cabinet Report on Mission to India, Memorandum by the Lord Privy Seal

CAB66/28 WP (43) 40, January 25, 1943, War Cabinet Report for the Month of December 1942 for the Dominions, India, Burma and the Colonies and Mandated Territories

CAB26/28 WP (42) 391, September 5, 1942, War Cabinet India, Indian States: Request by Chamber of Princes for Statement of Policy by HMG Memorandum by the Secretary of State for India

CAB66/34, WP (43) 63, 13th February 1943, War Cabinet: Cereals for the Indian Ocean Area. Note by Minister of War Transport

CAB66/36 WP (43) 197, May 10 1943, War Cabinet, Subversive attempts on the loyalty of the Indian Army, Memorandum by the Secretary of State for India

CAB66/36, WP (43) 170, April 22 1943, War Cabinet Report for the Month of March for the Dominions, India, Burma and the Colonies and Mandated Territories, report by the Secretary of State for India

CAB66/36 WP (43) 199, May 11, 1943, War Cabinet, The Application of Democratic Principles of Government, Memorandum by the Deputy Prime Minister

CAB66/39) WP (43) 345, 30th July 1943, War Cabinet, India's Requirements of Imported Food Grains, Report by the Shipping Committee

CAB66/39 WP (43) 349, 31 July 1943, War Cabinet, India's Requirement of Imported Food Grains, Memorandum by Secretary of State for India

CAB66/40 WP (43) 393, 10th September 1943, War Cabinet, Indian Food Situation, Memorandum by the Secretary of State for India

CAB66/40 WP (43) 381, 27 August 1943, War Cabinet, Report for the Month of July 1943, for the Dominions, India, Burma and the Colonies and Mandated Territories

CAB66/41, WP (43) 411, 22nd September 1943, War Cabinet, Economic Situation in India, Memorandum by the Secretary of State for India

CAB66/41 WP (43) 450 (Revised), 8th October, 1943, War Cabinet, India, Note by the Prime Minister and Minister of defence. The attached Directive to the Viceroy-Designate has now been approved by the War Cabinet

CAB66/42, WP (43) 493, 1st November 1943, War Cabinet, Canadian Gift of Wheat to India, Memorandum by Secretary of State for India

CAB66/42 WP (43) 495, 26th October 1942, War Cabinet, Report for the Month of October for the Dominions, India, Burma and the Colonies and Mandated Territories

CAB66/43 WP (43) 504, 4th November 1943, War Cabinet, Shipment of Food Grains to India, Memorandum by Secretary of State to India

CAB66/43 WP (43) 504, 4th November 1943, War Cabinet, Shipment of Food Grains to India, Memorandum by Secretary of State to India

CAB66/44 WP (43) 584, 26th December 1943, War Cabinet, Report for the Month of November 1943 for the Dominions, India, Burma and the Colonies and Mandated Territories

CAB66/45 WP (44) 18, 10 January 1944, War Cabinet India, Proposed Suspension of the Bengal Ministry and Assumption of Powers by the Governor under Section 93 of the Government of India Act, Memorandum by the Secretary of State for India

CAB66/46 WP (44) 55, 25 January 1944, War Cabinet, Report for the Month of December 1943 for the Dominions, India, Burma and the Colonies and Mandated Territories

CAB66/46 WP (44) 99, 11th February 1944, War Cabinet, Indian Food Grain Requirements, Report by the President of the Board of Education

CAB66/48 WP (44) 165, 18th March 1944, War Cabinet, Situation in India, Report from Chiefs of Staff

CAB66/49 WP (44) 228, 27th April 1944, War Cabinet, Indian Food Situation, Memorandum by the Home Secretary [Herbert Morrison]

CAB66/51 WP (44) 326, Government House Calcutta, 20 May 1944, addressed to WSC, from Governor or Bengal R.G. Casey

CAB66/56 WP (44) 562, 10th October 1944, War Cabinet, Indian Food Situation, Sir Henry French's visit to India, Memorandum of the Secretary of State for India

CAB66/56 WP (44) 562, 10th October 1944, War Cabinet, Indian Food Situation, Sir Henry French's visit to India, Memorandum of the Secretary of State for India

CAB66/64 WP (44) 212, 1st April 1945, War Cabinet, Report for the Dominions, India, Burma and the Colonies and Mandated Territories

CAB66/65 WP (45) 264, 20th April 1945, War Cabinet, Report for the Month of March 1945 for the Dominions, India, Burma and the Colonies and Mandated Territories

CAB66/67CP (45) 88, 26th July 1945, Cabinet, Report for the Month of June 1945 for the Dominions, India, Burma and the Colonies and Mandated Territories

CAB66/47 WP (44) 118, 19th February 1944, War Cabinet, Committee of Food Grain Requirements, REPORT

CAB66/52 WP (44) 351, 27th June 1944, War Cabinet, Shipment of Food Grains to India, Memorandum by the Secretary of State for India

CAB 127/136, Extract from a statement by Mr Jinnah, dated 6 December 1945

CAB 127/136 Letter from Muhammed Ali Jinnah to Sir Richard Stafford Cripps, New Delhi, 9 February 1946

CAB 371/635/67 Soviet Reaction to Partition, quoting Red Star, 31 July 1947

CP (47) 158 Indian Policy: Memorandum by the Prime Minister, Cabinet Office, 22 May 1947

DO 121/69Record of conversation between Lord Ismay and Pandit [Jawaharlal] Nehru on 2 October 1947

DO 121/69 Record of Conversation between Lord Ismay and Mr Jinnah at Karachi on 3 October 1947

DO 133/60 Press Information Bureau, Government of India, Ministry of Information, New Delhi, November 2, 1947, Movement of Refugees

DO 133/60 Terence Allen Shone, Economic effects of the disturbances in Eastern Punjab, 31 October 1947

DO 142/259 Telegram, Internal Situation in India. Sir Terence Allen Shone, High Commissioner of the UK to India, to Viscount Addison, Secretary of State for Commonwealth Relations, 10 September 1947

DO 121/69 Record of Conversation between Lord Ismay and Mr Jinnah at Karachi on 3 October 1947

FO 371/63529 Roundup of American Press Reaction to Britain's decision to leave India, 28 February 1947

PREM 8/565 Handwritten letter from Winston Churchill agreeing to support Indian independence

WO 208/761A Telegram from C-in-C India to War Office (18 August 1942) No.19842/1

WO 208/3812 Extract from broadcast by Subhas Chandra Bose

WO208/3811 Article in the *Times*, 22 December 1947

WP (42) 184, 1 May 1942, War Cabinet, Defence of India, Annex 1 Telegram from the Commander-in-Chief India No.10577/C dated 30th April 1942, Personal for CIGS from General Wavell

Hansard

Hansard, House of Lords Debates, 5 April 1916, vol. 21, cc604-22

Hansard: House of Lords Debate, 3 February 1942, vol. 121, cc 582-638

Hansard, HC Debates, 25 July 1923 vol. 167, cc541-94

Hansard: HC Debates, 21 January 1943, vol. 386, cc276-7

Hansard HC Debates, 4 November 1943, Vol. 393

Hansard, House of Commons debate, 15 March 1946, Vol.420, cc1413-761413

Hansard, House of Commons Debate, 10 February 1947, vol. 433, cc 1395-404

Original Documents, Articles and Publications

A White Australia, The Kanaka Labour Question, Sugar Growing in Queensland, The Part Played by the Black Man, A 'Herald' Investigation, Melbourne 1901

An Account of the Island of Mauritius and its Dependencies, by a late official resident, published by the author, London, 1842

An Appeal to England to Save India from the Wrong and Shame of the Age of Consent Act, published by the Bali Sadharani Sab ha, 25 April 1891

Agreement Creating the UNRRA, National Planning Association Pamphlets, 31-32, February 28 1944

Asiatic Review, vol.19, No.57, January 1923

Auckland City Labour Market Research Report, Migration and Auckland City, Mattia G. Barbera, February 2010

British and Foreign State Papers, 1817-1818, Compiled by the Librarian and Keeper of the Papers, Foreign Office, James Ridgway and Sons, Piccadilly, London, 1837

British Imperial Railways in Nineteenth Century South Asia, Laxman D. Satya, Economic and Political Weekly, November 22 2008

Burma Issues, Volume 16, Issue 2, February 2005, Burmese Indians: The Forgotten Lives, Samart Butkaew

Census of India – 1931 Volume I, J.H. Hutton

Colonial Reports: Annual, No. 1731, Annual Report on the Social and Economic Progress of the People of Mauritius, 1934, HMSO, London, 1935

Committees and Commissions in Pre-Independence India, 1836-1947: Vol.2, 1882-1895, M. Anees Chishti, Mittal Publications, New Delhi, 2001

Contributions to Asian Studies, Volume I, J.G. Arapura et al, Sponsored by the Canadian Association for South Asian Studies, E.J. Brill, Leiden, 1971

Current Population Estimates Malaysia, 2014-2016, Dept. of Statistics, Malaysia

Department for International Development, Bangladesh Profile, July 2018

Department for International Trade Guidance: Doing business in Pakistan: Pakistan Trade and Export Guide, updated 16 August 2018

East India Constitutional Reforms, Report on Indian Constitutional Reforms to both Houses of Parliament by Command of His Majesty, HMSO London, 1918

Edinburgh Papers in South Asian Studies No.24 (2010), The Punjabisation of the British Indian Army, 1857-1947 and the Advent of Military Rule in Pakistan, Syed Hussain Shaheed Soherwordi, School of History and Classics, University of Edinburgh

Facts and Fallacies Regarding Irrigation as a Prevention of Famine in India, John Dacosta, W.H. Allen, London, 1878

Famine Enquiry Commission on Bengal, Chairman Sir John Woodhead, 1944

Federal Franchise Act 1902, 'Disqualification of Coloured Races'

Food Crisis, Inflation and Political Control in Punjab (1940-1947), Sukhdev Singh Sohal, Journal of Punjab Studies, vol.20, 2013

Government of India Despatch of 26 October 1892, quoted in Simon Commission Report of 1926

History Today, Volume 36, issue 4, April 1986 Basdeo Mangru

Imperial Gazeteer of India, Provincial Series, Hyderabad State, Superintendent of Government Printing, Calcutta, 1909

Important speeches of Jawaharlal Nehru: Being a collection of most significant speeches delivered by Nehru from 1922 to 1946, The Indian Printing Works, Lahore, 1946

Indian Communities in Southeast Asia, Eds. K.S. Sandhu and A. Mani, Institute for Southeast Asian Studies, Singapore, 1993

Indian Indentured Workers in Fiji, Shiu Prasad, The South Pacific Social Sciences Association, Fiji, 1975

Indian Migrants in Myanmar: Emerging Trends and Challenges, Medha Chaturvedi, Senior Fellow, India Centre for Migration, Ministry of Overseas Indian Affairs

Bibliography

Indian Politics in South Africa: 1860 to the Present, Michael West, South Asia Bulletin, vol. 7, 1987

Jinnah-Gandhi Talks – September 1944 – Text of Correspondence and other relevant documents etc. Forward by Nawabzada Liaquat Ali Khan, M.L.A. Central Office, All India Moslem League

Karl Marx, writing in the New York Herald Tribune of 25 June 1853 and article under the heading 'British Rule in India'

Keeping New Zealand White: 1908-1920, Article for the University of Auckland, P.S. O'Connor, 1968

List of Etonians who Fought in the Great War MCM – MCMXIX

Minute of Dissent to the Family Enquiry Commission chaired by John Woodhead M. Afzul Husain

National Army Museum,1951-05-87-1, Last Indian Army Order

New York Times, 27 November 1943

New Zealand Immigration Restriction Act No.83 1899

New Zealand, Imperial Conference 1930, Summary of Proceedings, National Library of New Zealand, 1931

New Zealand Parliamentary Debates, First Session, Twentieth Parliament, Legislative Council and House of Representatives, 197th Volume, Comprising the Period from August 6 to September 24 1920, Wellington, by Authority, Marcus F. Marks, Government Printer, 1920

Parliament of Kenya, The National Assembly, History of the Parliament of Kenya, Fact Sheet No. 24, The Clerk of the National Assembly, Nairobi, 2017

Population by States and Ethnic Group, Dept. of Information, Ministry of Communications and Multimedia, Malaysia, 2015

Preliminary Note on the Conference by the Department of External Affairs' India and the Last Jubilee Queen, Dinyar Patel, 16 June 2012

Proceedings of a Conference Between the Secretary of State for the Colonies and the Premiers of the Self-Governing Colonies at the Colonial Office London, June and July 1897, 31 July 1897

Proceedings of the First Indian National Conference on the 28th, 29th, 30th December 1885, held at Bombay, Printed at the Swadeshmitran Press, Madras 1905

Re-Distribution from Above, The Politics of Land Rights and Squatting in Coastal Kenya, Karuti Kanyinga, Nordiska Afrikainstitut, Research Report No. 115, Uppsala, 2000

Report of the Army in India Committee, 1919-1920

Report of the Reforms Enquiry Committee, (1924), Delhi, Government of India Press, 1925

Report of the Coal Mining Committee, 1937 Volume One, Delhi, Manager of Publications, 1937

Report Upon the Military Cantonments of Kamptee and Seetabuldee, J.L. Ranking, Surgeon-Major, Sanitary Commissioner for Madras, Printed by H. Morgan at the Government Press, 1869

Rethinking Australia's International Past: Identity, Foreign Policy and India in the Australian Colonial Imagination, Alexander E, Davis, The University of Adelaide, Flinders Journal of History and Politics, Volume 29, 2013

Simon Commission Report on India (India Statutory Commission) Volume 1, Report of the Indian Statutory Commission, Volume 1 – Survey, Swati Publications, Delhi, Reprinted 1988

Slavery and the Slave Trade in British India; with Notices of the Existence of these Evils in the Islands of Ceylon, Malacca and Penang, drawn from Official Documents, Thomas Ward and Co. London, 1841

Speeches and Writings of Annie Besant, 3rd ed. G.A. Nateson and Co.

Summary of the Principles Measures of the Viceroyalty of the Marquess of Lansdowne in the Department of Revenue and Agriculture, December 1888 to January 1894, Office of the Superintendent of Government Printing India, Calcutta, 1894

Sunday Telegraph

The Age of Consent Act (1891) Reconsidered: Women's Perspectives and Participation in the Child Marriage Controversy in India, South Asia Research Vol.12, No.2, November 1992, Padma Anagol-McGinn

The Asiatic Act, The Asiatic Land Tenure and Indian Representation Act of South Africa, A Brief Summary of its Background, Terms and Implications, George Singh, BA, LLB, Council for Human Rights, Durban, SA, 1946

The Atlantic Charter A Criticism, Parliamentary Peace Aims Group (Members of the Labour Party), House of Commons, 1941

The Effects of Periodical Revisions of Land Tax in India, John Dacosta, W.H. Allen and Company, London, 1881

The Emancipation of India, A Reply to the Article by the Rt. Hon. Viscount Morley OM, on 'British Democracy and Indian Government in the Nineteenth Century and After', for February 1911, by H.M. Hyndman, The Twentieth Century Press Ltd, London 1911

The Financial Situation in India, As Expressed in the Budget Statement for 1886-87, John Dacosta, P.S. King and Son, London, 1887

The Ilbert Bill: A Collection of Letters Speeches, Memorials, Articles etc … W.H. Allen, London

The India List and India Office List, 1905, Harrison and Sons Limited, London, 1905

The Indian Demands: A Symposium on the memorandum of the Nineteen and Speeches at the Congress and Moslem League on their scheme of self-government for India, introduction by G.A, Nateson, G.A. Nateson and Co. Madras, 1917

The Indian Famine Crisis of World War Two, Mark B. Tauger, British Scholar, vol.1, Issue 2, March 2009

The Indigo Revolt of Bengal, Subhas Bhattacharya Digital South Asia Library, Social Scientist, V5 No.60 (July 1977)

The Journal of the Royal Society of Arts, No.3, vol. LXXI, Friday August 3, 1923, p645

The Official Gazette of the Colony and Protectorate of Kenya – Special Edition – Vol XXV, No. 914, Nairobi, November 23, 1923

The Railway Mania: Fraud disappointment expectations, and the modern economy, Andrew Odlyzko, School of Mathematics, University of Minnesota, 2012

The Rt. Hon. Henry Fawcett MP on the Nationalisation of the Land, and the Land Question in India, John Dacosta, W.H. Allen, London, 1884

Thirty Years Mission Life in Jamaica: A Brief Sketch of Reverend Warrand Carlile, Missionary at Brownsville, By One of His Boys, Nisbet and Co. London, 1884

Transnational Ghadr Movement: A Diasporic Dimension, Palavi Bhatte, Kyoto University Research Information Repository, February 2013

UK Trade in Numbers, February 2020, Department for International Trade

University of Oxford, Discussion Papers in Economic and Social History, No.63, July 2006. Educational Disparity in East and West Pakistan, 1947-1971: Was East Pakistan Discriminated Against? Mohammed Niaz Asadullah

Whither Hyderabad? (A Brief Study of Some of the Outstanding Problems of the Premier Indian State) Syed Abid Khan, 1935

Working Paper 209, Capital 'Development' and Canal Irrigation in Colonial India, Patrick McGinn, Institute for Social and Economic Change, 2009

Websites

Abc.net.au

Abs.gov.au Australian Bureau of Statistics

AlJazeera.com

Atlanticcouncil.org

Bhclondon.org.uk

Caribbeanatlas.com, The Experience of Indian Indenture in Trinidad: Arrival and Settlement, Sherry-Ann Singh, Department of History, University of the West Indies, St. Augustine, Trinidad and Tobago

children.org

cia.gov. The World Factbook

cnbc.com

Democracy, News Media and Famine Prevention: Amarya Sen and the Bihar Famine of 1966-67, Thomas L. Myhrvold, June 2003, sas.upenn.edu

difp.ie Documents on Irish Foreign Policy

difp.ie Documents on Irish Foreign Policy

diplomat.com

economics.indiatimes.com

economist.com 2 September 2017, The Legacy of Indian Migration to European Colonies

exodus2013.co.uk Lascars of London and Liverpool

globalsecurity.org

gov.uk Department for International Development

hindustantimes.com

immi.gov.au

indexmundi.com, Fiji Demographics Profile 2018

institute for Strategic Studies

interstat.com.au

legislation.gov.uk

National Museum of Australia

nationsencylopedia.com

Non Resident Indians Online, nriol.com

old-jamaica-gleaner.com, Pieces of the Past, Out of Many Cultures, The People Who Came, The Arrival of the Indians, Dr Rebecca Tortello

pakistanarmy.gov.pk

parliament.uk

pwc.co.uk

qz.com

refworld.org

sahistory.org.za

Southasiaanalysis.org, South Asia Analysis Group, Paper No. 3523, 26 November 2009, The Indian Community in Maynmar, Dr V. Suryanarayan

Statistics New Zealand, 3.stats.govt.nz. Results of a Census of the Colony of New Zealand Taken for the Night of the 29th April 1906

Stats.gov.nz

Tatasteeleurope.com

tepapa.gov.nz

theeconomistintelunit.com

thefinancialexpress.com

thehindu.com

timesofindia.indiatimes.com

walesonline.co.uk

Books

About, Ilsen, Brown James, Lonergan Gayle (eds.), *Identification and Registration Practices in Transnational Perspective, People, Place and Practices* (New York: Palgrave Macmillan, 2013)

Abu-Raki, Ibrahim M. *The Blackwell Companion to Contemporary Islamic Thought* (Oxford: Blackwell, 2006)

Abbas, Tahir (ed.), *Muslim Britain, Communities Under Pressure* (London & New York: Zed Books, 2005)

Adas, Michael *The Burma Delta: Economic development and Social Change on an Asian Rice Frontier, 1852-1941* (Wisconsin: University of Wisconsin Press, USA, 2011)

Aggrawal J.C. and Agrawal S.P. (Eds), *Utterakhand, Past Present and Future* (New Delhi: Concept Publishing Company, 1995)

Ahmad, Dr Sir Ziauddin, *Indian Railways* (Lahore: The Evergreen Press)

Aiyer, K.A. Neelakandha, *Indian Problems in Malaya, A Brief Survey in Relation to Emigration* (Kuala Lumpur: The India Office, 1938)

Aiyar, Sana, *Indians in Kenya, The Politics of Diaspora* (Cambridge Mass: Harvard University Press, 2015)

Ali Khan, Syed Sirdar, *The Life of Lord Morley* (London: Sir Isaac Pitman and Sons Ltd, 1923)

Ayer, S.A. *Story of the INA* (New Delhi: National Book Trust, India, 1972)

Almeida, Hermione de and Gilpin, George H., *Indian Renaissance: British Romantic Art and the Prospect of India* (Aldershot: Ashgate Publishing, 2005)

Andrew, William P. CIE, *Indian Railways as connected with the Empire in the East* (London: W.H. Allen and Company 1884)

Bacon, Edgar Mayhew and Murray Eugene Aaron, PHD *The New Jamaica* (New York:Walbridge and Co. 1890)

Badenach, Captain Walter, *Inquiry into the State of the Indian Army, with Suggestions for Improvement, and the Establishment of a Military Police for India* (London, J. Murray, 1826)

Bahudur, Sayyid Akhman Khan, *The Causes of the Indian Revolt* (Benares, Medical Hall Press, 1873)

Ballard, Roger (ed.) *Desh Pardesh, The South Asian Presence in Britain* (London: Hurst and Company, 1994)

Banaji, D.R., MA, LLB, DB, *Slavery in British India* (Bombay: Taraporevala, 1933)

Banerjea, Pramathanath, *A History of Indian Taxation* (Calcutta: University of Calcutta Press, 1930)

Banerjea, Sir Surendranath, *A Nation in Making: Being the Reminiscences of Fifty Years of Public Life* (London, New York, Toronto: Oxford University Press, 1921)

Banerjee, D.N., *Partition or Federation? A Study in the Indian Constitutional Problem* (Calcutta: General printers and Publishers Ltd, 1945)

Barua, Pradeep P., *Gentlemen of the Raj, The Indian Army Officer Corps 1817-1949* (Westport Cn & London: Praeger, 2003)

Basu, B.D. *History of Education in India* (Calcutta: Sri Gauranga Press, no publication date)

Basu, B.D. The Ruin of Indian Trade and Industries (Calcutta: R. Chaterjee, no publication date)

Bhave, Y.G. *The Mahatma and the Muslims* (New Delhi: Northern Book Centre, 1997)

Bhownaggree, Mancherjee, M., *The Constitution of the East India Company* (Bombay: Dufter Ashkara Press, 1872)

Bhuyan, Arun Chandra, *The Quiet India Movement, Rge Second World War and Indian Nationalism* (New Delhi: Manas Publications, 1975)

Bilgrami, Syed Hossain, and Wilmott, C., *Historical and Descriptive Sketch of HH the Nizam's Dominions, vol. 1* (Bombay: Times of India Steam Press, 1883)

Bilgrami Syed Hossain, *A Memoir of Sir Salar Jung I, GCSI* (Bombay: Times of India Steam Press, 1883)

Bolts, William, *Considerations on India Affairs* (London: J. Almon, 1772)

Borstelmann, Thomas *Apartheid's Reluctant Uncle: The US and Southern Africa in the Early Cold War* (New York, Oxford: OUP, 1993)

Bose, Mihir, *The Magic of Indian Cricket: Cricket and Society in India* (London, New York: Routledge, 2006)

Bryant, Arthur, *Macaulay* (London: Thomas Nelson and Sons, 1938)

Buckley, Robert B., *The Irrigation Works of India and their Financial Results* (London: Allen and Company, 1880)

Bueltmann, Tanja, *Scottish Ethnicity and the Making of New Zealand Society, 1950-1930,* (Edinburg, Edinburgh University Press, 2011)

Bushby, Henry Jeffreys, *Widow Burning, A Narrative* (London< Longman, Brown, Green and Longmans, 1855)

Campbell-Johnson, Alan, CIE, OBE *Mission with Mountbatten,* (Bombay, New Delhi, Calcutta, Madras: Aico Publishing House, 1951)

Carter Marina, and Ng Foong Kwong, James Abacus and Mah Jong, *Sino-Mauritian Settlement and Economic Consolidation* (Leiden,Boston: Brill, 2009)

Cassels, Nancy Gardner *Social Legislation of the East India Company, Public Justice versus Public Instruction* (Washington: Sage Publications, 2010)

Chhabra, GS, *Advanced Study in the History of Modern India, Vol. III (1920-1947)* (New Delhi: Lotus Press, 2005)

Chandra, Kailash, *Tragedy of Jinnah* (Lahore: Sharma Publishers, 1941)

Clarke, Hyde, *Colonization, Defence and Railways in Our Indian Empire* (London: John Wheale, 1857)

Clymer, Kenton J., *Quest for Freedom: The United States and India's Independence* (New York: Columbia University Press, 1995)

Cohen, Stephen Philip, *The Idea of Pakistan* (Washington DC: Brooking's Institution Press, 2004)

Collins, Larry & Lapiere, Dominique *Freedom at Midnight: The Electrifying Story of India's Struggle for Independence* (London: Grafton Books, 1986)

Constantine, Stephen *Emigrants and Empire, British Settlement in the Dominions between the Wars* (Manchester and New York: Manchester University Press, 1990)

Coupland, R. *The Future of India* (Oxford: OUP, 1944)

Curthoys, Anne, Lake Marilyn (eds.) *Connected Worlds: History in Transnational Perspective* (Canberra: ANU E Press, 2005)

Dacosta, John, *Facts and Fallacies Regarding Irrigation as a Prevention of Famine in India* (London: W.H. Allen, 1878)

Deakin, Hon. Alfred MLA, *Irrigated India, An Australian View of India and Their Irrigation and Agriculture* (London: W. Thacker and Company, 1893) de Burgh-Edwardes, S.B. FRGS, FECI, *The History of Mauritius: 1507-1914* (London: East and West Limited, 1921)

Dhillon, Dr G.S., *Canal System of the Punjab Region* (Ludhiana: Pau Press, 1992)

Digby, William CIE, *Prosperous British India: A Revelation from Official Records* (London: T. Fisher Unwin, 1901)

Dilley, Marjorie Ruth, *British Policy in Kenya Colony, 2nd Edition* (London: Frank Cass and Co. Ltd,1966)

Di Salvo, Charles R. *M.K. Gandhi, Attorney at Law, The Man before the Mahatma* (Los Angeles: University of California Press, 2013)

Dodwell, H., *Sepoy Recruitment in the Old Madras Army* (Calcutta: Superintendent of Government Printing, 1922)

Dorsett Shaunagh & McLaren, John (eds), *Legal Histories of the British Empire: Laws, Engagements and Legacies* (Abingdon: Routledge, 2014)

Douglas, Sir Arthur P., *The Dominion of New Zealand* (Boston: Little Brown, 1909)

Dumasia, Naoroji M., *The Aga Khan and His Ancestors, A Biographical and Historical Sketch* (New Delhi: Readworthy, 2008)

Durant, Will, *The Case for India* (New York: Simon and Schuster, 1930)

Dutt, Romesh Chunder, *India in the Victorian Age: An Economic History of the People* (London: K. Paul, Trench, Trubner and Company Ltd, 1904)

Dutt, Romesh Chunder, *The Economic History of India Under British Rule, from the Rise of British Power in 1757 to the Accession of Queen Victoria in 1837* (London: K. Paul Tench Tubner and Company, 1916)

Dwivedi, Om Prakash, *Tracing the New Indian Diaspora* (Amsterdam: Rodopi, 2014)

Elphick, Richard & Davenport, Rodney (eds), *Christianity in South Africa, a Political, Social and Cultural History* (Berkeley, Los Angeles: University of California Press, 1997)

Fair, C. Christine, *Fighting to the End, The Pakistan Army's Way of War* (Oxford & New York: Oxford University Press, 2014)

Fischer-Tine, Harald, & Michael Mann (eds.), *Colonialism as Civilising Mission: Cultural Ideology in British India* (London: Anthem Press, 2004)

Fisher, Michael H., *Migration, A World History* (Oxford: OUP, Oxford, 2014)

Foster, William, CIE, ed. *Early Travels in India 1583-1619* (Oxford: OUP, 1921)

Forrest, A.S. *Jamaica* (London: Adam and Charles Black, 1906)

Fraser, Lovat *Iron and Steel in India: A Chapter from the Life of Jamshedji Tata* (Bombay: The Times Press, 1919)

Fry. Julie & Wilson, Peter, *Better Lives: Migration, Wellbeing and New Zealand* (Wellington: Bridget Williams Books Ltd, 2018)

Gandhi, M.K. *An Autobiography: or the Story of My Experiments with Truth* (Ahmedabad: Navajivan Publishing House, 1959)

Gauba, K.L. *Hyderabad or India* (Delhi: Rajkamal Publications Ltd, Delhi, 1948)

Geerkan, Horst H., *Hitler's Asian Adventure* (Bonn: BukitCinta Books, 2017)

Ghosh, Kali Charan, *Famines in Bengal: 1770-1943* (Calcutta: Indian National Associated Ltd, 1944)

Ghosh, Suresh Chandra, *The Social Condition of the British Community in Bengal: 1757-1800* (Leiden: E.J. Brill, 1970)

Gilbert, Martin *Churchill: A Life* (London: Minerva, 1994)

Gilbert, Martin, *The First World War* (London: Harper Collins, 1994)

Gill, M.S., *Trials That Changed History, Socrates to Saddam Hussain* (New Delhi: Sarup and Sons, 2007)

Gilmour, David *Curzon* (London: Papermac,1995)

Gizen-no-Teki, *Colorphobia, An Exposure of the "White Australia" Fallacy* (Sydney: R.T, Kelly, 1903)

Grant, Captain Harold Maurice, *History of the War in South Africa: 1899-1902, Compiled by the Direction of His Majesty's Government* Vol. VI (London: Hurst and Blackett Ltd, 1910)

Gregory, Robert G., *Quest for Equality: Asian Politics in East Africa, 1900-1967* (Hyderabad: Orient Longman, 1993)

Greenwood, Anna & Topiwala, Harshad, *Indian Doctors in Kenya – 1895-1940: The Forgotten History* (New York: Palgrave Macmillan, 2015)

Hajari Nisid, *Midnight's Furies: The Deadly Legacy of India's Partition* (Boston, New York: Houghton Mifflin Harcourt 2015)

Hart, Daniel, *Trinidad and the other West Indian Islands* (Trinidad: The Chronicle Publishing Office, 1866)

Hibbert, Christopher, *The Great Mutiny, India 1857* (London: Penguin Books, 1983)

Hodgson, Colonel John Studholme, *Opinions on the Indian Army* (London: W.H. Allen, 1857)

Hood, Captain W.H., *The Blight of Insubordination, the Lascar Question and Rights and Wrongs of the British Shipmaster* (Liverpool: Spottiswoode and Co. Ltd, 1908)

Hoyland, John S., *Gopal Krishna Gokhale, His Life and Speeches* (Calcutta: YMCA Publishing House, 1933)

Huddleston, G., *The History of the East India Railway*, Thacker Spink and Co. Calcutta, 1906

Hume, Hamilton, *The Life of Edward John Eyre, Late Governor of Jamaica* (London:, Richard Bentley, 1867)

Husain, Dr Mahmud (ed.) *A History of the Freedom Movement, Volume III, 1831-1905* (Delhi, Renaissance Publishing House, 1960)

Hutton, James, *A Popular Account of the Thugs and Dacoits: The Hereditary Garotters and Gang Robbers of India* (London W.H. Allen 1857)

Hyndman, H.M., *The Bankruptcy of India, An Enquiry into the Administration of India under the Crown* (London: Swan Sonnenschein, Lowry and Company,1886)

Irschick, Eugene F., *Politics and Social Conflict in South India, the Non Brahmin Movement and Tamil Separatism, 1916-1929* (Berkeley and Los Angeles: University of California Press,1969)

Jackson, Patrick, *Morley of Blackburn: A Literary and Political Biography of John Morley* (Lanham, Maryland: Fairleigh, Dickinson, University Press, 2012)

Jenkins, Edward, *The Coolie, His Rights and Wrongs, notes of a Journey to British Guiana, with a review of the system and of the recent Commission of Inquiry* (London: Strahan and Co. Publishers, 1871)

Hardiman, David, *The NonViolent Struggle for Indian Freedom: 1905-1919* (Oxford: OUP, 2018)

Hobson, J.A. *Imperialism, A Study* (London: Allen and Unwin Ltd, 1905)

Huque, M. Azzizal, *The Man Behind the Plough* (Calcutta: The Book Company, 1939)

Jaffer, Aaron, *Lascars and Indian Ocean Seafaring, 1780-1860, Shipboard Life, Unrest and Mutiny* (Woodbridge: The Boydell Press, Woodbridge, 2015)

Jaganath, Dr. Santosh, *The History of the Nizam's Railways System* (Salapur: Laxmi Book Publications, 2015)

Jain, Prakash C., *Racial Discrimination Against Overseas Indians, A Class Analysis* (New Delhi: Concept Publishing Company, 1990)

Johnson, Richard L., *Gandhi's Experiments with Truth: Essential Writings by and About Mahatma Gandhi* (NY-Toronto, Oxford: Lexington Books, 2006)

Jhala, Angma Dey, *Royal Patronage, Power and Aesthetics in Princely India* (London, New York: Routledge, 2011)

Jones, Philip, Kenny, Anna (eds.) *Australia's Muslim Cameleers, Pioneers of the Inland, 1860s-1930s* (Kent Town: Wakefield Press, 2007)

Jupp, James, (ed.) *The Australian People: An Encyclopedia of the Nation, its People and their Origins* (Cambridge: Cambridge University Press, 2001)

Kabir, Nahid, *Muslims in Australia, Immigration, Race relations and Cultural History* (London: Routledge, 2010)

Kain, Jennifer S. *Insanity and Immigration Control in New Zealand and Australia: 1860-1930* (London: Palgrave Macmillan, 2019)

Kaminsky, Arnold P., *The India Office 1880-1910* (London, New York, Westport Connecticut; Greenwood Press, 1986)

Keith, Professor A. Berriedale, DCL, DLITT, *Speeches and Documents on Indian Policy, 1750-1921, Volume One* (London: Oxford University, 1921)

Keith, Professor A. Berriedale, DCL, DLITT, *A Constitutional History of India, 1600-1935* (Allahabad: Halcyon Press, 1937)

Kelly, John D., *A Politics of Virtue, Hinduism, Sexuality and Counter Colonial Discourse in Fiji* (Chicago, London: University of Chicago Press, 1991)

Keltie, J. Scott, (ed.) *The Statesman's Year Book, Statistical and Historical Annual of the States of the World for the Year 1897* (New York & London: Macmillan and Son Ltd, 1897)

Kendall, Paul, *The Battle of Neuve-Chapelle: Britain's Forgotten Offensive* (Barnsley: Frontline Books, 2016)

Kennedy, Andrew, *The International Ambitions of Mao and Nehru: National Efficacy, Beliefs and the Making of Foreign Policy* (Cambridge: CUP, 2012)

Kenworthy, Lt-Commander J.M., *India: A Warning* (London: Elkins, Mathew, Marot, 1931)

Khan, M. Fathulla, *A History of Administrative Reforms in Hyderabad State* (Secunderabad: New Hyderabad Press, 1935)

Khan, Mohammed Shabbir, *Tilak and Gokhale: A Comparative Study* (New Delhi: Ashish Publishing House, 1992)

Khosla, G.S., *A History of Indian Railways* (New Delhi: Ministry of Railways (Railways Board) Government of India, 1988)

Klaaren, Jonathan, *From Prohibited Immigrants to Citizens, The Origins of Citizenship and Nationality in South Africa* (Cape Town: UCT Press, 2017)

Kratoska Paul, (Ed) *South East Asia Colonial History, Vol. III, High Imperialism (1890s-1930s)* (London and New York: Routledge 2001)

Kratoska, Paul, *The Thailand Burma Railway 1942-46 Documents and Selected Writings* (London and New York: Routledge, 2006)

Lalvani, Kartar, *The Making of India: The Untold Story of British Enterprise* (London: Bloomsbury, 2016)

Lapping, Brian, *End of Empire* (London: Paladin, 1989)

Law, John F., *Modern Hyderabad (Deccan)* (Calcutta: Thacker Spink and Company, 1914)

Levine, Philippa (ed.) *Gender and Empire, The Oxford History of the British Empire, Companion Series* (Oxford: OUP, 2007)

Lewin, Ronald, *The Chief, Field Marshal Lord Wavell, Commander-in-Chief and Viceroy, 1939-1947* (New York: Farar, Straus, Giroux, 1980)

Lloyd George, David, *War Memoirs* (London: Odhams Press, 1938)

Long, Reverend J., *Evidence Explanatory of the Indigo System of Lower Bengal* (Calcutta: R.C. LePage and Company, 1861)

MacDonald, J. Ramsay, *The Government of India* (London: The Swarthmore Press, 1921)

Malleson, Col (ed.) *Kaye's and Malleson's History of the Indian Mutiny of 1857-58* (New York & Bombay: Longmans Green and Company, 1897)

Mallinson, Allan, *1914: Fight the Good Fight, Britain, the Army and the Coming of the First World War* (London: Bantam Books, 2014)

Markham, Violet R., *The South African Scene* (London: Smith Elder and Co. London, 1913)

Marston, Daniel, *The Indian Army and the end of the Raj* (Cambridge: CUP, 2014)

Martin, Montgomery, *British India: Its recent Progress and Present State* (London: Simpson Low and Son,1862)

Mathias, Peter, *The First Industrial Nation: An Economic History of Britain, 1700-1914* (London: Methuen and Company, 1976)

McAuliffe, R. Paton, *The Nizam, The Origin and Future of the Hyderabad State* (London: C.J. Clay and Sons, 1904)

McNair, J.F.A., *Prisoners Their Own Warders* (London: Archibald Constable and Company,1899)

Mehta, N.B., *Indian Railways: Rates and Regulations* (London: P.S. King and Sons Ltd, 1927)

Major, E., *Viscount Morley and Indian Reform* (London: James Nisbet and Co. Ltd, 1910)

Maxon, Robert M., *Struggle for Kenya: The Loss and Reassertion of Imperial Initiative, 1912-1923* (Cranbury NJ: Associated University Presses Inc. 1993)

McArthur, Brian, *Penguin Book of Twentieth Century Speeches* (London: Penguin Viking, 199)2

Menon, V.P., *The Transfer of Power in India* (Hyderabad: Orient Longman, 1997)

Minto, Mary, Countess of, *India, Minto and Morley, 1905-1910* (London: Macmillan London, 1935)

Mishra, V.B., *The Evolution of the Constitutional History of India (1773-1947)* (Delhi: Mittal Publications, 1987)

Money, William Taylor, *Observations on the Expediency of Shipbuilding at Bombay, for the service of His Majesty and of the East India Company* (London: Longman, Hurst, Rees, Orme and Browne, 1881)

Monson, Theodore, *Imperial Rule in India, being an Examination of the Principles Proper to the Government of Dependencies* (London: Archibald Constable and Company, 1899)

Montgomery, Bernard Law K.G., *The Memoirs of Field Marshal the Viscount Montgomery of Alamein* (London: Collins, 1958)

Mookerji, Radhakund, MA, *Indian Shipping: A History of Seaborne Trade and Maritime Activity of the Indians from the Earliest Times* (Bombay, Longmans Green and Company, 1912)

Moon, Parker Thomas, *Imperialism and World Politics* (New York: The Macmillan Company, No publication date)

Moon, Penderel (ed.), *Wavell, The Viceroy's Journal* (London, New Delhi, Karachi, Oxford University Press, 1973)

Morison, Cotter J., *Macaulay* (London: Macmillan and Company Limited, 1902)

Morris, James, *Farewell the Trumpets* (London: Penguin, 1979)

Mukherjee, Hena *The Early History of the East Indian Railway* (Calcutta: Firma KLM, 1960)

Mukherjee, Janam, *Hungry Bengal: War, Famine, and the End of Empire* (Oxford: OUP, 2015)

Murphy, John, *A Decent Provision: Australian Welfare Policy, 1870 to 1949* (London: Routledge, 2016)

Nagi, B.S., *Child Marriage in India: A Study of its Differential Patterns in Rajasthan* (New Delhi: Mittal Publications, 1993)

Naidu, B.V. Narayanaswamy, *Indian Trade* (Madurai: The De Nobili Press, Madura, 1942)

Naidu, Sarojini, *Mahatma Gandhi, His Life, Writing and Speeches* (Madras: Ganesh and Company, 1921)

Nanda, B.R., *Road to Pakistan: The Life and Times of Mohammed Ali Jinnah* (New Delhi: Routledge, 2010)

Naoroji Dadabhai, *Poverty and UnBritish Rule in India* (London: Swan Sonnenschein and Company, 1901)

Napier, Lt-General Sir Charles, *Defects, Civil and Military of the Indian Government* (London, Charles Westerton, 1853)

Neame, L.E., *The Asiatic Danger in the Colonies* (London: George Routledge and Sons Ltd., 1907)

Nicolson, Harold, *King George V: His Life and Reign* (London: Constable and Co. Ltd. 1984)

Northrup, David *Indentured Labour in the Age of Imperialism: 1834-1922,* (Cambridge: CUP, 1995)

O'Malley, L.S.S. CIE, *The Indian Civil Service:1601-1930* (London: John Murray, 1931)

Omissi, David, *The Sepoy and the Raj: The Indian Army 1860-1940* (London: Palgrave Macmillan, 1998)

Osman, Mohd Taib (ed.) *Malaysian World View* (Singapore: Southeast Asian Studies Program, Institute of South east Asian Studies, 1985)

Partington, Geoffrey, *Making Sense of History* (Bloomingdon Indiana: Xlibris LLC, 2013)

Patel, Dr S.H., *The Constitution, Government and Politics of India* (New Delhi: Vikas Publishing House Pvt Ltd, 2016)

Pati, Budheswar *India and the First World War, 1914-1918* (Delhi: Atlantic Publisher and Distributors, 1996)

Perry, F.W., *The Commonwealth Armies, Manpower and Organisation in Two World Wars* (Manchester: University Press, 1988)

Phythian-Adams, Lt-Col E.G. OBE, *The Madras Soldier, 1746-1946,* (Madras Superintendent Government Press, 1948)

Rafter, Captain, *Our Indian Army: A Military History of the British Empire in the East* (London: David Bryce, 1855)

Ragwan, Rodney, *Vision in Progress: Framing the Portrait of Indian Baptists in South Africa* (Eugene, Oregon: Resource Publications, 2011)

Raj. Baldev & Paul, T.V. *India in the World Order: Searching for Major Power Status* (Cambridge: CUP, 2002)

Ramusack, Barbara N. *The New Cambridge History of India: The Indian Princes and their States* (Cambridge: Cambridge University Press, 2004)

Rao, P. Rajeswar, *The Great Indian Patriots* (New Delhi: Mittel Publications, 1991)

Rao, P.R. Ramachandra, *Decay of Indian Industries* (Bombay: D.B. Taraporevala Sons and Company, 1935)

Ramanathan K.V., (ed.) *The Satyamurti Letters, The Indian Freedom Struggle through the Eyes of a Parliamentarian, Vol II* (Delhi: Pearson, Longman, Delhi, 2008)

Ravoof, A.A., *Meet Mr Jinnah* (Madras: The Deccan Times Press, 1944)

Regani, Sarajani, *Nizam – British Relations, 1724-1857* (New Delhi: Concept Publishing Company, 1988)

Riddick, John F., *The History of British India: A Chronology* (London: Praeger, 2006)

Robinson, Francis, *Separatism Among Indian Muslims: The Politics of the United Provinces Muslims 1860-1923* (Cambridge: CUP, 2008)

Rotberg, Robert I. *The Founder: Cecil Rhodes and the Pursuit of Power* (Oxford: OUP, Oxford, 1988)

Rotter, Andrew J., *Empires of the Senses: Bodily Encounters in Imperial India and the Philippines* (New York: Oxford University Press, 2019)

Roy, Kaushik, *The Indian Army in the Two World Wars* (Boston: Brill, Leiden, 2012)

Russell, Lord, of Liverpool, *The Knights of Bushido: A Short History of Japanees War Crimes* (London: Gorgi,1968)

Saikia, Yasmin & Rahman, M. Raisur (ed), *The Cambridge Companion to Sir Sayyid Ahmad Khan* (Oxford: OUP, 2019)

Sale, Lady J., *A Journal of the Disasters in Afghanistan: 1841-1842, Vol II* (London: Murray,1843)

Sampath, R.N. & Mari, Pe.Su, *Chidambaram Pillai V.O. Builders of Modern India* (New Delhi: Publications Division, Ministry of Information and Broadcasting,1992)

Sanders, E.W.C., *In Kut and Captivity: With the Sixth Indian Division* (London: Murray, 1919)

Sanderson, Edgar, MA, *The Fight for the Flag in South Africa: A History of the War from the Boer Ultimatum to the Advance of Lord Roberts* (Toronto: William Briggs, 1900)

Sara, Abdullah, *Kenya at the Crossroads, Administration and Economy under Sir Percy Girouard, 1909-1912* (Lanham, MD: Lexington Books, 2015)

Sarkar, Jadunath, *Economics of British India* (Calcutta: M.C. Sarkar and Sons, 1917)

Savarkar, Vinayak, *The Indian War of Independence of 1857* (No Publisher, 1909)

Sellers, Christopher & Melling, Joseph, (eds) *Dangerous Trade, Histories of Industrial Hazard Across a Global World* (Philadelphia: University Press, 2012)

Saxena, Dr Shyam Narain *Role of the Indian Army in the First World War* (Delhi: Bhavana Prakashan, 1987)

Scobie, John, *Hill Coolies, A Brief Exposure of the Deplorable Condition of the Hill Coolies in British Guiana and Mauritius, and of the Nefarious Means by which they were induced to Resort to these Colonies* (London: Harvey and Darton, 1840)

Seaman L.C.B., *Post Victorian Britain: 1902-1951* (London: Methuen, 1966)

Sen, S.N., *History of the Freedom Movement in India – 1857-1947* (New Delhi: New Age International Limited Publishers, 2003)

Sen, S.N., *History of Modern India* (New Delhi: New Age International Publishers, 2006

Seekins, Donald M. *Historical Dictionary of Burma (Myanmar),* (New York, London: Rowman and Littlefield, Lanham, 2007)

Siddiqui, Kalim, Conflict and War in Pakistan (London, Basingstoke: Palgrave Macmillan, 1972)

Silvestri, Michael, *Ireland and India, Nationalism, Empire and Memory* (New York: Palgrave Macmillan, 2009)

Singh, Harkirat, *The Indian National Army Trial and the Raj* (New Delhi: Atlantic Publisher and Distributors, 2003)

Singh, Nirmal Tej, *Irrigation and Soil Salinity in the Indian Sub-Continent, Past and Present* (Cranbury NJ: Rosemont Publishing and Printing, 2005)

Sleeman, Lt-Colonel William, *Rambles and Recollection of an Indian Official* (London: J. Hatchard and Son, 1844)

Spencer, R.G. *British Immigration Policy since 1939, The Making of Multi-Racial Britain* (London, New York: Routledge, 1997)

Stevenson, Richard, *Bengal Tiger and British Lion: An Account of the Famine of 1943* (New York, Lincoln, Shanghai: Universe Inc., 2005)

Stone, Ian, *Canal Irrigation in British India, Perspectives on Technological Change in a Peasant Economy* (Cambridge: CUP, 2002)

Streets, Heather, *Martial Races, The Military, Race and Masculinity in British Imperial Culture, 1857-1914* (Manchester & New York: Manchester University Press, 2004)

Sundaram, Chander S. *Indianisation, the Officer Corps, and the Indian Army, The Forgotten Debate: 1817-1917* (Lanham, Boulder, New York, London, Lexington Books, 2019)

Sundaram, Lanka, *Indians Overseas* (Madras: G.A. Nateson, 1933)

Sundararaja, Dr Saroja, *Kashmir Crisis, Unholy Anglo-Pak Nexus* (Delhi: Kalpaz Publications, 2010)

Sunderland, Jabez T., *India in Bondage: Her Right to Freedom* (Calcutta: Prabasi Press, 1929)

Surriyeh, Elizabeth, *Sufis and Anti-Sufis: The Defence, Rethinking and Rejection of Sufism in the Modern World* (London: Routledge Curzon, 1999)

Tejani, Shabnum *Indian Secularism, A Social and Intellectual History, 1890-1950* (Indianapolis Indiana University Press, 2008)

Thomas, Herbert Theodore, *The Story of a West Indian Policeman: or Forty Seven Years in the Jamaica Constabulary* (Kingston: The Gleaner Co. Ltd, 1927)

Thomas, P.J., *Mercantilism and the East India Trade* (London: Frank Cass, 1923)

Thomson, David, *England in the Twentieth Century* (London: Penguin, 1965)

Thompson, Edward & Garratt, G.T., *History of British Rule in India*: Volume II (New Delhi: Atlantic Publishers and Distributors, 1999)

Thorne, Christopher, *Allies of a Kind: The United States, Britain and the War Against Japan, 1941-1945* (Oxford, New York, Toronto, Melbourne: OUP, 1978)

Thompson, Edward, *Suttee – A Historical and Philosophical Enquiry into the Hindu Rite of Widow-Burning* (London: George Allen and Unwin Limited, 1928)

Tiwari, Chandrika, Prasada, *The Indian Railways: Their Historical, Economic and Administrative Aspects* (Ajmer: B. Mathura Prasad Shiwahare, 1921)

Toye, Hugh, *The Springing Tiger: A Study of the Indian National Army and of Netaji Sudhas Chandra Bos* (Mumbai: Allied Publisher Limited, 2009)

Tudor, Maya, *The Promise of Power: The Origins of Democracy in India and Autocracy in Pakistan* (Cambridge: Cambridge University Press, 2013)

Turner, David, *The Old Boys: The Decline and Rise of the Public Schools* (New Haven, London, Yale University Press, 2015

Uppal, J.N., *Gandhi: Ordained in South Africa* (New Delhi: Publications Division, Ministry of Information and Broadcasting, Government of India, 2007)

Vasunia, Phiroze, *The Classics and Colonial India* (Oxford: OUP, 2013)

Ventakataramani, M.S., *Bengal Famine of 1943: the American Response* (New Delhi: Vikas Publication House, 1973)

Vohra, Ranbir, *The Making of India, A Historical Survey* (London: M.E. Sharpe, 2001)

Wacha, Dinshaw Eduji, *Recent Indian Finance* (Madras: G.A. Nateson and Company, 1910)

Wagner, Kim A., *The Skull of Alum Bheg, The Life and Death of a Rebel of 1857* (Oxford & New York: Oxford University Press, 2017)

Waiz, S.A., *Indians Abroad* (Bombay: The Imperial Indian Association, 1927)

Warner, Philip, Auchinleck: *The Lonely Soldier, The Truth about Britain's Foremost Commander* (London: Sphere Books Ltd, 1982)

Wedderburn, Sir William, *Allan Octavian Hume, C.B. Father of the National Congress, 1829 to 1912* (London: Fisher Unwin, 1912)

West, Geoffrey, *The Life of Annie Besant* (London: Gerald Howe Limited, 1933)

Wheare, K.C., *The Statute of Westminster and Dominion Status* (Oxford: OUP, 1949)

Willard, Myra, *History of the White Australia Policy to 1920* (London: Frank Cass and Co. Ltd. 1967)

Winstedt, Sir Richard, *Malaya and its History* (London: Hutchinsons University Library, 1951)

Winstedt, Sir Richard, *Malaya, The Straits Settlements and the Federated and Unfederated Malay Straits* (London: Constable and Co. Ltd, 1923)

Wood, Ernest, *An Englishman Defends Mother India, A Complete Constructive Reply to Mother India* (Madras: Ganesh and Company, 1929)

Yong, Tan Tai, *The Garrison State, The Military, Government and Society in Colonial Punjab, 1849-1947* (New Delhi: Sage Publications, 2005)

Youe, Christopher P. *Robert Thorne Coryndon, Proconsular Imperialism in Southern and Eastern Africa, 1897-1925* (Gerrards Cross: Colin Smythe, 1986)

Zeigler, Philip, *Mountbatten: The Official Biography* (London: Guild Publishing, 1985)

Zimand, Savel, *Living India* (New York, London, Toronto: Longman Green and Company, 1928)

Index

Index